The Artful Economist

Ilde Rizzo • Ruth Towse

Editors

The Artful Economist

A New Look at Cultural Economics

 Springer

Editors
Ilde Rizzo
Department of Economics and Business
University of Catania
Catania, Italy

Ruth Towse
Bournemouth University
Bournemouth, Dorset, UK

CREATe
University of Glasgow
Glasgow, UK

ISBN 978-3-319-40635-0   ISBN 978-3-319-40637-4   (eBook)
DOI 10.1007/978-3-319-40637-4

Library of Congress Control Number: 2016951843

Cover illustration: The music is "Siciliana Academica" composed by Sir Alan Peacock in honour of the Faculty of Economics of the University of Catania, when he was awarded the laurea honoris causa (November 20, 1991)

Printed on acid-free paper

This Springer imprint is published by Springer Nature
The registered company is Springer International Publishing AG Switzerland

In memory of
Professor Sir Alan Turner Peacock
1922–2014

Foreword

Alan Peacock, a Lucid, Rigorous, and Pragmatic Academic

The first time I met Alan Peacock was in Catania, Sicily, in a seminar on heritage economics. I was amazed by the very high standards he set for himself and for the other economists as well (a kind of "desire for excellence"). The participants shared a strong concern for the "future of the past" and a sincere willingness to imagine sustainable economic models for the conservation of heritage. Alan Peacock was able to reconcile a normative and a positive approach and to apply his expertise and knowledge of the general question of public policies for culture to the concrete problems of the conservation of heritage.

With his impressive understanding of culture and the particular importance of music in his life, Peacock was an anti-conventional thinker. His writing was precise and elegant (a rare quality among economists). Peacock did not hesitate to be ironic or self-deprecating. He had a great sense of humour. Concerning heritage, he thought that in a growing economy it was paradoxical to ask the present generation to finance the conservation of monuments and sites for the next generation who will be richer than the present one. Peacock would probably have agreed with Groucho Marx's question: "Why should I care about future generations? What have they ever done for me?"

I would like to stress three features about Alan Peacock's writings that cross the different contributions to the seminar that was held in Catania in 2015, which forms the basis of this book: firstly, the wide scope of his commitments, secondly, his specific view of public economics, and thirdly, his interest in cultural economics.

1. Peacock had a wide vision of the world and of economic science. He wrote important reports, about 30 books and hundreds of papers. He was able to speak to different audiences (academics and less-specialized audiences). He was a liberal, but—I would say—an informed and enlightened liberal: he was always attentive to the issue of public action. He was an expert for the British Liberal party, but also, later, an independent advisor. This is probably the reason why he

wanted—in his book written with Charles K. Rowley (1975)—to challenge a mere Paretian approach of welfare economics by putting forward policy suggestions, such as negative income tax, antitrust action, etc. Peacock wanted to draw the boundaries of public action beyond which such action becomes ineffective. He was especially sceptical about the evaluation of quality in the arts: maybe he was overall aware of the inability of economists to build reliable indicators of quality.

2. Alan Peacock's interest in the economics of culture arose from public economics, with a clear issue: circumscribing public action without neglecting intervention in the presence of market failure (and for merit goods as well). Should the State provide subsidies to support infant industries or declining activities? Governments have to take into account that budgetary deficit shifts the burden of the public expenditures to future taxpayers who are not able to vote. As a public choice economist, Peacock was more aware than others of the respect for human values and individual choice. Market price should be considered the best indicator of an individual's choices. A thread of his different contributions to cultural economics is this respect for individual preferences: "we do not need to specify a set of values at all. All we need is a set of mechanisms by which individual members of society can express their preferences for cultural goods, and we shall soon find out the extent to which it seems necessary for them to take combined action in order to give effect to their desires" (Peacock 1992: 9).

3. Alan Peacock theorized reconciliation between individualism and interest in public action and translated this reconciliation in terms of public policy, especially—but not only—in the case of TV (the choices of individuals should prevail). Peacock's most famous contribution to British public life was his chairmanship of *The Committee on Financing the BBC* in 1985 and 1986. Among the report's conclusions (Peacock 1986), we can stress the forward-looking view about the future of TV and especially about "the disruptive potential of the new technologies of distribution". The report can be considered a summary of the ability of Peacock to be pragmatic and visionary simultaneously: the market must be based on consumer sovereignty on pay-tv and also provide diversity of programme suppliers. Besides the laissez-faire model based on broadcasters competing to sell audiences to advertisers, there is a place for publicly funded provision of high-quality programmes.

Alan Peacock's expertise in the practical application of economics of the arts was much wider than only the case of broadcasting. He was interested in all the arts. He served on the Arts Council of Great Britain and chaired the Scottish Arts Council from 1986 to 1992. His focus on the field of heritage especially benefited from his twofold concern for the conservation of the past and the need for sustainable economic growth. He was aware of the fact that what we call heritage is not considered as having any particular importance at the time it is created or produced. He was pragmatic, considering "that a government policy should be directed towards identifying, maintaining and preserving what might be called

'representative' historical artefacts, instead of giving into the magpie-like procliv-
ities of those who would preserve almost every physical manifestation of the past"
(Peacock 1997: 231). It was a way to emphasize the first duty of policymakers—
making the best choice among different alternatives—and the first duty of economists: to stay modest and aware of the limits of their models. As Professors Tim
Besley, FBA, and Peter Hennessy, FBA, write in their *Letter to Her Majesty*, about
another side of economists' issue, the inability of economists to foresee the crisis:
"The events of the past year have delivered a salutary shock. Whether it will turn
out to have been a beneficial one will depend on the candour with which we dissect
the lessons and apply them in future". (Letter to Her Majesty The Queen, British
Academy, London, 22 July, 2009).

More generally, Alan Peacock had a distinctly independent mind. He never
yielded to the temptation to make proposals that lobbies were expecting. For
example, in 1970, he recommended that London should have only two fully
grant-aided orchestras rather than four, giving birth to a strong controversy. In the
same way, he did not hesitate to recognize in his report on TV that there was not
enough advertising revenue to support both BBC and ITV companies in the short
term. Therefore, he concluded that it was not time to replace licence fee TV by
advertising revenues, in spite of the pressure of many figures in the Conservative
Party. This is why I especially like the conclusion of his contribution to the
Handbook of the Economics of Art and Culture edited by Victor Ginsburgh and
David Throsby (2006): "Keynes looked forward to the days when economists
would act and be regarded rather like dentists, more concerned with the immediate
realities of improving the human condition than with impressing the public with the
profundities of their statements about the good life. One suspects that Keynes's
hope may be the way that cultural economics will develop in relation to its policy
relevance. That will be all to the good, but the author still regards it as essential that
economists will retain a watching brief on those who claim that their expertise
entitles them to pride of place in policy decisions. If we do not continue to
demonstrate that their judgments of value are arbitrary, then we must not be
surprised if they continue to invent the economics for themselves." (Peacock
2006: 1139).

At the time this book is published, the economic crisis in emergent countries, the
rise of inequalities, the worries about the effect of globalization on the preservation
of cultural diversity, and the issue of migrants challenge the future of Europe. We
will miss academics with this scope and elevation of view.

Paris 13 University, Paris, France   Françoise Benhamou
Sciences Po-Paris, Paris, France

References

Peacock A (Chair) (1986) Report of the Committee on the financing of the BBC. Cmnd.9824. HMSO, London

Peacock A (1992) Economics, cultural values and cultural policies. In: Towse R, Khakee A (eds) Cultural economics. Springer, Berlin, pp 9–20

Peacock A (1997) Towards a workable heritage policy. In: Hutter M, Rizzo I (eds) Economic perspectives on cultural heritage. St. Martin's Press, New York, pp 225–235

Peacock A (2006) The arts and economic policy. In: Ginsburgh V, Throsby D (eds) Handbook of the economics of art and culture. North-Holland, Amsterdam, pp 1123–1140

Peacock A, Rowley CK (1975) Welfare economics. A liberal restatement. Wiley, A Halstead Press Book, New York

Contents

Introduction

Ilde Rizzo and Ruth Towse

Cultural economics has been fortunate in attracting eminent economists to contribute to it and none has made so comprehensive a contribution as Professor Sir Alan Peacock. The contributors to this book, many of whom are the current intellectual leaders of our field, honour Peacock's legacy not directly in encomia, several of which have been published following his death in 2014,[1] but by taking a new look at cultural economics. The authors are friends, colleagues, admirers and former students of Alan Peacock, several fitting into all three categories. Contributors were invited to write a chapter on a feature of Peacock's work that has been important in their own work in cultural economics or in a related discipline and to present it at a conference hosted by the Department of Economics and Business of the University of Catania in September 2015, whose financial contribution and support is gratefully acknowledged. Peacock was an honorary professor at the university and he loved to visit it and Sicily. The book accordingly includes a wide range of topics from broadcasting to welfare economics, offering both an evaluation of research on the topic and suggesting new insights for further research in cultural economics.

Peacock was not only an eminent professor of economics, however; he was also a lover of and participant in the arts. He was a keen amateur musician who studied composition with Hans Gál, now recognised as an important member of that group of refugee Jewish Austrian musicians who so altered the face of UK music. He put his understanding of both economics and music together in early advisory work on the

---

[1] Rizzo and Towse (2015), Peden (2015). The David Hume Institute has also published collected essays dedicated to the life and works of Alan Peacock (Perman 2015).

I. Rizzo (✉)
Department of Economics and Business, University of Catania, Catania, Italy
e-mail: rizzor@unict.it

R. Towse
Bournemouth University, Bournemouth, Dorset, UK

CREATe, University of Glasgow, Glasgow, UK

London orchestras and later as consultant to the PRS (the Performing Rights Society) in the UK, investigating the economic situation of composers (explored in this book in the chapter by David Throsby). His work on the market for musical composition also produced what could be the first empirical study of copyright in music (the subject of the chapters by Hector MacQueen and Ruth Towse). Each of these three authors pays specific tribute to the inspiration of Alan Peacock's trailblazing book with Ronald Weir *The Composer in the Marketplace* published in 1975. In the 1980s, Peacock took on two of the main institutions of the UK arts establishment: the Arts Council of Great Britain and the BBC. His weapons were his detailed knowledge of and empathy for the arts and his ability to apply economics to seemingly intractable problems. His detailed work on inflation in the arts in the 1970s, commissioned by the Arts Council, failed to 'come up with the right answer' and was hastily buried.[2] His chairing of the committee into the funding of the BBC was equally controversial and again, did not produce the answer everyone expected (see the chapter by Peter Goodwin). Later, Peacock became Chairman of the Scottish Arts Council and faced the practical problems of the public finance of the arts.

A notable feature of all Peacock's work in economics, which spanned public finance, public choice theory, political economy, welfare economics and its applications, as well as cultural economics, was that it was fully integrated. As Françoise Benhamou suggests in the Foreword, the binding thread was the question of the relative roles of the market and the state, of individual and public choice. Francesco Forte, Martin Ricketts and Hector MacQueen capture that feature in their respective chapters in this book, ascribing this *Weltanschauung* to Peacock's knowledge of and reverence for his Scottish Enlightenment intellectual forbears, Adam Smith and David Hume. In cultural economics these fundamental questions are manifest in relation to the public finance or subsidy for the arts and in the decision-making of public and subsidised bodies, whether ministries of culture, arts councils or the managers of arts, media and heritage organisations.

In Continental Europe, both West and East, state ownership and management of cultural organisations has long been the norm, though recently subject to some privatisation. In the UK, USA, Australia and other countries with similar institutional histories, performing arts provision—theatre, music, opera and ballet—is typically by non-profit organisations that are supported by national and local governments but which are also expected to finance themselves through ticket sales and to a varying extent, through private donation. The built heritage is similarly owned and maintained by a mixture of private non-profit and public, though museums and their collections are more often owned by the state. Despite these institutional differences, economics applies to the basic issues of supply and demand—incentives to and motivation of producers and consumers—and cultural economics has tackled these issues in the 'core' topics of the field: public finance of the arts and heritage, art prices, demand and participation in cultural activities, costs

---

[2]Peacock (1993) gave a detailed account of these activities in his book *Paying the Piper*, dedicated to the memory of Hans Gál.

and supply of the arts and heritage, artists' labour markets and more recently, the creative industries. A range of basic economic theories are utilised: welfare economics, public finance, public choice, industrial organisation, labour economics and human capital theory, albeit with adaptation to the specific features of the cultural sector. Over a lifetime's career of more than 60 years, Alan Peacock contributed to each of these areas through theoretical and empirical analysis. It is hardly surprising, then, that in a book that takes a new look at cultural economics, we take as a starting point Peacock's seminal contributions to the subject.

For a long time, starting from the 1960s, cultural economics was concerned with two aspects of the same problem, the finance of the arts and heritage. Those aspects were: explaining their increasing costs; and the justification of state involvement in their finance. The first exercise (still ongoing) was understanding the underlying economic structure of arts organisations, to which Baumol and Bowen (1965, 1966) made such a significant contribution with their theoretical and empirical analysis of what has come to be called Baumol's Cost Disease. The second, to which Baumol and Bowen also contributed, though with lesser emphasis, was the application of the Pigovian welfare economics concept of market failure as making the case for subsidy.

The performing arts, initially the focus of their analysis (though the ideas were later widely applied to museums, libraries and a whole range of civic services), was shown to have costs of production rising faster than price inflation. The reason lies in the inherent characteristics of the arts and other such services, namely they are labour intensive with fixed factors, at least as far as labour inputs are concerned. As productivity rises in the rest of the economy, wage rates rise but similar productivity increases are limited (at least for what might be called the 'standard repertoire') and push up labour costs in the arts disproportionately. Assuming that demand falls as ticket prices rise, earned revenue could not keep up with increases in costs and 'if the arts are to survive' (the commonly used phrase in the discussion), the revenue gap has to be closed by some external means, either state subsidy or private giving.

The Pigovian solution of state subsidy could be justified on the grounds of external benefits and cultural economists have been at pains to make the case on these grounds, some going further claiming that the arts and heritage are public goods. While there is indeed a case to be made for some external benefits of some art forms, perhaps more strongly for heritage (museums and built heritage) on the grounds of preservation for future generations, it is less convincing for every type of performing art. Peacock (1969: 330) made the point in his inimitable style:

> ...(it) is difficult to trace the way in which spillovers from the 'culture vultures' attending live performance to others is supposed to take place. It would be interesting to poll the public at large in order to confirm whether they derived an uncovenanted benefit from the attendance at publicly-subsidized symphony concerts or modern plays by those whose median income is almost twice as large as that of the employed population.

Nevertheless, the presence of external benefits (proven or not) has been the underlying assumption of much work in cultural economics. Having rejected the more widely held view that culture is a merit good (and if one takes that route, there is no need for fancy theories to make the case for paternalistic intervention), in this early article in cultural economics, Peacock proceeded to lay out his views on the role of government in relation to the arts, promoting his favoured solution of vouchers to selected groups of people with low-incomes organised by local government. Francesco Forte's chapter traces the development and applications of Peacock's policy prognostications as he moved away from welfare economics to public choice theory and outlines the opportunities that new technologies offer for the implementation of vouchers. Giacomo Pignataro's Afterword on economic advice reflects Peacock's thoughts on the subject which he often had cause to apply.

More generally, though, the whole edifice of welfare economics, both Paretian and Pigovian,[3] has long been criticised and re-evaluated. Martin Ricketts' chapter on welfare economics brilliantly provides a succinct overview of these debates. One element of that debate has been the question of distribution—or redistribution—of any subsidy or tax. The above quote from Peacock identifies one of the main problems of cultural subsidy: attendance at arts events and museums is dominated by better-off and more highly educated people (the two are generally correlated). Moreover, attendance does not appear to be greatly affected by prices; even free entry does not necessarily attract a wider spectrum of the population while demand by the 'culture vultures' is relatively inelastic.

Those are mere details, however, in a much broader assault on arts and heritage subsidy from critics adopting the approach of public choice theory. Indeed, that theory provides a major critique of welfare economics in general, regarding it as naïve in its implied view of the political decision-making process. In their chapter, Giardina and Mazza expound the origins of this approach in the Italian school of public finance, a topic on which Peacock also wrote. Peacock was the co-editor of *Classics in the Theory of Public Finance*, (Musgrave and Peacock 1958) one of the first books offering to the international audience an overview of the contribution of Italian scholars of public finance to the theory of public goods and its implications for public policy.

The stance of public choice theory sees the provision of cultural goods and services, especially in countries in which they are directly provided by the state, as being determined almost entirely by supply-side considerations, namely the interests of policy-makers and bureaucrats who have little incentive to consider demands by consumers and, given typical city hall accounting practices, little incentive on the part of the arts organisation to respond to them or to innovate. That is an underlying concern of Bruno Frey's chapter advocating greater innovation in museums and Michele Trimarchi's on opera. Those concerns are particularly strong in relation to the finance and management of cultural heritage, a topic which concerned Peacock for the last 20 years of his life. Chapters by Ilde Rizzo, Anna Mignosa and Ezra Zubrow deal with quite diverse aspects of cultural heritage: Mignosa's chapter on cultural policy reflects on the differences between the centralised and decentralised model and on the role of public-private partnerships;

---

[3]See Blaug (2011).

Rizzo discusses the implications of the increasing use of digital technologies by museums and heritage managers, while Zubrow, from a different disciplinary perspective (which is not necessarily consistent with a strict economic approach), considers a tragically old topic in a new way—the destruction of heritage through warfare.

Besides a concern with the underpinnings of policy, cultural economics has a long tradition of empirical analysis. Over the years, data on the creative economy—the arts, heritage and cultural and media industries—have improved significantly, enabling statistical tests to be done. Besides quantitative research, qualitative research also has a place in understanding and informing policy questions. The chapter by Roberto Cellini and Tiziana Cuccia offers a detailed quantitative analysis of public spending on culture, an abiding topic in cultural economics, using data on Italy. It offers insight into a fundamental aspect of the political economy of culture: the impact of decentralization and the consolidation of fiscal policies upon the amount of public spending on culture in a 'top-down' and state-driven system. And last but not least, Victor Ginsburgh analyses issues in evaluation, in theory and practice, using wine as an example and showing that the evaluation of wine is similar to art, and particularly to music (two of Peacock's great passions).

The claim of this book is that it provides a new look at cultural economics. Many of the chapters offer an evaluation of where we are now and provide pointers to new directions. The theoretical underpinnings of applied economics, including to our subject, have evolved over the last 50 years and continue to do so. There have been fundamental critiques of the now standardised 'market failure' position from various sources: from within welfare economics, from public finance, from public choice theory and from applied areas, including cultural economics. For the latter, difficulties in utilising our understanding for practical cultural policies abound. The tendency of arts and heritage policy-makers and administrators to vulgarise concepts economists know to be profound and to struggle with intellectually is often difficult to work with. The desire of such people for 'a number' that is used to clinch the argument often over-rides any reservations that accompany it. The prime example of this has been cost benefit studies which ignore the breast-beating of welfare economists and blithely go ahead with crude measures of social benefits, however carefully constructed and the results circumscribed, which are then touted about as gospel. The same tendency is rife in measurements of the value of the creative industries. Peacock loved to see this problem as the role of the economist as a 'hired gun'. So, evaluation of the fundamentals of cultural economics has to be part of any new look. Sources of new inspiration come from other areas of economics—behavioural, neo-institutional, law and economics—as well as from looking more carefully at the wider perspectives opened up by multidisciplinary analysis.

The need for a new look at cultural economics arises in practical terms because of the fundamental changes taking place in the cultural economy due mainly to digitisation. New technologies affect supply and demand: on the supply side they offer new services (as Ilde Rizzo shows in her chapter) but unless they are adopted on the demand side, they will not succeed. A further aspect is the cost of switching to them and the investment needed, especially in ICT. In the market economy, investment comes from private entrepreneurs, many of whom will not succeed. Technological progress in capitalist economy is based on the finance of failure as well as success. In the public sphere, loss and failure is more problematic for governments using public finance, especially when technologies are not stable. Regulation is also subject to this problem, in the cultural sector in particular in copyright law. Cultural economists have a great deal to contribute to the understanding of this type of regulation.

Digitisation has profoundly altered the cost of disseminating goods and services. Internet has become the virtual shopping mall for cultural products, such as books and has turned products into services. Products that were once sold for a price are now rented out on a licence (ebooks being a prime example), cutting distribution costs. The same process has made stealing vastly easier and piracy, especially of music and film has had its impact on those industries. Some losses can be regarded in the scheme of things as switching costs. Cultural economists have been busy measuring them, which has proved a challenging problem. New business models have emerged to combat them. There is much work ahead to understand how they can be applied to all areas of culture and to evaluate their effects on the economic organisation of the creative economy. The opportunities that digitisation offers the subsidised arts and heritage are immense and further research is needed to analyse its overall impact. The occurrence of a cultural 'digital divide' across social groups and heritage institutions is likely to put at risk less 'starry' performing arts and heritage institutions and to enhance inequalities. Narrowcasts of live performances can reach parts of the public who would otherwise not have access, either by virtue of geographical location or socio-economic barriers. They have proved very popular. They may also set unrealistic standards for the local live performing rights organisations, however—an unintended consequence. These developments in the creative economy have considerable implications for public finance.

The book shows how much our subject owes to Alan Peacock. It also demonstrates the breadth of his interests and accordingly, the chapters cover a wide range of topics. There is a consistency, however, in the approach to political economy, broadly defined. In that sense there is something for everyone, not just those interested in cultural economics. There is still a big divide between those who see government action as intervention and those for whom it is interference. Peacock managed to respect both positions and, liberal that he was, found a middle way. This book is dedicated to the memory of a man whom we admired, respected and loved. He was a devotee of economics, the arts and heritage and a good bottle of wine. He was an inspiration to cultural economists past, present and, we hope, future.

References

Baumol W, Bowen W (1965) On the performing arts: and anatomy of their economic problems. Am Econ Rev 55:495–502

Baumol W, Bowen WG (1966) Performing arts: the economic dilemma. Twentieth Century Fund, New York

Blaug M (2011) Welfare economics. In: Towse R (ed) A handbook of cultural economics, 2nd edn. Edward Elgar, Cheltenham, pp 425–430

Musgrave R, Peacock A (eds) (1958) Classics in the theory of public finance. Macmillan, London

Peacock A (1969) Welfare economics and public subsidies to the arts. Manch Sch Econ Soc Stud 4:323–335

Peacock A (1993) Paying the piper. Edinburgh University Press, Edinburgh

Peden R (2015) Alan Turner Peacock 1922-2014. British Academy, London, https://www.britac.ac.uk/templates/asset-relay.cfm?frmAssetFileID=15470. Accessed 14 Mar 2016

Perman R (ed) (2015) Alan Peacock dissenting. David Hume Institute, Edinburgh

Rizzo I, Towse R (2015) In memoriam Alan Peacock: a pioneer in cultural economics. J Cult Econ 39(3):225–238

Part I
Cultural Policy in Theory and Practice

The Individual Choice-Public Choice Perspective and Cultural Economics

Francesco Forte

Abstract This chapter deals with the application to cultural economics of the individual choice-public choice perspective. The first section reviews the creative contributions of Alan T. Peacock to this concept and its application to cultural economics. The second section is devoted to the presentation of the fundamentals of this theoretical and policy construct for theoretical welfare economics and public economics, focusing on the interacting games between households as electors-taxpayers and consumers of public services, government, bureaucracies, and firms. The third section is devoted to the applications of this perspective to cultural economics—performing arts, heritage and broadcasting—with the focus on the relations between individuals as suppliers and consumers of cultural services and the other players of the public economy. Pricing and vouchers versus subsidies for the supply of cultural goods and quasi-privatization and privatization devices are examined as ways to enhance the individual freedom of choice, while increasing the efficiency and effectiveness of the supply of cultural goods in the interaction between market forces and the public economy.

1 Introduction: A Creative Economist

Alan Peacock made numerous and significant contributions to a wide range of topics, including cultural economics, all of which had the focus on the individual choice-public choice question. Full details of this argument are provided in the Appendix with a review of Peacock's works, in which this creative economist made his main contributions to this approach (see Ricketts 2015) including its application to cultural economics (see Towse 2005).

In this chapter, Sect. 2 is devoted to the systematic presentation of the theoretical and policy principles of Alan Peacock's individual choice-public choice approach

F. Forte (✉)
University of Rome, La Sapienza, Rome, Italy

Mediterranean University of Reggio Calabria, Reggio Calabria, Italy
e-mail: micros.ricerche@vodafone.it

© Springer International Publishing Switzerland 2016   11
I. Rizzo, R. Towse (eds.), *The Artful Economist*,
DOI 10.1007/978-3-319-40637-4_2

to economic theory. Section 3 is devoted to some of the applications to cultural economics: performing arts, museums and built heritage and broadcasting. Pricing and vouchers versus public subsidies and the various quasi-privatization and privatization devices to enhance the consumer freedom of choice in a competitive setting and to increase efficiency and creativity, are discussed in this context.

As its label suggests, the individual choice-public choice approach consists of the fusion of two perspectives: one for the normative relevance of the individual choice principle and the other is about the positive relevance of the interacting decision game among different players in relation to public choices. The adoption of the individual choice principle implies acceptance of value judgements about the superiority of individual freedom in public choices and of consumer sovereignty. The recognition that real life public economy decision-making takes place through interaction among different players with their own interests implies limiting the public sector and adopting in it market economy devices as far as possible. A distinctive feature of this approach as a positive-real life oriented approach is the importance of empirical research, both at macro level through social accounting and at micro level through cost-benefit and cost-output analysis.

From the individual choice-public choice perspective, the basic value judgments about individual freedom and consumer sovereignty are neither a priori postulates of an ethical nature nor armchair hypotheses. They appear as anthropological values embedded in human nature, such as that of mutual respect (Buchanan 2005: ch. 2).[1] Their recognition implies taking these moral values as data, from which originate positive economic laws, on the lines of David Hume, of Adam Smith and of the Italian tradition of the school of 'Scienza delle Finanze' (Buchanan 1960).

From an anthropological perspective, the spectrum of individual subjective preferences goes much beyond the notion of utility conceived by Bentham as pleasure, to include the immaterial values of knowledge, of the arts and of culture, an area of wants for which the individual freedom of choice appears to be inborn. For economists such as Wilhelm Ropke (1958, 1960), Luigi Einaudi (1949) and Alan Peacock, this was a 'neo-liberal credo'. But the term 'neo-liberal', in this perspective, is likely to be overly restrictive.[2]

---

[1]There is, however, a difference between James Buchanan and Alan Peacock as for what the first defines as the 'ethics of benevolence' of the 'moral community' (Buchanan 2005: ch. 5 and 8). For Peacock it implies a much broader recognition of the principle of equality, as equality in the basic rights and as equality of opportunities (see footnote 2).

[2]An important example of the likelihood of this observation is the Memorandum of Dissent by Lord Norman Crowther Hunt and Alan Peacock (1973). Crowther Hunt, who shared the dissent, was an eminent exponent of the British Labor Party. As noted by Ricketts (2015) and in this book, Peacock thought had greater affinity with that of the German neo-liberals of Ordo and Ropke, whom he categorized as 'end state' liberals.

2   The Interacting Games of Public Economy and Individual Choice

From an individual choice-public economy perspective, a double critique leads to the refusal of the dominance of the elitist theories of welfare economics (Rowley and Peacock 1975: ch. 3; Peacock 1992).

The 'imperial construct' of social welfare functions of the Bergson/Samuelson type has to be rejected because it does not represent the real choices of individuals; it imagines what they might be from an artificial, abstract point of view from the top down and from the bottom up. This formulation implies the fiction of a unitary will of the society as a whole, while the society consists of interacting individual members. It overlooks the bargaining among the various players of the decision games. Arrow's 'impossibility theorem' relating to the instability of the decisions by majority rule indeed shows that individuals do differ and there is not such a thing as the general will of the community as theorized by Rousseau, because the community is not a unitary being.

On the other hand, the neo-Paretian conception of maximum welfare, which leads to approving any decision that improves the welfare of somebody without damaging others—which corresponds to Wicksell's unanimity rule—is untenable as a real life solution because merely leads to a point on the maximum efficiency curve. It does not say anything about the equilibrium point. Furthermore, that curve, considered in mere utilitarian terms, might violate basic values, such as those of freedom and of equality before the law (Rowley and Peacock 1975: ch. 6; Forte 1992, in the 'Comments' at the end of Peacock 1992).

The neo-Paretian approach privileges the status quo. However, the adoption of majority rule may privilege the welfare of the majority.[3] The foremost objection to this neo-Paretian theory is its lack of realism. It ignores that public choice processes are complex games, in which on the supply side there are elected politicians interested in remaining in power and bureaucrats with asymmetrical information and, on the demand side, electors-taxpayers with limited decision-making capability.

It follows that other ways must be pursued to maximize the welfare of individuals through their individual choices in the real life network of government sector choices: (a) reducing the amount of public choices; (b) extending the benefit principle in taxation; (c) increasing the role of individual demand and of the market in the public sector.

The prevalence of the benefit principles for public services, however, cannot be adopted when equality before the law is a requirement, which, in this approach, implies both aid to the less favoured and equality of opportunity, including in the area of cultural goods. Market provision and individual choice for the supply of public goods and decentralization of public choice are recommended whenever this

---

[3]Peacock acknowledges this problem discussing whether Keynes' thought was liberal (Peacock 1997).

does not conflict with efficiency and effectiveness. As Emilio Giardina 1992 notes in the concluding remarks of his comment on Peacock's analysis of the development of public choice theory (Giardina 1992, in Comments in Peacock 1992), this perspective implies no easy boundaries between interests and ideals.[4]

The Players in the Game The positive welfare maximization function W of individuals works within a triangle of bilateral bargaining takes place between four sets of players. They are: (1) the families H, which include the electorate; (2) the government G, formed by elected politicians; (3) the public bureaucracy B; and (4) the firms F and H, as suppliers and demanders of public services and as taxpayers (Peacock 1979b: ch. 1, 1992: ch. 1).

The general panorama now is that of interacting agency relations: (1) between electors and elected politicians, politicians and bureaucrats; (2) bureaucrats and private suppliers of goods and services to the government; (3) between the various layers of the bureaucracies; and (4) between bureaucrats and families and firms as consumers of public services and taxpayers. The electors are principals of the elected politicians, who are principals of the top bureaucrats. They in turn are principals of the bureaucrats at the lower layers. The bureaucrats, at all layers, are principals of the private suppliers of goods and services to the government. The tax authorities are principals of the taxpayers.

These agency relations are not unidirectional, as they work through interacting games in four interdependent markets. In the primary political market, H gives votes for the politicians of G in exchange for public policies in its interest and G influences the political demands of H by taxes and expenditures and by regulation enforced by B. In the political-economic market between G and B, G members demand, and B members supply, alternative packages of public policies. In the economic market of the execution of public policies, G and B are on the demand side, and F and H on the supply side of goods and services for public sector activities.

The market operators try to capture the public operators, conditioning their policies by rent-seeking practices, but also by reactions on the primary political market. In the political market of the execution of the public policies, G and B demand taxes and give public services to H and F, who react by tax avoidance and tax shifting, by rent seeking and other such behaviours and by the interactions in the political sector (Forte and Peacock 1985b; Peacock and Forte 1985).

Bargaining games similar to those in the tax and expenditure sectors also take place in the economics of public regulation, with similar interaction.

---

[4]The risk of exploitation of the majority on the minority is also the reason why Wicksell (1958) suggested the unanimity rule as the ideal solution and the qualified majority as a compromise. Notice, however, that Wicksell did include in that matter only the allocative expenditure and excluded the pure redistributive expenditures, for which he was invoking ad hoc principles. Wicksell's original work, of which the text published in English in1958 is an excerpt, was originally published in 1896 in German.

The 'Displacement Effect' Let us now consider how, in this model of interacting public choice among different players, the supplier of goods and services to the government, namely, the bureaucrats and the politicians, may increase the size of the government and resist any reduction to it, a theme obviously also of interest in the economics of culture, though the amount of cultural expenditure as percentage of the total is generally small and the growth of public spending is generally due to other, more popular, expenditures.

The 'displacement effect' (Peacock and Wiseman 1961) belongs in the area of the devices adopted by politicians and bureaucracies under the pressure of organized interests. The original example is that of an exogenous shock, say, that of a war, which may constrain a country to tax rises to finance expenditures of the war effort. When the exogenous disturbance is over, that expenditure is no longer necessary but the tax crop required to finance it is still there and may finance a new permanent item of expenditure, without asking taxpayers.

Notice, that under a progressive taxation system, a permanent displacement effect operates by the automatic increase of the fiscal burden on GDP, through the 'drag' of progressive tax rates ('fiscal drag'), which may also take place due to a mere increase of the price level.

A common explanation of the growth of public expenditure is Wagner's Law, which predicts that under the normal majority rule, the extension of the voting rights generates a tendency to increase public expenditures, because the lower class majority gets benefits through taxes paid by the middle-high class minority. That the majority rule, with the extension of voting rights, might create an anomalous increase in government size at the expense of the minority had been foreseen already in the first half of the nineteenth century by Alexis De Toqueville, in his book *Democracy in America* (De Toqueville 1840)[5] and may be represented by the 'Toqueville cross' diagram (Peacock 1983b, 1992). De Toqueville also observed, however, that when the class of property owners becomes the larger one, majority rule might not lead to an increase of the public spending even under universal suffrage because the tax burden could fall on the properties of the middle class belonging to the majority. Peacock demonstrates, with a diagram with a vertical and a horizontal axis forming a cross, that with the increase of median voters belonging to the middle class, the majority rule may not cause an increase of redistributive public expenditure at the expense of the minority.

The phenomenon of redistribution in real life does not stop when the middle class electors become the decisive voters, however. One explanation may be found in deficit finance, which creates public debt; the burden falls on future taxpayers, who are not at present voters. It is wrong to assume, though, that present voters do not share any burden of the public debt. The more it increases as ratio to GDP, the more its burden falls on the present generation through the crowding-out of alternative financial investments and through the increase of the risks to financial

---

[5]The French original edition of the book appeared in two parts in 1835 and in 1840. The English translation was of the same years.

systems due to the increased public debt. Thus, other means may be adopted to shift the burden to future voters without any substantial burden on the present ones: an example is the creation of pension rights (Peacock 1992). Another example may be the creation of rights of protection and restoration for heritage goods by law, thus shifting an increasing burden on the future. Obviously, one may argue that the future elector-tax payers are the ones to benefit most from heritage goods in the future.

The fact remains that future electors have to choose whether to reduce other expenditures or replace the revenue lost with other taxes or to reduce the budget by that amount.

Devolution of Functions In the political market one problem, that is also relevant in cultural economics, is that of the devolution of functions from the national level of government to the sub-national levels, in order to increase the weight of electors' preferences (Crowther Hunt and Peacock 1973; Peacock 1976a; Oates 1976; Peacock 1976b, re-edited in Peacock 1979a, b; Peacock 1996).

In principle, devolution should reduce the dispersion that takes place in centralized government between the preferences of the individuals as taxpayers and as beneficiaries of public expenditures and the quality and quantity of the supply of public goods and services (including the service of regulations, such as those for the protection of the heritage). In real life, however, decisions about devolution are not made looking at the demand side, being—mostly—made by politicians and bureaucrats looking to their supply side interests, under the pressure of organized national and regional interest groups. The results of the games among these interests do not necessarily generate a rational allocation of expenditures and revenues between the different levels of government.

The main point, therefore, in a constitutional reform of the function of the various levels of government is not of choosing which functions to devolve to which level, but how to reform them so as to allow the freedom of choice of individuals to matter. An example may be that of vouchers provided by the central government cultural institutions to lower income persons and young people enabling them to attend concerts and theatres in their communities, as an alternative to the devolution of these functions to the lower levels of governments (Peacock 1969; Crowther Hunt and Peacock 1973; Peacock 1996).

The Theory of Bureaucratic Behaviour Perhaps the most important implications that can be drawn for the economics of culture from this individual choice-public choice perspective of political economy is the theory of bureaucratic behaviour (Peacock 1977, 1978a, 1983a, 1992; Third Lecture, §2 and 3, Peacock 1993[6]; Forte 2000: ch. 5). Indeed there is in the cultural sector an acute problem of paternalism and predominance of the preferences of specialists as to which goods and services are to be produced and preserved and which artists to support, which may give rise

---

[6]This specifically for the cultural sector, in the area of performing arts.

both to X inefficiency and to their 'idleness coupled with prodigality' (Peacock 1992: 71).

The dominant models of bureaucracy in standard public choice theory, that of budget maximisation of Tullock (1965) and of Niskanen (1971), may thus be replaced by the Leibensteinian X inefficiency model (Leibenstein 1978) and by the Breton and Wintrobe model of interacting games of vertical trust (Breton and Wintrobe 1982). These games take place between top bureaucrats and the politicians and among bureaucrats, who pursue their own welfare, in pure monetary terms, in fringe benefits, in prestige and in 'on the job leisure'. One should also add the rent seeking games among bureaucrats and politicians on one side and the pressure groups of firms and individuals on the other side (Muller 1985; Forte and Peacock 1985a, b). To complete the picture one should consider the power games between members of the government and of the parliament Forte and Peacock 1985a, b) and politicians at the various level of government (Rizzo (1990) reedited as Rizzo (2011) with Introduction by Alan T. Peacock; Forte and Peacock 1985a, b). From this perspective, it is useful to pay some attention to the institutional design of the politician/bureaucrat relationship and to the features of delegation. The arms-length principle (implicitly recalled below) deserves some attention. Differences in culture play a role in determining different institutions and in affecting the conduct of public actors. Therefore, in the more general perspective of interacting public choice games, Niskanen's 'output maximization' may come out as a result of politicians' power games and of pressure groups' rent-seeking games.

Five policy devices may contrast the growth of government and the inefficiency of bureaucracies (Forte and Peacock, in Forte and Peacock 1985a):

1. Introduction of competition among bureaucrats in the supply of public services.
2. Competition of lower levels of governments.
3. Severing the nexus between public prices and taxes and the services for which they represent the payment.
4. Putting out government services to competitive tenders, maintaining government responsibility for the level of the service.
5. As the ultimate deterrent, privatization of public enterprises with removal of restrictions on freedom of entry to the relevant markets for the previously nationalized or municipalized public services.

3   Cultural Economics Conforming to Individuals' Choices

Let us now consider the specific applications to cultural economics of the individual choice principle from the perspective of market economy-public economy interacting games.

In this individual free choice approach, non-pecuniary values inherent to human nature do count because cultural immaterial values have more do to with people's enjoyment of life than those offered by other goods and services (Peacock 2000: Conclusions). Economic resources are limited and those for culture tend to be 'peanuts', also because culture has intangible value that is difficult to measure, even with refined economic indicators (Peacock 2003). Public economy reasons for intervening in the supply of cultural goods cannot be merely reduced to their nature as pure public goods because most of them are saleable on the market. However, external economies for consumers and producers, or 'spillover effects' may justify public aid.[7] Property rights of immaterial goods, such as those of the performing arts, are not easily enforceable (Peacock 1973; Towse 1999). This may also be true for the visual arts and for museums, while the external parts of the built heritage are a free good.

Spillovers of free supplies of arts and culture goods may benefit consumers because 'experience goods' (Nelson 1970) require previous consumption to appreciate them (Becker and Murphy 1991a, b; Mossetto 1993; Forte and Mantovani 2000, 2001). The addictive effect of past consumption may change tastes and modify the demand curves of consumers, shifting them upward, so that the marginal utility of consumption of cultural goods increases though time via adaptive preferences (Becker and Murphy 1991a, b; Peacock 1969, 1993; Forte 2010: ch. 3, sect 2). The upward shift of the demand gives spillovers to the producers too, who may increase and diversify their supply. These effects do not concern only future generations. Indeed, in the first instance, they determine the present younger generations' tastes when they become older.[8] Other spillovers may derive from the likely positive effect of cultural goods on tourism and on the international reputation of the country.

Spillovers of cultural goods also benefit other suppliers. The products and innovations of artists of the serious performing arts may benefit those of the popular performing arts (Peacock 1973). Similar consequences may take place for the visual arts and heritage goods via the effects of their artistic content on industrial design and architecture. Important spillovers have benefits for future generations by transmitting knowledge and creativity in the arts and culture to them.

In some cases, such as that of museums or theatrical performances, charging prices that cover all the average costs, would imply a loss of welfare because some capacity could remain unused, so that one may argue that the deficit and the subsidy might be justified by the Dupuit-Hotelling theorem. That shows that setting prices at marginal cost in order to exploit unused capacity would imply a deficit under decreasing marginal cost curves (or zero marginal costs in the limiting case) because average costs would be above the marginal costs. Of course, the theorem

---

[7]Peacock (1969) for the performing arts and the heritage; Peacock (1973) for musical composition; Peacock and Rizzo (2008) for heritage.

[8]When Peacock proposes to support the performing arts via the education system he implicitly accepts the theory of rational addiction for the arts as experience goods, as the knowledge of their meaning increases through their experience, transmitted to students by teaching (see on this J.S. Mill 1848: Book V, ch. II, sect 8; Mossetto 1993: ch. 2, §2.2.3).

may not be applicable to every cultural institution, as some do not have excess capacity.

On the other hand, under the general law of decreasing costs through time, that is, of increasing returns for the national product, the Baumol cost disease may lead to increasing costs through time of art goods and services (Peacock 2000) because their producers must be paid average wages and salaries; thus here the decreasing costs law may not be applicable. However, these costs might be inflated by inefficiencies in their supply by the bureaucracies in state-managed arts organisations, such as those existing in Italy, and by the bargaining power of performers and other cultural workers seeking improvements in their earnings (Peacock 1978a, 1982, 1983a, b).

In real life public choice interacting games that are the origin of public policies, preferences expressed through the individual free choices of the electors-taxpayers may have a difficult reception. In the area of cultural policies there are additional difficulties because of the asymmetric information aspects, in which the 'experts' are powerful 'gatekeepers', for example, defining which of the visual and performing art services to support or the value of the heritage that should be conserved.

In the performing arts, the composers and performers argue that they, not those 'who pay the piper', have the right to choose the music because they know the matter from the inside (Peacock 1993). The reaction of the elite to the thesis that the public must have more to say is generally negative, as they—the musicians—reply that they 'know better'.[9] However, from an individual choice perspective, those who pay the bill, that is, the consumers as taxpayers, should have the right to choose how to allocate and spend the money rather than the élite of managers in charge of the supply (Snowball 2009). In the heritage sector, the opinions of the managers and their advisers and the peer-group assessments by them dominate what should be in 'the public interest'—something that may not have much to do with taxpayers'/ voters' interest in the arts (Peacock 2000; Peacock and Rizzo 2008). In the case of broadcasting, the powerful position of the suppliers subsidized by an ad hoc tax may enhance the (quasi) monopoly power of the public broadcasting company. Public policies to re-equilibrate these games are needed to enhance the role of individual choices.

For guidelines, one may take the five set of policies above sketched above, paying attention to performance indicators whose adoption and manipulations may play an important role in achieving those ends. The five policy sets can be regrouped into two: adopt pricing as far as possible and use vouchers in a competitive space extended horizontally and vertically; undertake general and partial privatizations, particularly by non-profit entities,[10] again in an extended competitive space.

---

[9]An example may be the review in the *International Journal of Arts Management* of Peacock and Rizzo (2008) in which the thesis that the public should have more to say runs through the entire volume. The book has been judged "informative and helpful, but with an old-fashioned understanding of the heritage field and of the efforts of the heritage industry" (Witcomb 2010).

[10]It is often difficult to distinguish public, nonprofit and private cultural entities. See Schuster (1998) for the case of the USA.

The Market System in the Cultural Sector The market system may be extended both by adoption of new digital technologies and Internet and by reforming copyright rules and institutions, to encourage the sale of the services of the orchestras, museums, built heritage and TV programmes.

According to authors such as Peacock (Peacock 1969, 1993; Towse 2005) subsidies to producers and supplier of art and cultural goods and services should be replaced by vouchers,[11] which shift the choice to consumers and increase competition among the suppliers. An extended voucher system, targeted to the young, the less well to-do and residents of peripheral areas, might smooth the negative distributive effects of prices on consumers in the cultural sector and, via prices below average full average cost, expand the supply of cultural goods, more effectively than subsidies.

The application of the new digital and Internet technologies to the cultural sector (Towse and Handke 2013) presents new opportunities for 'vouchers' in digital format because technologies can reduce the administrative and operational problems related to the management of the voucher system and have also prevented its implementation. Personal cultural vouchers, free or at discounted prices may be permanent (unlike paper vouchers) as their issuers could restore and periodically vary their content electronically, empowering individual choices of consumers by adapting the voucher to the preferences that recipients reveal operatively online. A massive assignment of free and discounted vouchers with the option of digital access to new on line products of orchestras, theatres, virtual museums, and digital reproductions of archaeological and historic sites, art galleries and libraries, would enable access by residents of smaller towns and peripheral regions, a 'not dispersive devolution'.

The revenue of the cultural institutions may increase because the addictive effects of the free and low cost consumption of art and culture goods of targeted groups of customers increase demand.[12] New creative ways of producing and offering art and culture goods may develop in the digital world, the stimulated by consumers' preferences (Towse and Handke 2013). These preferences may be revealed also by the rating given by the owners of credit cards on the goods and services that they used, as is normally done for purchases via Internet. The extent of these effects would be influenced by the institutional setting—for example, how the principal-agent relationship is designed—and by the related incentive system and evaluation schemes.

Overall, the replacement of the public subsidies to the cultural institutions by digital cultural vouchers and the option for digital products online in an increasingly competitive space would affect the principal-agent relationship, restating as principal the consumers and extending the market and quasi market of cultural

---

[11]Digitalized vouchers may be personalized, thus avoiding the resale of them by the person entitled to others.

[12]Obviously, this prediction follows from the theory of rational addiction above referred to. It has been tested econometrically for US museums by Gray (1998).

goods and services. The paternalistic social welfare function thus may be mitigated by the preferences of the public in ways previously only imagined (as in Forte and Mantovani 2000 and in Peacock as quoted by Towse 2005). To prevent the risk of impoverishing the tastes of consumers, free and low cost digital vouchers could be targeted to selected types of institutions and services. The bureaucratic elites that influence public decision-making may reaffirm their role of custodian of the 'superior cultural values'. There is an inherent tension between the values pursued by the art managers and experts, by the artists, by the 'art lovers' and the prosaic point of view of the general consumers.

Application to Cultural Heritage The theme of who has the right to choose is particularly delicate in the case of cultural heritage, when it comes to the issue of the preservation of the past for the future. Obviously, the built heritage may become more profitable by restoring and adapting the historical buildings to perform new functions or using traditional ones in a different way. There is a growing recognition that the conservation of our heritage fabric has a role to play in the need to find sustainable building practices. There may be an economic value, from the point of view of sustainability, in finding ways to recycle and adapt our built heritage (Witcomb 2010). However, how should we reconcile these objectives with those of preservation?

A solution may consist in assigning to non-profit private organizations the decision on the recovery, restoration, preservation and valuation of immovable archaeological, historic, artistic buildings and to administer related public subsidies. The task may be undertaken by organisations such as the UK's National Trust, English Heritage, Historic Scotland (on which see Peacock 1994 and Towse 2005). The positive experience of Italy with the Istituto Regionale Ville Venete controlled by the Veneto Region (Mantovani 1997) may be taken as a model.

As for TV services, privatization may be a possible solution, however, distinguishing the supply of public services from the supply of commercial services, which may have different principal-agent relationships. Where to draw the line, again, is a matter of the institutional setting.

Thus one may pursue two concurrent strategies (as in the 1986 Peacock Report):

(i) Transforming public service television, financed by an ad hoc tax, into a non-profit company financed on the market and competing with private companies;

(ii) Abolishing the monopoly of the public service by a public service broadcaster and assigning this mission also to 'commercial' television companies, either public or private.

The transformation of public television into a semi-public enterprise working in the market economy, financed by products sold in the market and market-oriented, could open the door to further transforming it into a private non-profit organisation controlled by its members (Peacock 2000, 2004a). The shift from taxation to pricing for television programs may take advantage of the technological progress by the collection of the prices by the aid of electronic devices, as in the case of the lighthouse, to solve the transaction cost problem already pointed out by Coase (as in Peacock 1979a). The revenue of the television public services, whether supplied by commercial companies or by non-profit institutions, then, may derive from the charges for the specific programs by pay TV systems, which are now current for the programs paid for by the customers. In the case of the public service programs, their price would be covered by the government through vouchers distributed to the residents in the country, as anticipated by Peacock half a century ago (Peacock 1989). With the progress in ICT it is now possible to do this merely by giving a password to each owner of an electronic voucher entitling them to spend a given amount. By assigning the offer of subsidised cultural programs to commercial television too, the privileged situation of the public service television would no longer be justified and the role of the individual consumer choice would increase (Peacock 2000; Towse and Handke 2013).

4   Final Remarks

It would not be correct to assume that the adoption of individual choice-public choice perspective implies that markets always work better than the public sector for cultural goods. It is true that freedom of individual choice for culture, as a good with ethical value, is more important than for other goods. But here too, as in the broad sectors of welfare expenditures, the guiding principle of this perspective is that the market is needed to reduce the need for public intervention and to pursue an improved satisfaction of the freely chosen individual wants.

Annotated Bibliography of Works by Alan Turner Peacock
1950s and 1960s. The roots of Peacock's individual choice theory may be found in seven books written or edited by him, alone or with co-authors, between the 1950s and 1960s.

In the first of 1952, *The Economics of National Insurance* (Peacock 1952), Peacock criticizes the social security system adopted in UK on the grounds that is did not conform to the benefit principle that should inform a social public economy oriented by individual free choice.

The second book, *National Income and Social Accounting*—co-authored by Peacock with Harold C. Edey (Edey and Peacock 1954), is a pioneering book on the system of national accounting. The tripartite subjects of the accounts, that is, Households, Firms and Government with their interacting market transactions later on also became the players of the public economy interactive games, which consist of non-market, market and quasi market transactions.

The third book, in which we may identify the roots of the new perspective of economics to which Peacock was contributing, is *Classics in Public finance*, edited together with Richard Musgrave in 1958 (Musgrave and Peacock 1958).[13] The

---

[13] James Buchanan, in the Preface, is thanked for the assistance in the Italian selection. This is the first encounter of Peacock with the founder of the Virginia Public School approach.

anthology presents the debate among Continental writers on public finance on the process of the allocation of resources between the government and the private sector, as compared to the ideal means of taxing individuals, to satisfy their collective wants. The subjective interpretation of social wants and the benefit approach dominate the debate between the Austrian, Italian, Scandinavian, German writers, presented there.

There followed in 1961, the book with J. Wiseman on the *Growth of Public Expenditure in United Kingdom*, in which the two authors explain from the supply side, via the displacement effect, the growth of public spending, which they analysed with careful accounting (Peacock and Wiseman 1961). The displacement effect consists in the increase of the public spending and taxation, due to some public want, such as that of defence of the country, which it is necessary to satisfy. Once that necessity is over and the expenditure for it is no longer required, the related tax endowment is still available for other purposes, without asking taxpayers for further contributions. Thus, the fiscal burden of the new expenditures is concealed from the taxpayers, implying the maintenance of growth of government that the majority, if it knew its real opportunity cost, might not approve.

The fourth book, in which there are presentiments of Peacock's contributions to the new individual choice perspective, is an essay with J. Wiseman 'Education for Democrats' (Peacock and Wiseman 1964). Under the criterion of equality of opportunities for all individuals, they argue that public expenditure for higher education, in general, has to be paid by the beneficiaries, perhaps via student loans.[14]

The fifth book that needs to be mentioned in this 'pattern recognition' of the contributions by Peacock to this new perspective, is a lesser known work, written with the assistance of Dieter Biehl on 'Quantitative Analysis in Public Finance' (Peacock and Biehl 1969), devoted to measurement of the public economy.

There followed in 1971 the book with K. Shaw on *The Economic Theory of Fiscal Policy*. Here Peacock, with his co-author, presents a fiscal policy of growth and employment conforming to the basic freedom of individual choice principles, which requires a competitive economy and a balanced budget to avoid the burden of public debt falling on future voters, who have no voice in the present.

The Second Period From the mid-1970s to the new century, Peacock works on the interacting public choice game structure of individual choices—the public choice way of looking at the market economy-public economy process—and confronts it with the other theories relating to the public economy-market economy interaction.

A first contribution, mostly on the critical side, has to do with the welfare economics foundations of political economy and of public economics, is in the book *Welfare Economics. A Liberal Restatement* with Charles Rowley (Rowley and Peacock 1975). The authors (Chapter 6) criticize the 'neo Paretian' view of the welfare maximization process based on the principle that the welfare of the

---

[14]On the proposal of this essay as for the aid to the students of higher education. See Fedeli and Forte (2008) in Petretto and Pignataro (2008).

community increases when someone may get a benefit while no one is worse-off. The authors argue that this is a mere efficiency principle, defective from the distributive point of view because it privileges the status quo, which may even violate basic values of the individuals such as that of free choice. On the other hand, the elaborated social welfare function of Bergson-Samuelson type is an artificial exercise, as the common will of a community does not exist.

The model of interacting games of public choice vis á vis individual choice is systematically presented by Peacock with various applications in the 1979 book on *The Economic Analysis of Government and Related Themes* (Peacock 1979b).

Peacock then proceeded to edit three anthologies with co-authors on the development of his approach to public economy decision-making. With myself, the two anthologies on *The Political Economy of Taxation* in 1981 and on *Public Expenditure and Government Growth in 1985* (Forte and Peacock 1985a, b); and with Martin Ricketts as main co-author, the one on the public economics of regulation (Peacock et al. 1984).

The 1992 four lectures on 'Public Choice Analysis in Historical Perspective' (Peacock 1992 and comments of Forte 1992 and commentary of Giardina 1992), offered Peacock the intellectual occasion for confronting the individual choice-public choice perspective which he adopts with the public choice economics of James Buchanan and other authors, and of integrating the two, going beyond the seminal version of *The Calculus of Consent* of Buchanan and Tullock (1962).

The book of 1997 on *The Political Economy of Economic Freedom* (Peacock 1997) first presents the liberal perspective of Peacock's individual choice theory, its underlying ethical philosophy and its impact on the critique of economic policy.; it then compares his views with those of Sen and of Keynes.

In the autobiographical book of 2010 *Anxious To Do Good. Learning to be an Economist the Hard Way*, Peacock collects his memoirs, notes and correspondence as economist working for the cause of the British Liberal movement, in the period between the first half of the 1950s of the twentieth century to the first decade of the twenty-first century.

Finally, in his last book *Defying Decrepitude: A Personal Memoir* (Peacock 2013) he describes with witty humor his vicissitudes with the Nation Health Service and, among others, how music may defy the difficulties of old age.

Peacock and Cultural Economics Alan Peacock is one of the founder of cultural economics, which he has explored in a multiplicity of aspects, from the performing arts to cultural heritage and broadcasting. From the title of his first important paper on cultural economics of 1968, 'Public Patronage of Music: An Economist's View' (Peacock 1968), one may infer that the focal point of his research in this sector is on how reconcile public intervention with the freedom of the arts and culture.

As Chairman of the Arts Council of Great Britain's National Enquiry into Orchestra Resources (Peacock Report 1970) he actually argued that the orchestras could be financed by recordings and sale of tickets to their concerts, rather than by public subsidies.

As member of the Royal Commission on the Constitution 1969–73 he, with Lord Crowther Hunt, wrote the Memorandum of Dissent (Crowther Hunt and Peacock 1973), maintaining that a mere devolution of the existing functions was not the right solution. A drastic change was needed in the functions of the government to give, through the devolution, a much larger place to the individual's freedom of choice. The true devolution for Peacock consisted in empowering the consumer-voter tax payer. The relevance of this 'Memorandum' for cultural goods is clear from what Peacock wrote later (Peacock 1996: 9). Among the reforms, which he would have chosen to put prior to the devolution process, there were: voucher schemes for performing arts for people with lower income; a reform of TV, putting listeners and viewers' interests before those of producers of programs; and improved communication between performing and creative musicians of orchestras and their public.

Then, in 1973, there are a paper on the economic value of musical composition, centred on the difficulties of enforcing copyrights in this sector and on the contrast between the 'serious' music and 'popular music' (Peacock 1973) and a paper on cultural accounting (Peacock and Godfrey 1973).

In 1974, Peacock, with co-author Godfrey, turns to the economics of museums and galleries, with the approach adopted for the performing arts (Peacock and Godfrey 1974) and comes back to the economics of performing arts with a paper on understanding its economics, in an anthology edited by Bing Chen (Peacock 1974). Then there is Peacock's book with Ronald Weir, *The Composer in the Market place* (Peacock and Weir 1975), where he develops the themes discussed in the paper of 1973.

In 1978, Peacock begins to focus his interest on the intergenerational issue of heritage from the individual free choice point of view, considering both museums and historical and artistic buildings (Peacock 1978b).

In 1982, writing a Report on the effects of inflation on the performing arts in the UK, Peacock showed that, contrary to the Baumol's disease predictions, the wages of artists had increased less than the inflation rate, while those of 'ordinary' workers had increased more. In 1985, he reflects again on the Baumol cost disease law in the performing arts (Peacock 1985), already dealt with in Peacock (1969).

Appointed Chairman of the Committee on financing the BBC, Alan did not support Margaret Thatcher's intention of replacing the licence fee with advertising. The 'Peacock Committee' instead proposed that BBC television could make its revenue by direct subscription (Peacock 1986a). The proposal was in line with that expressed in the paper on the lighthouse (Peacock 1979a)[15] and in the Peacock Report on orchestras, on the possibilities offered by the technological developments transforming public or quasi-public goods into marketable goods.

In 1986 there is a first paper applying these ideas to broadcasting (Peacock 1986b). Then, from 1986 to 1989, four other papers on broadcasting: (1) On technological development to allow to price its services (Peacock 1986c); (2) on consumer sovereignty and broadcasting (Peacock 1987a); (3) on broadcasting

---

[15]With a similar approach to Coase (1974).

finance through free subscription and programme purchase (Peacock 1987b); and (4) on public service functions of broadcasting as those of cultural programs performed also by private companies by vouchers to the public (Peacock 1988).

In 1993, Peacock publishes his main book on cultural economics: *Paying the piper. Culture, Music, Money* (Peacock 1993). The interacting games between artists, households as consumers and as electors, political class, bureaucrats constitute the main thread of the book.

In his Keynes Lectures to the British Academy of 1994, Peacock came back to the topic of heritage with a paper on 'A Future for the Past' (Peacock 1994), adopting the public choice model as seen above. The bureaucrat managers of the 'heritage', via asymmetric information and unclear definition of costs and output of conservation, *de facto* replace the consumers as principals in the agent-principal relation and concentrate their efforts in getting resources from the politician, with the support of art experts (see chapters by Mazza 2003 and 2005 respectively in Towse 2003; Towse 2005).

In the same year, Peacock edits, with Ilde Rizzo, the book *Cultural Economics and Cultural Policies* (Peacock and Rizzo 2005), in which the criteria for government support to culture, actually applied or to be applied, are confronted in an individual choices-public choices perspective.

At the beginning of the new century, pursuing the same approach, Peacock writes two papers, supported by a significant collection of data, on the financing of performing arts, heritage and broadcasting in England (Peacock 2000) and in Scotland (Peacock 2001).

In 2003 there followed a paper on performance indicators in cultural policy (Peacock 2003); the next year a paper on public service broadcasting by private TV (Peacock 2004a) and another in defence of the credibility of cultural economists (Peacock 2004b in Ginsburgh 2004).

In 2008, Alan Peacock publishes, with Ilde Rizzo, *The Heritage Game* (Peacock and Rizzo 2008), which aimed at investigating, with a political economy approach, the impact of economic analysis on the formulation and implementation of heritage policies.

References

Becker GS, Murphy KM (1991a) A theory of rational addiction. J Polit Econ 96(4):675–700
Becker GS, Murphy KM (1991b) Rational addiction and the effect of prices on consumption. Am Econ Rev 81(2):237–241
Breton A, Wintrobe R (1982) The logic of bureaucratic conduct. An economic analysis of competition, exchange and efficiency in private and public organization. Cambridge University Press, New York
Buchanan JM (1960) The Italian tradition in fiscal theory. In: Buchanan JM (ed) Fiscal theory and political economy. University of North Carolina Press, Chapel Hill, NC
Buchanan J (2005) Why I, too, am not a conservative. The normative vision of classical liberalism. Edward Elgar, Cheltenham, UK

Buchanan JM, Tullock G (1962) The calculus of consent. University of Michigan Press, Ann Arbor, MI

Coase R (1974) The lighthouse in economics. J Law Econ 17:357–376

Crowther Hunt N, Peacock AT (1973) Memorandum of dissent. Royal Commission on the Constitution 1969-73 Vol. II. HMSO, London

Edey HC, Peacock AT (1954) National income and social Accounting. Hutchinson, London

Einaudi L (1949) Lezioni di politica sociale. Einaudi, Torino

Fedeli S, Forte F (2008) Il dibattito teorico sugli aiuti agli studenti nell'istruzione superiore: una verifica empirica per l'Italia. In: Petretto A, Pignataro G (eds) Economia del capitale umano. Istituzioni, incentivi e valutazione. Franco Angeli, Milano, pp 145–175

Forte F (1992) Comments. In: Peacock AT (ed) Public choice analysis in historical perspective. Cambridge University Press, New York, pp 117–127

Forte F (2000) Principi di Economia Pubblica. Giuffrè, Milano

Forte F (2010) Principles of public economics. A public choice approach. Edward Elgar, Cheltenham, UK, updated revision of Forte F 2007 Manuale di Scienza delle Finanze, 4th edn. Giuffrè, Milano

Forte F, Mantovani M (2000) Efficiency and effectiveness of museums' supply in an agency context. Studi Economici 71:5–48

Forte F, Mantovani M (2001) Measures of art and cultural welfare. Methodological and empirical aspects, Atti del Convegno New Economic Windows Salerno, September 2001

Forte F, Peacock AT (eds) (1985a) Public expenditure and economic growth. Basil Blackwell, Oxford

Forte F, Peacock AT (1985b) The political economy of public-sector growth and its control. In: Forte F, Peacock AT (eds) Public expenditure and economic growth. Basil Blackwell, Oxford

Giardina E (1992) Commentary. In: Peacock AT (ed) Public choice analysis in historical perspective. Cambridge University Press, New York, pp 145–167

Ginsburgh V (ed) (2004) Economics of art and culture. Elsevier, Amsterdam

Gray CM (1998) Hope for the future? early exposure to the arts and adult visit to art museums. J Cult Econ 22:87–98

Leibenstein H (1978) General X inefficiency theory of economic development. Oxford University Press, New York

Mantovani M (1997) Il patrimonio culturale delle ville venete e la sua sostenibilità. Un'analisi economica e fiscale. Edizioni Filò, Belluno

Mill JS (1848) Principles of political economy, re-edited by Robson J (1965) Collected Works of J.S. Mill. Routledge Kegan Paul, London

Mossetto G (1993) Aesthetics and economics. Kluwer Academic, Dordrecht

Musgrave R, Peacock AT (eds) (1958) Classics in the theory of public finance. Macmillan, London

Nelson P (1970) Information and consumer behavior. J Polit Econ 78(2):311–329

Niskanen WA (1971) Bureaucracy and representative government. Aldine, Chicago, IL

Oates WA (ed) (1976) The political economy of fiscal federalism. Heath, Lexington, MA

Peacock AT (1952) The economics of national insurance. William Hodge, Edinburgh

Peacock AT (1968) Public patronage of music. Three Banks Rev March:1–19

Peacock AT (1969) Welfare economics and public subsidies to arts. Manchester Sch Econ Soc Stud 4(December):223–235, reprinted in J Cult Econ 1994, 18:151–161

Peacock AT (1970) Report of the Arts Council enquiry into orchestra resources in Great Britain. Arts Council of Great Britain, London

Peacock AT (1973) The economic value of musical compositions. In: Kulp B, Stutzel W (eds) Beitrage zu einer theorie der sozialpolitik. Duncker and Humboldt, Berlin, pp 11–27

Peacock AT (1974) The problem of performing arts and the economic analysis. In: Chen B (ed) Understanding economics. Little Brown, Boston, MA

Peacock AT (1976a) The political economy of devolution. The British Case. In: Oates WA (ed) The political economy of fiscal federalism. Heath, Lexington, MA

Peacock AT (1976b) The political economy of dispersive devolution. Scot J Polit Econ 23(3): 205–219 (re-edited in: Peacock AT (1979) The economic analysis of Government and related themes. Martin Robertson, London)

Peacock AT (1977) Giving advice in difficult times. Three Banks Rev March:3–23. Also chapter 16 in. Peacock AT (1979) The economic analysis of government and related themes. Martin Robertson, London

Peacock AT (1978a) The economics of bureaucracy. An inside view. In: The economics of politics, Institute of Economic Affairs, London. Also chapter 17 in. Peacock AT (1979) The economic analysis of Government and related themes. Martin Robertson, London, pp 235–242

Peacock AT (1978b) Preserving the past: an international economic dilemma. In: Caroni P, Dafflon B, Enderlee G (eds) Nur Ökonomie ist keine Ökonomie. Festschrift fur B. M. Biucchi. Verlag Paul Haupt, Bern, pp 305–314

Peacock AT (1979a) The limitations of the public goods theory: the lighthouse revisited. In: Bohley P, Tockemitt G (eds) Festscrift fur Heinz Haller. Re-edited with minor changes as Chapter 9 in. Peacock AT (1979) The economic analysis of government and related themes. Martin Robertson, London, pp 127–136

Peacock AT (1979b) The economic analysis of government and related themes. Martin Robertson, London

Peacock AT (1982) Controlli microeconomici e macroeconomici della spesa pubblica, Einaudi Notizie

Peacock AT (1983a) Public X inefficiency. Informal and institutional constraints. In: Hanusch H (ed) Anatomy of government deficiencies. Springer, Berlin, pp 125–138

Peacock AT (1983b) Reducing government expenditure: a British view. In: Giersch H (ed) Reassessing the role of government in the mixed economy. Mor, Tubingen, pp 1–24

Peacock AT (1985) The cost disease: analytical and policy aspects. In: Hendon MA et al (eds) Bach and the box: the impact of television on the live arts. Akron, Oh, Association of Cultural Economics

Peacock AT (1986a) Report of the Committee on financing the BBC. HMSO, London

Peacock AT (1986b) Making sense of broadcasting finance. Robbins Lecture. University of Stirling. Reprinted in Towse R (ed) (1997) Cultural economics. The arts, the heritage and the media industries. Edward Elgar, Cheltenham, vol I, pp 435–448

Peacock AT (1986c) Technology and the political econmy of broadcasting, Intermdia, November 1986

Peacock AT (1987a) Fernseefinanzierunf und Verbraucher, Zetschrift fur Wirtschaftspolitik, 2, pp 113–123

Peacock AT (1987b) The politics of investigating broadcasting finance, Royal Bank of Scotland Review, March 1987, pp. 285–291

Peacock AT (1988) Subsidization and promotion of the arts. In: Giersch H (ed) Merits and Limits of Markets. Springer, Berlin

Peacock AT (1989) Freedom in broadcasting. Institute of Economic Affairs. Hobart Papers, London

Peacock AT (1992) Public choice analysis in historical perspective. Cambridge University Press, New York

Peacock AT (1993) Paying the piper: culture, music and money. Edinburgh University Press, Edinburgh

Peacock AT (1994) A future for the past: the political economy of heritage. Proc Br Acad 87: 189–226, reprinted in: Towse R (ed) (1997) Cultural economics. The arts, the heritage and the media industries, vol I. Edward Elgar, Cheltenham, pp 387–424

Peacock AT (1996) The device of devolution. Hume Occasional Paper n. 50. The David Hume Institute. Pace Print, Edinburgh

Peacock AT (1997) The political economy of economic freedom. Edward Elgar, Cheltenham, UK

Peacock AT (2000) Public financing of arts in England. Fiscal Stud 21(2):171–205

Peacock AT (2001) Calling the tune: a critique of art funding in Scotland. Edinburgh Policy Institute, Edinburgh

Peacock AT (2003) Performance indicators and cultural policy. Economia della cultura 13:1–10

Peacock AT (2004a) Public service broadcasting without the BBC? The Institute of Economic Affairs, London

Peacock AT (2004b) The credibility of cultural economists' advice to governments. In: Ginsburgh V (ed) Economics of art and culture. Elsevier, Amsterdam, pp 167–178

Peacock AT (2013) Defying decrepitude. University of Buckingham Press, Buckingham

Peacock AT, Biehl D (eds) (1969) Quantitative analysis in public finance. Praeger, New York

Peacock AT, Forte F (eds) (1985) The political economy of taxation. Basil Blackwell, Oxford

Peacock AT, Godfrey C (1973) Cultural accounting. Soc Trends 4:61–65

Peacock AT, Godfrey C (1974) The economics of museums and art galleries. Lloyd Bank Rev 111: 364–375

Peacock AT, Rizzo I (eds) (2005) Cultural economics and cultural policies. Kluwer Academic, Dordrecht

Peacock AT, Rizzo I (2008) The heritage game. Oxford University Press, London

Peacock AT, Weir R (1975) The composer in the market place. Faber Music, London

Peacock AT, Wiseman J (1961) The growth of public expenditure in the United Kingdom. Oxford University Press, London

Peacock AT, Wiseman J (1964) Education for democrats. Institute of Economic Affairs, London

Peacock AT, Ricketts M, Robinson IR (eds) (1984) The regulation game: how British and West-German companies bargain with government. Basil Blackwell, Oxford

Petretto A, Pignataro G (eds) (2008) Economia del Capitale Umano. Franco Angeli, Milano

Ricketts M (2015) Peacock, Alan T. (1922–2014). The new Palgrave dictionary of economics, online edition

Rizzo I (2001) The Idden debt. Springer, Netherland

Ropke W (1958) Civitas humana: a humane order of society. William Hodge, London (first German edition Zurich Erlenbach, 1944)

Ropke W (1960) A humane economy. The social framework of the free market. Von Mises Institute. Henry Regnery, Chicago (first German Edition 1943, Rentach, Zurich)

Rowley C, Peacock AT (1975) Welfare economics. A liberal restatement. Martin Robertson, Oxford

Schuster JM (1998) Neither public nor private: the hybridization of museums. J Cult Econ 22: 127–150

Snowball J (2009) Review of Alan Peacock and Ilde Rizzo, the heritage game. J Cult Econ 33: 321–324

Toqueville De A (1840/1965) Democracy in America. Oxford University Press, London

Towse R (1999) Copyright, incentives and performers' earnings. Kyklos 52(3):369–390

Towse R (ed) (2003) A handbook of cultural economics. Edward Elgar, Cheltenham, UK

Towse R (2005) Alan Peacock and cultural economics. Econ J 115:262–276

Tullock G (1965) The politics of bureaucracy. Public Affairs Press, Washington, DC

Wicksell K (1958) A new principle of just taxation. In: Musgrave R, Peacock AT (eds) Classics in the theory of public finance. Macmillan, London

Witcomb A (2010) Book review: the heritage game: economics, policy and practice by Alan Peacock and Ilde Rizzo. Int J Arts Manag 12(3):80–81

Welfare Economics and Public Policy: A Re-examination

Martin Ricketts

Abstract Classical liberal political economists such as Rowley and Peacock (Welfare economics: a liberal restatement, York studies in economics. Martin Robertson, London, 1975) expressed serious reservations about the way Welfare Economics came to be used in the formulation of public policy. In this chapter the sources of this discontent are outlined and the liberal critique explored. Austrian, Ordo-Liberal, Public Choice and Transactions Cost elements are separately considered. None of these approaches on its own quite sums up the overall critique, which really amounts to a survey of the difficulties of reconciling neoclassical marginal economics and modern techniques with Classical Liberal Political Economy.

1 Introduction

The question of whether and to what extent economic analysis is capable of offering clear advice on matters of public policy lies behind much work in cultural economics. It is a question that has been associated since the middle of the twentieth century with two seemingly irresistible trends. The first of these is the general increase in the size and scope of state activity compared with the years preceding the first and second world wars, a subject first systematically analysed by Peacock and Wiseman (1961) which charted the Growth of Public Expenditure in the United Kingdom. The second trend is that economics as a discipline has become progressively 'professionalised'.

Accompanying and associated with these trends were two other distinct developments. Firstly the education of the typical economist became much more focussed on particular mathematical techniques of analysis. In microeconomics this could be seen in the formalisation of rational choice theory, the refining of techniques of constrained maximisation and the identification of equilibrium states

M. Ricketts (✉)
University of Buckingham, Buckingham, UK
e-mail: martin.ricketts@buckingham.ac.uk

© Springer International Publishing Switzerland 2016
I. Rizzo, R. Towse (eds.), *The Artful Economist*,
DOI 10.1007/978-3-319-40637-4_3

for both the individual and the system as a whole. In macroeconomics profession-alism was associated with the construction of macroeconometric models and the generation of the data that were needed for their estimation. Economics also became professionalised in a more literal sense because it became increasingly possible to use an education in economics for career purposes. These career opportunities arose not merely in higher education but within government and even in private business. The expanding role of the state required some technical support. Public policy required justification, formulation and implementation and economics provided certain techniques that were useful in these respects.

In macroeconomics the responsibility of the government for the maintenance of full employment meant that fiscal policy was no longer simply about financing a limited number of traditional public activities, it was also about the control of 'aggregate demand'. Keynes famously remarked that the economist should be regarded rather like a dentist—someone who had special knowledge of available treatments and technical opportunities that could be of service to the general public but which would not generally be the source of controversy. The growth of the welfare state, however, meant that intervention was far more detailed than required for the manipulation of aggregate demand in the interests of 'stabilisation policy'. The state developed social policy (in education, health, housing and income support), competition policy, agricultural policy, environmental policy, regional policy, urban regeneration policy, transport policy, consumer protection policy, health and safety policy and even policy towards heritage, culture and the arts. In general it extended its reach into areas far outside the range traditionally associated with the 'classical' functions of the state.

For our purposes, however, it is the role that Welfare Economics has played in these developments that is the focus of attention. For if it was Keynes's analysis of national income determination that underlay stabilisation policy after the Second World War, it was the refinement of 'the New Welfare Economics' in the hands of Hicks (1939) and Kaldor (1939) building on the earlier work of Vilfredo Pareto that provided the intellectual support for much interventionist activity. This is not, of course, to argue that it necessarily 'caused' the various microeconomic policy departures but merely that it was on hand to provide the necessary intellectual buttressing.

Rowley and Peacock (1975), for example, building on Peacock and Rowley (1972a, b) were highly critical both of the nature and extent of policy interventions and of the role that welfare theory played in supporting them. Their reservations revolved around three broad areas. Firstly they were suspicious of the normative basis of much policy advice which implicitly adopted the Hicks-Kaldor test or the 'Potential Pareto Improvement' in social welfare to justify state intervention. Quite apart from some technical ambiguities associated with the test that were well rehearsed at the time, it elevated the pursuit of 'allocative efficiency' above all other considerations. Secondly they criticised the epistemology underlying welfare theory and its static foundations. Could policy makers really plausibly be assumed to have access to the relevant information about the marginal social benefits and costs of certain activities in order to introduce suitably calibrated policy instruments aimed at improving social outcomes? Finally, they were incredulous at the naivety of an approach to public policy that assumed the existence of public servants devoted to 'the public interest'. This had nothing to do with an excessively negative view of human nature. The Rowley and Peacock critique did not endorse the self-regarding and virtually solipsistic view of human nature embedded in some micro-economic theory. On the other hand there was a clear theoretical impropriety in assuming broadly self-regarding preferences on the part of private contractors but disinterested and public spirited preferences on the part of public officials or politicians. Variations in the behaviour of economic agents should be explained by differences in 'the situation in which they are placed' (as Adam Smith put it) rather than by differences in essential character and motivation. Further it was clear that the growth of the state and the development of democratic politics created a very complex environment in which opportunities for special interest groups to exert influence—including the state bureaucracy itself—should not be overlooked.

Perhaps these general points can best be summarised by the observation that the application of welfare economics to the formulation and justification of public policy did not easily harmonise with the traditions of Classical Liberalism. These were rooted in the writings of the eighteenth century Scottish Enlightenment philosophers as represented by David Hume and Adam Smith. In the nineteenth century they flowed through the work of de Tocqueville on democracy, John Stuart Mill on liberty and, of course, the great Italian tradition in Public Finance. The critique was a re-assertion of the claims of political economy over the exponents of the newer mid-twentieth century corpus of technical micro and macroeconomics. Again this was not because the application of technique or theoretical rigour in economic analysis was always inherently undesirable. It was because the pursuit of refinements in technique could give a very misleading impression of 'scientific' precision to the study of economic policy. Policy errors in this view were to be expected from an approach that derived policy prescriptions from a highly formal-ised theoretical foundation and which omitted extremely important normative considerations and practical difficulties. The rest of this chapter re-examines some of the objections to welfare economics raised by Rowley and Peacock in their critique and elsewhere and discusses the alternative classical liberal view of the relationship between welfare theory and public policy.

2 The Paretian Tradition

It is clearly not possible within the space of a short section to provide a compre-hensive review of the development of modern Welfare Economics. Some statement of the main elements of the approach is necessary, however, in order to consider the objections that have been raised and the difficulties encountered in using it as a tool in the formulation and the appraisal of public policy. In essence the New Welfare Economics arose out of the marginal revolution of the late nineteenth century with its emphasis on a subjectivist or 'marginal utility' concept of value. With attention focussed on individual willingness to pay for goods and services rather than the technological question of how many hours of labour were required to produce them, the notion of 'utility' subtly changed its meaning.

From being a quality of things, it became a term associated with an individual's wellbeing or 'happiness' and then simply a mathematical representation of a person's subjective preferences. For Adam Smith an object might have 'great utility'—meaning usefulness. For Mill or Bentham, utility was associated with actions which conduced to human happiness or which avoided pain. These pleasures and pains were not, however, to be inferred from actual choices. People might often err or through ignorance, poor example, or harsh economic conditions make choices that jeopardised ultimate happiness. The quantity and quality of pleasures and pains was to be tested not by revealed choice but by 'the preference felt by those who in their opportunities of experience, to which must be added their habits of self-consciousness and self-observation, are best furnished with the means of comparison' (Mill 1861: 11). Policy here was to be determined by those who knew what was good for us and aimed at maximising aggregate happiness—implying an ability to compare one person's happiness with another. For the supporters of subjective value, utility became the individual economic agent's maximand. People became rational 'utility maximisers' able to place possible choices in order of preference and to pick the (self-evaluated) best from those available. Utility was purged of normative content in itself. It merely reflected the actual preference ordering of an economic agent with higher numbers being assigned to choices more preferred in the ranking. Given that any monotonic transformation of a utility function could serve to represent the same preference ordering it was clear that the new theory provided no basis for comparing one person's utility with another.

Normative content re-emerged with specific value judgements that are now associated with Pareto and which underlie the New Welfare Economics. In the first place it is specifically assumed that individuals are the best judges of their own welfare. With the exception of severe mental illness or the absence of age and experience, people are assumed to know what is good for them. Secondly the individualistic basis of the theory is confirmed by the assumption that the welfare of society is dependent upon the self-assessed individual levels of welfare experienced by all of its members. This is sometimes referred to as 'welfarism'—the proposition that in the normative evaluation of social states only information about individual orderings matters. Finally, with the maximisation of aggregate happiness ruled out by the impermissibility of inter-personal comparisons of utility, the New Welfare Economics was founded on a more restrictive criterion for judging changes in social welfare. The Pareto criterion states that the welfare of society as a whole is improved if at least one person is made better off in their own estimation and no one is worse off.

Given the seemingly restrictive nature of the Pareto criterion it seems strange that a theoretical edifice has been constructed that has proved so powerful in influencing public policy and that has earned the displeasure of classical liberals. Although often presented as being quite weak, the value judgements on which it is based are certainly not beyond dispute. It might also have been expected that, since a single objector could stymie any policy, it would prove quite hard to develop proposals that would gain the necessary agreement for their adoption. To its critics, the transformation of Paretian welfare economics into a hegemonic doctrine of great practical significance has been accomplished by a form of intellectual leger-demain. For Rowley and Peacock, the root of this subterfuge could be found in the uncritical use within normative policy analysis of the concept of 'Pareto efficiency'.

A state of 'efficiency' exists if Pareto improvements in social welfare have been exhausted and there are no further opportunities available for making some people better off without harming others. Pareto efficiency is clearly a necessary condition for maximising social welfare in the framework of the New Welfare Economics because inefficiency would imply the existence of social states that everyone would prefer. If everyone could be better off by some reallocation of resources it is hard not to agree that to tolerate the inefficiency would be poor policy and that moving to the efficient one would increase social welfare. It is tempting, however, to be led to the false conclusion that efficient states are to be socially preferred to inefficient ones. Certainly *some* efficient states will be preferred to an inefficient one—those in which everyone is actually better off. But there will exist many other possible changes that in principle lead to efficiency but that fail to satisfy the Pareto Criterion. Indeed in most practical situations it is almost inconceivable that literally every person will be made better off by a particular intervention of the state. Mostly there will be gainers and losers. If the gainers could actually compensate the losers all would be well and the Pareto criterion satisfied. But if such compensation cannot be paid for practical or political reasons the normative principles so far discussed provide no support for moving from an inefficient position.

This de facto underpinning of the status quo by the strict Pareto criterion led, in the 1940s and early 1950s, to a loosening of the criterion and to the adoption of various hypothetical 'compensation' tests associated with Hicks (1939), Kaldor (1939), Scitovsky (1941) and Little (1950). If the gainers could hypothetically compensate the losers from a change (and if the losers were unable hypothetically to bribe the gainers not to go ahead) it was argued that the change should be implemented and that social welfare could be said to have increased even in the absence of the actual payments. Rowley and Peacock (1975: 51) characterise this as "a bold attempt to hoodwink the policy-makers into believing that the Paretian criteria were more powerful than in fact was the case" and refer to the success of this operation as akin to 'a hoax'. The main point is that it implied that Pareto efficiency was a suitable aim of economic and social policy and that it could be pursued without paying attention to the strict application of the Pareto criterion.

By substituting the 'Potential Pareto Improvement' criterion in place of the strict 'Actual Pareto Improvement', public policy was released from a straightjacket and set free to roam widely. Its role became to identify allocative inefficiency and to use corrective policy instruments that led to net social benefits. Because the compen-sation of losers was not actually required, this agenda could lead to apparently illiberal implications, while the rooting out of inefficiency was capable of produc-ing an almost limitless case for government intervention. The technical requirements for Pareto efficiency were so abstruse and demanding that they were most unlikely to be satisfied in their purity in any practical situation. For all gains to trade to be exhausted every person's marginal valuation of a good or service must be the same (thus ruling out gains from exchanging one good for another); factor inputs must be allocated so that their relative marginal products are identical across all producers (thus ruling out higher output from exchanging one input for another); and the marginal willingness to pay for goods should equal their respective marginal costs (thus ruling out gains from increasing or diminishing the output).

Famously it turned out that these conditions would indeed be satisfied (given suitable restrictions on utility and production functions) in a perfectly competitive equilibrium—a proposition now called the first fundamental theorem of welfare economics. Essentially this was because, in such an equilibrium, all consumers and producers act as price takers and face the same price ratios in the market. These price ratios determine the real terms of trade available, and each transactor will demand or supply goods and services according to whether it is individually advantageous. At the margin the gain to supplying or demanding more of a good or factor will be zero, and price ratios will be equal to the marginal subjective valuations of all consumers and to the marginal costs of all producers. In a textbook world of perfect competition therefore the role of public policy as a means of securing 'efficiency' would be negligible.

Far from limiting the domain of public policy, however, the first theorem of welfare economics established a kind of rarefied and unachievable benchmark against which to compare the markets of the real world. It provided some intellectual support for a presumption in favour of 'competitive markets' and the freedom to trade, but even here the efficiency rationale and the strict conditions required by the first theorem appeared to favour a somewhat desiccated idea of what a truly competitive market looked like. Indeed, as Hayek pointed out, a perfectly competitive market seemed, on the face of it, to rule out most competitive behaviour since no one would be conscious of having any particular rivals. Price shading, product differentiation, advertising, technical innovations—all were ruled out in perfectly competitive theory. Economic agents faced 'parametric' market prices not competitors.

So far from descriptive reality were the competitive markets of welfare economics that 'market failure' seemed ubiquitous and became a foundation stone of the theory of economic policy. Not only did efficiency require 'perfect' rather than actual competition, the system of competitive pricing could only work if all the goods and services traded were strictly private and excludable. This ruled out the existence of non-rival and non-excludable 'public' goods, the technical conditions for the supply of which had been derived by Samuelson (1954) and which had been discussed by many earlier public finance economists most notably Wicksell (1896) and Lindahl (1919). The inability of competitive markets to supply efficient quantities of public goods was hardly a surprise. Economists going back to Adam Smith recognised that there were goods that would not repay a single person to produce 'though they may be in the highest degree advantageous to a great society' and that some collective choice mechanism was required in these areas. What extended the range of policy discussion most significantly however, were activities that were neither purely private nor purely public but which conferred benefits or costs on external parties. Private consumption and production decisions did not always simply affect the welfare of the individual economic agents taking the decisions but could 'spill-over' to influence the welfare of others. Inter-dependencies of utility or production functions shattered the ability of the impersonal perfectly competitive price system to yield efficient outcomes. Prices in competitive equilibrium would reflect the marginal private costs and benefits of individual decision makers not the full marginal social costs and benefits of decisions summed over all affected parties.

Externalities have effectively become the intellectual foundation stone of the economics of public policy. Wherever it can plausibly be maintained that private and social costs diverge, welfare economics provides a case for intervention in the interests of efficiency. Resource re-allocation could potentially make everyone better off as the valuations of the victims or beneficiaries of external effects are taken into account. Air pollution, traffic congestion, the 'over-exploitation' of natural resources, external benefits in health and education, spillovers in the property market, agglomeration economies in cities, waste disposal, airport noise, the protection of artistic and other heritage assets—the list of areas demanding corrective policy action is almost limitless. In each case the policy response, following a tradition associated with Pigou (1920), is usually to recommend a tax or a subsidy on the relevant activity equal to the marginal external costs or benefits associated with it. In this way the external effect is 'internalised' in the sense that tax or subsidy-inclusive prices faced by transactors in the market now represent the full 'social' costs or benefits from an activity, and each person has an incentive to adjust his or her behaviour accordingly.

The potential for economic and social policy to recommend intervention across a wider and wider range of activity in response to perceived external effects is illustrated by the gradual modification and elaboration of the nature of inter-dependencies. Whereas externalities were initially represented by smoking factories raising the costs of laundries, or the effects (good or bad) on the water table of draining mines, attention has moved away from production towards consumption. In social policy the idea that one person's consumption of health or education might affect the utility of another has long been a justification for intervention. But this approach has been extended so that it is capable of undermining what had been a clear distinction between 'efficiency' and 'equity' considerations. Paretian Welfare Economics was traditionally silent on distributional questions because of the inadmissibility of making inter-personal comparisons of utility. If individual utility functions are specified in such a way that other peoples' incomes matter, however, it becomes possible to see certain types of redistribution as being a matter of 'efficiency' rather than of 'equity'. As early as the 1960s Hochman and Rogers (1969) were writing about 'Pareto Optimal Redistribution' on the basis that one person's level of income might appear in another person's utility function. On the assumption of benevolence, 'efficient' transfers to the poor from the rich can be derived and finance through the tax system justified on the grounds that 'free riding' would otherwise prevent sufficient voluntary donations.

More recently Layard (2005) has argued that status races lead to excessive effort and that this justifies higher taxes on income from work (my effort to get ahead adversely influences other peoples' chances of doing the same—in the same manner as my attempt to get a better view at a football match might end in everyone standing instead of sitting). Similarly, Frank (1985) following Hirsch (1976) sees the quest for 'positional goods' (goods whose value depends on their exclusivity and that signal a person's status) as leading to 'inefficiency'. Places in top schools, senior positions in political or business organisations, houses in beautiful locations are not the type of 'good' that can be replicated and made available to all. One person's pursuit of a positional good adversely affects others by increasing its price and inducing further mutually frustrating responses from others. Allocating a fixed stock of a resource to those who value it most highly is usually a requirement of efficiency, and externalities that are the result of price movements and are therefore 'pecuniary' in nature would normally not demand a policy response. The person who wins is the person who pays. But where the resource takes the form of a prize in a tournament, the combined social effort expended to win it might be excessive in the sense that everyone could be better off by somehow agreeing to compete less fiercely. Frank (2005) argues that a progressive consumption tax is justified to moderate this behaviour. These taxes are clearly in the Pigouvian tradition—an attempt to confront decision makers with the external costs of their actions. Certain types of effort and consumption are classed along with pollution as requiring policy intervention.

3   A Liberal Critique

The Paretian paradigm and the 'economic efficiency' objective sketched in the above paragraphs is an integral part of the education of most economists and it still plays a central role in academic discussions of public policy. Whether it has the stranglehold on the profession that Rowley and Peacock found so uncongenial 40 years ago might no doubt be disputed. But it is at least possible to argue that a relatively uncritical approach to welfare theory and an implicit acceptance of efficiency as a primary concern, at least in microeconomic policy, remains the norm. Indeed the ability to derive recommendations for state intervention in areas as wide ranging as utility regulation, competition policy, environmental protection, education policy and even income redistribution on the basis of apparently 'scientific' criteria, has meant that the framework of Paretian Welfare Economics remains a congenial one to many interest groups across the political spectrum.

As has already been observed, there were many aspects of the Paretian framework that classical liberal critics rejected and, in addition, there were many important considerations that the approach entirely overlooked which made it dangerous as a foundation for public policy. In the first place the paradigm provides no analysis of the actual process of policy making. It simply relies on perfectly informed and publicly motivated technocrats to do the right thing. The result is that the choice of policy instruments can often seem of secondary importance to specifying the nature of the optimum allocation of resources. The traditional Pigouvian framework of policy analysis, for example, does not, in and of itself, provide an explanation of why taxes and subsidies should be preferred as policy instruments over regulations and directives or tradable licences. There is an implicit recognition that prices provide important information to decentralised decision makers but no explicit consideration of why (if information is known reliably by regulators) alternatives would not be equally effective and why (if information is not so reliable and cheap) tax or subsidy instruments are likely to lead to a potential Pareto improvement in social welfare. In fact Rowley and Peacock (1975) have a strong preference for tax instruments rather than directives to cope with the problem of pollution externalities (168–175) but the arguments they deploy concern the public choice implications of the different instruments, the importance of limiting the discretionary power of regulators and avoiding corruption, and the consequences of differing policies for the maintenance of freedom and the rule of law. Without explicit investigation of information, implementation and enforcement problems, in other words, all of which require additional ethical and political judgments to be made, the superiority of any public policy over alternatives (including the alternative of doing nothing) cannot be known.

A second general area of disquiet at a more philosophical rather than practical level relates to the assumption of 'welfarism'. Is it acceptable for social welfare to depend entirely on the self-assessed utility levels of all individual members of society? At first sight the principle that individual preference orderings are what matters and that somehow these must be the foundation of any aggregate assessment of social welfare seems unlikely to conflict with other normative principles about the good order of society. But Rowley and Peacock are at pains to argue that welfarism is no guarantee that social choices will be compatible with their conception of a liberal order or that preference orderings contain all the necessary information for the normative evaluation of policy. A liberal approach to policy they argue would ultimately be concerned with 'the maintenance and extension of individual freedom' (78) as 'an ethical value in itself' not simply a means to another end such as material prosperity. If negative liberty—being left alone to make choices and learn from experience—is an important value in itself, it might clearly conflict with a paternalistic desire to engineer outcomes that raise a person's self-assessed 'utility'. Similarly, if some ideal system of taxation that satisfied 'efficiency' theorems also required continual surveillance and the regular searching of houses by tax inspectors in dawn swoops it might reasonably be rejected in favour of systems of taxation less empowering of officials. Again, if it is argued that my purchase of an expensive Italian car requires me to pay a tax reflecting the 'harm' to my envious neighbour, would an immigrant from a racial minority be required to pay a tax to reflect the 'harm' experienced by all the racialists in the neighbourhood? At a certain point, most liberals, while eschewing coercive means as far as possible, would not 'recognise' the validity of certain preferences and would therefore deny the strict application of welfarism.

In the sections that follow some of these ideas will be explored in greater detail. The classical liberal critique has affinities with several related schools of thought including Austrian Economics, the German Ordo-Liberal School, Public Choice Theory and Transactions Cost Economics. Each of these will be considered in turn.

3.1   The Austrian School

At the centre of the Austrian critique of neoclassical theory from the mid twentieth century has been a deep suspicion of static equilibrium analysis and an insistence that the main problem of coordination is the discovery and use of dispersed information. This approach led Mises, Hayek and others to take a profoundly different view of central planning in the 1930s from theorists of general equilibrium such as Lerner and Lange. Central planning would fail they predicted (in the event correctly) because instead of resulting from the evolving and varied judgement of entrepreneurs about costs and benefits, the mandated prices of the planners would be the product of poor information and be much less subject to correction or adjustment in the face of new or modified goods and services. The price system was a method of information discovery and dispersal and would only reflect the final pattern of text book equilibrium when all change had ceased. In a world of perpetual innovation it was most unlikely that such a state would ever be approached and planners in any case would have no means of anticipating what it was.

Echoes of this dispute are to be found in the Austrian critique of Welfare Economics. If the existing allocation of resources is inefficient and there are unexploited gains to trade there will be an incentive for entrepreneurs to discover this and to gain entrepreneurial profit from developing new markets and facilitating new patterns of exchange. This general 'laissez faire' approach to economic life is apparent in the Austrians' distinctive distrust of anti-monopoly policy. The first theorem of welfare economics, as has been seen, provided rigorous normative support for a particular conception of competition. A perfectly competitive equilibrium is Pareto efficient. From standard welfare economics therefore we get the idea that public policy should encourage competition in the name of economic efficiency and 'competition policy' has become, since the mid-twentieth century, a normal part of the regulatory framework.

The Austrians, however, argue that the perfectly competitive framework is misleading. The assumptions are not merely unrealistic—which might be true of any abstract model—they lead to a misunderstanding of competitive processes and encourage action that undermines dynamic competitive forces. For example, the profitability of firms is taken in the neoclassical paradigm as a measure of monopoly power and as a way of estimating 'efficiency losses' from monopoly pricing (Cowling and Mueller 1978). For Austrians these profits are more reasonably regarded as entrepreneurial profits indicating successful past innovation and a degree of 'transitory monopoly' that should be of no concern to policy makers

(Littlechild 1982). The main requirement is that government policy must not create artificial barriers to new entry and that tariff barriers and other protective measures are avoided. With these provisos, efforts to interfere by influencing the number of firms, controlling profits and prices or forbidding contractual and commercial arrangements that are entirely un-coerced are unwarranted. 'Protection from force and fraud' (Shenfield 1983) is the proper role of government in commercial relations not interfering in market structure or influencing contractual terms on a case by case basis.

It will be evident from these brief comments that the Austrian approach to public policy is entirely about processes. For Hayek (1976: 31) the 'law of liberty' provided 'end-independent rules' applying equally to all members of society 'which serve the formation of a spontaneous order'. There was no expectation that the application of these 'rules of just conduct' would produce any particular socially desired outcomes such as 'efficiency'. The economic system would simply go on and its normative properties would be judged entirely by the nature of the free interactions to which it gave rise. Hayek termed the order resulting from market processes as a 'catallaxy'. Of course, most Austrian School economists would expect that a system based on free and law-governed exchange relations would be likely to give rise to material gains for most people over time as entrepreneurs discovered new ways of serving the demands of others. But the system was not itself justified normatively by appeal to its likely material or distributional results. The law should aim 'to improve equally the chances of all'—that is 'the chances of anyone selected at random' (1976, 129). On monopoly, Hayek (1979: 85–86) was only concerned to prevent a dominant firm from using price discrimination to prevent entry or to conspire with others to protect a market from interlopers. His recommendation was that all agreements in restraint of trade should be unenforceable at law without exception with multiple damages available to complainants in the civil courts.

3.2 Ordo-Liberalism

The intellectual connection between the Ordo-Liberals and the Austrian liberals is so close that a cursory reading of contributors to these schools of thought might easily fail to uncover the sources of disagreement. Peacock and Willgerodt (1989a) in their introduction to a set of commentaries on the Ordo-Liberal School note that it was Hayek who made contact with Walter Eucken and others after the Second World War and arranged for Eucken to deliver a course of lectures at the London School of Economics eventually published in 1952 as *This Unsuccessful Age*. Ultimately the difference between the Austrian school and the Ordo-Liberals is well summarised by Barry (1989: 112). "The Ordo movement's liberalism is of the end-state type. Despite their constant stress on the 'indivisibility' of freedom, its proponents maintain that it is always permissible for the state to intervene to restrict liberty in order to preserve the free competitive order." No doubt this is of some importance to social philosophers, but from the perspective of this chapter the question is how far it led to differences in their approach to welfare economics and the role of public policy.

Both the Austrian tradition and the Ordo-Liberal tradition are critical of the static nature of welfare economic theory. Both view competition as a process of rivalry and emulation rather than a state in which all traders are price takers, and therefore both tolerate departures from equilibrium, and the resulting static efficiency losses, as an encouraging sign that the participants in the system are actually awake and having to make decisions.[1] Lutz (1956: 161) for example, commented that 'as far as the dynamic, forward-pressing nature of competition is concerned then the 'perfect' competition of the theorist is downright sluggish'. The difference between the two traditions is more a question of political judgment than economic analysis. For the Ordo-Liberals the experience in Germany of economic collapse in 1933 following monetary disaster and an interventionist industrial policy, closely followed by the rise of National Socialism, led to a suspicion of both market power and state power. Monopolies were undesirable not merely because they might be 'Pareto inefficient'. More importantly they were politically dangerous in that their interests might come to dominate the state. Both private power and public power were dangerous and had somehow to be circumscribed by a neutral rule of law. In other words, fear of totalitarian degeneration tended to make Ordo-liberals more rather than less interventionist in particular fields.

This was particularly true of their attitude to monopoly where their willingness to countenance intervention to prevent market dominance and restrictive practices was less apologetic than the typical Austrian position. Here, as Lutz (1956: 153–155) points out, they were closer to Adam Smith and the 'classical' liberal tradition than the Austrians. Maintaining the competitive order and preventing 'conspiracies against the public' was a longstanding part of the liberal tradition even if this was based more on a general desire to protect the 'system of natural liberty' and its dynamic potential than any concern for twentieth century notions of 'Pareto efficiency'. Rowley and Peacock (1975) certainly supported a very robust competition policy—although as non-discretionary as it could be made. Hayek (as we have seen) felt that a neutral rule of law might be compatible with making all agreements in restraint of trade unenforceable but Rowley and Peacock go further. Unlike Hayek, they were prepared to penalise infringements through criminal as well as civil proceedings and were prepared to prohibit mergers and acquisitions where market share 'correctly defined' exceeded a prescribed level.

The focus on competition policy of the early Ordo-Liberals is understandable in the context of German history and does enable some comparison of liberal with Welfare Economic approaches to be discussed. In essence the structure of Welfare

---

[1]It should be noted however, that Eucken's central policy target is a competitive price system where economic power would disappear completely and the market would approach the perfectly competitive benchmark. See Richter (2015). Efficiency was not the reason for favouring such a market structure, however, and the role of technical change as a threat to powerful interests was recognised.

Theory itself offers little clue as to how inefficiency should be corrected or even discovered while the liberal response is to institute a system of competition law that resists the emergence of monopoly in the interests of growth and the dispersion of economic power rather than the achievement of efficiency. The sources of inefficiency in welfare economic theory, however, are almost endless as we have observed, and it is not clear what a liberal approach might be to the possible social inefficiencies associated with multifarious types of externalities.

Some attributes of the Ordo-liberal response can be inferred from their writing however. Giving public officials discretionary power to intervene in the competitive order in the interests of environmental protection, for example, would be contrary to Ordo-liberal principles. To prevent the growth of discretionary power incompatible with decentralised market coordination the Ordo-liberals required measures to be 'marktkonform'. The term originated with respect to measures of social protection and redistribution but, under more modern conditions, could be applied to pollution externalities. Attention has already been drawn to Rowley and Peacock's preference for taxes or tradable licences rather than direct controls on pollution and this would entirely accord with Ordo-liberal traditions.

It is interesting to note, however, that the Ordo-liberals took this notion only so far. Peacock and Wiseman (1964) wrote a paper for the Institute of Economic Affairs called 'Education for Democrats' advocating the use of vouchers and more choice and competition in schools. Twenty-five years later Peacock and Willgerodt (1989b: 12) observe that when it came to aspects of social policy such as education, no systematic questioning of public provision came from the Ordo-liberals although "it would be difficult to think of a better example of 'marktconform' social policy than privatising schools subject to some government regulation and the offering of vouchers to parents as a method of dealing with the problems of equality of access to education". Perhaps this was so far beyond the limits of the politically feasible that it was deemed not worth serious consideration. But it raises the obvious point that 'public choice' considerations determine policy more than liberal principles— whether of the Austrian, Ordo or Classical variety. The usefulness of Welfare Economics as well as various forms of liberalism as a guide to public policy is constrained by the public choice context.

3.3   The Public Choice School

Looking at the expanding role of the state in the twentieth century it is possible to use the framework of welfare economics to explain the underlying forces. Perhaps the state grew because disinterested public officials were uncovering inefficiencies in the economic system and correcting them, or because voters were accurately expressing their preferences for the provision of public goods and demanding greater quantities as their incomes rose. Perhaps technology was creating more potential areas of market failure and requiring greater state activity. If the income elasticity of demand for public goods was greater than unity the ratio of public expenditure to GDP would tend to rise over time.

When attention is directed at the actual methods by which collective decisions are taken however, and the processes by which policy is developed and implemented, the 'public interest' model of taxation, public expenditure and regulation is thrown into question. 'Positive' public choice uses the usual tools of economic modelling to look at individual rationalistic utility maximising behaviour in the arena of collective decision making in representative democracies. It analyses both the 'demand side' of this process such as voting behaviour, lobbying, and the formation of pressure groups, and the 'supply side' such as the offering of policy platforms by vote maximising politicians or the development and implementation of policy by bureaucrats or other agents of the state. Rowley and Peacock (1975) refer extensively to the work of Downs (1957), Breton (1974), Niskanen (1971) as well as Buchanan and Tullock (1965) and much work in the 1970s and thereafter concerned the application of the 'economics of politics' to diverse areas of government activity (see Peacock 1979a).

Instead of the conventional model of public policy in which the government was conceived as a single actor aiming to maximise some clear objective function by control of sufficient policy instruments subject to known economic constraints, Peacock (1979a, b) proposes a revised policy paradigm featuring bargaining between firms, households or outside interest groups, the government and the bureaucracy, each with their own objectives and possible response mechanisms. This framework can be seen in the title and sub title of a study undertaken for the Anglo-German Foundation (Peacock and Robinson 1984)—*The Regulation Game: How British and West German Companies Bargain with Government*. It was revisited also in the Mattioli Lectures in 1992 (p. 15). Recognition that the activities of the State could not be analysed independently of the various interests that comprised it was also a notable feature of the whole Italian tradition in Public Finance. This led to a much greater recognition of the importance of "the supply side of political decision making if we are to understand why government has grown" (Peacock 1992: 95).

The 'normative' side of public choice theory was not so uniformly welcomed by classical liberals however. The influence of Paretian thinking in the Public Choice School can be seen in attempts by Buchanan (1975) and others to support unanimity or (following Wicksell 1896) reinforced majorities for post-constitutional contracting over public goods; and to generate a 'theory of law' from a notional process of agreement at an earlier constitutional stage. Unlike the analysis of Rawls (1971) the latter was based not on the agreed principles emerging from behind a 'veil of ignorance' but from the more Hobbesian starting point of a hugely inefficient equilibrium in the war of all against all. The 'public choice Paretians' therefore see public policy as emerging from collective decision making mechanisms based on universal agreement or at least 'consensus'. This will not ensure 'efficiency' in the 'pure' static sense of the absence of any further gains to trade, nor will it mean that there cannot be losers from collective decisions or even that, if there are, the gainers will in every case be able to compensate them. What the theory does is provide a normative justification for the rules of post-constitutional contracting that accords with the value judgements of traditional welfare economic theory and which provides a normative benchmark for a critique of actual processes of public policy formation.

Rowley and Peacock (1975) were not convinced, however, that this derivation of collective decision rules from basic Paretian value judgements was of much practical help. "Between the ideal society of the constitutional contract and the reality of public choice in any contemporary society there is in our view an insurmountable gap" (p. 148). It seems unreasonable to expect any normative theory to produce results that avoid a 'gap' between them and reality. But here, perhaps, the important word is 'insurmountable'. What Rowley and Peacock find frustrating about the public choice Paretian approach is that its conclusions are, in their judgement, incapable of providing practical guidance on how collective decisions could be improved. Full agreement on constitutional change to ameliorate the manifest inefficiencies associated with existing arrangements documented by studies of 'the economics of politics' was impossible. Better, they argued, to advocate a distinctive set of 'liberal' value judgements and try to get the associated reforms implemented under existing rules, even though their acceptability might fall a long way short of universal assent.

3.4   Transactions Costs

Although public choice theory played a major role in undermining the idea that policy advice could reasonably be extracted from the theory of welfare economics without reference to the quite separate problem of implementation, it did not directly undermine the tenets of welfare economic theory itself. A different theoretical advance that impinged directly on the relevance of welfare theory to public policy derived from the transactions cost critique developed by Coase (1960). Since 'inefficiency' implied unexploited gains to trade, the general explanation of failure to secure these gains could be found in various sources of impediment—including information costs, bargaining costs, enforcement costs, and so forth—summarised in the portmanteau term 'transactions costs'. Where transactions costs were low, for example where noise or other 'external costs' linked to an activity affected a close neighbour, the civil law was quite capable of handling the situation. Either the polluter could compensate the neighbour, or the neighbour could bribe the polluter to desist, depending upon the prevailing property rights assignment applying to the transactors.

Of course there would be instances in which the costs of gaining agreement were so great that the case for public intervention would be compelling assuming that the state itself did not face insurmountable information and implementation costs. The standard 'public good' justification of state intervention remained, but reformulated in transactions cost terms. Instances of 'market failure' could no longer be regarded as automatically requiring state action through taxes and subsidies or other regulatory intervention. Public policy could not be the product of standard welfare theory alone but had to be based on a case by case 'comparative institutions' approach which took transactions costs into account. After Coase, economic decisions could no longer be allocated between the two categories of 'private choice' and 'public choice' representing 'market contracting' and 'collective agreement through the state'. Multifarious institutions were capable of being developed between these categories—including firms, partnerships, clubs, friendly societies, and associations of all kinds—aimed at securing mutual gains from cooperation. These face all the usual problems of potential free riding on joint output and opportunistic behaviour, but in the right legal framework they can also develop solutions—from simple peer pressure to novel methods of exclusion.

Coase was highly critical of 'blackboard economics'—by which he meant the derivation of policy proposals from neoclassical competitive equilibrium theory and the associated structure of welfare economics without reference to the legal and institutional framework. The general equilibrium world of perfectly competitive theory had no rationale for the existence of firms or any collective institution short of the state itself. Yet the very use of money and the development of firms was testament to the existence of transactions costs and to the possibility of spontaneous responses to them. It could not be inferred that in the 'real world' of transactions costs, collective choice through the state would necessarily produce superior outcomes to more local initiatives. The idea that the state could somehow avoid all transactions costs and had access to information more cheaply than others was labelled the 'Nirvana fallacy' by Demsetz (1969).

The Coasean view of transactions costs is clearly consistent with positive public choice analysis in that the latter is mainly concerned to emphasise the problems of contracting, agency costs and bargaining in the public sector. Coase's work supplements the study of public choice, however, by providing a framework capable of looking at many differing institutional arrangements between pure individual arm's length contracting in a 'perfect' market and pure centralised collective decision making. It also provides a 'normative theorem' applicable to public policy. It recommends structuring the law so as 'to remove the impediments to private agreements'.[2] In other words, policy should aim to reduce transactions costs so as to permit more of the gains to trade to be garnered through the normal processes of business and civil interaction. Traditional welfare economics was based upon the rather different notion that the law should aim to 'minimise the harm caused by failures in private agreements'. The latter approach requires the state to have information and administrative capacity that is far in excess of what can realistically be expected. The normative Coase theorem is quite compatible with much liberal and Ordo Liberal thinking—especially the removal of unnecessary restrictions on new entrants—but the justification is derived less from a desire to disperse economic power than to lower barriers to voluntary agreement. In this sense the Ordo liberal position is influenced by political considerations whereas the Coasean

---

[2]See, for example, Cooter and Ulen (1997: 89–90).

position is concerned still (and in spite of reservations about static theory) with maximising the gains to trade and pursuing 'efficiency'.

Peacock was aware of the Coasean critique but seems to have been more inclined to attack welfare economics from a classical liberal perspective rather than a strictly Coasean one. He wrote a paper on the lighthouse (Peacock 1979b) which was critical of Samuelson's approach to public goods and in the process made reference to Coase (1974). Coase had noted that lighthouses (the archetypal 'public good') were in fact built and operated privately in the UK in the eighteenth and nineteenth centuries and that methods had been found to circumvent problems of exclusion and to enforce payment. Peacock agreed that lighthouses were built and profitably operated but argued that Coase had underestimated the importance of the state in granting the various privileges that made enforcement possible—such as denying customs clearance of goods until lighthouse dues were paid. From a normative point of view, however, these 'privileges' could be argued to represent the operation of a policy based on the normative Coase theorem that facilitates activities that would otherwise be prevented by transactional hurdles. Peacock was inclined to emphasise other elements in the story such as the incentive that private provision gave to technical progress, the possibly transitory nature of 'publicness', and the administrative waste or 'X' inefficiency likely to accompany public provision. More recent years have seen considerable progress in the study of the range of institutional responses to problems of public goods and external effects, notably in areas such as water management and other local environmental resources (Ostrom 2005). The lighthouse continues to attract comment with Booth (2014) arguing that stock-exchanges had similar characteristics and that private governance evolved to cope with high transactions costs in financial markets long before the state became the dominant regulator.

4   Conclusion

The criticisms of welfare economics considered above—its basis in 'welfarism', its emphasis on 'efficiency' as a policy criterion above all others, its fundamentally static nature, its neglect of information and transactions costs, and generally the difficulty of bringing the theory into contact with the 'real world' of practical policy—have continued to perplex public finance economists and others. Some of this critical effort is not so much aimed at the structure of welfare economics itself which is bound to be formal and abstract and not immediately applicable, but to the manner in which it has been interpreted. There is nothing in the theory itself which supports the idea that because a policy advisor is able to imagine externalities of all types and plausible 'market failures', policy interventions are automatically recommended almost as a purely 'technical' matter. Indeed the fundamental theory is in essence more limiting in this respect than the utilitarianism of old and has paradoxically only extended its reach by discreetly forgetting the problem of specifying a 'social welfare function' that would enable social choices to be made between alternative efficient states.

In further defence of welfare economics it might also be added that it has developed as a rigorous tool of normative analysis—clarifying value judgments and investigating precisely in what sense some social states might be said to be preferred to others. As a contribution to philosophy as much as to economics, welfare theory could hardly replace rather than simply inform the practical business of policy design and implementation. The latter is really a separate area of expertise requiring knowledge of positive and normative economics as well as much institutional and historical background. John Neville Keynes (1897) referred to this as 'the Art of Economics', and one way of expressing the frustration of the critics is that modern welfare economics is perceived to have substituted for it entirely.

The concentration of welfare economic theory on equilibrium states in which efficiency conditions are either satisfied or violated has diverted attention from the information problem. If information about valuations and costs is generated and revealed in the very process of exchange and cannot simply be accessed by policy makers at low or zero cost, the whole business of policy making is complicated. Whether we consider the Austrian, Ordo-Liberal or Transactions Cost critique, the common thread is the difficulty of knowing the social marginal costs and benefits attached to any activity other than through the freely expressed choices of individual contractors. For the Austrians the problem is so severe that judging alternative 'results' or 'equilibrium' states is effectively rejected in favour of a purely procedural view of 'justice'. For the Ordo-Liberals the 'ideal' of highly dispersed economic power is associated with the competitive system and policy to ensure its survival is a major responsibility of the state. For transactions cost theorists only trial and error processes can reveal how best to react and to secure the gains to trade. Policy is therefore primarily focussed on trying to reduce impediments to private agreements by specifying privately and collectively exchangeable property rights and permitting competing forms of governance to evolve.

Public policy cannot plausibly be concerned only with process however. While the calculation of 'efficient' end states might be beyond policy makers, the concept itself is powerful and important. Some major contributions of economists to policy analysis—for example the consequences of price controls—depended heavily on the consequences for 'efficiency'. The case against rent control in the UK, for example, was not mainly that it could be seen to infringe liberal principles of freedom of contract or property rights. The decisive argument leading to reform was the (eventually obvious) extreme inefficiency of the whole system and the potential gains therefore available to liberalisation. From a purely moral standpoint, to tolerate inefficiency is to tolerate 'waste' and this has led to a strong defence of the concept in social policy generally. Culyer (1992: 9) robustly defends the 'hard' notion of efficiency as an essential ingredient in social policy. "I want to argue ... that it is necessary if there is to be any *morally acceptable* social policy".

Classical liberal principles are not, in themselves, in conflict with Culyer's position and the concept of efficiency finds its place in many areas of liberal policy analysis from the supply of public goods to education and the protection of heritage assets. But suspicion of bureaucratic supply and awareness of public choice pressures generally lead classical liberals to favour the empowering of consumers rather than officials when it comes to practical policy. Rowley and Peacock (1975: 3) write, for example, that "it will soon be clear to the reader that what he is being offered is classical political economy with modern trappings". While adopting the techniques of rational maximisation subject to constraint for positive microeconomic analysis, when it came to policy Rowley and Peacock drew from classical traditions and preferred broad liberal principles to welfarism.

References

Barry N (1989) Political and economic thought of German neo-liberals. In: Peacock AT, Willgerodt H (eds) German neo-liberals and the social market economy. Macmillan, London, pp 105–124

Booth P (2014) Stock exchanges as lighthouses. Man Econ 1(2):171–187

Breton A (1974) The economic theory of representative government. Macmillan, London

Buchanan JM (1975) The limits of liberty: between anarchy and Leviathan. University of Chicago Press, Chicago

Buchanan JM, Tullock G (1965) The calculus of consent. University of Michigan Press, Ann Arbor

Coase RH (1960) The problem of social cost. J Law Econ 3:1–44

Coase RH (1974) The lighthouse in economics. J Law Econ 17(2):357–376

Cooter R, Ulen T (1997) Law and economics. Addison-Wesley, New York

Cowling K, Mueller DC (1978) The social costs of monopoly power. Econ J 88(352):727–748

Culyer AJ (1992) Need, greed and Mark Twain's cat. Reprinted in: Cookson R, Claxton K (eds) (2012) The humble economist. University of York and Office of Health Economics, pp 3–13

Demsetz H (1969) Information and efficiency: another viewpoint. J Law Econ 12(1):1–22

Downs A (1957) An economic theory of democracy. Harper and Row, New York

Eucken W (1952) This unsuccessful age or the pains of economic progress. Oxford University Press, New York

Frank RH (1985) Choosing the right pond: human behaviour and the quest for status. Oxford University Press, Oxford

Frank RH (2005) Positional externalities cause large and preventable welfare losses. Am Econ Rev 95(2):137–141

Hayek FA (1976) Law, legislation and liberty, vol 2. The mirage of social justice. Routledge and Kegan Paul, London

Hayek FA (1979) Law, legislation and liberty, vol 3. The political order of a free people. Routledge and Kegan Paul, London

Hicks JR (1939) The foundations of welfare economics. Econ J 49(196):96–712

Hirsch F (1976) Social limits to growth. Harvard University Press, Cambridge

Hochman HM, Rogers JR (1969) Pareto optimal redistribution. Am Econ Rev 59(4) Part 1:542–557

Kaldor N (1939) Welfare propositions of economics and interpersonal comparisons of utility. Econ J 49(195):549–552

Keynes JN (1897) The scope and method of political economy, 2nd edn. Macmillan, London

Layard R (2005) Happiness: lessons from a new science. Allen Lane, London

Lindahl E (1919) Just taxation—a positive solution. Translated by Henderson E in: Musgrave RA, Peacock AT (1958) Classics in the theory of public finance. Macmillan, London, pp 168–176

Little IMD (1950) A critique of welfare economics, Clarendon Press, Oxford

Littlechild S (1982) Misleading calculations of the social costs of monopoly power. Econ J 91(362):348–363

Lutz FA (1956) Observations on the problem of monopolies. Translated and reprinted in: Peacock AT, Willgerodt H (eds) (1989) Germany's social market economy: origins and evolution. Macmillan, London, pp 152–170

Mill JS (1861) Utilitarianism. Reprinted (1910) in Everyman's Library n 482. Aldine, Chicago

Niskanen WA (1971) Bureaucracy and representative government. Aldine, Chicago

Ostrom E (2005) Understanding institutional diversity. Princeton University Press, Princeton

Peacock AT (1979a) The economic analysis of government and related themes. Martin Robertson, Oxford

Peacock AT (1979b) The limitations of public goods theory: the lighthouse revisited. In: Festschrift fur Heinz Haller. JCB Mohr, Tubingen. Reprinted in Peacock AT (1979) The economic analysis of government and related themes. Martin Robertson, Oxford, pp 127–136

Peacock AT (1992) Public choice analysis in historical perspective, Raffaele Mattioli lectures. Cambridge University Press, Cambridge

Peacock AT, Robinson JR (eds) (1984) The regulation game. Basil Blackwell, Oxford

Peacock AT, Rowley CK (1972a) Pareto optimality and the political economy of liberalism. J Polit Econ 80(3):476–490

Peacock AT, Rowley CK (1972b) Welfare economics and the public regulation of natural monopoly. J Public Econ 1(2):227–244

Peacock AT, Willgerodt H (eds) (1989a) Germany's social market economy: origins and evolution. Macmillan, London

Peacock AT, Willgerodt H (eds) (1989b) German neo-liberals and the social market economy. Macmillan, London

Peacock AT, Wiseman J (1961) The growth of public expenditure in the United Kingdom. Princeton University press, Princeton

Peacock AT, Wiseman J (1964) Education for democrats. Hobart paper 25. Institute of Economic Affairs, London

Pigou AC (1920) The economics of welfare. Macmillan, London

Rawls J (1971) A theory of justice. Harvard University Press, Cambridge

Richter R (2015) German "Ordnungstheorie" from the perspective of the new institutional economics. In: Essays on new institutional economics. Springer, Heidelberg, pp 161–183

Rowley CK, Peacock AT (1975) Welfare economics: a liberal restatement, York studies in economics. Martin Robertson, London

Samuelson PA (1954) The pure theory of public expenditure. Rev Econ Stat 36(4):387–389

Scitovsky T (1941) A note on welfare propositions in economics. Rev Econ Stud 9(1):77–88

Shenfield A (1983) Myth and reality in antitrust. Occasional paper 66. Institute of Economic Affairs, London

Wicksell K (1896) A new principle of just taxation. Translated by Buchanan JM in: Musgrave RA, Peacock AT (1958) Classics in the theory of public finance. Macmillan, London, pp 72–118

Public Choice, Economics of Institutions and the Italian School of Public Finance

Emilio Giardina and Isidoro Mazza

Abstract A vast, multi-disciplinary, literature has investigated the reasons why, in democracies, policies may actually pursue vested narrow goals, to the benefit of restricted groups but at the expense of the community. This analysis constitutes the foundation of influential contributions in the growing field of economics of institutions. This study highlights how the concepts of narrow interest groups and ruling elites can be found in the largely forgotten strand of research conducted by leading scholars of the so-called Italian School of Public Finance (ISPF), which emerged over the end of the nineteenth century and the first half of the twentieth. The chapter also indicates how the fundamental insights on the political decision-making provided by the economics of institutions and the ISPF are able to shed a light on central problems concerning the definition and implementation of cultural policies.

> My main thesis—the permeation of public choice theory not only with echoes from past generations of thinkers but with ideas of such thinkers that have maintained their potency
> (Peacock, Public Choice Analysis in Historical Perspective, 1992: 93)

1 Introduction

Governments are not so popular nowadays, as they face a diffuse and increasing criticism. In the US, surveys show that public trust in government decreased almost steadily from 1958 to 2014, going from 73 to 24 %, with a maximum of 77 % in 1964 and a minimum of 18 % in 2011 (Pew Research Center 2014). A similar decline is detected in surveys conducted in OECD countries where the average confidence was 45 % in 2007 and went down to 40 % in 2012, amid the 2008 crisis (OECD 2013). Not surprisingly, in those countries, we also observe a strongly negative correlation between perceived corruption and government confidence. The situation is even worse in Europe, where an already low public trust in government went further down, from 40 % in 2005 to about 32 % in 2013. Confidence in

E. Giardina • I. Mazza (✉)
University of Catania, Catania, Italy
e-mail: giardina@unict.it; imazza@unict.it

© Springer International Publishing Switzerland 2016　　　　　　　　　　　　　51
I. Rizzo, R. Towse (eds.), *The Artful Economist*,
DOI 10.1007/978-3-319-40637-4_4

political parties is further lower in each European country (but Denmark), as it fluctuates around 20 %, in that period. These figures offer a rather disturbing picture of a generalised dissatisfaction about the outcome of policymaking and raise serious doubts about the ability of democracies to pursue collective goals.

A fundamental contribution of the economic analysis of political decision-making, or public choice theory, has been to highlight how political opportunism, rather than efficiency and equity, may guide public policies. Lack of information is often described as a formidable hurdle for the public in its attempts to oversee and evaluate the political process,[1] putting aside the voting paradox (Downs 1957; Riker and Ordeshook 1968), which questions the very fundament of representative democracy, namely voting participation of rational individuals. This lack of information translates into a problem of political accountability. If the political system is indeed unable to systematically 'punish' policies that are not consistent with the maximization of social welfare, we may expect a substantial degree of autonomy for policymakers pursuing selfish goals. Moreover, the outcome of the public sector may be difficult to predict for the vast, and hardly avoidable, array of incomplete contracts characterising bureaucracy. Their existence, as well as the asymmetric information affecting elected representatives when they deal with managers and experts in the public sector, hinder the control that politicians—and the public in general—may exert on bureaucrats.

In a system where political accountability is weak, organized groups representing specific economic interests have the opportunity to influence the decisions of elected representatives as well as public managers (here generally defined as bureaucrats), leading to policies that are biased in favour of those few citizens (Grossman and Helpman 2001, 2002). Similarly, powerful elites may find grounds for reinforcing and perpetuating their influence on the political and economic sphere of a country. Recent additional empirical support for oligarchic policymaking is provided by the study of Gilens and Page (2014), which examines 1779 policy issues in the US and finds that economic elites and organized interest groups have substantial impact on US government policy, while average citizens and unorganized groups have little or no independent influence.[2]

The cultural sector is a notable example of a situation in which obstacles to public oversight of policies are likely to surface. In this sector, asymmetric

---

[1]This widespread assumption underlying most theoretical analysis of Public Choice (for a review, see Mueller 2003), has been partially curtailed by the new approach to political economy (see, among others: Besley 2007; Wittman and Weingast 2008). This approach, following the earlier contributions by the 'Chicago School' which somewhat reconciled public choice with Paretian welfare economics, supports a more 'positive' view of the political sector than that presented by the scholars associated to the 'Virginia School'. In particular, institutions and fully rational agents would guarantee some degree of public control over policymaking and a fairly competitive electoral system resulting in an outcome that, in principle, would 'tend' towards efficiency.

[2]According to a traditional classification in political science, the evidence in favour of the influence of economic elites would support the theory of economic-elite domination, while the evidence in favour of the influence of organized interest groups would provide support for the theory of biased pluralism.

information naturally tends to be pervasive. The widespread belief that the appreciation of cultural production needs a high level of cultural capital tends to neuter the impact of external criticisms on the activity of the experts, who have a great influence on the definition of the goals of cultural policies and, especially, on their implementation. In the case of heritage, experts can go as far as defining what artefacts can be identified as such (Peacock 1994a, b).[3] A similar phenomenon happens to be true also for visual and performing arts, where experts are the main gatekeepers deciding what kind of art is worthy to receive public support. The marginalisation of the public's voice in policymaking casts some doubts on whether cultural policy in the end always tends to pursue the collective benefit (Towse 1994) or rather the goals of a self-referential cultural elite of experts and of specific lobbies with the means 'to capture' decision-makers. These risks have encouraged scholars to resort to direct democracy through referenda (Frey and Pommerehne 1995), or to apply institutional remedies such as the arm's-length principle (van der Ploeg 2006).[4]

A vast, multi-disciplinary, literature has investigated the reasons why, in democracies, policies may actually pursue vested narrow goals, to the benefit of restricted groups at the expense of the community. The analysis is prevalently microeconomic, but some of its main economic insights have been used also in a macroeconomic perspective in the blossoming research on the economics of institutions and development (Acemoglu et al. 2005; Banerjee and Duflo 2011; Bardhan 2005; Brady and Spence 2010; Galor and Moav 2004, 2006; Galor et al. 2009). In their recent acclaimed book *Why Nations Fail. The Origins of Power Prosperity and Poverty* (2012), Acemoglu and Robinson show how concentration of power and wealth in hands of few hampers economic development. For its focus on biased redistribution in favour of restricted elites, this study connects to an earlier contribution exploring institutional explanations for the long vexed question of the determinants of growth, namely Olson's *Rise and Decline of Nations: Economic Growth, Stagflation and Social Rigidities* (1982). Both contributions interpret the slow-down in growth, and the subsequent decline of economies, as a consequence of the predominance of restricted groups of people over government output.

Their analyses, however, show undetected links to the advances made in the economic analysis of government made by Italian scholars who constituted the so-called Italian School of Public Finance (ISPF) at the turn of the nineteenth century and the beginning of the twentieth. The relevance of ISPF to the development of modern Public Finance and Public Choice was acknowledged by some prominent scholars (Musgrave and Peacock 1958; Buchanan 1960, 1967; Peacock 1992; Wagner 2003).[5] However, its early contribution to the analysis of the

---

[3]For references on the political economic literature of cultural heritage see: Rizzo and Throsby (2006), Peacock and Rizzo (2008), Holler and Mazza (2013).

[4]Mazza (2011) and Holler and Mazza (2013) provide some comments on the limits of such institutions to effectively overcome the discussed problems.

[5]Surveys on the contributions of the ISPF are also Backhaus and Wagner (2005), Fausto (2003, 2010), Fausto and De Bonis (2003), Fossati (2010).

disproportionate influence that a limited segment of the population, either organized interest groups or power elites, may have over public policy, is yet to be fully
acknowledged. Our aim is to highlight the neglected links between that analysis and
the literature on the economics of institutions, pointing at the influence of powerful
restricted highlighted by the political economy of institutions and the early contributions to this issue of the ISPF. We will show how the political economic
framework introduced by the ISPF and, especially, the studies on the ruling class
and power elites, by Mosca and Pareto respectively, anticipate Olson's theory of
interest groups and the political economic analysis on institutions and development
of nations provided by Acemoglu and Robinson (2012).

This chapter is organised as follows. Next section summarizes the analyses by
Olson and by Acemoglu and Robinson on how interest groups and elites may come
to influence the process of political decision-making and hinder growth. The third
section highlights some important insights of the ISPF on the study of public policy
and, in particular, on the development of an elitarian system of government. The
fourth section applies some indications emerging from the analysis to the process of
decision-making and implementation of cultural policies. Few comments end the
chapter.

2   Lobbies, Elites and the Economics of Institutions

The possibility that government policies may not fulfil the preferences of the
majority of voters, but rather the specific interests of a relatively small group has
been thoroughly investigated in the last 50 years by an extensive political economy
literature initiated by the pioneering study of Olson (1965) and the subsequent
influential contributions by Tullock (1967), Stigler (1971), Krueger (1974),
Peltzman (1976), and Becker (1983, 1985).[6]

Olson   Olson (1965) provides an explanation for the formation of an interest group.
This is in general a narrow group of subjects with a common interest that has found
sufficient selective incentives—which apply just to those who contributed to the
common cause—to pursue their goal(s). The limited size of the group is crucial to
overcome free-riding and slash organisation and decision costs that affect large
groups (generally driven also by heterogeneous preferences) and make them
impossible to organize. Moreover, it allows the group to obtain large per-capita
benefits for each member of the group with a small spread of costs for the society. In
this way, the negligible cost paid by each citizen for so narrow a redistribution—
from the many contributors to the few beneficiaries of the group—are substantially
smaller than the costs of mobilizing a collective reaction.

---

[6]See also Buchanan and Tullock (1962).

If its limited size helps an interest group to develop, the information the public lacks regarding the policy formation process makes the group powerful. Interest groups have resources available (financial support and information useful for a politician to be elected, instruments of pressure such as strikes and newspaper articles, revolving-doors, etc.) to influence (capture) politicians. But, in principle, voters could punish the government enacting biased policies. However, voters are expected be "rationally ignorant" of politics (Downs 1957).[7] Any single voter has a negligible influence on the result of elections. The expected collective benefits of casting a vote for the right candidate are, therefore, inferior to the individual costs of acquiring information about the candidates (and even to go to the ballot to cast a vote). Moreover, information about politics, which is a collective good, is itself a collective good and, hence, subject to the well-known free-riding problem. The ultimate outcome, then, is that in a representative democracy, every vote does not count for the same: interest groups are politically powerful disproportionately with respect to their relatively tiny size.

In the literature following Olson (1965), the activity of lobbies has mostly been analysed from a microeconomic perspective, investigating, for example: the formation of groups, the instruments of influence, the institutional conditions favouring or discouraging such influence, the efficiency losses that interest groups may generate in their attempt at influencing policies and obtaining rents, and the overall (positive and negative) impact in the political decision-making process. Several years later than this seminal work, Olson applied the theory developed in the *Logic of Collective Action* (1965) to the economic analysis of institutions, in a macroeconomic perspective, in order to provide explanations for the *Rise and Decline of Nations: Economic Growth, Stagflation and Social Rigidities* (1982). That study provides a number of testable hypotheses on the influence of interest groups. We mention four of them that are particularly relevant also for what follows in this chapter.

Firstly, stable societies tend to accumulate more interest groups over time; therefore long periods of peace tend to favour the consolidation of cartels. Secondly, special interest groups reduce efficiency and GDP in the societies where they operate. Thirdly, 'umbrella' organisations (in contrast to narrow interest groups) have incentives to make the society in which they operate more prosperous. Fourthly, interest groups slow down the ability of a society to adopt new technologies and also obstruct the reallocation of resources in response to changing conditions, with a negative impact on the rate of growth. Decline, therefore, is interpreted as being mainly due to the consolidation over time of the power of interest groups protecting and incrementing their rents at the expense of efficiency and, thus of growth. Extraordinary events that subvert the status quo—such as wars, revolutions, international political (dis)integration—can wipe out old elites and lobbies, signing the end of biased and inefficient redistribution, and the beginning of a new period of sustained growth. Olson's analysis would then offer an

---

[7]See footnote 1 for a disclaimer on that hypothesis.

explanation for the remarkable growth of Japan and Germany, whose productive apparatus was indeed destroyed in WW2, but so was the old system of privileges and rents for narrow interest groups. On the contrary, the victorious Great Britain kept its old established almost intact and suffered a period of post-war stagnation.

Acemoglu and Robinson Some of the main intuitions presented in Olson (1982) are returned to and considerably extended by Acemoglu and Robinson (2012). In their ambitious study, they draw on several historic examples, spanning from Neolithic times to the present day and across more continents, to derive arguments in support of their analysis. After a rebuttal of some popular theories that have occasionally put forward to explain prosperity or poverty, the fundamental proposition from their analysis is that world inequality has institutional origins. Institutions regulate the economy and provide incentives that motivate people in their economic decisions.

In particular, there are two kinds of economic institutions: inclusive or extractive. There are two necessary conditions for inclusiveness: a pluralist system and a centralized political authority. In pluralist political institutions, "instead of being vested in a single individual or narrow group, political power rests with a broad coalition or a plurality of groups" (Acemoglu and Robinson 2012: 80). However pluralism is not a sufficient condition for inclusive economic institutions, since we need some kind of political centralization that is able to enforce the law to guarantee economic activity and trade. In this case, norms of the legal system are designed with the goals of constraining power, guaranteeing equal rights and opportunities, and safeguarding property rights. This environment is in turn expected to have a positive impact on education, the spread of technology, and thus growth. The reader can easily see the resemblance with the above third hypothesis indicated by Olson (1982).

In contrast, the absence of one of the conditions needed for inclusiveness is sufficient to have what Acemoglu and Robinson call 'extractive' economic institutions. In this case, the preservation of property rights is insecure and the distribution of legal and economic power tends to be narrow: powerful elites choose the legal and economic system that enriches them and regulate the market in a way that sustains themselves in a perverse loop reinforcing their power. Therefore, entry to the market is allowed as long as it supports the existing elites and technological improvement may be inhibited for the fear of destabilization.

In contrast to Olson (1982), Acemoglu and Robinson provide a dynamic analysis of transition.[8] Being based on dynamic optimization, it presents the feature that small differences at critical junctures may have long-run impact on a country's development (for example, the Spanish failure to invade England). Moreover, a wrong path can be chosen that leads to poverty not prosperity. Recalling the Schumpeterian concept of creative destruction helping growth, Acemoglu and

---

[8]For an analytical treatment of the issues presented in Acemoglu and Robinson (2012), see Acemoglu (2010).

Robinson warn that some countries may fear to change old businesses for new ones. Elites will naturally resist the emergence of new technologies of production (for instance, the industrial revolution), which may subvert old privileges and jeopardize the power of elites. In contrast, 'soft' transitions are less likely to be opposed if they do not immediately threaten power elites. Again, the similarity with Olson's fourth hypothesis is quite evident.

In conclusion, we notice that the choice of which economic institutions are indeed inclusive remains rather subjective. For example, whether the US has inclusive or extractive economic institutions is open to debate. While Acemoglu and Robinson (2012) support the first option, Gilens and Page (2014) show that interest groups and elites rule in the United States rather than the majority. Moreover, the arguments presented by Acemoglu and Robinson, as compelling and fascinating as they are, surprisingly overlook to properly refer to previous analysis which also investigated similar topics.[9] In the following section, we refer to the legacy of the ISPF that provided a very early investigation of the role of elites and interest groups and which has been widely disregarded by the political economy literature.

3   Narrow-Interest Policymaking in the Italian School of Public Finance

The remarkable and lasting attention of scholars in economics and political science to the role that elites and interest groups have in shaping policies and influencing growth and income redistribution is not at all a recent phenomenon. It is deeply rooted in the political and economic thinking between the second half of nineteenth century and the first half of the twentieth century (see Olson 1965). In that period, we also observe the development of the ISPF, which contributed to the foundation of the modern public finance and offered an analysis of the fiscal decision-making process and of the participation of political forces: both anticipated the path-breaking contribution of Public Choice (Giardina 1992). Its importance was indeed recognized by the Virginia School, and Buchanan (1960) published the first review in English of the Italian tradition, 2 years before the publication of the *Calculus of Consent*. It is arguable, however, whether Public Choice theory indeed originated from the analytical framework developed by the ISPF, and by other prominent European scholars such as Alexis De Tocqueville, Knut Wicksell, Eric Lindahl, Duncan Black, Frederick von Hayek. In any case, as recognized also by Peacock

---

[9]Leaving aside Olson (1982), which is just briefly mentioned, no prominent scholars among the founders of Public Choice is cited, in spite of the closeness of the topics and insights. Equally surprising is that Acemoglu and Robinson (2012) does not refer to important investigations on the topic of political and economic elites (in the US) carried in political science, such as Mills (1956) and Winters (2011).

(1992) and Wagner (2003), the ISPF provided an early view of the non-organic form of the state, which is one of the pillars of modern public finance, where policies result from the interaction of groups having different political powers.

The ISPF was reputedly initiated by the seminal works of Maffeo Pantaleoni (1883) and Antonio De Viti de Marco (1888, 1914, 1934, 1939), although Buchanan (1960) highlights how the stimulus provided by the studies of Francesco Ferrara was overlooked for a long time. Mazzola, Montemartini, Mosca, Puviani, Barone, Pareto, Einaudi, Griziotti e Fasiani are among the most prominent names who contributed to the establishment of an Italian tradition that was for some time unknown outside of Italy (with the exception of Pareto who held the chair of political economy at the University of Lausanne).

De Viti de Marco claimed, as did several authors in the present study, that oligarchies may rule also in the institutional framework of representative democracy. Having founded his theory of government on the juxtaposition between 'absolute' and 'democratic' State, he also predated recent theories of collective choice (Acemoglu 2010).

The English translation of *Principi di Economia Finanziaria* in 1936 gave some international recognition to De Viti de Marco (1934) notwithstanding that work was scorned by some and praised by others. The *Principi* signalled a sharp discontinuity with the normative view of public finance sustained by Edgeworth, and then by Pigou, in which the government has the main role of defining an optimal plan of intervention in order to minimize efficiency losses (Wagner 2003). De Viti de Marco did not separate the market from the state. On the contrary, he envisaged government decisions as emerging from the interaction of the same people operating in the market.[10] An analogy would be the associations of a democratic State to a cooperative firm—which operates for the welfare of its members in the same fashion as elected representatives should do—and of an absolute State to a monopolist—which maximizes rent similarly to a ruler exploiting his subjects for his personal interest (Giardina 2008). This connection between market and government shows some similarities to the catallactic approach put forward by Friedrich von Hayek. The notion that fiscal phenomena have to be investigated in the same way as market phenomena is an important breakthrough that widely characterizes the ISPF (Wagner 2003). Eighty years after the publication of the *Principi*, we see that the contribution of ISPF to the foundation of modern public finance (which now does include the political economy approach) is still remembered, as indicated by some recent surveys (Backhaus and Wagner 2005; Fausto 2003, 2010; Fossati 2010; Wagner 2003).

Browsing through a modern textbook of Public Finance, however, the exponents of the ISPF most likely to be found are Puviani and, of course, Pareto, although the latter was critical about the possibility of building an economic theory of public

---

[10]For De Viti de Marco, as with Pantaleoni and later Fusiani, the government is a cooperative agent of the public, although its mandate can be implemented in different ways, maximising the number of votes or rather the aggregate intensity of preferences (Giardina 2008).

finance, since actions in this field in his view pertain more to the sociological sphere (Dallera 2013), as explained in his *Trattato di Sociologia* (1923). Puviani owes his fame primarily to the concept of fiscal illusion that has provided a heuristic underpinning to several studies connecting the growth of the public sector to the substantial misperception that individuals have about their fiscal burden. Vilfredo Pareto's contribution to modern microeconomics and the innovation of ordinal utility and (Pareto) optimality are well known and studied by every first year student in economics.[11]

Relatively less is known internationally about Pareto's analysis of power elites. The study of elites has a statistical foundation (Forte and Silvestri 2013). If we consider the distribution of individuals according to their wealth and according to their political power, Pareto states that we would see that the people who are the richest are also the most powerful. In the top percentiles, we find the 'elected', namely the elites. For Pareto, inequality is quite natural, since society is heterogeneous in terms of different variables (or indexes) related to different individual capacities (such as wealth, education, political power), and elites enjoy higher values for each. Then, in every society, we find in the lower tier those who are ruled and in the upper tier those who rule. Pareto, moreover, warns that if those who own great wealth are also those who control the political power, they will be able to perpetuate themselves at the top of the socio-political-economic hierarchy. This vicious cycle is indicated also by Acemoglu and Robinson (2012), and similarly to the latter Pareto envisages a transition mechanism: social change is due to the transformation or replacement of elites. The transformation happens when new external elements become part of the elite, until they are assimilated. In the end, since the struggle for power is endless and heterogeneity is structural, no social system is eternal: sooner or later it will disappear ("history is a cemetery of elites").

The ultimate problem is then how to give power to those who will use it properly for the collective welfare. On this account, Pareto is sceptical that a pluralist system enfranchising the masses will exclude an elitist government: those who will be elected will govern for their own good. Democracies are doomed to clientelism and populism and unable to unseat the system of power elites. Possibly, this cynical view of democracy (which to some extent recalls the most liberalist positions within Public Choice) and his full endorsement of fascism contributed to the future oblivion of Pareto's political studies. Incidentally, it is worth mentioning the striking resemblance between the central insights by Buchanan and Tullock (1962), Olson (1965), Peltzman (1976) and Becker (1983, 1985) and Pareto's analysis of 'conflictual relations' in policymaking. Pareto (1896–7) highlights the reasons why it is politically viable for a democratic government to implement a transfer to a restricted—not necessarily poor—group of people which has to be

---

[11]Pareto's analysis is however more complicated than it generally appears in textbooks. Pareto in fact distinguishes two separate concepts: ophelimity, concerning pure economic satisfaction, and utility, referring to broader satisfaction than the economic one. For a discussion of these concepts and of the maximum of ophelimity/utility *of* or *for* the collectivity, see Giardina (2008), and Forte and Silvestri (2013).

financed by a mass of citizens. This transfer would in fact be possible only if the political gains (in terms of votes) expected by groups competing for public expenditure and satisfying their specific interests are greater than the losses of votes of the many taxpayers financing that expenditure. The justification lies, for Pareto, in the asymmetry that we have to expect between the political reaction of a small, organized group having high stakes (per capita benefits) in that policy, and the reaction of the opposing mass of citizens bearing small individual costs for that biased policy and, therefore, having feeble incentives to resist against its implementation.[12] For his contribution, here briefly summarized, we believe that Pareto deserves to be recognized as one of the precursors of the economic theory of interest groups (Giardina 1992).

As suggested by Forte and Silvestri (2013), the theory of elites elaborated by Pareto was part of a more widespread reflection in Europe about the feasible ways to integrate the people in the process of political decision-making that was instead dominated by elites. This analysis was not very distant, although different, from Mosca's theory of a ruling class (which is equivalent to the restricted ruling minority that Pareto calls the elite) and Pantaleoni and Bertolini (1892) attention to the distinction between contractual agreements and coercive political arrangements (Giardina 1992). In fact, these scholars demonstrate how democracy was never sufficient to stop a restricted share of society from having control over the masses of the governed.

Mosca's line of research, however, focused on the relationship between government and citizen, while for Pareto, the existence of inequalities and, thus, of elites was perfectly natural, and the hierarchical relationship between ruled and rulers almost constant along the endless succession of elites. In Mosca, there is a different attention to the necessity of finding arguments to legitimate power and of a normative definition of good government (Forte and Silvestri 2013). These issues are resolved by indicating the middle class as that having superior abilities with respect to all other classes (Mosca 1939).[13]

4   Narrow Interests in Cultural Policy

The ISPF scholars did not specifically investigate the case of cultural policy. A notable and early exception is De Luca (1858), a professor of public economics and statistics at the university of Naples, who specifically addressed the topic of public support to the fine arts. De Luca interprets arts as instrumental for the intellectual development of a society, as a source of beauty and relief sought by all individuals. They also represent a 'high' form of recreation, which actually generates an incentive to work more in order to pay for its enjoyment. Although arts are a

---

[12]See Pareto (1896–7) par. 1046 and 1047. See also De Viti de Marco (1890) for a similar point.

[13]For an empirical verification of Mosca's theory in the Italian politics, see Fedeli et al. (2014).

secondary—rather than primary—want, De Luca is in favour of public support, mainly for equity reasons, only when private associations are not able to sustain arts adequately. De Luca's view of government support is interesting for its rarity, at a time when the reasons for a cultural public policy were not as widely recognized as today, and for the surprising 'modernity' of his reference to the third sector and the world of associations (see the chapter by Mignosa in this book). Moreover, regarding the specific content of this chapter, his opinion is particularly interesting for the observation that arts are themselves expression of the dominant thinking in a society (De Luca 1858: 255–6). And this dominant thinking naturally stems from the intellectual, economic, and political elites.

But is culture policy indeed necessarily responding to the goals of some elites? Are policymakers and bureaucrats expected to be 'captured' by narrow groups? The prospect of biased policies in favour of vested interests and, ultimately, the problem of guaranteeing democratic representation in the definition and implementation of policies are central issues in the analysis of government support to culture. Normative analysis has provided several justifications for government intervention and compared different instruments in terms of efficiency (Towse 1994; van der Ploeg 2006). Positive analysis has, however, warned that the decision-making process concerning the allocation of public funds or, more generally, the direction to follow in the implementation of cultural policies does not guarantee, in principle, (public) choices that are consistent either with welfare maximization or at least the goals of a majority (Peacock 1993).[14]

Actually, taking a closer look at the characteristics of the cultural sector, we see elements that are quite propitious to the formation of narrow interest policies, which are directed to satisfy the political goals of decision-makers (see Guccio and Mazza 2014, for empirical support) or the interests of organized groups (Grampp 1989), or socio-economic elites and other gatekeepers. Firstly, we often observe a substantial lack of public information and limited political accountability in the cultural sector because the general public is inclined to accept the idea of having little voice on cultural policies due to the (presumed) higher knowledge of experts. In other words, people may not believe they have sufficient cultural capital needed to evaluate cultural expenditure. In fact, while everyone may feel confident in evaluating and eventually protesting for the poor condition of a school, hospital or road, the same feeling may not exist in case of judging a play, a concert, or an exhibition.[15] Secondly, the high opinion that people generally have for culture together with their lack of information about the (economic) outcome of policies, make supporting culture a useful and acceptable stratagem to propose policies that appear

---

[14]Is it well known that the median voter outcome, obtained under specific circumstances in direct or representative democracy systems, does not necessarily maximize social welfare.

[15]It is, however, correct to mention that particular cultural events, especially art exhibitions or art displays in public spaces, did occasionally generate a public outcry, in different countries. However, the reason was almost inevitably an alleged offense to public decency or to religious creeds. Therefore, the protest did not directly imply a judgement about the artistic value of the sponsored event but rather the open violation of shared norms or beliefs.

to endorse culture but end up favouring specific economic interests. An example is international regulation to protect cultural diversity, which is an effective way to protect domestic cultural industries (music and cinema, in particular), especially in non-English speaking countries. Thirdly, public policies are likely to determine narrow benefits with diffuse costs: the size of the group of direct beneficiaries of public expenditure (artists, producers in the cultural sector, critics...) is rather restricted and redistribution in their favour can determine high per-capita benefits with rather marginal individual costs for the society, and thus with little negligible political costs for the public decision-makers.

The literature has recognized the discussed problems and suggested some institutional remedies. If we accept that this is a problem of representation embedded in any representative democracy, we could resort to direct democracy and use referenda. Frey (2000) supports the idea that people are adequately aware of the benefits of cultural expenditure and, therefore, capable to preserve culture: there is no real danger of cultural impoverishment if we directly ask citizens to express their preference on public support to culture. There are a number of difficulties with such a solution. Even if we leave aside the costs of referenda—which may indeed may be lower than those of representative politics—and the fact that a minority of people may be sufficient to pass a bill—which, again, it is not excluded by a representative system—referenda have the shortcoming of being potentially subject to transitory emotions. Moreover, their outcome can be influenced by grassroots lobbying, where the general public is contacted and informed in such a way as to induce a certain reaction that is consistent with the goal of whom finances such a campaign. Finally, and most importantly, experimental economics has highlighted how the format of a question has a serious impact on the type of answer we get (see the problem of framing, for example). Therefore, the outcome of a referendum can indeed be influenced by those who decide the way a question is going to be asked. And this power of the agenda setter takes us back to the original problem of democratic representation introduced before.

An alternative institutional solution could be provided by the application of the arms-length principle, which was adopted by the Arts Council in the UK and then in the USA. Autonomous agencies could avoid that cultural policies are subject to the influence of politicians, bureaucrats, interest groups, and powerful elites as it could be the case if we had direct public management (van der Ploeg 2006). Such agencies, although publicly funded, are substantially independent in their decision of the allocation of resources and are managed and supervised by experts. This system of independent agencies has, however, some pros and cons, as far as democratic participation is concerned. It is designed in a way to forestall political influence in the allocation of public funds for culture, but it raises the problem of accountability of those agencies with respect to the taxpayers. In fact, the public is basically unable to contrast their decisions (even if they are elitist). Moreover, decisions taken by several independent agencies may lack coordination and lead to a fragmented national cultural policy. In order to try "to resolve the oxymoron of accountability and autonomy" (Quinn 1998: 293), the Netherlands adopt a mixed system of separation of powers, where agencies have the power of proposing which projects to subsidise but the government keeps the financial and regulatory power. But political control, although restricted, may open the door to interferences from politically powerful lobbies. In order to reconcile cultural policies with the collective preferences in arm-length bodies, Peacock (1998) suggests having representatives from local cultural organizations in the boards of public agencies implementing cultural policy. An additional alternative is the National Trust model, where private associations, independent from the political—and, in principle, more accountable to the community preferences—administer cultural programmes.

In conclusion, arms-length bodies, with or without the participation of external members representing different community interests, or National Trust-type organisations can represent an institutional remedy for the independency of cultural programs from politics and vested interests of organised groups. But do they also prevent the formation of cultural policies satisfying the aims of *intellectual* elites rather than those of a community? Our opinion is that they do not, in general, for at least two reasons. First the experts managing the activities of such agencies, for their specific cultural formation, are naturally focused on their specific fields and have little understanding or concern about the opportunity cost of their decisions for the whole society. Second, due to their independence, they do not have adequate incentives to take fully into account the interests of the public. Moreover, the procedures of selection and appointment of board members, managers, and consultants (what we could call the politics *within* the organisations) should be investigated more thoroughly to verify whether they are sufficiently open to account for the preference of the public rather than dominant elites.[16]

5   Concluding Remarks

This brief chapter has investigated the theoretical links between two fundamental contributions in the field of the economics of institution, both based on the influence of narrow interest groups, and those between this strand of research and early and often neglected analysis provided by the ISPF on ruling elites, or ruling class. The succinct analysis has highlighted points in common between modern economic of institution and the theory elaborated by Pareto and Mosca. It is however difficult to say whether the ISPF studies on power elites and ruling class really anticipates the theory of narrow interest groups. In particular, the emergence of ruling elites or class is explained by Pareto and Mosca more as a natural (statistical) event than the consequence of economic phenomena. Under a more general perspective, this study offers interesting insights to interpret the growing discomfort of the public with respect to policymaking in many advanced economies.

---

[16]Holler and Mazza (2013) also highlight the question concerning the choice of the decision rule in any committee in these bodies, and how such a choice affects the outcome of the decision process.

The attention has then been devoted to the decision-making process for the definition and implementation of cultural policies. The issues presented in this chapter lead us to think that cultural policies are potentially subject to the influence of elites, although different institutional frameworks may help to reduce their impact on the government output.

References

Acemoglu D (2010) Political economy lecture notes. http://economics.mit.edu/files/8753. Accessed 16 Mar 2016

Acemoglu D, Robinson JA (2012) Why nations fail. The origins of power, prosperity and poverty. Profile, London

Acemoglu D, Johnson S, Robinson JA (2005) Institutions as a fundamental cause of long-run growth. In: Aghion P, Durlauf SN (eds) Handbook of economic growth, vol 1. Elsevier, Amsterdam, pp 386–472

Backhaus JG, Wagner RE (2005) Continental public finance: mapping and recovering a tradition. J Publ Finance Publ Choice 23(1/2):43–67

Banerjee AV, Duflo E (2011) Poor economics: a radical rethinking of the way to fight global poverty. Public Affairs, New York

Bardhan P (2005) Scarcity, conflicts and cooperation: essays in political and institutional economics of development. MIT Press, Cambridge

Becker GS (1983) A theory of competition among pressure groups for political influence. Q J Econ 98:371–400

Becker GS (1985) Public policies, pressure groups and deadweight cost. J Publ Econ 28:329–347

Besley T (2007) Principled agents? The political economy of good government. Oxford University Press, Oxford

Brady D, Spence M (eds) (2010) Leadership and growth. World Bank Commission on Growth and Development, Washington

Buchanan JM (1960) The Italian tradition in fiscal theory. In: Buchanan JM (ed) Fiscal theory and political economy. University of North Carolina Press, Chapel Hill, pp 24–74

Buchanan JM (1967) Public finance in democratic process. University of North Carolina Press, Chapel Hill

Buchanan JM, Tullock G (1962) The calculus of consent. Logical foundations of constitutional democracy. Michigan University Press, Ann Arbor

Dallera G (2013) La 'scuola' italiana di scienza delle finanze. Moneta e Credito 66(261):45–93

De Luca P (1858) La scienza delle finanze. Stabilimento tipografico dei classici italiani, Napoli

De Viti de Marco A (1888) Il carattere teorico dell'Economia Finanziaria. Loreto Pasqualucci editore, Roma

De Viti de Marco A (1890) L'industria dei telefoni e l'esercizio di stato. Giornale degli economisti settembre:279–306

De Viti de Marco A (1914) Scienza delle finanze. Lezioni compilate dal dottor C. Dama. Attilio Sampaolesi, Roma

De Viti de Marco A (1934) Principi di economia finanziaria. Giulio Einaudi editore, Torino, English edition (1936) First principles of public finance. Jonathan Cape-Harcourt Brace, London

De Viti de Marco A (1939) Principi di economia finanziaria, edizione riveduta definitiva. Giulio Einaudi editore, Torino

Downs A (1957) An economic theory of democracy. Harper, New York

Fausto D (2003) An outline of the main Italian contributions to the theory of public finance. Il Pensiero Economico Italiano 11:11–41

Fausto D (2010) Public expenditure in Italian public finance theory. Eur J Hist Econ Thought 17 (4):909–931

Fausto D, De Bonis V (eds) (2003) The theory of public finance in Italy from the origins to the 1940s. Il Pensiero Economico Italiano (special issue) 11

Fedeli S, Forte F, Leonida L (2014) The law of survival of the political class: an analysis of the Italian parliament (1946–2013). Eur J Pol Econ 35:102–121

Forte F, Silvestri P (2013) Pareto's sociological maximum of utility of the community and the theory of the elites. In: Backhaus JG (ed) Essentials of fiscal sociology. Peter Lang, Frankfurt am Main, pp 231–265

Fossati A (2010) The idea of state in the Italian tradition of public finance. Eur J Hist Econ Thought 17(4):881–907

Frey B (2000) Arts & economics. Analysis & cultural policy. Springer, Berlin

Frey B, Pommerehne WW (1995) Public support for the arts in a direct democracy. In: Frey B (2000) Arts & economics. Analysis & cultural policy. Springer, Berlin, pp 115–129

Galor O, Moav O (2004) From physical to human capital: inequality in the process of development. Rev Econ Stud 71:1001–1026

Galor O, Moav O (2006) Das human-kapital: a theory of the demise of class structure. Rev Econ Stud 73:85–117

Galor O, Moav O, Vollrath D (2009) Inequality in landownership, the emergence of human-capital promoting institutions, and the great divergence. Rev Econ Stud 76:143–179

Giardina E (1992) Commentary. In: Peacock AT (ed) Public choice analysis in historical perspective. Cambridge University Press, Cambridge, pp 145–167

Giardina E (2008) Le scelte finanziarie e il massimo Paretiano di utilità collettiva. In: Giardina E (ed) Scritti scelti (1960-2007). Franco Angeli, Milano, pp 72–99

Gilens M, Page BI (2014) Testing theories of American politics: elites, interest groups, and average citizens. Perspect Polit 12(3):564–581

Grampp WD (1989) Rent-seeking in arts policy. Publ Choice 60:113–121

Grossman G, Helpman E (2001) Special interest politics. MIT Press, Cambridge

Grossman G, Helpman E (2002) Interest groups and politics. Princeton University Press, Princeton

Guccio C, Mazza I (2014) On the political determinants of the allocation of funds to heritage authorities. Eur J Polit Econ 34:18–38

Holler M, Mazza I (2013) Cultural heritage: public decision-making and implementation. In: Rizzo I, Mignosa A (eds) Handbook on the economics of cultural heritage. Edward Elgar, Cheltenham, pp 17–36

Krueger A (1974) The political economy of the rent-seeking society. Am Econ Rev 64(3):291–303

Mazza I (2011) Public choice. In: Towse R (ed) A handbook of cultural economics, 2nd edn. Edward Elgar, Cheltenham, pp 362–369

Mills CW (1956) The power elite. Oxford University Press, New York

Mosca G (1939) The ruling class. McGraw-Hill, New York

Mueller D (2003) Public choice III, 3rd edn. Cambridge University Press, Cambridge

Musgrave RA, Peacock AT (1958) Classics in the theory of public finance. Macmillan, London

OECD (2013) Government at a glance. OECD, Paris

Olson M Jr (1965) The logic of collective action: public goods and the theory of groups. Harvard University Press, Cambridge, MA

Olson M Jr (1982) Rise and decline of nations: economic growth, stagflation and social rigidities. Yale University Press, New Haven

Pantaleoni M (1883) Contributo alla teoria della distribuzione della spesa pubblica. La Rassegna Italiana ottobre:25–70, English translation: (1958) Contribution to the theory of the distribution of public expenditure. In: Musgrave R and Peacock AT (eds) Classics in the theory of public finance. Macmillan, London, pp 16–27

Pantaleoni M, Bertolini A (1892) Cenni sul concetto di massimi edonistici individuali e collettivi. Giornale degli economisti aprile:285–323

Pareto V (1896–7) Cours d'économie politique. Librairie de l'Université de Lausanne, Lausanne

Peacock AT (1992) Public choice analysis in historical perspective, Raffaele Mattioli lectures. Cambridge University Press, Cambridge

Peacock AT (1993) Paying the piper. Edinburgh University Press, Edinburgh

Peacock AT (1994a) A future for the past. The David Hume Institute, Edinburgh

Peacock AT (1994b) The design and operation of public funding of the arts: an economist's view. In: Peacock AT, Rizzo I (eds) Cultural economics and cultural policies. Kluwer Academic, Dordrecht, pp 167–184

Peacock AT (1998) The economist and heritage policy: a review of the issues. In: Peacock AT (ed) Does the past have a future? The political economy of heritage. Institute of Economic Affairs, London

Peacock AT, Rizzo I (2008) The heritage game. Oxford University Press, Oxford

Peltzman S (1976) Toward a more general theory of regulation. J Law Econ 19:211–240

Pew Research Center (2014) Public trust in government: 1958-2014. http://www.people-press.org/2014/11/13/public-trust-in-government. Accessed 16 Mar 2016

Quinn RBM (1998) Public policy and the arts: a comparative study of Great Britain and Ireland. Ashgate, Aldershot

Riker WH, Ordeshook PC (1968) A theory of the calculus of voting. Am Polit Sci Rev 62(1):25–42

Rizzo I, Throsby D (2006) Cultural heritage: economic analysis and public policy. In: Ginsburgh VA, Throsby D (eds) Handbook of the economics of the arts and culture. Elsevier, Amsterdam, pp 983–1015

Stigler GJ (1971) The theory of economic regulation. Bell J Econ Manag Sci 2:137–146

Towse R (1994) Achieving public policy objectives in the arts and heritage. In: Peacock AT, Rizzo I (eds) Cultural economics and cultural policies. Kluwer, Dordrecht, pp 143–165

Tullock G (1967) The welfare costs of tariffs, monopolies, and theft. West Econ J 5(3):224–232

van der Ploeg F (2006) The making of cultural policy: a European perspective. In: Ginsburgh VA, Throsby D (eds) Handbook of the economics of the arts and culture. Elsevier, Amsterdam, pp 1183–1221

Wagner RE (2003) Public choice and the diffusion of classic Italian public finance. Il Pensiero Economico Italiano 11:271–282

Winters JA (2011) Oligarchy. Cambridge University Press, New York

Wittman DA, Weingast BR (eds) (2008) The Oxford handbook of political economy. Oxford University Press, Oxford

Political Economy of Broadcasting: The Legacy of the Peacock Report on Financing the BBC

Peter Goodwin

Abstract This chapter examines the legacy of the Report of the Committee on Financing the BBC (1986) chaired by Alan Peacock. It argues that the report is of particular interest because it is a rare case of detailed policy analysis and prescription about the finance of public broadcasting led by a cultural economist. It contextualises the report historically and politically, and then turns to examining the impact of its recommendations. It finds that some of these (most particularly not putting advertising on the BBC) have been of decisive long-term significance; some (the auction of ITV franchises) have been of great short term impact, but divorced from the Report's long term strategy, which was and still is almost completely ignored. Finally, from the perspective of three decades after publication it assesses the more general impact of the report on approaches to broadcasting policy in the UK.

1 Introduction

Public service broadcasters are major cultural institutions—in some cases arguably *the* major cultural institution in their respective countries. How public service broadcasting is financed, how it is organised and what scope it has all vary from country to country, with often long-standing national traditions about how these things are ordered. But the finance, organisation and scope of public service broadcasting have also regularly been matters of considerable political controversy, with many of the same issues crossing national borders. Those controversies have grown over the past three and more decades, fuelled among other things by increased commercial competition in broadcasting, the rise of political 'neo-liberalism', and the increasingly rapid adoption of new communications technologies

P. Goodwin (✉)

Communication and Media Research Institute (CAMRI), University of Westminster, London, UK

e-mail: goodwip@westminster.ac.uk

© Springer International Publishing Switzerland 2016   67

I. Rizzo, R. Towse (eds.), *The Artful Economist*,

DOI 10.1007/978-3-319-40637-4_5

from satellite broadcasting through to the electronically networked global society of today.

These controversies about public service broadcasting can be and sometimes are analysed with the tools of and from the perspective of cultural economics (see Towse 2006) but it is rare indeed for a cultural economist to have been officially summoned to come up with practical solutions to them. So the case where a leading cultural economist was summoned to assess the financing (and as it turned out rather more) of the oldest, most internationally influential and one of the biggest public service broadcasters is surely worth assessing. The case is, of course, Alan Peacock's chairmanship of The Committee on Financing the BBC (the British Broadcasting Corporation). Established in 1985 and reporting in 1986 (Peacock 1986), the committee has since been universally known as the Peacock Committee, and its report as the Peacock Report. The Peacock Committee followed in the footsteps (and incidentally was the last) of a distinguished series of official committees on broadcasting in the UK which had been set up and reported roughly every decade during the life of the medium. Peacock's three immediate predecessors were Beveridge (reported 1951), Pilkington (reported 1962) and Annan (reported 1977).

Each of these three committees—at least in conventional historical wisdom—left a signature legacy which still endures. In the case of Beveridge that signature legacy is a bit of a cheat, because in fact it was that of a minority report by the Conservative politician and committee member, Selwyn Lloyd, recommending, against the majority of the committee, the end of the BBC's television monopoly and the establishment alongside it of a competing commercial, advertising-funded television channel. This duly happened in 1955, a generation ahead of virtually anywhere else in Europe, with the establishment of the ITV (Independent Television) network. Pilkington and Annan's signature legacies are more straightforward. Pilkington berated the commercial excesses of the UK's newly established commercial television, thereby ensuring a rather more public service framework for it, and awarded the then available third channel to the BBC. BBC2 started broadcasting in 1964 and is still going strong. Annan expanded the notion of public service broadcasting in a more pluralistic way and recommended that the then available fourth television channel should be awarded, not to the commercial ITV, but to a channel alternative both in content and in production source. In other words, it laid the groundwork for Channel 4, which started in 1982 and which, too, is still going strong (although perhaps now altogether more populist and less alternative than how it was conceived, but read on).

The Peacock Committee was established in March 1985, reporting, on schedule, less than 16 months later in July 1986. Its remit was apparently considerably narrower than its predecessors, but its recommendations went way beyond its brief and were both wide ranging and long-term. It would be tempting (and some have been tempted) to suggest some headline signature legacies of the Peacock Report. Three possible ones come to mind: the 1990 auction of the commercial ITV franchises, the overthrowing of the traditional public service framework of UK broadcasting in favour of a market framework, and turning the BBC over to subscription. But, as we shall see, none of them is at all satisfactory even as a headline summary. Was the 1990 franchise auction the real thrust of the report? What sort of 'market framework' did it argue for? And, while eventually paying for the BBC by subscription was certainly a major recommendation of the committee, it was one which was never adopted. This chapter examines the significance of the committee's report nearly three decades after it was published. It looks at its impacts—or in some cases surprising lack of impact—on UK broadcasting policy, both short term and long term, and examines in what ways and to what degree the report's long term perspectives on broadcasting stand up today.

2   The Background

There were several factors behind the establishment of the Peacock Committee. The most direct was the scale of increase in the licence fee which the BBC felt compelled to propose at the end of 1984. Costs in broadcasting had tended to rise faster than general inflation—not just a UK or BBC problem but in part an incidence of what cultural economists will be familiar with as Baumol's cost disease (Collins et al. 1988: 16–18). In the 1970s the BBC's licence fee did not need to reflect this because during this period television viewers moved in large numbers from black and white to colour and therefore from a (lower) black and white licence fee to a (higher) colour licence fee. By the early 1980s this shift was nearing completion. So the bid for a licence fee rise, which the BBC announced at a press conference in December 1984, was for an increase from £45 to £65, that is, a rise of 41 % (Milne 1989: 127).

In any political circumstances this might have prompted calls for a review of the financing of the BBC. But these were not just any political circumstances. Margaret Thatcher's Conservative Party had won a second, and now crushing, majority in the election of 1983. Thatcher had consolidated her dominance over her administration with a cabinet now more supportive of her pro-market challenge to the post-war consensus. This was the beginning of the years of full-blown 'Thatcherism'.

During Thatcher's first term 1979–83, television policy had largely been concerned with the establishment of the new Channel 4 (a hangover from the recommendations of the Annan Committee in 1977) and with (ultimately not very successful) attempts to promote the new broadcast technologies of cable and satellite (for a full account of this period see Goodwin 1998: 25–68). Now, after 1983, policy attention shifted to the terrestrial BBC/ITV duopoly at the core of UK television. British free-market think-tanks had largely ignored television broadcasting since the 1960s. But in the early 1980s two new publications (Veljanovski and Bishop 1983; Adam Smith Institute 1984) reopened the intellectual free-market challenge to the public service tradition of British broadcasting—and re-opened it in a far more receptive political climate.

The largely pro-Conservative printed press, several of whose proprietors nurtured their own prospective business opportunities in a more commercial television market, were loudly hostile to the BBC. In January 1985 the *Times* (owned by Rupert Murdoch) took the exceptional step of publishing three successive leaders on 'Whither the BBC?' (January 14, 15 and 16). 'The BBC' the first one pronounced 'should not survive the present Parliament in its present size, in its present form and with its present terms of reference intact'. This hostility to the organisation and scope of the BBC was also reinforced by hostility to some of its output. The Conservative Party and its press allies have long tended to view the BBC as a haven of leftism. In the mid-1980s recent controversies over aspects the BBC's treatment of the Falklands War and the conflict in Northern Ireland had fanned that prejudice.

General pro-market hostility to the UK's traditional public service framework for broadcasting, and to the BBC in particular, did not in and of itself, prescribe a particular remedy. And there were significant differences among the critics. One of the two think-tank reports of the early 1980s favoured pay-tv as an alternative to the licence fee, the other favoured advertising (for a fuller discussion see Goodwin 1998: 70–73). Margaret Thatcher herself favoured funding the BBC by advertising. Understandably, because they believed that competition in the sale of television advertising would lead to a fall in its price, the advertising industry itself was also strong in support of advertising on the BBC and particularly vocal in publicly advocating this at the end of 1984. And at this time the advertising industry had considerable credibility and influential links to the Conservative Party (for more detail see O'Malley 1994: 24–29).

This was the political climate in which the Committee on Financing the BBC was established—announced to the House of Commons on 27 March 1985 by Home Secretary Leon Brittan, with the following remit:

(i)   To assess the effects of the introduction of advertising or sponsorship on the BBC's Home Services either as an alternative or a supplement to the income now received through the licence fee.

Including

    (a) the financial and other consequences for the BBC, for independent television and local radio, for the prospective services of cable, independent national radio and direct broadcasting by satellite, for the press and advertising industry and for the Exchequer; and

    (b) the impact on the range and quality of existing broadcasting services; and

(ii) to identify a range of options for the introduction, in varying amounts and on different conditions of advertising and sponsorship on some or all of the BBC's Home Services, with an assessment of the advantages and disadvantages of each option, and

(iii) to consider any proposals for securing income from the consumer other than through the licence fee. (Peacock 1986: 1)

It should be noted that on the one hand this was an apparently narrow remit, but that on the other hand, (i) (b) and (iii) opened up very considerable possibilities to a committee determined to go beyond those narrow limits—possibilities which Peacock and Samuel Brittan exploited to the full (and which, possibly, Home Secretary Leon Brittan may have hoped they would).

It is not difficult to see why, given the political background we have just described, this remit was generally interpreted by most contemporary outside observers as being a remit to put advertising on the BBC. To most contemporary outside observers, the composition of the committee reinforced that impression. Neither Peacock nor the economic journalist and senior *Financial Times* columnist Samuel Brittan, who was to prove the other intellectually decisive figure on the committee, either were or ever had been, members of the Conservative Party, but both were well known as free-marketers. Peacock's longstanding support for the Institute of Economic Affairs and recent Vice-Chancellorship of the private University of Buckingham (a favourite project of Margaret Thatcher) would at the time have appeared to put him very much at one with the Thatcherite *Zeitgeist*.

The other members of the committee were to a greater or lesser degree more sympathetic to the public service broadcasting status quo. But two were members or supporters of the Conservative Party and none were members or perceived as supporters of the Labour Party. "I myself regretted," observed Samuel Brittan in 1987, "that there was no one on the Committee publicly associated with the Labour Party." (Brittan 1987: in: O'Malley and Jones 2009: 105).

And as one of the other members, Jeremy Hardie, remarked 20 years later:

> It wasn't fixed but still it was a committee of a particular kind. For example, it was heavy on economists or quasi economists, which is one of the ways of approaching public policy issues, but only one way. The second thing, as I say, it didn't do this classic 'spread' thing of having the trade unionist, and in terms of politics I always believed that I was there as 'the dangerous lefty', as I was a member of the SDP [a then recent right-wing split from the labour Party]. (O'Malley and Jones 2009: 220).

Peacock and Brittan were well aware of this almost universal perception of the committee as being rigged to support advertising on the BBC, at the same time as vigorously denying that this was in fact the case.

As Peacock wrote in 1987:

> The Committee's approach to the financial problems of broadcasting and its far reaching conclusions came as a surprise. It was supposed to have been appointed to reach foregone conclusions. This was not the case. It was widely expected that the BBC should take advertising. It did not so recommend. It was believed that the terms of reference would so confine its activities that it would not be able to consider the wider aspects of broadcasting resources and how they should be financed. In fact it offered revolutionary proposals designed to alter the whole the whole system of broadcasting finance. (Peacock 1987 in: O'Malley and Jones 2009: 86)

And a few years later Samuel Brittan offered an explanation of why outside observers had got it so wrong—they confused his and Peacock's free-market views with "(a) enthusiasm for advertising finance, (b) support for commercial pressure groups and (c) desire to please the Thatcher Government." (Brittan 1991: 340).

Brittan was, of course absolutely right about the confusion. But, as we shall see, this almost universal misjudgement amongst contemporary outside observers, had the ironic effect of enormously increasing the impact of one of the Committee's conclusions.

3   The Recommendations

The Committee pushed its remit to the limits and beyond. When it reported in July 1986 its conclusions and recommendations extended way beyond the financing of the BBC, included such apparently distantly related matters as independent production and the auction of ITV franchises, and presented a very long term vision about the development of broadcasting and the place of public service within it. And not only were the recommendations extremely diverse both in subject matter and scope, so too was their reception, and their ultimate legacy or, it would be more accurate to say their various and varied *legacies (In the plural)*.

For the Committee, however, there was a tight and clearly articulated logic behind this diversity. The report's conclusions (Peacock 1986: 124–151) began by itemising what it believed the research, evidence and discussion of its first 11 chapters had shown. It is worth singling out four among these:

- An emphasis on the disruptive potential of the new technologies of distribution (cable, satellite and VCRs)
- The potential for introducing more competition into the industry of the new category of independent producers brought into existence by the birth of Channel 4
- The dire consequences for ITV revenues of advertising on the BBC
- The potential for subscription

These suggested 'an unstable and rapidly changing broadcasting scene' ahead (Peacock 1986: 124). In order to formulate policy for this environment it was necessary to be clear about what the fundamental aim of broadcasting was. And in the committee's view it was "to enlarge both the freedom of choice of the consumer and the opportunities available to programme makers to offer alternative wares to the public", (Peacock 1986: 125).

In pursuit of that end

> British broadcasting should move towards a *sophisticated market system* based on consumer sovereignty. That is a system which recognises that viewers and listeners are the best ultimate judges of their own interests, which they can best satisfy if they have the option of purchasing the broadcasting services that they require from *as many sources of supply as possible*. There will *always be the need to supplement the direct consumer market by public finance for programmes of a public service kind.*...supported by people in their capacity as citizens and voters, but unlikely to be commercially self supporting in the view of broadcasting entrepreneurs. (Peacock 1986: 133) [my emphases PG].

It is important to emphasise two things about this vision. First it was about a 'sophisticated' market system, and the committee were fairly precise about what they meant by that and what they didn't. They meant direct consumer payment, preferably by pay-per-view. And they meant a diversity of suppliers.

> *We reject the commercial laissez-faire model which is based on a small number of broadcasters competing to sell audiences to advertisers.* Such a system neither achieves the important welfare benefits theoretically associated with a fully functioning market, nor meets British standards of public accountability of the private use of public assets.

Furthermore, *so long as the number of television channels is limited, and there is no direct consumer payment, collective provision and regulation of programmes does provide a better simulation of a market designed to reflect consumer preferences than a policy of laissez-faire.* (Peacock 1986: 133) [my emphases PG].

Second, within the sophisticated broadcasting market there would still be a continued place for publicly funded provision of programmes like news, documentaries, 'high quality Arts', education, criticism and controversy, even experimental entertainment (for the list and the rationale see paras 563–565, pp. 127–128) "The only a priori stipulations are that state support should be direct and visible and not achieved by cross subsidisation or "leaning" on programme makers, and that such patronage should account for a modest proportion of total broadcasting." (Peacock 1986: 128).

Given this vision of a sophisticated market system for broadcasting based on pay-tv and diversity of programme suppliers, the contrast of this with 'laissez-faire' based on advertising and limited programme suppliers and the recognition that the current position of public provision and regulation might for the moment mimic the benefits of the 'sophisticated market' rather better than 'laissez-faire' it followed logically that the Peacock Report's suggested journey should be long-term and have clearly marked stages.

The Report envisaged three stages, outlined in tabular form on p. 136. During Stage 1 'Satellite and cable develop but most viewers and listeners continue to rely on BBC, ITV and independent local radio.' For this stage (apparently envisaged to extend into the 1990s) the Report outlined a detailed series of 17 policy recommendations (Outlined in Peacock 1986, sect. 12.5:136–146) In Stage 2 there would be 'a proliferation of broadcasting systems, channels and payment methods' and subscription would replace part of the licence fee. By Stage 3 there would be an 'Indefinite number of channels. Pay-per-programme or pay-per-channel [would be] available. Technology reduces cost of multiplicity of outlets and of charging system'. By this stage there would be 'multiplicity of choice leading to a full broadcasting market'.

4   Different Legacies and Different Sorts of Legacy

We will return in a while to the legacy (or legacies) of the Peacock Report's long term big picture—its 'sophisticated market' vision and its advocacy of subscription funding for the BBC in the longer term.

But we will start our examination of legacy by looking at what happened to some of the 17 specific and detailed recommendations put forward by the Committee as part of its Stage 1 in a far bigger process. And when we do so we need to constantly remind ourselves that, on the whole, where they were taken up, for good or bad they floated free of their place in that bigger vision.

We also need to remind ourselves when discussing legacies that we are dealing with a range of different, and sometimes very different, types of phenomenon.

Sometimes specific recommendations were rapidly adopted in more or less the way and with more or less the results which the Committee appeared to envisage. Sometimes they were adopted in a significantly different way or had significantly different results. And, as we shall see, sometimes they were completely ignored. Sometimes the legacy may have been intellectual rather than in concrete policy terms. And, particularly given the very long term nature of the committee's vision it may only be now, three decades on, that we can really assess them. We must also deal with the tricky question of separating out conjunction from causation. Just because things happened along the lines that the Committee recommended does not necessarily mean that it happened *because of* the recommendations. And, as we shall see, in many respects this is a very real issue in judging the effects of the Report. Finally, and again important because of the very long term nature of its vision, we need to assess legacy not only in terms of policy and intellectual impact, but also in terms of the committee's foresight.

4.1   Immediate Legacy 1: Advertising on BBC Television

But the obvious place to start is where outside observers at the time started—would there or would be not be advertising on the BBC? And here, the Report was devastatingly decisive.

Recommendation 2 (p. 137) was unambiguous that "BBC television should not be obliged to finance its operations by advertising while the present organisation and regulation of broadcasting remain in being." Partly this was because the extensive range of research that the committee examined led them to believe that advertising on BBC television would both not generate sufficient revenue to finance its operations and would seriously damage ITV's revenues.

"But," the report immediately added, "we must emphasise that our recommendations against advertising in Stage One is not dependent on these estimates; and it would stand even if we were much more optimistic about the likely growth of advertising expenditure and its sensitivity to price reductions" (p. 137).

Their reasoning was very much along the lines of their distinction between 'sophisticated market system' and 'commercial laissez-faire' which we have already discussed.

> The main defect of a system based on advertising finance is that channel owners do not sell programmes to audiences, but audiences to advertisers. The difference between the two concepts would narrow if there were a sufficiently large number of channels, without concentration of ownership. ...But these conditions do not prevail and are unlikely to for some time. So long as the present duopoly remains in being and competition is limited to a fringe of satellite and cable services, the introduction of advertising on television is likely to reduce consumer choice and welfare. (p. 137)

The political impact of this recommendation should in no way be underestimated for two key reasons. First because it came from a committee which, as we have explained, was virtually universally perceived as having been set up in order to deliver advertising onto BBC television. Given that perception—even if the empirical evidence the Committee collected had been less extensive or more ambiguous—the fact that the Committee recommended *against* advertising on the BBC made it virtually impossible for the Government to ignore that recommendation.

Secondly, we should not forget how significant the decision to reject advertising on BBC television was. Advertising on BBC television was vigorously favoured by the very dominant Prime Minister of the time. It was a popular option among voters, particularly lower income voters—a relatively sophisticated opinion survey by BRMB, commissioned by BBC and used as evidence by the Committee found that 63 % of the UK population favoured funding the BBC through advertising rather than the licence fee (Peacock 1986: 212). And, it should also be noted, advertising on public service television channels was, or was soon to be, a reality in the majority of the larger European countries.

Just 6 months after the publication of the report Douglas Hurd, the new Home Secretary (and one probably more protective of the BBC than his predecessor Leon Brittan), announced to the House of Commons that the government had definitely accepted that the BBC should not be financed by advertising and "for the time being the licence fee should remain the main source of income." That licence fee would be fixed until the following March and then indexed to the general cost of living for the following 3 years—another recommendation of the Peacock Committee, which was supposed to exert some pressure for efficiency on the BBC given the tendency of broadcasting costs to rise faster than general inflation (Goodwin 1998: 89–90).

This decisive rejection of advertising on BBC television, so rapidly accepted by the Conservative government, was to be a long-lasting one. In 1998, surveying the history of television policy under the Conservative administrations of Thatcher and Major, I observed "By explicitly rejecting Thatcher's preferred option Peacock Committee effectively spiked advertising on the BBC as a practical political option for the next decade." (Goodwin 1998: 91) It turns out I was not exaggerating. Nearly two decades further on the option has not returned. Revealing evidence for just how dead the advertising option has remained can be seen in this year's Conservative government green (consultative) paper on the BBC Charter Review. This is a green paper which is widely viewed as presenting the biggest threat to the BBC for more than a generation, in which, apparently no option that would reduce or commercialise the BBC is ruled out. Yet on funding the BBC solely from advertising it baldly says:

> This is not deemed appropriate because, as shown in evidence to the {House of Commons] Culture, Media and Sport Select Committee's Future of the BBC review, there is little appetite for a move to an advertising model. Such a move is seen as undesirable because the market is not large enough to sustain an organization the size of the BBC in its entirety. Moving to such a model would likely have significant negative impacts for others in the market, including other Public Service Broadcasters' ability to finance public service content, and an overall diminishing of advertising minutage. (DCMS 2015: 101)

Thirty years on this is the Peacock Committee's most definite and important legacy.

4.2   Immediate Legacy 2: Independent Production on BBC and ITV

One other of Peacock's Stage One recommendations was also rapidly taken up by Government and is with us to this day. Recommendation 8 was that "The BBC and ITV should be required over a ten year period to increase to not less than 40 % of the proportion of programmes supplied by independent producers" (p. 142). Until this time the vast majority of BBC and ITV programmes had been produced in-house. Indeed the independent television production sector had been effectively brought into being by the creation of Channel 4, which had started broadcasting less than 4 years previously in 1982.

One of the prime reasons for this recommendation was that it would exert a downward pressure on costs. (p. 141–142).

To this rationale was added an interesting caution: "The purpose of further encouraging independent production is to increase competition and multiply sources of supply. This purpose would be frustrated if the independent production industry became concentrated through merger or takeover, into (say) three or four major companies." (p. 142)

Just 4 months after the publication of the report, during the first full House of Commons debate on it in November 1986, Home Secretary Douglas Hurd reserved some of his most favourable comments for the independent production quota recommendation "We agree with that view and believe that independents, too, deserve, a place in the sun." Hurd said that he believed a 25 % quota, with a shorter timescale for implementation (the proposal backed by the independent producers' lobby) was more realistic and that he was soon to meet executives of the BBC and IBA (Independent Broadcasting Authority—the regulatory body then responsible for commercial television) in order to implement that. (House of Commons Debates, 20 November 1986, cols 718–719) This Government pressure brought significant results even before it was eventually embodied in legislation in the 1990 Broadcasting Act.

Thirty years later considerably more than 25 % of BBC and ITV programmes are made by independent producers, and such production has played its part in the enormous reduction in union strength within the industry, reducing wages and therefore costs. The independent sector has long ago decisively broken from its dependence on Channel 4 and grown significantly. It has indeed concentrated, as the Committee were concerned it would, but not to the extent that they feared.

So the spread of the independent television production sector into becoming a significant and stable part of the UK television industry has to be seen as the second clear-cut and important long-term legacy of the Peacock Report. With one caveat. Peacock's rejection of advertising on BBC television was the rejection of a policy which the Government might well have implemented had Peacock not stopped them. So here the Peacock recommendation was decisive. But is surely likely that, regardless of what Peacock had recommended, at some stage, and quite likely not many years later, independent production would have been required on the BBC and would have happened, by commercial decision, on ITV. Mandatory contracting out of public provision, and outsourcing by the private sector, were after all far more general phenomena during this period, and so too was weakening of trade union organisation within both the public and the private sector.

4.3   Uncomfortable Legacy 1: The ITV Franchise Auction

As we have seen the Government decided within a matter of months to adopt the Peacock Report's 'Stage One' recommendations on advertising on BBC television, licence fee indexation and independent production quota. It took considerably longer to decide on most of the rest, with a cabinet committee chaired by Margaret Thatcher debating the issues for much of 1987. "It was not the most cost effective way of spending time" one of its members, the then Chancellor of the Exchequer, Nigel Lawson, dryly recollected (Lawson 1992: 720–721).

Eventually, in November 1988, well over 2 years after the publication of the Peacock Report the Government published its considered practical proposals in response, the White Paper, *Broadcasting in the '90s: Competition, Choice and Quality* (Home Office 1988). Two years later, after much debate and change, these proposals became law in the 1990 Broadcasting Act.

On the face of it, the 1988 White Paper contained a considerable number of proposals which appeared to originate in the Peacock Report. As Peacock's closest ally on the committee observed shortly after the White Paper's publication, "According to one leading broadcasting journalist the Report scored a 'strike list' of about two-thirds on recommendations eventually accepted in the Broadcasting White Paper published in November 1988" (Brittan 1989: 39).

Samuel Brittan (and his journalistic source) were perhaps being optimistic. But even then Brittan (and Peacock, too) were clear that the Government had effectively cherry-picked the Report's proposals, while ignoring its overall strategy.

> Unfortunately, the selective way in which the Government picked up specific proposals from the Report, while failing to accept its basic import, was unpromising. *To the extent that the Government endorsed some Peacock recommendations it is the letter that was accepted, and the spirit that was rejected.* (Brittan 1989: 39–40, Brittan's emphasis).

I have treated the White Paper, the Act and its implementation at length in my book *Television Under the Tories* (Goodwin 1998: 93–122). Here I simply want to focus on two further major legacies from the Peacock Report's Stage One recommendations—these were the Recommendation 10 that "Franchise Contracts for ITV contractors should be put to competitive tender" (p. 143) and Recommendation 14 "Channel 4 should be given the option of selling its own advertising time and would then no longer be funded by a subscription from ITV" (p. 144).

The ITV Franchise 'Auction' was to prove the highly controversial centrepiece of the 1988 White Paper and the 1990 Act. It is therefore ironic that it was one of only two recommendations of the Committee that was not advanced unanimously by its members, and indeed secured only a bare majority with three of the members (Judith Chalmers, Jeremy Hardie and Alastair Hetherington) registering, and justifying, their dissent (footnote p. 143).

The majority (Peacock, Brittan, Lord Quinton and Peter Reynolds) justified their proposal as "a revenue raiser and an incentive to economise in resource outputs", a better way than the then existing broadcasting levy of creaming off monopoly profits. The majority were clear that they would expect the then regulator, the IBA, "to lay down the minimum quality, schedules and range of criteria" which bidders must meet. In addition "the IBA could decide that a company offering a lower price was giving 'more value for money' in terms of public service and accordingly, award the franchise to them." (p. 143).

The dissenting minority objected that (a) it would be very hard for the IBA to choose a lower bid on the grounds of more public service and if it did so it would be criticised as being arbitrary; (b) public service undertakings by successful bidders could not be made precise enough to be enforceable; and (c) a competitive tender system, being designed to reduce profits, made it more likely that companies would make losses or poor profits, and in those circumstances the IBA would find it harder to enforce standards (footnote p. 143).

After huge debate and many modifications, competitive tender for the ITV franchises, survived into the 1990 Act and was implemented in 1991 by the ITC (Independent Television Commission - the new more 'arms length' regulator of commercial television established by the 1990 Act to replace the IBA). Critics, often using some of the arguments raised by the dissenting Peacock Committee minority, had predicted dire consequences for quality. The Government maintained that it had enabled the ITC to set a 'Bechers Brook' (the most difficult jump in the Grand National horse race) in terms of quality threshold and introduced a clause whereby in 'exceptional circumstances' the ITC could accept a higher quality but lower bid. As events turned out, the results of the process did not provide significantly more upsets of incumbents than the 'beauty contest' of the previous round of franchise renewals, were not generally perceived as particularly fair and, in the one case where an 'exceptional' circumstances award might have been deemed appropriate, this was not pursued because the ITCs lawyers advised against it. The Peacock minority might consider themselves vindicated.

The competitive tender system was used once again, in the award of the new Channel 5, producing a result which (unlike with the ITV franchises in 1991) most outside observers were quite happy with, but which was convoluted and scarcely transparent (for details see Goodwin 1998: 116–117). When the Conservative Government published a White Paper on Digital Terrestrial Television in 1995 it proposed (and put into legislation in 1996) commercial multiplex franchises to be awarded by the ITC on the basis of three criteria, none of which included cash. The principle of cash bidding for television licences which had been deemed so important in the 1988 White Paper and 1990 Act had now been quietly dropped (Goodwin 1998: 150–151). And it was dropped too when the ITV franchises awarded by cash bid in 1991 were due for renewal. They were simply subjected to a negotiated roll over.

So the Peacock proposal of competitive tender for television licences, which not only was taken up and carried into policy, but also generated huge amounts of debate at the time, petered out within a decade. The legacy was a highly controversial but distinctly short lived one.

4.4 Uncomfortable Legacy 2: Channel 4 Sells Its Own Advertising

Unlike most of its Stage One proposals, the Peacock Report's recommendation that Channel 4 should be given the option of selling its own advertising time was accompanied by very little subsidiary explanation or qualification. All that was added was that "Channel 4 is now at a point where its costs are of a similar order to the revenue from its advertising." (p. 144) In other words it *could* now survive by selling its own advertising. But this is rather different than that it *should*. The previous regime, whereby ITV had sold Channel 4's advertising as well as its own, and then Channel 4 had taken a prescribed slice of the total, had clearly sheltered Channel 4 during its start up, but it also served to protect its 'alternative' remit, from direct competition for advertising revenue. The Peacock Report did not discuss this issue, but when its recommendation was taken up by the White Paper, critics most certainly did. As a result by the time that the White Paper endorsement had been incorporated into the legislation of the 1990 Act, the Government had made the concession that if Channel4's advertising revenue fell below 14 % of total terrestrial television advertising revenue then it could be topped up with a levy on the ITV companies (of up to an extra 2 % of the total). Although if Channel 4 did better than 14 % it had to share the extra with the ITV companies. This buffer has subsequently been removed.

So a last practical legacy from Peacock's Stage One recommendations which has survived to this day is Channel 4 selling its own advertising. And, even against extra competition, the channel has thrived financially. However most observers would judge that as it has thrived it has progressively shed most of its 'alternative' remit (with the major exception of its still highly reputed evening news bulletin). It has, in other words, become part of the 'commercial laissez-faire' which Peacock was so careful to distinguish from a 'sophisticated market system'.

In this case the legacy was certainly long-lived. But was it one that the report had anticipated or desired?

5   No Strategic Legacy

So far we have discussed those of Peacock's Stage One recommendations which were adopted. Significantly all are about the organisation or financing of *existing, free-to-air, terrestrial television* channels. When we turn to the Stage One recommendations that were *not* adopted, then we find a very different picture.

The very first of the Stage One recommendations was that "All new television sets sold or rented in the UK market should be required from. . .not later than 1 January 1988, to have a peritelevision socket and associated equipment which will interface with a decoder to deal with encrypted signals." The explanation was simple: "In order to prepare for subscription it is necessary to ensure that television sets are suitably adapted" (p. 136). In a similar spirit Recommendation 15 was that "National telecommunication systems (for example, British Telecom, Mercury. . .) should be permitted to act as common carriers with a view to the provision of a full range of services, including delivery of television programmes." Again, the explanation was simple: "The uncertainties of technological development preclude any dogmatic view of the future. There is nevertheless a good chance that Recommendation 15 might lay the foundation of a system giving multiplicity of choice even before Stage 1 is completed."

The Government ignored both proposals. There were to be no mandatory peritelevision sockets and the ban on BT and Mercury carrying broadcast entertainment was continued for years afterwards. In other words, the Peacock Report's proposals to foster the new technologies of distribution which it emphasised as necessary for the development of a full broadcasting market were ignored, while proposals on the immediate future of the existing terrestrial television system were taken up. This is the other—negative—side of the Government's cherry-picking of the Report's proposals. As we have seen, *some* important Stage One proposals were taken up and in some form or other implemented in legislation. But equally significantly some major ones were ignored. The process of selection ripped those that were selected out of the context of being Stage One in longer term process.

The 1988 White Paper purported to acknowledge its intellectual debt to the Peacock Report, but it departed from its spirit in two crucial ways. One we have just discussed, the full broadcasting market (and within it a subscription future for the BBC) was shifted to the indefinite future. Scarcely any positive preparation was proposed for it. Secondly, the strong libertarian streak in the report, its hostility to pre-publication censorship in broadcasting, was directly contradicted by the emphasis in the White Paper on extending controls over 'taste and decency'.

5.1   Intellectual Legacy 1: The Sophisticated Market System for Broadcasting?

So far we have discussed legacy of the Peacock Report in terms of its relatively immediate impacts on public policy and the long term consequences of those. We have also noted that in terms of actual public policy the overall strategic thrust of the report was definitely *not* adopted. Lip service may have paid to it in the 1988 White Paper, but thereafter even lip service tended to be in short supply.

However, it is often maintained that the report left lasting legacies in the ways in which broadcasting policy in the UK is discussed—that it introduced concepts, focuses and ideas into subsequent debate that were not there before.

There are two strands to this suggested new thinking. The first is a general approach to seeing the future of broadcasting as being in a 'sophisticated market system'. The second is a new model for thinking about public service broadcasting. We will discuss them in turn.

The authors of an academic study on *The Economics of Television: The UK Case* published 2 years after the report began by stating: "The setting up of the Peacock Committee, the evidence that its inquiry has elicited, and the debate on the future funding of UK broadcasting that it has sparked off, have performed the valuable function of placing the economics of broadcasting firmly at the centre of the policy making agenda." (Collins et al. 1988: 1).

Now, this may have been a bit of special pleading, but it came from a contemporaneous study by no means sympathetic to the Report's overall position. And it is certainly the case that the mode of argument in the Peacock Report was quite different from that of its immediate predecessors, those by Pilkington and Annan. For instance, efficiencies in resource allocation had not figured prominently in either. They were a recurring theme in Peacock, though.

And this overtly economic mode of argument about broadcasting generated an overtly economic response from some of those who might think themselves at risk from it. So, notably, in the 1990s the BBC commissioned a number of professional economists to produce studies on the then current broadcasting environment which were then published, and which employed the sort of clearly argued basic economics (and welfare and cultural economics in particular) applied to broadcasting familiar to anyone who has read the Peacock Report. Perhaps the most important of these studies is *Broadcasting, Society and Policy in the Multimedia Age* (Graham and Davies 1997). Symbolically, one of the authors, Gavyn Davies, then chief international economist at Goldman Sachs, was soon after appointed Chair of the BBC Board of Governors. And, symbolically in another way, some years later Peacock recommended Graham and Davies' book as an intellectually worthy adversary to his own views on broadcasting (Peacock 2004: 34).

But the raised importance of economic arguments in broadcasting policy since the Peacock Report does not necessarily mean that their increased prominence is primarily a legacy of the Report. First, some of the economic issues, in particular the focus on efficiency and market solutions to achieve them, have become a dominant theme right across public policy in the UK (and internationally) in the last 30 years. With or without the Peacock Committee they would surely soon found their way into the broadcasting debate.

Secondly, much of the thrust of economic or free market thinking in broadcasting has certainly not embraced the grand vision of the 'sophisticated market system' for broadcasting advanced in the report. Indeed much of it has been ad hoc special pleading or is in effect the 'commercial laissez-faire', from which the Peacock Committee was keen to distance itself. In as much as a similar grand vision does influence more recent debates, it tends to come from thinking about the internet and media convergence, leaving the Peacock Report as an intellectually intriguing precursor rather than a direct intellectual influence.

5.2   Intellectual Legacy 2: A New Model of Public Service?

Prior to Peacock *all* broadcasting in the UK had been seen as operating (and indeed was legally required to operate) as a public service. A small dent had just been made in with the new policies promoting cable in the early 1980s—the new cable systems not being included in this legal public service framework. But in practice all broadcasting as a public service was still the picture when the committee was established and to a considerable extent has persisted since (although OFCOM, the regulator and competition authority for the UK communications industries, now distinguishes between 'public service' channels—ITV, Channel 4 and Channel 5 and others that it regulates). Definitions of public service were and still are notoriously difficult to pin down, and *all* of the output of the BBC in particular was perceived by those who ran the organisation as public service. The Peacock Report, as we have seen, neither rejected the notion of public service, nor did it think it would disappear, even in a situation of channel abundance. But it did a) attempt to define it more precisely; b) situate it as a part—and eventually a modest part—of the broadcasting system rather than as the whole of it; c) stress the need for transparency in the allocation of the public finance which by (Peacock's) definition it required; and d) divorce it from the BBC as an institution by proposing that a Public Service Broadcasting Council distribute public finance to 'public service' programmes on *all* channels, commercial or otherwise.

The report's proposal to establish a Public Service Broadcasting Council, like the rest of its long-term strategy was shunted by the Government into an indefinite future and then rapidly forgotten, much to Peacock's contempt (see Peacock 1989: 61–62), although the idea of distributing the licence fee beyond the BBC has recently resurfaced in the government's Green Paper on BBC Charter renewal (DCMS 2015: 144). In the years since 1986 the argument that the BBC should confine itself to more strictly public service programming, and therefore cut back the scope of its activities and leave some of the more popular of them to the commercial sector, has been a recurrent one. This year's consultative paper on BBC charter renewal is the most recent manifestation of this tendency (DCMS

2015: 78–79). And it could be argued that it was the Peacock report that established this theme. As we have seen, the sort of programmes which the report thought might be regarded as public service was potentially wide-ranging. They also fell within the sorts of list that subsequent proponents of narrowing the scope of BBC activities have followed. There is some ambiguity, however, in the Report's more abstract definition, 'programmes which viewers and listeners are willing to support in their capacity of taxpayers and voters, but not directly as consumers.' Suppose they are willing to support them in both capacities, as indeed, it could be argued, they do in the case of many of the BBC's most popular—and populist—programmes. In that case the definition does not really do the filtering job aimed for by Peacock, and desired by the many subsequent advocates of restricting the scope and scale of programming that they wanted to count as public service. Interestingly the Report's argument did not include the notion of public service provision 'crowding out' commercial competition, which has been an increasingly common one for narrowing the scope of BBC output (again see DCMS 2015 for a recent manifestation of this position).

In assessing how influential the Peacock Report's intellectual approach to public service broadcasting actually turned out to be, we should also note that arguments for trying to precisely define public service and to confine it to that which cannot be delivered by the market reach far wider than broadcasting and have a range of other sources (for instance European Union rules on state subsidies).

In terms of transparency of public financial support for public service, the Peacock report's urgings seem to have had little influence. It is worth observing that the two big recent reductions in the BBC's income—shifting to it the full cost of the World Service in 2010 and of licence fee exclusion for over 75s in 2015—have been notable for their complete lack of transparency. These were ad hoc deals 'negotiated' behind closed doors—or more accurately enforced by government on the BBC behind closed doors. They involved very considerable amount of money—hundreds of millions of pounds on each case. They each involved major issues of principle—should overseas broadcasting be paid from the licence fee or by the Foreign office in the first case, and should the decision about a welfare payment (free licences for the aged) be in the hands of the BBC or Parliament. But in both cases there was no prior public or parliamentary discussion before the decision was announced.

6 Foresight

One final element we need to assess in looking at the legacy of the Peacock Report is the quality of its foresight. The Report put was in large part premised on the prospect of rapid change in the broadcasting environment. Peacock himself began a 1989 essay with the statement "Within a very short time there are likely to be enormous changes in the structure and finance of television broadcasting...". These included 'a wider choice of channels', 'direct charging' and 'increased competition'

(Peacock 1989: 51–52). As we have seen, many of the recommendations of the Report, were designed to advance those changes, but the report also assumed they were going to happen anyway in one form or another.

The report was certainly not alone in 1986 in this expectation of imminent and rapid technological and market change in the television world. And despite its general technological optimism, its three-stage recommendations showed a rather more sober estimate of the speed of change in the market than some contemporaneous commentators. Hindsight—especially 30 year hindsight—can be brutally unfair, but with that strong caveat, how prescient was the report about subsequent developments in UK broadcasting?

At one level very prescient. Although cable build, and consumer take up of what was built, had been slow before 1986 and continued to be so for several years thereafter (see Goodwin 1998: ch. 5), multi-channel and direct payment in the UK on a potentially mass scale began with the start of satellite broadcaster Sky's UK-directed services in 1989. By mid-1996 nearly 22 % of UK television households were paying subscriptions for multi-channel television (mostly via satellite, but with a significant minority via cable) (BARB establishment survey June 1996 cited in Goodwin 1998: 156). In Spring 1997 those cable and satellite channels were taking an 11.4 % share of total viewing. (*Broadcast* 6 June 1997 cited in Goodwin 1998: 156) As the report had anticipated that 'for some years to come—probably until well into the 1990s—the bulk of television will be supplied by a very limited number of channels' (Peacock 1986: 135) this was very much along the general lines and the timescale that they had foreseen.

Some details, however, did not go quite as expected. The committee had hoped that extra channels and direct charging would come via a national fibre-optic network run by BT and/or Mercury. It also hoped that at least one new terrestrial channel would be given over to direct charging (as Canal plus had recently been in France). And it seemed to have high expectations of cable. Despite the report's recommendations, as we have seen, government prevented the development of a national fibre-optic broadcasting network, and government and regulators showed no great interest in creating a British equivalent of Canal plus. Cable development continued to be disappointing. It was satellite, not the official 'high powered' DBS (Direct Broadcasting by Satellite), but the 'medium powered' Sky, that was the real driver of the multi-channel and pay-tv future which the report had anticipated. Writing some 2 years after the report was published, but before Sky even started its UK based services, Sam Brittan recognised the importance of this new development (Brittan 1989: 42).

These are technical details. They may, however, be of considerable significance for the report's vision. The national fibre-optic network that the report envisaged, if it had acted as a common carrier for television broadcasting, would, perhaps, as the committee clearly hoped, have opened up the new market for a large number of new players. The multi-channel pay-tv market that in fact developed was in practice dominated by a single new player—Rupert Murdoch's Sky.

Today, nearly three decades after the report, and well after it had expected a full broadcast market to have developed, the continued rise of multi-channel and pay television are apparent. Ninety-three per cent of UK households have digital television and therefore have access free-to-air to the dozens of channels that would have seemed the epitome of multi-channel back in 1986. Over half of these pay for satellite or cable. Total subscription television revenues are 50 % more than television advertising revenues and more than double the licence fee (Ofcom 2015: 143).

In the years immediately after the publication of the report, Peacock and Samuel Brittan often criticised government and regulators for not adopting some of the report's proposals and therefore inhibiting the development of the fully competitive television broadcasting market they had aimed to accelerate (see for example Brittan 1989: 40–44). Nevertheless, they saw it as happening anyway—but at quite what pace they seemed sometimes seemed surprisingly uncertain. As late as 2004 Peacock was writing: "Consumer sovereignty requires that a broadcasting market exists that enables consumer preferences to be directly expressed through the market. *There is considerable speculation about whether our system will move towards such a situation and how quickly.*" (Peacock 2004: 36 my emphasis). Eighteen years after the publication of the report, and with the progress in pay and multi-channel television that we have just sketched, Peacock was still hesitating about when his hoped-for full broadcasting market would actually come about.

7   Conclusion

Anyone reading the Peacock Report 30 years on has to be struck by the apparent coherence and vision of its argument—even if, like me, they do not share the basic faith in the market that underlies it. They also have to struck by its chutzpah—of explicitly not doing what it was supposed to do (at least by Margaret Thatcher) and recommending against advertising on the BBC. That is its most solid and enduring legacy, because if they had not done that then very likely we would have had advertising on the BBC and that would have had some rather serious (and in my view highly detrimental) consequences.

As an integral part of its bigger vision the Committee put forward a range of immediate practical proposals, many of which were simply ignored or rejected, but some of which, separated from their strategic context, were implemented. Of these, one (competitive tendering for ITV franchises) prompted enormous controversy in the run up to its implementation and generated no taste for repetition. It is now part of history. Two others (the independent production quota and Channel 4 selling its own advertising) are still with us and are important features of the UK television landscape. Whether these are good or bad features we might debate. And whether they might have come about without the Peacock Report we might also debate.

The Peacock Report's long term grand vision was officially squashed practically on publication. Partly that was punishment for coming up with the wrong conclusion on advertising on BBC television. Partly it was punishment for its libertarian strand, so out of line with Margaret Thatcher's brand of social conservatism. It may well also have been because it was altogether too grand for the civil servants and politicians of the time. No wonder the Peacock Committee was the last of its kind.

It is tempting to see aspects of that grand vision having survived at an intellectual level, and thus delivered the long term legacy which was lacking in practical implementation. I am sceptical. It is true that discussion of broadcasting has for a long time emphasised efficiency, relation to the market and restricting public service to a more strictly defined core. And, whatever the outcomes in terms of the renewal of the BBC charter, the 2015 government Green Paper on the BBC (DCMS 2015) shows just how far this framework for discussion of broadcasting has become dominant in official thinking. But efficiency, market and restriction in scope have been common features of the dominant approach to the whole range of public services for the last three decades. It therefore seems implausible that we can put their manifestations in broadcasting entirely—or even mainly—down to the Peacock Report.

The Peacock Report foresaw a broadcasting world in which new distribution technologies enabled multiplicity of channels and widespread direct consumer payment for television. Thirty years on that has most certainly happened—although, scarcely surprisingly, with a different mix of technologies than the Report envisaged. The Report saw the achievement of this multiplicity of channels and direct consumer payment as providing the basis for a sophisticated broadcasting market system based on consumer sovereignty, with only a modest place for public service. Thirty years on too, whether the reality of today's multi-channel and pay-tv, with its own new dominant players, lives up to that vision, or is in fact just a new version of the 'commercial laissez-faire' which the Report disparaged remains a highly controversial question.

References

Adam Smith Institute (1984) Communications policy (Omega report). Adam Smith Institute, London

Brittan S (1987) The fight for freedom in broadcasting. Polit Q 58(1):1–20, Reprinted in: O'Malley T, Jones J (eds) (2009) The Peacock committee and UK broadcasting policy. Palgrave Macmillan, London, pp 101–120

Brittan S (1989) The case for the consumer market. In: Veljanovski C (ed) Freedom in broadcasting. IEA (Institute of Economic Affairs), London, pp 25–50

Brittan S (1991) Towards a broadcasting market: recommendations of the British Peacock committee. In: Blumler J, Nossiter TJ (eds) Broadcasting finance in transition. OUP, Oxford

Collins R, Garnham N, Locksley G (1988) The economics of television: the UK Case. Sage, London

DCMS (Department of Culture, Media & Sport) (2015) BBC charter review: public consultation. London, DCMS, Cm 9116 at www.gov.uk (page references to portrait version)

Goodwin P (1998) Television under the Tories: broadcasting policy 1979-1997. BFI (British Film Institute), London

Graham A, Davies G (1997) Broadcasting society and policy in the multimedia age. John Libbey Media, London

Home Office (1988) Broadcasting in the '90s: competition, choice and quality. Cm 517. HMSO, London

Lawson N (1992) The view from No 11: memoirs of a Tory radical. Bantam, London

Milne A (1989) DG: the memoirs of a British broadcaster. Coronet, London

Ofcom (2015) The communications market 2015. Ofcom, London (August)

O'Malley T (1994) Closedown? The BBC and government broadcasting policy 1979-92. Pluto, London

O'Malley T, Jones J (eds) (2009) The Peacock committee and UK broadcasting policy. Palgrave Macmillan, London

Peacock AT (Chair) (1986) Report of the committee on the financing of the BBC. Cmnd. 9824. HMSO, London

Peacock AT (1987) The "politics" of investigating broadcasting finance. Roy Bank Scot Rev 153: 3–16, reprinted in: O'Malley T, Jones J (eds) (2009) The Peacock committee and UK broadcasting policy. Palgrave Macmillan, London, pp 84–100

Peacock AT (1989) The future of public service broadcasting. In: Veljanovski C (ed) Freedom in broadcasting. IEA (Institute of Economic Affairs), London, pp 51–62

Peacock AT (2004) Public service broadcasting without the BBC?. IEA Occasional Paper n 133. IEA (Institute of Economic Affairs), London, pp 33–53

Towse R (2006) A cultural economics approach to public service broadcasting (with particular reference to the UK). In: Juergen H, Kopper G (eds) Media economics in Europe. Vistas, Berlin, pp 157–171

Veljanovski C, Bishop W (1983) Choice by cable: the economics of a new era in television. IEA (Institute of Economic Affairs) Hobart Paper 96, London

The Public Spending for Culture in the Face of Decentralization Processes and Economic Recession: The Case of Italy

Roberto Cellini and Tiziana Cuccia

Abstract This chapter analyses the evolution of public spending for culture, in front of institutional changes, specifically decentralization processes, and fiscal consolidation policies, taking Italy over the period 1996–2012 as a case study. The case of Italy is representative of the top-down, state-driven model of public support to culture, even if increased autonomy has been attributed to local subjects in recent times. We pay attention to the role of different government layers and to differences across regions, with a focus on what happened during the years of the so-called 'Great Recession' (2008–12). Particular aspects of spending for culture, as compared to the whole of public spending, do emerge, as well as the link with the dynamics of aggregate income.

> The purpose of this study is to present the facts about the behaviour of [...] government expenditures [...], and to explain that behaviour by reference to basic propositions about the character of government and the facts of history. But the statistics cannot tell the whole story. Their value [...] is to guide us toward the facts of history that have been significant in encouraging the growth of public expenditures. Nevertheless, we feel that the general approach, using these concepts alongside the facts about absolute expenditure growth and its historical time pattern, provides a useful technique for imposing order upon the study of government expenditure generally. (Peacock 1961: xix, xxvii, xxx)

1 Introduction

Cultural policies across European countries have different dimensions and take different forms. Van der Ploeg (2006) suggests that three different basic models of allocating public cultural expenditure exist: the Italian-French system, that is a top-down and state-driven system, in which politicians and bureaucrats make decisions; the British system, in which arts councils (independent bodies funded by the government) have the responsibility for cultural expenditure allocation; and

R. Cellini (✉) • T. Cuccia
Department of Economics and Business, University of Catania, Catania, Italy
e-mail: cellini@unict.it; cucciati@unict.it

© Springer International Publishing Switzerland 2016
I. Rizzo, R. Towse (eds.), *The Artful Economist*,
DOI 10.1007/978-3-319-40637-4_6

the 'intermediate' (Dutch) system in which the responsibility is on the government, but an independent arts council plays a relevant role with experts' advice. The purpose of this chapter is to analyse the impact of institutional reforms and the consolidation of fiscal policies upon the public spending for culture in a country like Italy, which is historically a top-down and state-driven system but has been facing deep reforms over the last years. Specifically, we are referring to the decentralization processes that have occurred in Italy starting from the mid-1990s, and to the fact that an increasing degree of autonomy has been attributed to specific bodies in the cultural field.[1] Furthermore, we are referring to the fiscal consolidation policies adopted in Italy, as well as in several Western countries, starting from 2008, in consequence of the harsh world economic contraction also labelled as the 'Great recession'. Specific analyses on how the Great recession and fiscal consolidation policies have impacted on public spending for culture in Europe are missing, as far as we know.

Indeed, a (government) Report is available for Italy (AA.VV. 2013), but more recent data, and different choices concerning the analytical perspective, lead us to provide a pretty different picture here. Again, a book recently edited by Trupiano has to be mentioned, in which the public spending for culture is analysed in the general framework of private and public spending for culture (Trupiano 2015, and specifically Volpe 2015 on public spending across regions). Thus, some points emerging from our present study are already known; several other aspects, by contrast, are not yet discussed in available studies.

Schematically, the questions we aim at answering, are as follows:

1. How has the weight of public spending in GDP changed, and how has the weight of public spending in GDP changed specifically for culture?
2. Have these changes been uniform across different regions?
3. How have the (public spending) shares of different government layers been changing? Have substitutions occurred between different government layers regarding public spending on culture?
4. How has the internal structure of public spending for culture been changing? How has the current account been changing with respect to capital account? Is there a specific pattern for culture, different from the totality of public spending?
5. Which relationships emerge, between public spending for culture and aggregate income dynamics?

With reference to the this last point, we will investigate the causal links between the dynamics of public spending, or specific public spending for culture, on the one side, and the dynamics of GDP on the other side. In other words, our ultimate goal is

---

[1]We are referring, for example, to the reforms of museums which have taken place in Italy over the last years: starting from 2009, different administrative acts have been adopted (till to the comprehensive reform in 2014 which takes the name from the current Minister for Culture, Franceschini), to provide state museums with a larger degree of managerial and technical-scientific autonomy. The reforms aim to simplify administration, to promote innovation and to enhance the valorisation of the specific endowment of museums.

to assess whether the public spending for culture has a specific effect on GDP, as compared to general public spending. We aim to assess whether such effects are homogeneous across Italian territories, or some regional specificity emerges.

We refer here to the case of Italy, by resorting to the data made available under the project CPT—'*Conti Pubblici Territoriali*' (that is, RPA, 'Regional Public Account', in English) of the Italian Ministry of Economic Development. This databank, compiled according to the European accounting rules, covers the period 1996–2012; the spending of all public institutions (of different layers) is aggregated according to the regions of destination, and it is classified according to different criteria, including the sectoral criterion.

We are perfectly aware that the amount of public spending tells only a partial story about the supply of cultural goods and service. Nor is our aim to simply support people who complain about cutbacks in cultural public spending. It goes without saying that the amount and the quality of cultural production depend on organizational arrangements, specific management choices, and institutional design, along with the available financial resources. In the sphere of the public sector, a lot of effort has to be made for producing goods and service in a more efficient way. Thus, it is true that less resources do not necessarily imply lower amount of quantity and quality of cultural service. Perhaps, the financial constraints are an exogenous constraint leading to more efficient production and distribution processes (Cuccia and Rizzo 2015). An efficiency analysis, taking into account the number of delivered cultural products, is part of our future research agenda. Nevertheless, the evolution of public spending is a key factor, which cannot be overlooked to understand what has happened in cultural markets (see, in particular, Peacock and Wiseman 1979; Peacock 2000, 2006, 2007).

The structure of the present study is as follows. Section 2 explains the features of the data-bank. Section 3 introduces the series under analysis and their characteristics. The questions listed above are answered in Sect. 4. Section 5 provides some theoretical considerations. Section 6 concludes.

2 The Data Under the RPA Project, and Some Basic Evidence

The regional public account (RPA) databank (http://www.dps.gov.it/it/cpt/index. html) provides yearly financial data on revenues and expenditures of the Italian public sector. The final aim of RPA system is to develop a structured database, with full accessibility and exploratory flexibility of the data, to help policymakers of different levels to allocate funds and evaluate the effectiveness of different policies. The currently available version covers the time period 1996–2012. Data are divided both according to a *sector-based* classification broken down into 30 items, including culture,[2] that can be mapped both according to the Classification of the Functions of Government (COFOG) and according to 20 *economic functional categories* (in current or in capital account, such as general administration, wages; or investment in buildings, investment in machinery, respectively).

The RPA consists of two parts: General government and the Public sector. 'General government' is formed of entities that primarily produce nonmarket services, while 'Public sector' includes, in addition to General government, a 'non-general-government' sector consisting of central and local entities that operate in the public services sector and are subject to direct or indirect control. What is included depend on the legal nature of the entities themselves and the laws that govern the various sectors of public action. In the RPA database, the EU criteria were expanded to achieve a broader coverage, thereby including a significant number of public firms under the control of the state (or Regions or local municipalities). These entities are subject to periodic monitoring as part of the RPA project.

In this chapter, we consider the public spending of the public sector in its broad definition used by the RPA. Figure 1a, b portrays the pattern of total public spending, in nominal and real terms, and its share in GDP (all figures are assembled in the Appendix). The amount of public spending is larger than usually considered, precisely because the RPA also includes the spending from the firms under a public control.[3]

Total public expenditure has steadily increased in Italy, over 2000–08, both in nominal and in real terms; this holds both for public spending of the public sector in a broad sense (as defined above) and for the public administration in a strict sense. It is interesting to emphasise that the fiscal consolidation policies reduced (nominal) public expenditure only in 2009 and 2010. Taking into account the severe contraction of GDP, which occurred in 2011 and 2012, it is not surprising that the share of public expenditure in GDP has increased during the years of the so-called Great Recession.

Figure 2 portrays the total amount of public spending for culture (in nominal and real terms) and its share in GDP and in total public spending. The absolute amount of public spending for culture has been increasing over 1996–2004, but since then its pattern has been steadily decreasing. The same picture emerges with reference to the shares. The size of these shares clearly shows the marginality of culture, and its smaller and smaller role. Culture represented around 1.2 % of total public spending in 1996; this share was increasing until 2004, when it reached the maximum value

---

[2]Expenditure for culture include public funds for heritage, museums and monuments, historical gardens, libraries, cultural centres; cinema, theatre and music; leisure and sport without commercial or tourist scope. Thus, the entries are rather heterogeneous, and culture has to be interpreted in a broad sense.

[3]In Italy, a number of public firms have been privatized over the last decades—but they have remained under a public control. These entities are included in the public sector in a broad sense, and RPA takes them into account. Similarly, in several cases, local administrations have created firms to manage local public services. Even if these firms are formally private, they are included in the broad public sector by RPA, as long as public administrations control them and generally appoint the managerial structures.

(around 2.2 %). Since then, the trend has been steadily downwards and the last available datum, in 2012, reports a share of around 1.0 %. This means that public spending for culture is around 0.7 % of the Italian GDP, well below the 2 % goal set by EU. This percentage further decreases, of course, if we limit ourselves to considering the expenditure from the public sector in a strict sense. The share has been steadily decreasing also over the years of the Great Recession. However, it would be wrong to affirm that the responsibility of the decrease is due to the recession; the decreasing pattern started well before the Great recession: from 2004 to 2008 these shares fell of one third, returning (in 2008) to the starting values of 1996.

A comparison with other European countries is in order at this point. The Council of Europe (2014) noticed that the differences across European countries in public expenditure on culture have widened in the last few years (following the crisis started in 2008); this is likely due to severe public budget constraints and fiscal consolidation policies following the financial crisis. On average, the public expenditure on culture is about 1.1 % of GDP in EU-27 (with reference to 2012). As underlined by Cuccia et al. (2015), this percentage has been rather stable over the period 2000–11 in the largest part of the European countries. Italy represents an exception, with its large cut of public expenditure on culture; the cut has been even larger than in other countries suffering from sovereign debt crisis, such as Portugal, Ireland, and Spain (AA.VV. 2013; Volpe 2015).

Thus, total public spending in Italy has not been significantly decreasing over the years of Great recession, in nominal terms, nor in real terms. On the contrary, its share in GDP has been increasing (due to the GDP contraction). This is consistent with the well-known fact that fiscal consolidation policies, in Italy, have been mainly based on tax increases, rather than expenditure cuts. By contrast, public spending for culture has been steadily decreasing during the same years of Great recession, whatever analytical perspective one takes. It has been decreasing in absolute (nominal and real) terms; it has been decreasing if normalized with respect to the total public spending, as well as if normalized to the GDP.

In what follows, we propose a more detailed picture, taking into account: (1) the territorial dimension; (2) the government layers; (3) the internal structure of public spending for culture.

3   The Geographical Distribution

Economic differences across Italian regions are large. Italy represents a case in which regional inequalities are large and long-lasting. In a long-run perspective, the economic growth has been unable to reduce regional disparities; the Southern regions and the islands, Sicily and Sardinia (the so-called "*Mezzogiorno*") are still lagging behind. The decades in which regional convergence processes took place (like during the golden age over the 1950s and 1960s) are an exception, rather than the rule. A huge body of literature exists on the lack of convergence across

Italian regions, and the reasons for it (see Paci and Pigliaru 1997; Cellini and Scorcu 1997; Daniele and Malanima 2007; Felice 2011). The secular lack of regional convergence is a fact, even though massive public intervention aimed to overcome the disparities has taken place for decades. Several contributions focus on the reasons of the failure of public intervention, and a number of factors have been suggested, ranging from institutional explanations, to corruption, to the lack of social capital and other relevant production inputs (see the review of Trigilia 2012; see also Felice and Vecchi 2013). Therefore, it makes sense to evaluate whether significant differences across regions are present concerning public spending for culture. Such evaluations are of particular importance in front of the decentralization process under way.

Here we consider the division of Italy in five areas, namely, the North-West, the North-East, the Centre, the South, and the Islands.[4] The patterns of total public spending, and public spending for culture, in these geographical areas are represented in Fig. 3a, b. In general, the patterns show similar shape across areas. However, total spending shows a smoother pattern than public spending for culture: the variability of public spending for culture across regions is higher as compared to the variability of total public spending. As a result, the ranking of the areas, according to the share of public spending for culture, normalized with respect to total public spending (Fig. 4), is not stable at all: the Islands' area was at the top position in 1996, while it ranks at the median position in 2012; in the last years under scrutiny, the South area (which is the poorest, in terms of per-capita GDP) has replaced the North-Western area (the richest one, in per-capita GDP terms) as the worst performer in terms of share of spending per culture in total public spending. From a focus on 2008–12 it is clear that North-West and North-East did not face a decrease of their shares, while Centre, South and Islands each shows a decreasing share.

So far, we have dealt with *aggregate* data. Now we propose some considerations, taking into account *per-capita* data (data on population are from Istat (2014), the Italian National Institute of Statistics). The distribution of per-capita public expenditure across territorial areas is very stable (Fig. 5a), with the regions of the Centre showing the highest level, and the Southern ones the lowest. The fact that the Centre has the largest per-capita values can be partly explained by the fact that Rome, the capital, is located in the Centre. Thus, it is incorrect to complain (in the

---

[4]The North-Western regions include Piemonte, Valdaosta, Lombardia and Liguria, representing about the 32 % of Italian GDP and 26 % of population, with an income per capita larger than 1.22 times the average national datum (data are referred to 2008); the North-Eastern regions include Emilia R., Veneto, Trentino A.A., Friuli V.G., representing 23 % of GDP and 19 % of population, with income per capita 1.18 times the national datum; the Central regions are Toscana, Marche, Umbria and Lazio (21 % of GDP, 19 % of population, with income per capita 1.05); the Southern regions are Abruzzo. Molise, Campania, Puglia, Basilicata and Calabria (23 % of population but less than 16 % of GDP, with income per capita equal to 0.66 times the national datum); the Islands are Sicilia and Sardegna (7 % of GDP and 12 % of population), with income per capita, in relation to the national datum, similar to the South. The aggregation of Southern regions and Islands is also called *Mezzogiorno*.

political arena) about the high public spending in the South: the per-capita expenditures are higher in Northern regions, if one takes the public sector in a broad sense into account. If we focus on expenditure for culture (Fig. 5b), the picture is different: first, the ordering is not as clear as for public spending in general, but the Centre continues to show the highest level, and the South the lowest. North-East ranks at the second position, showing a higher propensity to make public spending for culture than North-West. However, consider that North-East includes cities like Venice and Verona, that are superstars in cultural tourism; public spending for culture here may also aim to enhance the tourism industry (Cellini and Torrisi 2013). Second, and most important, the pattern is far from being steadily increasing for all territorial areas, as happens for total public spending. The contraction of per-capita public spending for culture since 2005, shown by Fig. 5b, is impressive.

4 The Layers of Government

Figure 6a, b portrays the detailed composition of the relative shares. Two important facts emerge, which strongly differentiate the situation of cultural *vis-a-vis* total spending. First, the role of the central administration has been *steadily* decreasing over all the first decade of 2000 as far as total public spending is concerned, consistently with the de-centralization processes that have taken place in Italy. This pattern of steady decline does not hold for culture: the shrinking role of central administration is concentrated in the sub-period 2004–08. Moreover, over the last years under consideration, the central government re-gained its shares (due to the budget cuts for regions and local administration), as far as both the total public spending and the public spending for culture are concerned.

Second, in the cultural sector, the role of regions is much smaller than that of local administrations; this is the opposite as compared to the evidence relating to total public spending.

These two facts are interesting to analyse and explain. We did not find ready explanations in the available literature. Our guesses are as follows. Expenditure for culture did not find strong support in the political agenda over 2004–08 (as compared, for instance, to social welfare); moreover, when central government has to cut expenditure, culture is a sector in which the cuts are easier (as compared to other sectors, for example, health or police).

Copic et al. (2013) have noted that it is a common experience across European countries that the cut in cultural public budgets is concentrated at the level of central government. This holds also for Italy if one looks at the aggregate volumes of public expenditure for culture, while it is more debatable if one looks at the share of spending for culture in total public spending. Central administrations experienced a (little) increase in their share, in the years since the Great recession; this is simply due to the severe budget cuts that hit local administrations much more than the central government during the fiscal consolidation policies. The recovery of central administrations is smaller in the sector of culture as compared to the whole public spending.

As to regional and local administrations, it is clear that regions do not care, generally speaking, about culture as much as local layers of government. As is well known, in Italy the largest part of the budget of regions is addressed to health services. Even if culture falls into the regions' field of action, its practical importance is negligible, at least in financial terms. This is the outcome emerging at the aggregate level; it is true, however, that there are regions which have exclusive competence for specific cultural activities—we are thinking, for instance, of Sicily for museums and archaeological sites; in such a specific case, of course, the division of public spending is different from the aggregate outcome (see Cuccia et al. 2015, for details on the particular case of Sicily).

The large role of local administrations in public spending for culture lends itself to various considerations. On the one hand, it enables sustaining local artistic expression (Marrelli and Fiorentino 2016); on the other hand, it could lead to supporting artistic works of questionable quality, as long as it is largely influenced by local "political economy" considerations.[5]

5 The Internal Structure of Public Spending for Culture

The first articulation under scrutiny concerns the distinction in current *vs.* capital account expenditure.

Figure 7a portrays the public spending in current account, along with the specific entry of public spending for personnel, and the public spending on the capital account, for the whole public sector in a broad sense. The amount of public spending for personnel and in capital account are very similar in quantitative terms (and pretty constant over the years under consideration). The spending in current account is steadily increasing over the whole time period under consideration. In other words, the total public spending in current account has increased steadily (for the total spending), for reasons different from personnel.

Figure 7b portrays the pattern of the same variables, with reference to the specific spending for culture. Differently from the aggregate public spending in the broad public sector, the expenses for culture in current account have increased until 2006, and they have been sharply declining afterwards. In other words, in the expenditure for culture, a contraction in current account has occurred, that is not observed in the total public spending. The beginning of the decrease occurred *before* the Great recession and the consequent fiscal consolidation policies. For

---

[5]For instance Guccio and Mazza (2014) document that the allocation of funding for cultural heritage conservation activities in Sicily for the period 1992–2002 was politically motivated and influenced by the prominence of representatives of the ruling coalition in a district and the loyalty of voters to the main party. See also Mazza (2011).

culture, public expenditures in capital account are more stable than expenditures in current account, and the variability of current account spending is clearly motivated by expenditure other than personnel. It is worth noting that the Government Report on public spending for culture (AA.VV. 2013: 13) shows an opposite conclusion as to the variability of expenditure in capital account: the Report suggests that expenses in capital account are more variable than the expenses in current account. However, this Report focuses only on the most recent years (after 2000), and omits to consider some entries, such as expenses for interests, whose variability is not overlooked by the data under scrutiny here. As a matter of fact, if one focuses on the years of the Great recession, expenses in capital account appear to be decreasing, while expenses in current account are more stable.

Figure 8 looks at the situation from a different perspective. It portrays the pattern of the share of public spending on the capital account for the specific sector of culture, as compared to total public spending. Culture is a sector in which the share of public spending on the capital account is, in general, over-represented. This fact is already known, and it is underlined by the Report of the Italian Government on public spending for culture (AA.VV. 2013)—in this case with substantial consistency with our findings. However, our elaborations provide quantitative figures, which significantly differ from what is stated in that Report. In fact, in our sample, the average share of expenses in capital account is about 20.6 % with reference to the culture sector (*vs.* 13.5 % for the total public spending), while the Government Report provides 30 % and 10 %, respectively. Once again, the time-span under consideration is different, and the Government Report does not consider some entries among the expenses (the largest one, the passive interest bill). If we limit attention to the years of the Great recession covered by the available sample (2008–12), and rely on our present definition of the variables, the shares of spending in capital account are 23.2 % (for culture) and 12.4 % (for whole public spending), interestingly indicating that the fiscal consolidation policies have hit the capital account spending for culture in a (relatively) weaker way than the public spending in general. In general, expenses on the capital account have decreased for different reasons: the constraint from the 'internal stability pact', the impossibility for regions and local administrations to resort to external debt, the difficulties related to the starting steps of the 2007–13 European programmes. Differently from other analyses (AA.VV. 2013; Volpe 2015), our present study suggests that culture is not a sector in which these difficulties have played a main role.

Regarding the distribution of the share of expenditure on the capital account for the cultural sector across the geographical areas, data show that the area in which the ratio has the highest average value is North-East (with an average share of 23.5 %), followed by North-West (22.1 %), South (20.8 %) and Centre and Island (with a similar average share of about 18.8 %). However, differences are not very large, and their ranking over the years is pretty unstable. Thus, one can conclude that the geographical divide, between North and South, is rather small, as to the composition of cultural expenditures between current and capital accounts.

A final point has to be made concerning the public expenditure for personnel. The personnel expenditure in the specific sector of culture is very similar to the pattern of expenses for personnel in the whole public sector: Expenses for personnel have been increasing, in nominal terms, between 1998 and 2006, and this growth arrested in 2006; so, the halt cannot be attributed to the Great recession and the consequent fiscal consolidation policies. We can add that during the years of the Great recession and the fiscal consolidation, these expenses for personnel do not show any tendency to decline in nominal terms (a slight decline takes place in real terms). The average value of the share of expenses for personnel, relative to total public spending, is 17.4 % for the whole public spending and 16.1 % for the specific sector of culture, over the time-span under consideration. Thus, expenses for personnel are not oversized in the cultural sector, as compared to the whole of public spending. The share of public spending for personnel (in public spending) shows a larger variability over years in the cultural sector, as compared to the average for all sectors. For a large part of the timespan under consideration, the share of expenses for personnel was smaller in the cultural sector, as compared to the whole of public spending (see Fig. 9); admittedly, this situation has reversed in the most recent years.[6] Consider, however, that in several circumstances, public administration has substituted services provided by external companies to labour; surely, this is particularly true for the cultural sector. Thus, data on the share of expenses for personnel do not allow to draw conclusions about the labour intensive nature of different sectors of public administration.

From a geographical point of view, the average share of personnel expenses in culture is the highest for Islands (this is due, indeed, to Sicily), where it is about 19.9 %; the lowest pertains to the South (around 10 %), while North-West, North-East and Centre are between 15 and 17 %. Thus, the common place according to which the whole *Mezzogiorno* has an over-sized personnel body in public admin-istration is false, at least for the specific sector of culture. However, the situation is very heterogeneous in the Southern regions: while Sicily has a large share for personnel expenses, other regions are at the bottom end of the regional distribution.

6 An Exploratory Analysis on the Links Between Public Spending and Aggregate Income

In this section, we investigate the issue of causality between GDP and public spending, to assess whether a specific role emerges for public spending for culture. Second, we propose an estimation of the elasticity coefficient capturing the links between aggregate income (GDP) and public spending (and public spending for culture). We would like to emphasise that the content of this Section has an exploratory nature: here we are considering a very limited sample of data—concerning both the variables and the time period under consideration—while a

---

[6]The situation is substantially similar, if the share for personnel is evaluated with reference to spending in current account, instead of considering the total amount of spending.

more comprehensive approach would be necessary to derive well-founded conclusions. Our aim here is to draw some lines of future research.

6.1 Causality

First of all, we have to emphasise that the sample under consideration consists of only17 observations. However, the results we obtain are so clear and surprising that their suggestive content cannot be overlooked.

In view of the limited time-span under consideration, we investigate the issue of causality taking into account the simple concept of *Granger causality* (Granger 1988). We limit consideration to one lag; the main substantial results, however, do not change, if two lags are considered. Table 1 shows that the total public spending does not Granger-cause GDP, while GDP Granger-causes total public spending. The result is clearly surprising, according to basic macroeconomic theory. However, such an outcome is not so strange, and it is far from being a novelty, provided that public spending is acknowledged to be influenced by income dynamics.

The causality link is reversed, if public spending for culture is considered instead of total public spending. Indeed, public spending for culture does Granger-cause GDP, with a positive sign, while GDP does not Granger-cause spending for culture. These pieces of evidence seem to suggest that public spending for culture is able to positively affect national income, while the same does not hold for the whole total spending.[7]

We are fully aware that several cautions are necessary. Of course, we do not consider the non-stationary nature of data (but no problems emerge, according to the statistics, and this is not surprising in view of the limited time span under investigation). Furthermore, we do not consider the effect of additional variables and possible spurious correlation. However, the clearness of the result is in any case interesting.

It is also interesting to notice that these causality relation links generally hold also at the geographical level, with one exception. In fact (see Table 2), public spending for culture Granger-causes GDP (with one lag, at least at the 10 % significance level) in any area but the South (where the coefficient is positive, but statistically insignificant).

---

[7]In this exercise, all variables are considered in nominal, aggregate terms. The GDP has been built by applying to the series in real terms, provided by CRENoS, the national IACP series provided by Istat.

Table 1 Granger causality

	Dept. variable			
Regressors	GDP	SPA_GTOT	GDP	SPA_CULT
CONSTANT	78648 (0.27)	−203631 (−4.79)**	134187 (3.16)**	6996 (1.67)
GDP(-1)	1.15 (6.27)**	0.74 (6.49)**	0.89 (25.44)**	−0.003 (−0.74)
SPA_GTOT(-1)	−0.29 (−1.30)	0.09 (0.63)		
SPA_CULT(-1)			4.33 (2.19)**	0.73 (3.77)**
R2	0.98	0.99	0.99	
F test ($F_{2,13}$)	361.1**	259.5**	439.3**	7.68**
DW	2.07	1.73	2.35	2.16
Test on restriction to 0 of the coefficient of:				
GDP(-1)		$F_{1,13} = 42.08$ [p = 0.000]**		$F_{1,13} = 0.55$ [p = 0.471]
SPA_GTOT(-1)	$F_{1,13} = 1.68$ [p = 0.21]			
SPA_CULT(-1)			$F_{1,13} = 4.81$ [p = 0.047]**	
Summary conclusions on Granger causality				
	GTOT→GDP No [0.217]	GDP→GTOT Yes [0.000]**	CULT→GDP Yes [0.047]**	GDP→CULT No [0.471]

Note: One (two) asterisk denotes statistical significance at the 10 % (5 %) level

Table 2 Summary conclusions on Granger causality among variables in territorial areas

	Territorial area				
Causality link	North-West	North-East	Centre	South	Islands
GTOT→GDP	No [0.217]	No [0.315]	No [0.313]	No [0.245]	No [0.600]
GDP→GTOT	Yes [0.000]**	Yes [0.000]**	Yes [0.001]**	Yes [0.000]**	Yes [0.002]**
CULT→GDP	Yes [0.073]*	Yes [0.086]*	Yes [0.032]**	No [0.102]	Yes [0.061]*
GDP→CULT	No [0.620]	No [0.650]	No [0.297]	No [0.671]	No [0.973]

Note: The table reports the summary conclusion on Granger causality, following for each territorial area the same procedure as used in Table 1. One lag is considered in regression; significance, evaluated at 10 % (or 5 %), is denoted by * (or **)

6.2 Elasticity of Public Spending to Income

The previous results seem to suggest that GDP does cause the total public spending in Italy and in any geographical area within Italy that we considered. Hence, we can provide an estimate of the elasticity of public spending to GDP. We also provide an estimate of the elasticity of public spending for culture to GDP, even if previous

Table 3 Elasticity of public spending (and public spending for culture) to GDP

	1996–2007	2008–2012	1996–2012
$E_{\text{GTOT,GDP}}$	1.15**	0.51	1.28**
	($E = 1$: $p = 0.08$)	($E = 1$: $p = 0.00$**)	($E = 1$: $p = 0.00$**)
$E_{\text{GCULT,GDP}}$	1.99**	−1.42	0.92**
	($E = 1$: $p = 0.02$**)	($E = 1$: $p = 0.00$**)	($E = 1$: $p = 0.04$**)

Note: *(**) denote statistical significance at the 10 % (5 %) level; $E = 1$ denotes the test on the restriction of the elasticity coefficient to 1

evidence suggests that the direction of causal link is the opposite. In any case, the interpretation of the estimates we are going to provide is meaningful only if we rest on the assumption that public spending (and public spending for culture) are consumption decisions, endogenously determined and depending on aggregate income: only under these assumptions, does it make sense to compute such elasticity coefficient. We use a log-log regression equation (including a constant term), on contemporary data, to obtain the estimations. The outcome is provided in Table 3. All the elasticity coefficients are different from zero; we also evaluate the equality of these elasticity coefficients to 1.[8]

Considering the whole time period, total public spending appears to be a luxury good, while public spending for culture appears to be a necessary good. However, the supporting regression shows clear signs of misspecification: a clear structural break is present in 2008, and over the 2008–12 sub-period the elasticity of public spending for culture is negative, while the total public spending shows an elasticity equal to 0.5 (neither is significant). For this reason, we also report the result concerning the time-span 1996–2007. In this sub-sample, a very 'sensible' result obtains: the total spending has elasticity equal to 1.15, not statistically different from 1, while the elasticity of public spending for culture emerges to be equal to 1.99, statistically different from 1.Clearly, these pieces of evidence lead to the "microeconomic" conclusion that 'public spending for culture' is a luxury good, while public spending in general behaves as a normal good. The same substantial conclusion is reached, if the elasticity is simply obtained as the ratio between the average percentage change of public spending (or public spending for culture) and the percentage change of GDP: such a rough computation leads to 0.69 (or 1.37) as elasticity coefficients.

6.3 Elasticity of GDP to Public Spending for Culture

We have shown that GDP is Granger-caused by public spending for culture, in Italy and in a number of geographical areas. Now we provide some evidence concerning

---

[8]The results concerning elasticity coefficients are substantially identical if the independent variable is considered in lagged value.

Table 4 Elasticity of GDP to public spending for culture ($E_{GDP,GCULT}$)

	(A) Contemporary independent variable	(B) Lagged independent variable
Italy	0.28**	0.30**
North-West	0.28*	0.29**
North-East	0.35**	0.36**
Centre	0.13	0.15*
South	0.15	0.19
Islands	0.29	0.35*

Note: The elasticity is computed basing on a log-log regression; in column (A) variables are simultaneous; in column (B) the dependent variable (public spending for culture) is lagged one period. *(**) denote statistical significance at the 10 % (5 %) level

the elasticity coefficient—see Table 4. As far as Italy is concerned, the elasticity coefficient is 0.28 (or 0.30 if the independent variable is considered in lagged value) and is statistically significant. The elasticity coefficients by area vary from 0.13 (not statistically significant) to 0.35 (statistically significant at the 5 % level). This means that 1 % increase of public spending for culture entails an increase of GDP equal to around 0.3 %, at the national level.

7 Concluding Remarks

In this chapter, we have taken Italy as a case study to evaluate how institutional changes, and specifically the decentralization processes that have taken place in this country over the last decade, along with the Great recession (which began in 2008) and the fiscal consolidation policies have impacted upon the public cultural expenditures. Italy is an interesting case to analyse, as long as it is representative of a top-down, state-driven model of public support to culture. In general, the decentralization reforms that have taken place starting from the mid-1990s have led to a smaller role of central administration. Over the last years a number of reforms have taken place in the specific sector of culture, providing local subjects with a higher degree of administrative and technical-scientific autonomy. However, we cannot affirm that the structural model has radically changed. A major change, perhaps, is due to fiscal consolidation policies that have taken place over the last years, following the Great recession and the public debt crisis.

We have aimed at evaluating whether the pattern of public spending for culture has some particular characteristics, as compared to total public spending. We have resorted to the data made available under the project CPT (i.e., RPA, Regional Public Account), which has classified all public spending (from General government and from firms under a public control), according to European criteria, and considering the final scope of expenses and their specific regional destination.

Of course, some cautionary notes are necessary. First of all, although the classification of expenditures is rather accurate in the CPT databank, a revision of classification is currently under way, and a new edition of the databank is expected in next future. At present, public expenditure for 'culture' includes a wide set of heterogeneous entries and its correct definition is under debate. Furthermore, the present analysis has not considered the private financing of cultural activities. In this respect, it is important to recall that in Italy, (private) Bank Foundations play an important role in financing culture. However, different reports document that the total amount of resources devoted by Bank Foundations to the cultural sector have been reduced over the last years (see ACRI 2013; see also Cuccia et al. 2015).

We have shown that public expenditure for culture presents specific characteristics. First of all, its pattern is pretty different from the pattern of total public spending. While total public spending does not show any tendency to decrease in the second half of 2000s, and especially after the 2008 crisis with the fiscal consolidation policies, public expenditure for culture has sharply decreased, even in nominal terms. The decrease has been registered in both the current and the capital account. Clearly, the drop of public expenditure has been possible for culture, unlike in several other sectors, in which obligatory expenses are more significant. However, it is important to stress that the downward tendency started before the Great recession, and it seems to have a structural nature, rather than being connected to fiscal consolidation policies. As a consequence, the share of public spending for culture in GDP in Italy is now around 0.7 %, well below the maximum value, 1.43 %, reached in 2004 and well below the target of 2 % mentioned in several EU documents.

Second, we have seen that public spending for culture is very unstable across the geographical areas, differing from the whole public spending which shows an impressive stability across them.

Third, we have documented that different layers of government play a different role in public spending for culture as compared to total public spending. In fact, the role of local administrations is definitely larger, as compared to the rest of public expenditure. We have discussed the possible reasons, and the consequences, of such a composition. Here, we would like to stress that the discretionary power of policy-makers, and especially local policy-makers, in financing cultural activities cannot be overlooked. Thus, we believe that the statement of van der Ploeg (2006)—according to which in Italy (and France) the role of politicians and bureaucrats in making decisions concerning culture is particularly large, due to the top-down, state-driven model of public spending allocation in the field of culture—continues to be valid, even in view of the increased role of local administrations entailed by the decentralization process.

Last but not least, public spending for culture Granger-causes aggregate income. Our estimation exercise provides an elasticity coefficient around 0.3, significantly different from zero, as far as the elasticity of GDP to public spending for culture is concerned. In a nutshell, public spending for culture positively affects the dynamics of aggregate income.

Appendix

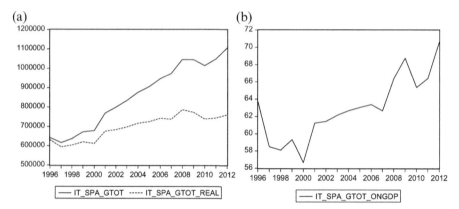

Fig. 1 (**a**) Total public expenditure, in nominal and real terms; (**b**) share of total public expenditure in GDP. Figure is based on data from CPT

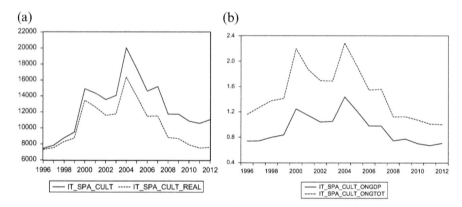

Fig. 2 (**a**) Public expenditure for culture, in nominal and real terms; (**b**) share of public expenditure for culture in GDP and in total public expenditure. Figure is based on data from CPT

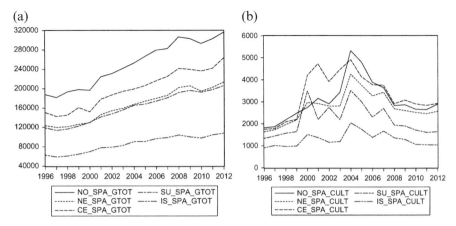

Fig. 3 (**a**) Pattern of total public expenditure in territorial areas; (**b**) pattern of public expenditure for culture in territorial areas. Figure is based on data from CPT

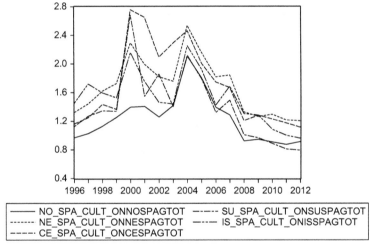

Fig. 4 The share of public expenditure for culture in share of total public expenditure, territorial areas. Figure is based on data from CPT

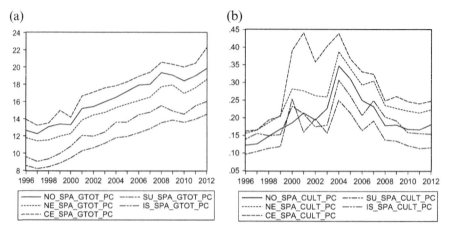

Fig. 5 (**a**) Public expenditure per in per-capita terms; (**b**) public expenditure for culture per in per-capita terms. Figure is based on data from CPT

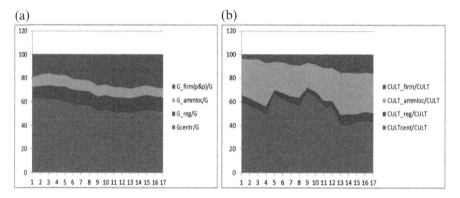

Fig. 6 Shares of central, regional, local government and public firms—(**a**) total public expenditure and (**b**) public expenditure for culture. Figure is based on data from CPT

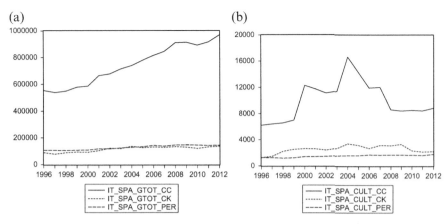

Fig. 7 Pattern of public expenditure, in current account and in capital account, and expenditure for personnel—for (**a**) total public expenditure, and (**b**) public expenditure for culture. Figure is based on data from CPT

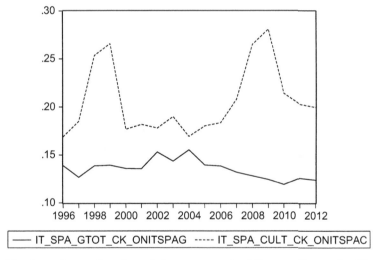

Fig. 8 The share of expenditure in capital account—total public expenditure and public expenditure for culture. Figure is based on data from CPT

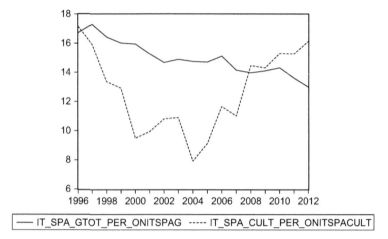

Fig. 9 The share of expenditure for personnel in public expenditure. Figure is based on data from CPT

References

AA. VV. (2013) I flussi finanziari pubblici nel settore Cultura e Servizi ricreativi in Italia. Dipartimento per lo sviluppo e la Coesione Economica, Roma

ACRI—Associazione delle Casse di Risparmio Italiane (2013) Diciottesimo rapporto sulle fondazioni di origine bancaria—Anno 2012. ACRI, Roma

Cellini R, Scorcu AE (1997) How many Italies? Rassegna lavori dell'ISCO 13:93–124

Cellini R, Torrisi G (2013) Regional public spending for tourism in Italy: an empirical analysis. Tourism Econ 19:1361–1384

Copic V, Inkei P, Kangas A, Srakar A (2013) Trends in public funding for culture in the EU. European Expert Network on Culture (EENC) Report, Brussels

Council of Europe (2014) Compendium of cultural policies and trends in Europe (15th edition). http://www.culturalpolicies.net. Accessed 30 January 2016

Cuccia T, Rizzo I (2015) Less might be better: sustainable funding strategies for cultural producers. City Cult Soc. doi:10.1016/j.ccs.2015.07.002

Cuccia T, Monaco L, Rizzo I (2015) Are less public funds bad? New financial strategies for cultural operators. MPRA wp64782. https://mpra.ub.uni-muenchen.de/64782/1/MPRA_paper_64782.pdf. Accessed 30 Jan 2016

Daniele V, Malanima P (2007) Il prodotto delle regioni e il divario Nord-Sud in Italia 1861-2004. Rivista di Politica Economica 97:267–316

Felice E (2011) The determinants of Italy's regional imbalances over the long run: exploring the contributions of human and social capital. Oxford University Economic and Social History working paper series n 088. Nuffield College, Oxford University

Felice E, Vecchi G (2013) Italy's growth and decline, 1861-2011. CEIS Research Paper 293

Granger CWJ (1988) Some recent developments in a concept of causality. J Econ 39:199–211

Guccio C, Mazza I (2014) On the political determinants of the allocation of funds to heritage authorities. Eur J Polit Econ 34:18–38

Istat (2014) Annuario statistico Italiano 2013. Istat, Roma

Marrelli M, Fiorentino P (2016) Cultural commons and local art markets: zero-miles contemporary art in Naples. Cult City Soc 7(2):117–122. doi:10.1016/j.ccs.2015.12.002

Mazza I (2011) Public choice. In: Towse R (ed) A handbook of cultural economics. Edward Elgar, Cheltenham, pp 362–389

Paci R, Pigliaru F (1997) Structural change and convergence: an Italian regional perspective. Struct Change Econ Dynam 8:297–318

Peacock AT (1961) The growth of public spending in the United Kingdom. NBER, Washington, DC

Peacock AT (2000) Public financing of the arts in England. Fiscal Stud 21:171–205

Peacock AT (2006) The arts and economic policy. In: Ginsburgh VA, Throsby D (eds) Handbook of the economics of art and culture. Elsevier, North Holland, Amsterdam, pp 1123–1140

Peacock AT (2007) The credibility of cultural economists' advice to Governments. In: Towse R (ed) Recent developments in cultural economics. Edward Elgar, Cheltenham, pp 60–73

Peacock AT, Wiseman J (1979) Approaches to the analysis of government expenditure growth. Publ Finance Rev 7:3–23

Trigilia C (2012) Why the Italian Mezzogiorno did not achieve a sustainable growth: social capital and political constraints. Cambio 2:137–148

Trupiano G (ed) (2015) La finanza della cultura: La spesa, il finanziamento, la tassazione. TrE, Rome

Van der Ploeg F (2006) The making of cultural policy: a European perspective. In: Ginsburgh VA, Throsby D (eds) Handbook of the economics of art and culture. Elsevier–North Holland, Amsterdam, pp 1183–1221

Volpe M (2015) I flussi finanziari pubblici nel settore della cultura e dei servizi ricreativi a livello regionale. In: Trupiano G (ed) La finanza della cultura: La spesa, il finanziamento, la tassazione. TrE, Roma, pp 25–36

Part II
Economics of Copyright and Music

Performance Rights in Music: Some Perspectives from Economics, Law and History

Hector MacQueen

Abstract This chapter discusses the liberal economic approach to problems of copyright law espoused by Alan Peacock, in particular in relation to performing rights in music. His contribution showed a man of independent mind, not at all afraid to disagree with the established wisdom or to draw conclusions that surprised those for and with whom he worked. In the spirit of an argument amongst friends, the chapter analyses the extent to which Peacock's view of the economics of copyright resembled or differed from those who had gone before, including David Hume and Arnold Plant. It is suggested that the approach was another example of Peacock's rejection of William Baumol's analysis of the economics of the performing arts as always bound to require public subsidy. Peacock showed that composers and their publishers adjusted their positions to the demands of the market and also generated significant revenue for themselves in meeting consumer demand, in particular through collective action by way of membership organisations such as the Performing Right Society. In the 1970s he also advocated the imposition of a levy on blank media enabling private copying of content, an issue which has recently returned to the fore in debates about further copyright reform to meet the digital challenge. The chapter concludes with some comments on Peacock's reluctance to extend his economic analysis to more general questions about copyright law and policy.

1 Introduction

My first personal encounter with Alan Peacock came about as a result of a meeting I had in the University of Edinburgh with Professor Gordon Hughes in January 1988. Hughes was a successor of Peacock in the Chair of Political Economy in the Faculty of Social Sciences; I was then the Associate Dean of the Faculty of Law; and the

H. MacQueen, F.B.A., F.R.S.E. (✉)
University of Edinburgh, Edinburgh, UK
e-mail: hector.macqueen@ed.ac.uk

© Springer International Publishing Switzerland 2016
I. Rizzo, R. Towse (eds.), *The Artful Economist*,
DOI 10.1007/978-3-319-40637-4_7

subject of our discussion was the joint degrees in law and economics.[1] We were exploring how to move the degrees on from being ones that were 50 % law and 50 % economics into something at least in part genuinely law-and-economics, with the economic analysis of law its central intellectual focus. That exploration ultimately ended in failure; but a few weeks later, on 12 April, I had instead been introduced to Alan Peacock in the somewhat cramped surroundings of a small office which the Heriot-Watt University had given him and his newly-founded David Hume Institute in its Chambers Street buildings in Edinburgh. I had already heard a great deal about him, in the contexts of, first, the Royal Commission on the BBC that he himself had so rumbustiously chaired from 1984 to 1986, and second, his then still current Chairmanship of the Scottish Arts Council from 1986, an experience he would write about a little later in his book *Paying the Piper*, in a chapter entitled 'Valse Triste: How to Lose Friends and Alienate People' (Peacock 1993: 115–41). I was therefore a rather nervous young Daniel feeling that he was entering a lion's den if not the lion's maw. Instead the next hour or so was the beginning of a friendship which survived my succeeding him as Director of the Institute that was his brainchild, co-authorship on our common ground of copyright, and differing views on a host of subjects ranging from Adam Smith to the xylophone.

The purpose of that first meeting was to discuss a possible commission for me to write something for The David Hume Institute on the law and economics of intellectual property. At the end of the following year, my *Copyright, Competition and Industrial Design* hit the bookstalls: a lawyer's attempt to analyse a highly technical bit of law with perspectives from history, economics and a policy point of view (MacQueen 1989, 1995). And within another couple of years I found myself Alan Peacock's successor as Director of the Institute, trying to find other people willing to discuss the law and legal system in a similar way and to fulfil the objective stated in his visionary proposal of 1983: 'a policy research centre which concentrates, though not exclusively, on forging links between economists and law with the primary aim of improving understanding of both short and long term problems of implementing sensible economic policies' (Peacock 1983: section 2.4).

I thought it right to begin *Copyright, Competition and Industrial Design* by pointing out that in David Hume's writings there is nothing specific about copyright, even although it was (as ever) a fiercely controverted subject in his own lifetime and one in which, as a published author, he had a direct personal interest (MacQueen 1989, 1995: 1–2). But something can perhaps be inferred from what he did say on the subject of property in general. For Hume, justice was an artificial rather than a natural virtue, the product of man's experience of and preference for social living, albeit driven by self-interest as a 'more artful and more refined way of satisfying' individual passions. Property and its transference by consent alone was likewise a construct, designed by man to ensure that society held together and was not destroyed by the individual's tendency towards entirely selfish action and appropriation (Norton and Norton 2011: 311–31).

---

[1] An LLB in Law and Economics and an MA in Economics and Law. The degrees are still available today in Edinburgh University.

The invention of copyright in the Statute of Anne at the beginning of the eighteenth century can illustrate precisely Hume's point about the artificial nature of property as a device for the betterment of society and the 'artful' promotion of self-interest, in this case that of authors and other creators who, protected by the new right, would be encouraged to produce social benefit because that will bring them reward. But Hume's subsequent discussion of the nature of property begins to raise questions about whether he thought the notion of property applicable to new intellectual creations. For him *stability of possession* was the key element in establishing the existence of property; and this was further developed by ideas of *occupation* (what constitutes taking possession), *prescription* (the right-affirming effect of the passage of time without challenge to the possession), *accession* (the addition of matter to the original object such as the fruits of our garden or the offspring of our cattle which become our property even without possession), and *succession* (the transfer of a deceased's property to the next generation). None of this related obviously to the creation of something new. Hume further specifically rejected the justification of property commonly used in relation to copyright and other forms of intellectual property, a theory most often associated with Hume's philosophical predecessor, John Locke; that is, the labour theory by which I own what is produced by my labour. Hume wrote:

> Some philosophers account for the right of occupation, by saying, that everyone has a property in his own labour; and when he joins that labour to anything it gives him the property of the whole. But, (1) there are several kinds of occupation, where we cannot be said to join our labour to the object we acquire; as when we possess a meadow by grazing our cattle upon it. (2) This accounts for the matter by means of *accession*; which is taking a needless circuit. (3) We cannot be said to join our labour in anything but in a figurative sense. Properly speaking, we only make an alteration on it by our labour. This forms a relation betwixt us and the object; and thence arises the property, according to the preceding principles (Norton and Norton 2011: 324 note 72).

At best, then, the creative person began to gain property in the medium on which the intellectual creation was first expressed. The idea of ownership of what had been created, as distinct from the material on which it had been composed, was simply outside Hume's conception of property.

As I have explored elsewhere (MacQueen 2010), this difficulty for Hume in the notion of *intellectual* (or indeed incorporeal) *property* was expressed more directly by some of his Scottish Enlightenment contemporaries such as Adam Smith and Lord Kames. It was also discussed by jurists like Kames' fellow-judge, Lord Bankton, and by academic lawyers such as John Erskine (Professor of Scots Law at Edinburgh University 1737–1765), Baron David Hume (also Professor of Scots Law at Edinburgh University, from 1786 to 1822 and our Hume's nephew), and George Joseph Bell (successor to Baron Hume in the Edinburgh Chair 1822–1837). On the whole, these men (all published authors) preferred to see copyright (and patents) as grants of particular (or 'exclusive') privileges by the state to individual subjects which created markets that otherwise would not exist, because it was in the public interest that they should. But the grants were carefully limited—for example, to specific periods of time—to avoid or minimise the possible ill-effects of the private monopolies to which they gave rise. As Kames put it: "the profit made in that period is a spur to invention: people are not hurt by such a monopoly, being deprived of no privilege enjoyed by them before the monopoly took place; and after expiry of the time limited, all are benefited without distinction" (Kames 1778: ii, 99). There were analogies with 'property', but the analogy should not mislead one into attributing to the rights created by the privileges all the absolute effects which law generally assigned to 'property'. The privileges were granted in the *absence* of what law would call 'property'. Such grants were made for the public good, and in the same name the privileges could be—and were—much more restricted in scope than outright property. (See further on 'exclusive privilege' Black 2014).

Such an understanding of his author's rights as privileges may well have underpinned Hume's own conscious and painstaking handling of them as a source of income. Having sold the rights to the first edition in two volumes of *A Treatise of Human Nature* to one publisher in 1739 whereupon, in Hume's own famous words, it "fell deadborn from the press", he switched to a new one for a third volume, although his first publisher remained willing to take it forward (Graham 2004: 92–3, 112–13; Brown 2014: 61 (MS facsimile), 88 (edited transcript). Again, in the 1750s initial sales of Hume's *History of England*, published in Edinburgh, were retarded by the London publishers' 'conspiracy' to restrict competition from Edinburgh and elsewhere in Britain and Ireland. The pressure eventually led Hume to switch to a London-based (if Scottish-born) publisher, Andrew Millar, in whose hands the *History* went on to become one of the great publishing success stories of the second half of the eighteenth century (Mossner 1980: 312–16; Graham 2004: 216–22, 226, 248–52; Harris 2015: 349–50, 368–70, 405, 407–8).

In the seminal cases of *Hinton v Donaldson* (1773) and *Donaldson v Becket* (1774) the Scottish and English courts respectively and definitively decided in 1773–74 that 'literary property', or copyright, was a legislative creation which expired altogether at the end of the period set down for it by the Statute of Anne 1710, having no existence thereafter as a form of 'property' at common as distinct from statutory law (MacQueen 2014). Hume thought the courts' decisions correct as a matter of the interpretation of the Statute, but actively supported the London publishers in their ultimately unsuccessful campaign to have Parliament pass another statute which would extend the copyright term for a further period of years with retrospective effect (Greig 1969: ii 286–8; *Parliamentary History* 1813: cols 1098, 1108, 1400). Hume's death in 1776 meant that he did not see the continuing success of the *History* after its copyright expired; indeed, it did not go out of print until 1894 (Mossner and Ransom 1950; Phillipson 1989: 3, 137–9; Towsey 2010: 262–92).

Today we have travelled a long way from the eighteenth century and Enlightenment debates about the nature of property and literary or intellectual property; but there are still important insights in that discussion from which we can draw lessons for today's policy-makers. Above all, perhaps, it is vital not to be taken in by use of property rhetoric when we consider what is to be done to address copyright issues such as the exploitation of product designs, the subject-matter of *Copyright,*

Competition and Industrial Design, or the problems of 'file-sharing' of music, which have occupied rather more public and legislative space in the early part of the twenty-first century. Hume's scepticism about the natural-ness of property, somehow or other antecedent to any other interest, and his identification of it as merely an artifice designed for the benefit of society, must be taken on board. In particular, his rejection of the idea that property claims flow from labour (or creativity) remains wholly convincing, and is confirmed with only a moment's thought from our general experience in everyday life. If that is right, then we must also accept that the creator as such has no claim beyond that given by the legislation in force at the time of the creation, and that that claim was and remains shaped ultimately by consideration of the public rather than the individual interest.

2   Alan Peacock and Performing Rights

I think a Humean perspective underpinned Peacock's own investigations of copyright questions. They focused on one particular aspect rather than the whole subject, namely the right of a copyright holder to control public performance of the copyright work, whether 'live' or by way of a recording of a performance. This is most obviously important to music and drama, and it was the application of the law in the musical context that engaged Peacock most, given his prior serious interest in that subject-matter for its own sake.

Copyright began to extend to music as such only in the nineteenth century, however. The eighteenth-century debate already referred to was concerned only with 'literary property'; that is to say, in the words of the Statute of Anne, with books and other writings. While sheet music received early recognition as 'writing' in the English courts, extension of protection to the abstract musical work itself had to await further statutes, with Prussia apparently leading the way and the United Kingdom following suit in the Copyright Act 1842 (Kretschmer and Kawohl 2004: 34–9). Before then, composers had to earn their living from patronage, performance, teaching and other, not necessarily musical work (see further Scherer 2004). The chief initial benefit of protecting the work itself was to give the composer the right to earn a return from publication of the sheet music; the interest in performances was rather in getting the work performed and thereby increasing the sales of its score. It was only with the development of, first, sound recordings in the late nineteenth century, and then broadcasting in the early twentieth, that the performance right came to be seen as a significant potential source of income for the composer (and the music publisher).

So far as I have been able to discover, Peacock did most of his research and thinking on the subject after he moved from Edinburgh to become the first Professor of Economics at the newly-founded University of York in 1963. York also had a music department and in 1968 Peacock gave a talk there on the subject of public patronage and music. In it he argued against the view of his former LSE colleague William Baumol (Baumol and Bowen 1966) that, since the performing arts were incapable of productivity gains, public subsidy was inevitable if they were to survive at all (Peacock 1993: 23–31). At this stage, however, Peacock (like Baumol and Bowen) took little if any account of performing and performance rights as means by which composers and performers earned remuneration that reflected market demand for what they could offer.

Appointed in 1969 to chair an Arts Council of Great Britain inquiry which published its *Report on Orchestral Resources in Great Britain* in 1970, Peacock gained many more direct insights into the funding of music (Peacock 1993: chapter 4 ['Molto Furioso']). Amongst numerous other matters, the Report made a number of recommendations about the payment of composers (and performers), and about ways of making the providers of music more responsive to public demand on what should be played, and who should play it, in return for public funding support. The Report was, as Peacock used cheerfully to recall, rejected by the Arts Council even before its publication, and attracted considerable hostility from a musical establishment un-used to the idea that the allocation of public subsidy should be driven by consumer rather than producer interests (Peacock 1993: 71–4).

A useful outcome of the Orchestral Resources Report for Peacock, however, was that his name and musical interests came to the attention of the Performing Right Society (PRS). This was the copyright collecting society for composers and print publishers of music first established in the United Kingdom in 1914. Its members transferred to it the handling and enforcement of their individual rights, receiving in return an income flow related, at least in broad terms, to the actual use of their individual works. In the early 1970s the PRS was engaged in a dispute with the BBC, its principal licensee, over the formula to be used in calculating the 'blanket' licence fees and royalties to be paid annually to the Society by the BBC (British Broadcasting Corporation) for the latter's music broadcasting. The established formula, last confirmed in 1967, was one of a fixed charge or royalty per BBC receiving licence. Growth in composers' income was thus dependent upon the volume of licence sales, while there was no benefit to them from increases in the licence fee. Nor did the income flow relate to the actual use of music by the BBC. Further, there was a long-running dispute between the PRS and the BBC about the way to take account of the audience for broadcast music: should this be based on the actual audience (the BBC position) or the potential audience, which was the audience for *further* performance material (recordings, sheet music, etc) set up by the broadcast (the PRS position)? The BBC position had hitherto prevailed; now the battle-lines had been drawn up again before the Performing Right Tribunal (PRT), the body charged since the Copyright Act 1956 with the resolution of disputes between the Society and major licensees like the BBC.

The PRS hired Peacock as an economic consultant in putting its case to the PRT. The consultancy was to be Peacock's introduction to the economic importance of copyright in the musical context (Peacock 1993: chapter 6 ['Moto Perpetuo: Composers of the World Unite']). His confidential report for the PRS was delivered in May 1972, a couple of months after the Performing Right Tribunal published its decision on the case. But as he later noted, he was "in a position to help with the [PRS] submission to the PRT which had to be made well before [he] was due to report" (Peacock 1993: 112–13). He was also able to conduct a survey of the composer members of the PRS inquiring into their sources of income (see Peacock and Weir 1975: 22–4), thus providing the empirical base upon which he always liked to build his analyses. In economic terms, he saw the problem as one of a dual monopoly: a monopoly supplier of copyright administrative services against a monopsonist user of the copyright material.

Peacock's suggested approach to the question before the PRT was to gear the income flow to PRS much more with the use the BBC made of music in its broadcasting output; to bring into play the extent to which changes in the licence fee were linked to the cost of living; and to deploy assessment of composers' relative position in the scale of earnings: "the onus of proof being on the BBC to demonstrate why composers should experience a fall in relative earnings through time!" (Peacock 1993: 112). That still left open how to assess the audience, or 'music use' factor, and what the royalty multiplier should be in any formula. Peacock acknowledged the need to "take the existing situation as the point of departure for any arbitration and seek compromises which do not require either side to face major changes in their economic position or at least to have to make them quickly" (Peacock 1993: 112). With the BBC as one of the parties, public opinion was also a factor of significance.

PRS had put forward four alternative formulae for determining what it should receive from the BBC, three of which were ultimately rejected by the PRT: one based on a sum per receiving licence, one based on a percentage of 'music use' income, and one based on a percentage of 'music use' operating expenditure. The formula finally adopted by the PRT in *BBC v Performing Right Society Ltd*, 27 March 1972 (Freegard and Black 1997: Case No 13, 90–98), was still one based on a percentage of the BBC's own licence revenue and grant-in-aid, but it also took composers' relative earnings into account, because this 'had the merit of simplicity' (Freegard and Black 1997: Case No 13, para 5.13.18). Peacock noted that the addition to this formula of a 'music use' weighting was not accepted, quoting the Tribunal as arguing that a straight unweighted formula 'would be sufficient to cover not merely the rise in the cost and standard of living, but also an increased use of PRS music by the BBC' (Peacock 1993: 113). The PRT also referred to the extreme difficulty of the task it faced in the absence of a 'market price' for the right to broadcast PRS music (because there was no market in the ordinary sense of the term in which that right was freely bought and sold). There was only one seller, that is, the PRS, which by reason of the jurisdiction conferred on the Tribunal was not free to demand any price it might choose to fix, and there were only two potential buyers for the broadcasting right, namely the BBC and the Independent Television contracting companies (which invariably negotiated with the PRS as one body) (Freegard and Black 1997: Case No 13, para 5.13.9).

Peacock thought that in all this "the PRT, which had taken a firm line in favour of the 'specific tax' approach in their 1967 decision, changed its tune to a remark-able extent" (Peacock 1993: 112). The collector-reporters of the PRT's decisions, Michael Freegard and Jack Black, remark that the decision was significant because the PRT gave up what had been its previously rigid approach of looking primarily at previous agreements between the parties to determine the outcome of present disputes, and looked further for evidence of change in relevant circumstances since those previous agreements (that is, more of a market-based approach). The starting point, however, was the proposals made by the parties, the nearest one could get to the prospect of a bargain-based analysis (Freegard and Black 1997: Case No 13, paras 2.3–2.11). The case was also noteworthy for a dissent by Sir William Skimmings, one of the four sitting members of the Tribunal; such individual dissents were very unusual in the body's history. Sir William favoured the approach based on percentage of 'music use' income, which he thought produced an overall fair result that was also fair in its constituent parts (Freegard and Black 1997: Case No 13, para 5.13.22). Peacock could thus fairly claim what would now be called 'impact' upon the PRT's thinking, even if the Tribunal was not wholly won over to his ideas.

Peacock's next venture into the copyright field followed rapidly: an economic analysis of public policy and copyright in music, published in a German festschrift in 1973 (Peacock 1979); and, then, with the support of the PRS, in 1975 he published with his York colleague and co-author Ronald Weir a book entitled *The Composer in the Market Place*. The latter was something of a sandwich: the first and last chapters, of which Peacock was the principal author, offered economic analyses of the position of the composer of music and of the market for musical composition, while the middle three, primarily the work of Weir, constituted a history of the performing right from the nineteenth century which developed into an account of the rise and changing practices, policies and legal positions of the PRS to 1970 (Peacock and Weir 1975: 12; see also Peacock 1993: chapter 3 ['Intermezzo (1): Economics of Musical Composition in One Lesson']). The book also included brief accounts of the development of collecting societies other than the PRS: for example, the Mechanical Copyright Recording Society, founded in 1911 to deal specifically with the right to control fixation, or recording, of a musical work, and Phonographic Performance Ltd, founded in 1934 to cover the copyright in the sound recording itself (Peacock and Weir 1975: 91–3, 134, 148–50).[2]

Peacock's position on copyright is developed most fully in his 1973 article on the subject rather than in the book. Although not expressed in such terms, the article is also a clear manifestation of his general dissent from the Baumol position on funding the arts (see further Towse 2005). In Humean fashion Peacock acknowledged that "[s]ociety has to devise rules to determine not only how property rights are to be exchanged, but how they are to be acquired in the first place" (Peacock 1979: 140). The creation of copyright was justified because it enabled individuals to realise their freedom "to use their physical and 'brain' capital as they wish in order to optimise their own welfare" (Peacock 1979: 140). In the case of musical

---

[2]The PRS and the Mechanical Copyright Protection Society formed the MCPS-PRS Alliance in 1997 and in 2009 the name 'PRS for Music' was adopted as a brand in under which the alliance sat. In 2013 PRS and MCPS-PRS Alliance realigned their brands and became respectively PRS for Music and The Mechanical-Copyright Protection Society (MCPS).

compositions, however, he accepted the collectivisation of composers on economic grounds: "the costs of collection of performance royalties to individual composers so far outweigh the revenue benefits that they should be allowed to combine in order to negotiate terms of payment, licences, etc, and to decide methods of royalty distribution between members" (Peacock 1979: 142–3). This was particularly so in the United Kingdom, where the collecting society could offset the powerful buyer that was (and is) the BBC. Hence the existence of the PRS and similar bodies in other aspects of copyright administration was justified, albeit government had to monitor and regulate its discharge of its functions in order to ensure that its market power was not abused against the public and in particular the consumer interest.

Regulation did not have to go so far as nationalisation of the collection agency, however. At its most extreme, a publicly owned agency might have the power to become in effect an instrument of censorship. There was certainly no reason to think that such a state organisation would do a better job in royalty collection than the existing private organisation and, indeed, not being a membership organisation, it would be under less pressure to achieve that. Accordingly, Peacock argued, so long as copyright existed and was operated efficiently, 'the market can be used as the vehicle for determining the remuneration of composers' (Peacock 1979: 148). Given his previous experience of dismissal at the patrician hands of the Arts Council and the musical establishment, he could perhaps be forgiven for the gleeful note in his near-concluding comment: "[W]hatever composers may think about the economic system we live in, they certainly actively participate in organisations designed to protect their economic interests" (Peacock 1979: 148).

The history of the PRS also well demonstrated the capacity of composers and their publishers to respond to changing market conditions. The creation of the Society in the first place was as a response to the challenge posed by the emergence of sound recordings as an increasingly significant means by which consumers enjoyed musical performance. The Society's development had responded quickly to the rise of wireless broadcasting (in particular by the BBC), film music, juke-boxes, 'music while you work', and piped music as new ways in which compositions reached their growing audiences (see also Montgomery and Threlfall 2007). In essence musical performance had ceased to be an ephemeral and occasional experience involving only the performers and any audience in the same physical space. It could now be stored and in that form also sold to anyone able to buy it, and, whether 'live' or stored, transmitted to anyone equipped with the machinery to receive the transmission.

Many of these developments Peacock, born in 1922 and a lover of music from an early age, could recall from personal experience (Peacock 1993: 2–15). But he may have learned still more at first hand from those whose personal recollections went even further back than his, such as the Austrian composer Hans Gál (1890–1987). He taught Peacock composition in Edinburgh between 1960 and Peacock's departure for York in 1963 (Peacock 1993: 13–15). In an interview first published in 1987, Gál recalled his native Vienna in his childhood and young manhood:

[E]verything was restricted to the comparatively rare chance of public performance. The Philharmonic Orchestra in Vienna gave eight concerts a year. There were two more orchestras, and everyone had, I think, a dozen concerts a year. This was the supply of orchestral music. Chamber music was a rare occasion in public. … The only primary possibility of getting acquainted with great music was the piano duet. … Every work that was published was first published as a piano duet; it was the way of selling music at the time. … Things changed enormously with the advent of radio—it changed the world of music (Anderson 1987: 36–7; reprinted Gál 2014: 218–19).

Gál's life also illustrated very well a point emphasised in Peacock's copyright writings: few composers made a living from composition alone but instead had portfolio careers the other elements of which often (but not invariably) had a musical dimension (Peacock 1979: 137–8; Peacock and Weir 1975: 20–4). Thus Gál taught not only composition but also performance in Austria; and when, as a Jew, he and his family were forced to flee to Britain in 1938, he became first a cataloguer in the Reid Music Library at Edinburgh University and then later a teacher both privately and in the Faculty of Music at the University as well as a performer and a conductor. He had to survive major external shocks: the First World War, the expulsion from his homeland, internment as an 'enemy alien' in Britain from May to September 1940 (the journal he kept during this period being the moving centre-piece of a recent publication on the man), and later family tragedies. Yet he maintained himself as a musician and composer throughout a long life, and indeed music probably enabled him to survive some terrible personal experiences (Gál 2014: 13–22; 175–82).

3 Peacock v Plant: The Blank Media Levy

It is not quite the case that Peacock was the first British economist to take an interest in copyright questions (see further Hadfield 1992: 19–32). His other hero from the Scottish Enlightenment, Adam Smith, justified the 'exclusive privilege' or 'monopoly' of copyright as 'an encouragement to the labours of learned men'; before its invention 'a scholar and a beggar seem to have been terms very nearly synonymous [*sic*]' (Meek et al. 1978: 83; Todd 1976: 149). Smith thought that in general the rights struck a balance which was appropriately responsive to the consumer interest, especially with regard to their time-limited period: "[I]f the book be a valuable one the demand for it in that time will probably be a considerable addition to his fortune. But if it is of no value the advantage he can reap from it will be very small" (Meek et al. 1978: 83).

Smith had been followed by Jeremy Bentham in seeing the copyright monopoly as without social harm to off-set against the monopolist's benefit. Bentham went beyond Smith's 'encouragement' in recognising the incentive effect of copyright: "he who has no hope that he shall reap, will not take the trouble to sow" (Bowring 1838–1843: vol 3, 71). The classical liberal, John Stuart Mill, was also favourable towards copyright: "it would be a gross immorality in the law to set everybody free to use a person's work without his consent, and without giving him an equivalent" (Robson 1965: 928–9). But Macaulay's famous epitomisation of copyright in 1841 as "a tax on readers for the purpose of giving a bounty to authors" (Macaulay 1853: vol 1, 292), set the tone behind the thinking that led most twentieth-century economists considering the matter before Peacock to oppose copyright law as "unnecessary and damaging to competition and [to] claim .. that there were other ways to stimulate creativity and artistic innovation" (so summarised in Towse 2004: 54; see further Hadfield 1992: 33–45).

Even before the outset of Peacock's professional career, Sir Arnold Plant (who was an early if indubitably senior colleague at the London School of Economics[3]) had given rather critical assessments of copyright's economic impact, arguing that the public interest would be better served by restricting its scope and perhaps ultimately getting rid of it altogether (Plant 1934, 1953). Copyright did not provide incentives for authors to produce, and the indiscriminate breadth of its coverage meant that it did not encourage improvements in the quality of work. Publishers benefited more than authors and, while admittedly the former took significant risks in publishing, they could earn their profit without necessarily satisfying the overall demand for a work. Publishers' rights should last for a shorter time than authors', and other publishers should thereafter be free to publish upon payment of a statutorily fixed royalty to the relevant author. Such a system had been introduced under the Copyright Act 1911 in respect of making sound recordings (the 'mechanical' or 'fixation' right), where those who held rights in material that was recorded by their licence were thereby obliged to accept further recordings by others upon the latter making payment to them of a compulsory royalty (the 'statutory recording licence'). Plant sought the expansion of this system beyond its then limited sphere.

In his 1973 article Peacock responded to Plant by noting that implicit in his argument was the assignment of property rights with reference to their allocational effects only in one limited sphere, that is, composition rather than publication, without compensation for those who would lose out. While publishers and authors or composers did have distinct interests, they had to combine, as they did in the PRS, to protect themselves against monopolistic buyers such as public broadcasters and recording corporations. In any event the continued rapid advance of technology, in particular the increased possibility of consumers producing copies of performances for themselves, meant that a right to control public performance was no longer enough to ensure returns for either composer or publisher. Forbidding private reproduction would not work because that was unenforceable in practical terms. The right way forward would be a taxation or levy system on the price of recording media, related however, in accordance with Peacock's basic economic principles, to the length of playing time available on the device and so to actual or potential consumer use (Peacock 1979: 144–7; see also MacQueen and Peacock 1995: 173–4).

---

[3]Peacock's copy of Plant 1953 (which I now possess) is inscribed 'A. T. Peacock from A. P.'

In this refutation of Plant we can once again see Peacock dissenting from received wisdom, at least within the economics profession. While Plant's ideas, given vent in the run-up to what became the Copyright Act 1956, gained no further hold in that legislation, the 'statutory recording licence' for sound recordings was retained. That was ultimately abolished however by the Copyright, Designs and Patents Act 1988. This was despite a contrary recommendation by the Whitford Committee on copyright and designs law, which sat from 1974 and reported in March 1977 (Whitford Report: chapter 6). But subsequently the United Kingdom Government led by Mrs Thatcher began to signal what its ultimate conclusions would be on the matter. "[I]t seems anomalous," said a Green Paper published in 1981 by the Secretary of State for Trade, "that sound recordings should be singled out for special treatment" (Department of Trade and Industry 1981: 18). Further, "As the Government views the situation, it is probable that the recording of music would be better left to the operation of the competitive forces in the market" (ibid). What most probably undermined the statutory recording licence, however, was the difficulties it created for the free movement of goods within what was then the European Community (see especially Joined Cases 55, 57/80 *Musik-Vertrieb Membran GmbH v GEMA* [1981] ECR 147; Department of Trade and Industry 1981: 19). Thus Plant's approach finally sank beneath the incoming tide of European market integration as well as free market thinking.

But Peacock's counter-idea of a levy on recording media and/or machinery has likewise gone nowhere with successive Governments in the United Kingdom. The levy has of course been frequently discussed in debates about copyright reform. In 1977 the Whitford Report recommended:

> It is our view that, for private recording, the only satisfactory solution is the introduction of a levy on the sale price of recording equipment. A major problem in the case of private recording, which no other system seems able to overcome, is that of policing; we feel the levy approach will effectively meet this difficulty. ... As in Germany it should be the manufacturer or importer who should be liable for the levy" (Whitford Report 1977: para 322).

Peacock claimed to have made a submission on the subject to the Whitford Committee, but his name is not listed amongst those who gave either written or oral evidence to the committee (Peacock 1993: 100–2; Whitford Report 1977: 244–53). Although many of the Whitford Report's other recommendations eventually found their way on to the statute book via the Copyright, Designs and Patents Act 1988, this did not hold good for the levy proposal any more than for the retention of the statutory recording licence. As Peacock wryly noted, the then Government abandoned the initial inclusion of the levy idea in its Bill: "some say that it was concerned about the political consequences of taxing a consuming pleasure of the young about to vote for the first time!" (Peacock 1993: 102).

That fear of electoral unpopularity has continued to haunt British government on the subject ever since, whether approaching it from the right or the left or in uneasy coalitions. The issue has never gone away, however, thanks to the European Union interest in the harmonisation of copyright law and the growing use of levy systems amongst the other Member States (albeit uncomfortably for some). This went along with the ongoing issue of unauthorised private copying now made even easier by the increasing use and availability of digital technology in the 1990s. In particular, in 2001 the European Parliament and Council Directive 2001/29/EC (the Infosoc Directive) gave Member States the option of allowing copying by a "natural person for private use and for ends that are neither directly nor indirectly commercial". But this was conditional on rightholders receiving 'fair compensation' (Infosoc Directive 2001: article 5(2)(b)). The United Kingdom accordingly decided against exercising the option.

The question resurfaced, however, when the United Kingdom Government began its own reviews of copyright law: first the Gowers Review in 2006, then the Hargreaves Review in 2011. Both recommended the creation of a copyright exception for private copying for so-called 'format' or 'place-shifting' that would allow, for example, the owner of a CD to copy it into a portable playing device also belonging to the person concerned (Gowers Review 2006: paras 4.68–4.76 recommendation 8; Hargreaves Review 2011: paras 5.27–5.31). Each also argued that copyright right-holders could factor into their reproduction charges an amount taking account of the extra uses enabled by the proposed exception. Hargreaves however could see 'no economic argument for adding an extra charge to [personal media devices which rely on private copying] in order to authorise reasonable private acts which are part of the normal use of devices' (Hargreaves Review 2011: para 5.28). Given that the proposed exception was limited to genuinely personal private copying and would not extend to making copies for, say, friends or family members, it would not damage sales of the CD or other content involved.

The United Kingdom Government went ahead and introduced such a private copying exception—section 28B—into the still surviving 1988 Act by way of the Copyright and Rights in Performance (Personal Copies for Private Use) Regulations 2014 (SI 2014/2361). These were made on 26 August 2014 and came into force on 1 October 2014. The absence of the compensation for right-holders required under article 5(2)(b) of the Infosoc Directive was justified by reference to the Directive's recitals, which stated that in evaluating the levels of compensation to be paid, "a valuable criterion would be the possible harm to the rightholders resulting from the act in question" (Infosoc Directive 2001, recital 35). The recital continued: "In cases where rightholders have already received payment in some other form, for instance as part of a licence fee, no specific or separate payment may be due. … In certain situations where the prejudice to the rightholder would be minimal, no obligation for payment may arise" (Infosoc Directive 2001, recital 35).

Unfortunately for the Government, however, the wheels came off its scheme on 19 June 2015, thanks to a successful judicial review challenge in the High Court of England and Wales (*Regina ex parte British Academy of Songwriters, Composers and Authors, Musicians' Union, UK Music 2009 Ltd v Secretary of State for Business, Innovation and Skills (The Incorporated Society of Musicians intervening)* [2015] EWHC 1723 (Admin), [2015] 3 CMLR 28). The case was brought at the instance of a number of organisations representing composers, musicians, the collecting societies and commercial music interests. Mr Justice Green gave a long but very clearly expressed and reasoned judgment which included an extensive review of legal and economic literature on the subject as well as the relevant case law of the Court of Justice of the European Union (CJEU). He held that the Government had correctly understood the Directive in believing that it could introduce a private copying exception without providing for rightholder compensation if the harm to the rightholder was minimal. He also held that the Government had been entitled to decide that its measure of harm in this context was the expectation that costs to rightholders due to lost sales would be minimal or zero. This had taken as a starting point that the endemic copying performed by users, in the United Kingdom, did not, to any material degree, thwart duplicate sales which might otherwise have been made by the purchaser had copyright law been rigorously enforced. This was more realistic than the measure for which the claimants had argued, the basis of which was a hypothetical licence fee which would be charged to the user in a counterfactual market where enforcement was all pervasive.

Mr Justice Green concluded, therefore, that the key issue before him was "Whether on the facts there is evidence of harm beyond the *de minimis* level for which no compensation mechanism has been provided?" ([2015] EWHC 1723 (Admin), para 141). He went on to note (citations omitted):

> The *de minimis* concept is not defined in the Directive. The Court of Justice has ruled that where the Directive does not define a matter Member Stateshave a discretion . . . to choose their own parameters. The Secretary of State thus had a certain margin of appreciation to select a sensible *de minimis* threshold. In defining *de minimis* a Member State must strike a *"fair balance"* between the competing interests of consumers, rightholders and manufacturers of copying devices . . . . All of this means that even within the confines of a narrow legal issue there are still choices to be made by the Secretary of State and that the Court should exercise caution in second guessing those choices. Yet these are still choices to be exercised within relatively tight bounds, in particular because the property rights of natural and legal persons are at stake and because this is an exception from a basic norm and because if harm exceeds a *de minimis* level compensation *must* be paid ([2015] EWHC 1723 (Admin), para 143).

Thus Mr Justice Green felt able to examine the evidence, and in particular the economic evidence, upon which the decision to introduce section 28B had been taken. His analysis was that the conclusion drawn by the Secretary of State—namely, that the harm to rightholders from a 'format' or 'place shifting' exception would indeed be *de minimis* because 'pricing-in' (the practice of factoring in the likelihood of private copying when determining the charge to be made for the initial reproduction) was already widespread—was not supported by the evidence. The introduction of section 28B was therefore unlawful.

The decision left open the possibility that the United Kingdom Government could bring forward another scheme allowing private copying without compensation for rightholders. But the Government soon made clear it had no intention of doing so.[4] Action continues at a European level, however. The decision of the

---

[4]See notice published 20 July 2015, accessible at https://www.gov.uk/government/news/quashing-of-private-copying-exception.

CJEU in Case C-572/13 *Hewlett-Packard Belgium SPRL v Reprobel SCRL, intervener Epson Europe BV*, 12 November 2015, re-emphasised the need for actual harm to right-holders before a compensation scheme needed to be introduced alongside a private copying exception, but then set out a complex range of requirements before such compensation schemes could be upheld under European Union law, invalidating some Belgian laws on the subject in consequence. The result further highlighted the fragmentation of laws and practice amongst the Member States. The European Commission's *Communication towards a modern, more European copyright framework*, published on 9 December 2015, cautiously said only that the current uncertainty '*may* warrant intervention at EU level to provide greater clarity and put an end to major distortions', while also promising that 'The Commission will also promote a reflection on how levies can be more efficiently distributed to right holders' (European Commission 2015: 8, 9). This last must be the most significant difficulty given that the whole system is justified ultimately only if it gives creators appropriate returns for the use made of their work by others.[5]

Thus Peacock's position on private copying levies may yet be vindicated in the United Kingdom by virtue of European Union law, which would surely have appealed to his sense of irony. So too the possibility that the United Kingdom would leave the Union just as a private copying levy system would otherwise be imposed upon it.[6]

4   Implementing Performing Rights: Conclusion

When Alan Peacock and I wrote a joint piece on implementing performing rights that was first delivered as a presentation at a conference in Venice in 1994, technology had again been moving on in relation to music (MacQueen and Peacock 1995). We began by playing part of a CD performance by a classical composer (something of Haydn, if memory serves; but it may not) to highlight the point that composers once earned remuneration without copyright, in particular by performing themselves. But the advance of technology had made that form of survival alone virtually impossible. In many ways this article simply amounted to an up-dating of Peacock's earlier work, together with perhaps greater legal detail coming from my side of the collaboration. The conclusion was certainly the same: 'the lesson learned from the tremendous influence of technology on the implementation of performing rights is that of the continuous adaptation of the various interest groups if they are to survive economically' (MacQueen and Peacock

---

[5]See the European Commission website (http://ec.europa.eu/internal_market/copyright/levy_reform/index_en.htm) for previous sporadic outbursts of interest in the subject since 2006.

[6]This refers to the United Kingdom referendum on continued membership of the European Union, to be held in June, 2016.

1995: 174). The Internet, or as we called it back then, the 'information super highway', was something of which we were both aware, without having much knowledge of the detail. This lay behind our next sentence: 'It is not entirely in the realm of fantasy to envisage that, in the course of the next century, technology will allow copyright owners to communicate much more directly with those who wish to perform their works and even to see the costs of detecting piracy considerably reduced' (MacQueen and Peacock 1995: 174). With this comment we were thinking of sometime in the twenty-first century, most probably sooner rather than 100 years hence. We did not however envisage the world of 'file-sharing' which digital MP3 technology would enable within half a decade, making names such as Napster, Grokster and Pirate Bay world-famous for a time, if not notorious (see generally Witt 2015).

The Internet also led to the creation of a new right of importance in the performance of music, the public communication right, which extends beyond broadcasting and cable to Internet and wireless transmissions generally (Infosoc Directive article 3). It is worth noting that present-day legitimate sites for music down-loading and 'streaming', such as Spotify, operate on the basis of PRS for Music licences in the United Kingdom, so that collecting societies are clearly not by any means redundant in the Internet context.[7] Individual composer-performers have found the Internet and social media sites such as You Tube a possible way to attract an audience and then make a market for their talents by way of on-site advertising and sponsorship as well as achieving recording contracts.[8] So our final prediction— composers' combined action might become confined to seeking ways of minimising the legal costs of enforcement of their rights—may yet hold good. But even here the collecting societies will probably continue to play a significant role in generating income for the rightholder (see Koch 2015).

In the work Peacock and I did together, I could not persuade him to engage very much with wider questions about the substance of copyright law. We never discussed whether the net cast by the concept of a public performance as any performance outside the strictly domestic sphere was too wide, for example, as when, in a Scottish court case decided in 2007, it hauled in a garage mechanic playing music on his radio where customers could hear it while he worked (*PRS v Kwik-Fit Group Ltd* [2007] CSOH 167, [2008] ECDR 2). We touched only briefly on the rise of performers' rights, which have now come very close to those of copyright authors (MacQueen and Peacock 1995: 161; see further Towse 1999; Williamson 2015). Back in the mid-1990s, the length of the copyright term was a major issue thanks to the European Union's Council Directive on the subject extending the basic period from author's lifetime plus 50 years (the international minimum still under the Berne Convention and the TRIPS Agreement) to one of lifetime plus 70 years. Was this justifiable on any economic principle or evidence?

---

[7]See for example, http://www.prsformusic.com/users/broadcastandonline/onlinemobile/Pages/PerformingRightOnlinelicence.aspx.

[8]See for example, http://www.vh1.com/news/52874/10-stars-discovered-on-youtube/.

Peacock pointed out to me that 'efficiency' (would the change increase quantity or quality of output?) was not the only criterion that might be applied to the question. There was an 'equity' issue too, whereby the change might be justified because of increased life expectancy: if the 50-year period had been created to benefit two generations of the composer's descendants, then change was needed to continue reaching the same result (MacQueen and Peacock 1995: 159).

Re-reading Peacock's copyright writings for the purposes of this article, I see that he not infrequently (if only ever very briefly) compared the limited length of copyright protection unfavourably with the potential permanency of physical property; so perhaps his view was really that the limits were mis-placed (Peacock 1979: 140, 143–4; Peacock and Weir 1975: 18). If so, that would have placed him at odds with some of the leading figures of the Scottish Enlightenment; although what of Hume, one must ask, given our earlier discussion of his thinking on the matter (see above, Sect. 1)? My own view was, and remains, that the two-generation rule may be appropriate if the author's descendants are in fact its beneficiaries; but with copyright being also transferable during life, that is not a given in any case. Nor is it at all clear what 'equity' arguments can be made for the commercial interests whose investments in most works are based on much shorter-term 'efficiency' calculations of potential risks and gains. In any event it is very unusual for physical property, or the owner thereof, to have, as a matter of fact, any assurance of permanent, inalterable existence. The conversation with Peacock on this is one that I would very much like to renew if I could.

As the late Neil MacCormick pointed out in his Hume Lecture in 2006, David Hume certainly took the view that "the idea that you can make your laws without long and careful deliberation is … a dangerous one" (MacCormick 2006: 17). There was instead—and there still is—a need for thorough investigation and analysis of the evidence about what is really happening in society, set against a considered view of basic policy requirements and, a Law Commissioner may be allowed to suggest, legal principles. For copyright in music, that certainly means detailed consideration of the music industry and its marketplaces from the creation of works onward, which must continue as the relevant technologies emerge and are exploited in the musical setting. The question of the private copying levy provides a current and important example, but not the only one. There is, in other words, an ongoing project for which the work of Alan Peacock provides a model of high standards and rigorous inquiry; and his successors, in both economics and law, should follow that lead in the future.

Peacock relished controversy with those with whom he disagreed, the sense of combat in meetings or open floor debates possibly heightened by his being sometimes unable to make out what his opponents were saying because of the deafness in one ear resulting from the perforation of an eardrum at birth. The walking stick, on which latterly he leaned, and the floor microphone which he preferred to flourish for emphasis rather than to make himself heard, could give him a somewhat belligerent air on these occasions. If therefore some (especially Presidents of the British Academy and the Royal Society of Edinburgh) thought of him as a turbulent priest, for me and many others to whom I was introduced by Peacock over the years, he was quite simply one of the finest minds and most generous personalities that we had ever encountered. Any debate was always, in what is said to be Hume's phrase about the pursuit of truth, an argument amongst friends. That is the spirit I want to invoke here. Peacock's light never flickered or faded, and now in memory it remains still and always bright.

References

Anderson M (1987) Hans Gál: a conversation with Martin J Anderson. J Br Music Soc 9:33–44
Baumol W, Bowen WG (1966) Performing arts: the economic dilemma. Twentieth Century Fund, New York
Black G (2014) Exclusive privilege: Adam Smith, John Millar and the creation of a new real right. In: Anderson RG, Chalmers J, MacLeod J (eds) Glasgow tercentenary essays: 300 years of the School of Law. Avizandum, Edinburgh, pp 20–52
Bowring J (1838–1843) Jeremy Bentham, The works of Jeremy Bentham. Published under the superintendence of his executor, John Bowring. 11 vols. William Tait, Edinburgh
Brown IG (ed) (2014) David Hume my own life 1776. Royal Society of Edinburgh, Edinburgh
Department of Trade and Industry (1981) Reform of the law relating to copyright, designs and performers' protection. Cmnd 8302. HMSO, London
European Commission (2015) Communication towards a modern, more European copyright framework. COM (2015) 626 final, Brussels, 9 Dec 2015
Freegard M, Black J (eds) (1997) The decisions of the UK Performing Right and Copyright Tribunal. Butterworths, London
Gál H (2014) Music behind barbed wire: a diary of summer 1940. Toccata, London
Gowers Review (2006) Gowers review of intellectual property. HMSO, London
Graham R (2004) The great infidel: a life of David Hume. Tuckwell, East Linton
Greig JYT (1969) The letters of David Hume. 2 vols, reprint of 1932 edn. Clarendon, Oxford
Hadfield GK (1992) The economics of copyright: an historical perspective. Copyright Law Symp 38:1–46
Hargreaves I (2011) Digital opportunity: a review of intellectual property and growth. https://www.gov.uk/government/publications/digital-opportunity-review-of-intellectual-property-and-growth. Accessed 17 Dec 2015
Harris JA (2015) Hume: an intellectual biography. Cambridge University Press, Cambridge
Home H (Lord Kames) (1778) Principles of equity, 3rd edn. Bell & Creech, Edinburgh
InfoSoc Directive (2001) European Parliament and Council Directive on the harmonisation of certain aspects of copyright and related rights in the information society
Koch J (2015) How to make money with your music on YouTube. ASCAP http://www.ascap.com/playback/2015/06/action/make-money-youtube.aspx, 22 June 2015. Accessed 17 Dec 2015
Kretschmer M, Kawohl F (2004) The history and philosophy of copyright. In: Frith S, Marshall L (eds) Music and copyright. Edinburgh University Press, Edinburgh, pp 21–53
Macaulay TB (1853) Speeches parliamentary and miscellaneous. Clarke, Beeton, London
MacCormick N (2006) The European Union and the idea of a perfect Commonwealth. Hume Occasional Paper n 68. The David Hume Institute, Edinburgh
MacQueen HL (1989, 1995) Copyright, competition and industrial design, 1st edn. Aberdeen University Press for The David Hume Institute, Edinburgh (1989); 2nd edn. Edinburgh University Press for The David Hume Institute, Edinburgh (1995)
MacQueen HL (2010) Intellectual property and the common law in Scotland c.1700-c.1850. In: Bently L, D'Agostino G, Ng C (eds) The common law of intellectual property: essays in honour of David Vaver. Hart, Oxford, pp 21–43

MacQueen HL (2014) The war of the booksellers: natural law, equity, and literary property in eighteenth-century Scotland. J Leg Hist 35:231–257

MacQueen HL, Peacock AT (1995) Implementing performing rights. J Cult Econ 19:157–175

Meek RL, Raphael DD, Stein PG (eds) (1978) Adam Smith, lectures on jurisprudence. Oxford University Press, Oxford

Montgomery R, Threlfall R (2007) Music and copyright: the case of Delius and his publishers. Ashgate, Aldershot

Mossner EC (1980) The life of David Hume, 2nd edn. Clarendon, Oxford

Mossner EC, Ransom H (1950) Hume and the 'conspiracy of the booksellers': the publication and early fortunes of the *History of England*. Univ Tex Stud Engl 29:162–182

Norton DF, Norton MJ (eds) (2011) David Hume, Treatise of human nature. Oxford University Press, Oxford

Parliamentary history (1813) Parliamentary history of England from the earliest period to the year 1803, vol XVII, AD 1771–1774. London

Peacock AT (1979) Public policy and copyright in music: an economic analysis. In: Peacock AT (ed) The economic analysis of government and related themes. Martin Robertson, London, pp 137–152, reproduced from Kulp B, Stützel W (eds) (1973) Beiträge zu einer Theorie der Sozialpolitik: Festschrift für Elisabeth Liefmann-Keil zum 65. Geburtstag. Duncker & Humblot, Berlin

Peacock AT (1983) A vision of the Institute. Published in Kuenssberg N, Lomas G (eds) The David Hume Institute: the first decade. The David Hume Institute, Edinburgh (1996). Reprinted in Kuenssberg N (ed) Argument amongst friends: twenty five years of sceptical enquiry. The David Hume Institute, Edinburgh (2010)

Peacock AT (1993) Paying the piper: culture, music and money. Edinburgh University Press, Edinburgh

Peacock AT, Weir R (1975) The composer in the marketplace. Faber, London

Phillipson N (1989) Hume. Weidenfeld & Nicolson, London

Plant A (1934) The economic aspect of copyright in books. Economica 1:167–195

Plant A (1953) The new commerce in ideas and intellectual property. The Stamp Memorial Lecture 1953. Athlone, London

Robson JM (ed) (1965) John Stuart Mill, Principles of political economy: with some of their applications to social philosophy, 2 vols. University of Toronto Press, Toronto

Scherer FM (2004) Quarter notes and bank notes: the economics of music composition in the eighteenth and nineteenth centuries. Princeton University Press, Princeton

Todd WB (ed) (1976) Adam Smith, an inquiry into the nature and causes of the wealth of nations, 2 vols. Oxford University Press, Oxford

Towse R (1999) Copyright and economic incentives: an application to performers' rights in the music industry. KYKLOS 52:369–390

Towse R (2004) Copyright and economics. In: Frith S, Marshall L (eds) Music and copyright. Edinburgh University Press, Edinburgh, pp 54–69

Towse R (2005) Alan Peacock and cultural economics. Econ J 115:262–276

Towsey MRM (2010) Reading the Scottish enlightenment: books and their readers in provincial Scotland, 1750-1820. Brill, Leiden

Whitford Report (1977) Copyright and designs law: report of the committee to consider the law on copyright and designs. Cmnd 6732. HMSO, London

Williamson J (2015) For the benefit of all musicians? The Musicians' Union and performers' rights in the UK. In: Rahmatian A (ed) Concepts of music and copyright: how music perceives itself and how copyright perceives music. Edward Elgar, Cheltenham, pp 167–194

Witt S (2015) How music got free. Bodley Head, London

Copyright and Music Publishing in the UK

Ruth Towse

Abstract The chapter investigates the role of copyright in the economic development of music publishing in the UK from a historical perspective. Peacock and Weir's 1975 book, *The Composer in the Market Place* has been a strong influence on the research on the economic survival of music publishing over its long existence. There is little economic literature specifically on music publishing as an industry, though there is a useful related literature on composers and their publishers. The chapter looks at the development of copyright law in musical works (which differs significantly from that in literary works) and its effect on the market for published music. It shows how music publishers adapted to the new streams of royalty revenue arising from changes in consumption as successive technologies for access to music were adopted; these changes in turn occasioned the revisions of copyright law. The historical approach reminds us that disruptive technologies in the music industry are nothing new. What this research shows is that in the early twentieth century, music publishers survived the effect on the market for published music of sound recording and radio by switching from the long-established sales model to that of rights management. Updated copyright law supported the change of business model but it was not the motivating force. This conclusion has resonance for the similar switch being adopted today by other creative industries in adapting to digitisation.

1 Introduction

This chapter is an historical examination of the impact of copyright law on the economic development of music publishing in the UK. Music publishing per se has been little researched by economists, though there are notable publications on the economics of musical composition (Peacock and Weir 1975; Baumol and Baumol

R. Towse (✉)
Bournemouth University, Bournemouth, Dorset, UK

CREATe, University of Glasgow, Glasgow, UK
e-mail: ruth.towse@gmail.com

© Springer International Publishing Switzerland 2016   133
I. Rizzo, R. Towse (eds.), *The Artful Economist*,
DOI 10.1007/978-3-319-40637-4_8

1994; Scherer 2004) and on the social history of the music profession (Ehrlich 1985, 1989). Another source of information is a literature on the relationship between individual composers and their publishers.[1] In addition there are publishers' own accounts, notably that by Boosey (1931) (rather confusingly the head of Chappell & Co.) and histories of publishing houses (often commissioned and hagiographic), for example, Grove (1887) on the House of Novello.

The chapter draws on all these sources and in particular on Peacock and Weir, whose pioneering work on composers and performing rights is exemplary. Here the focus is on music publishing as an industry, as an updated 'companion piece' to Peacock and Weir's seminal book. It looks at the role of business models and copyright in music publishing and the effects on them of the growth of copying technologies.

Peacock and Weir charted the effect on the market for musical composition of the technological 'revolutions' of sound recording and radio, which fundamentally changed music publishing and created the modern music industry. In the Postscript, they discuss contemporary concerns (in the 1970s) about the effect of 'home copying' by means of tape recorders and cassette players that were being introduced at the time. This chapter alters the focus of these developments to the role copyright played in the market for published music.

The research project to which this chapter relates, entitled 'Economic Survival in a Long Established Creative Industry: Strategies, Business Models and Copyright in Music Publishing' attempted to analyse the relative roles of copyright law (and its related institutions, such as collecting societies) and business models in music publishing, in the context of the impact of digitization in the creative industries. The project set out to offer an historical overview of how music publishing had weathered similar technological storms in the past not, of course, to predict the weathering of this one, but instead to examine the elements of the survival strategy. History does not repeat itself in technological developments but their impact on the market may be similar and responses are telling. The response to disruptive technologies relates to the Schumpeterian view that entrepreneurs' adaptation to and adoption of them is a significant aspect of innovation. In the case of today's creative industries, the kneejerk response is to lobby for stronger copyright protection (not a strategy that Schumpeter considered—see Blaug 2005).

Economic, social and technological developments over the 400 year life of the music publishing industry have led to ever-increasing access to music in a progression from performance at home and in church to public concerts, then via sound recording, radio and television and now internet. In the earliest days of printed music from the end of the fifteenth century, the market for printed sacred music was for use by the Church and by wealthy families. By the seventeenth century, music publishing had extended into the sale of printed secular music for home entertainment and sheet music was commissioned and performed on their premises by the

---

[1]Montgomery and Threlfall (2007) on Drysdale (2013) on Elgar are especially illuminating.

makers of musical instruments to 'advertise' their wares. Home performance considerably increased throughout the nineteenth century as the piano became the instrument of choice for homes great and small (Ehrlich 1985). By the mid-nineteenth century public concerts of classical music and popular music halls had become established, providing a vehicle for the performance of published sheet music for promoting sales to choral societies, brass bands, music teachers and to the public. Concerts were promoted (and halls hired) by leading music publishers, who paid singers and band leaders to 'plug' new titles to promote sales of printed music for use at home.

With the development of sound recording and radio, the demand for published music shifted in the early twentieth century as home consumption of music changed in favour of listening to records and to the radio. Music publishers then discovered that revenues from performing and mechanical rights were the future of their business and set up organizations to collect them. This switch in the business model also led to changes in the contracts they made with composers and song writers.

These developments are followed up in greater detail in this chapter.[2] The chapter is organized as follows: Sect. 2 looks at the various elements of copyright in musical works; Sect. 3 analyses the value of these rights with data on sources of revenues and the value of different rights; Sect. 4 discusses contracts between music publishers and composers and song writers; Sect. 5 is on the economic organisation of music publishing; and Sect. 6 concludes.

2   Development of Copyright in Published Music

Copyright law forms the basis of business models in music publishing today and its historical development is therefore crucial to understanding the economics of the industry. Historically, copyright in music lurched along somewhat unevenly, sometimes governed by universal changes to copyright law and at other times responding to specific developments in the market for music (Deazley et al. 2010). No changes were made for many years then there were bursts of new legislation. Initially copyright simply protected the reproduction and distribution of printed musical works but gradually the range of rights with which we are now familiar were added to copyright law as technologies for the reproduction of music and new markets came along.

---

[2]The chapter is an expanded and more detailed version of Towse (2016).

2.1   Copyright Law and Music

The 1710 Statute of Anne established copyright as an exclusive right granted to the author of a work of literature but copyright in musical compositions was not recognised until later. Copyright's protection for the reproduction and distribution of printed musical works was only established by a court ruling (Bach v. Longman) in 1777. Nevertheless, enforcement was difficult and piracy of sheet music persisted right up to the first decade of the twentieth century as various Acts of Parliament relating to copyright failed to make possible or feasible the apprehension and conviction of pirates.

Unauthorised copying had long affected both popular and 'serious' music: tunes from operas by popular composers such as John Gay and Rossini were played on the street, sometimes even before the first performance. Popular ballads and songs formed the biggest share of the market in published sheet music and it was those works that were pirated on a massive scale. As with contemporary online piracy, the most successful works were the ones most widely copied. One has to ask, as with online piracy today, to what extent the unlawful trade deprived the lawful trade of revenues. It seems that most publishers (Novello & Co. being an important exception: see Grove 1887) purposefully set their prices above that which many people could afford and inevitably the higher price excluded some 'legal' demand. The 6d ballad[3] was sold by the pirates at 1d, a price difference that was often commented on in Parliament when reform to copyright law was discussed. It is hard to find quantitative data on the value of losses due to piracy, though there is information on the numbers involved in individual seizures, often of many thousand copies (Ehrlich 1985). There were certainly many closures of music publishing firms (see Humphries and Smith 1970), which might suggest piracy as a cause, but on the other hand, there were very successful large firms and music publishing was (and remains) a profitable business, despite piracy.

In 1881 the Music Publishers Association (MPA) was founded to enable its members to collaborate in prosecuting the pirates and to lobby for more effective enforcement of the law by the police and customs officers. The problem, which was only solved with the 1906 Musical Copyright Act, was enforcement; prior to that it had almost impossible to produce the necessary evidence to prosecute the pirates. It was widely known who the chief pirates were, not least because unauthorized copies were sold openly in public. Once illegal copies had been seized, the pirates simply renewed their stocks by setting up in a new location. After the Act, the MPA brought a number of cases resulting in prison sentences for the perpetrators and that succeeded in putting a stop to this particular contravention of copyright law (Boosey 1931; Peacock and Weir 1975; Ehrlich 1989).

---

[3]d = one penny in old money. See footnote 5.

2.2   The Performing Right

Initially, copyright protected reproduction and distribution of printed works. For music, however, other rights were called for to protect its public performance. The performing right for dramatic works had been established in 1833 in the UK in response mainly to demands by playwrights and it also benefitted composers of opera and other musical theatre.[4] In 1842, the performing right was extended to non-dramatic works, thus to orchestral, vocal and choral music (McFarlane 1980). But music publishers chose not to exercise it. Until the 1900s, their focus was almost entirely on sales of sheet music and hire of orchestral parts for theatrical and concert performance and they simply ignored the performing right. The reason, discussed below, was the publishers' widespread use of 'plugging' as a way of advertising published music for sale to the public, to which the performing right was considered to be a disincentive. Royalties from performing rights for the use of published music were, however, collected in the UK by the French collecting society SACEM (Société des auteurs, compositeurs et éditeurs de musique), the first one of its kind, founded in France in 1851. It opened a branch in the UK to enforce the *petit droits*, as they were known (by contrast to the grand rights for use of musical works in the theatre), for the public performance of music by French composers in the UK. The enforcement of performing rights was for a long time resisted by UK publishers because they viewed the performing right as conflicting with sales, their main source of revenue (Boosey 1931; Peacock and Weir 1975; Ehrlich 1989; Drysdale 2013).

A further reason held back the exercise of performing rights: they had been brought into disrepute by the activities of Henry (Harry) Walls, who in 1875 had set up a private business, the Copyright and Performing Right Protection Office, which bought up the copyrights of older works which performers mistakenly thought to be in the public domain but were not. Walls exploited the provision of the 1833 Act, which had set the fine for unauthorized public performance of a protected work at 40/-,[5] by bringing cases against unsuspecting infringers and charging them the statutory 40/- penalty, a figure that was more or less equal to the fee the performer (usually a singer) had received. To combat this, the 1882 Copyright (Musical Compositions) Act, so-called 'Walls Act', sought to stop this practice by requiring the copyright owner of a published work who wished to retain the performing right to print a notice stating that it was reserved on the title page of every published copy; if the copyright and the performing right were owned separately, the owner of the performing right had to give the owner of the copyright notice to comply. But as this Act failed to alter the amount of the penalty, Walls was not stopped and it took the 1888 Copyright (Musical Compositions) Act to rectify the situation, now

---

[4]Opera and music for the theatre in general were the most profitable sources of income for composers (see Rosselli 1984; Scherer 2004).

[5]In old money (pre 1971), there were 20 shillings (marked by /- or s) in a pound and 12 pence (marked with a 'd') in a shilling, i.e. 12d = 1s; 20s = £1. Thus 40/- = £2 (worth £200 in 2014).

making the judge responsible for assessing 'reasonable' damages in cases of unauthorized use.

2.2.1 The Performing Right Society

The standard practice in music publishing for centuries had been for the publisher to buy-out all the composers' rights for a flat fee. That led to ambiguity over the composers' entitlement to exercise the performing right. The 1911 Copyright Act established that the 'copyright' of a work as transferred to the publisher did not include performing rights. This opened the way to the formation of the Performing Right Society (PRS) in 1914. It was supported by several (but by no means all) music publishers, to administer performing rights on behalf of both writer and publisher members. After a period of considerable opposition by some leading publishers, notably Boosey & Co and Novello & Co, the performing rights of most of the repertoire were assigned to it by the 1930s (Ehrlich 1989).[6] Thus collective rights management became established in the UK and has been central to the business models of music publishers in the UK and elsewhere ever since.

Peacock and Weir (1975) argue that these teething troubles made establishing royalty rates difficult for PRS for some considerable time. Without the cooperation of all publishers assigning their catalogue to PRS, there was ambiguity as to the scope of its 'blanket' licence and that made PRS hesitant to charge too high a licence fee. Moreover, the performing right was very unpopular with performers and that also affected some composers' attitude to it, in particular those at the more popular end of the market. It was regarded by music publishers as a disincentive to the wide-spread practice of 'plugging', which constituted an essential part of their business model for the sale of sheet music throughout the nineteenth and into the twentieth centuries in the UK and in the USA (where it is known as payola and is illegal[7]).

Plugging was the established means of advertising new titles by paying a 'royalty' to singers and band leaders to promote a particular song or work in music halls, restaurants, music shops and other places where music was played, with the purpose of promoting the sales of the sheet music to the public.[8] To preserve this business model, some publishers advertised 'free music', that is, music for which they waived the collection of the performing right (Peacock and Weir 1975). Although it was not and is not unlawful in the UK, plugging

---

[6]Drysdale (2013) argues that the failure of publishers to enforce the performing right deprived composers of income, indicating that they failed to have composers' interests at heart.

[7]The topic of an article by Ronald Coase (1979).

[8]The performer's 'royalty' (as it was called) could be similar to that paid to the composer; for example, in 1922 a singer named Dearth was paid a royalty of 2d (a time, presumably) for 3 years by Boosey & Co to sing 'Why Shouldn't I?' by K. Russell, for which Russell received a royalty on sales of 3d then 4d after sales of 10,000 (Boosey &Hawkes' archive held at the Royal College of Music).

nevertheless was regarded with more than a little discomfort in the MPA (Boosey 1931). The final *coup de grace* to plugging, however, was effected by the BBC (British Broadcasting Corporation), which from the beginning licensed music from PRS, becoming its chief client for many years. The BBC (until the 1950s, the sole broadcaster in the UK) banned plugging on the radio and at one time even refused to allow titles of work being played to be announced, a rather odd situation that was resolved only when music publishers agreed to stop paying pluggers (Ehrlich 1989: 51–4).

2.2.2 Performing Right Society Income

PRS income grew slowly at first as rates were set at a relatively low level to encourage users to sign up; later that policy caused problems as PRS sought to raise royalty rates to more equitable levels. From 1930 to 1950 PRS income grew fourfold in real terms (Towse 2016). As royalty rates were increased, however, its monopoly power was challenged. The 1956 Copyright Act ushered in the Performing Right Tribunal to regulate charges and resolve disputes between the PRS as monopoly supplier of licensing services and users of those services, chief of which was the monopsony user of music, the BBC[9] (Peacock and Weir 1975).

Dominant though it now is, the PRS took some 20 years to fully establish itself with the music profession. By 1930, however, the PRS had become the main vehicle for negotiating the rates for and licensing the performing right. The BBC's use of PRS for acquiring a licence to broadcast sound recordings and for its own transmission of live music performances was the major force in fully establishing its central role (Peacock and Weir 1975). In 1930, the BBC was responsible for over 50 % of PRS revenues; revenue from broadcasting was not much less at 44 % in 1960, by which time the BBC no longer had a monopoly of broadcasting in the UK. In 2000, broadcasting licence fees were 35 % of total PRS income and 25 % in 2014 (Towse 2016).

The performing right had been on the statute books for 100 years before it became central to the business model of music publishing. By 2014, the PRS for Music[10] had 115,000 publisher and writer members and reported revenues of £665.7m of which they distributed £596m (PRS for Music 2014). The shift in consumer tastes and the development of sound recordings and the radio competed with live performance in the home. It had been the mainstay of the music business for several hundred years but by the 1900s, sales of sheet music were falling,

---

[9]It was in a dispute between PRS and the BBC that Peacock's consultancy Economists' Advisory Group advised the PRS, leading to his work on the Composer in the Marketplace (see Peacock 1993; also Rizzo and Towse 2015).

[10]In 1996 PRS for Music was formed by merging PRS and MCPS: they have now formally separated.

requiring a new response. The economic history of music publishing changed significantly once these trends were accepted.

2.3   The Mechanical Right

The new technologies of reproducing music provided a further source of revenue for both music publishers and composers and songwriters. The 1911 Copyright Act introduced a new right to mechanical reproduction by the 'contrivances' then available, namely piano rolls and phonograms. The MPA set up a for-profit agency to administer these rights, which in 1924 became the Mechanical Copyright Protection Society (MCPS). Its function was to license and collect fees from record companies and later from broadcasters and others mechanically reproducing music (nowadays, for example, for ring tones) for distribution to publishers and composers. Sound recordings became very popular quite quickly and technological improvements to phonograms (record players) and records made them easier to use (Peacock and Weir 1975). In the early years of the twentieth century, listening to records and to the radio soon displaced do-it-yourself home entertainment and accordingly, sales of sheet music fell.

There were, however, similar hiccups in the initial stage of the establishment of mechanical rights as there had been with the performing right. The 1911 Act recognized the exclusive right of the composer only so far as the first permission for use of the mechanical right was given: thereafter, a compulsory licence enabled subsequent recordings (what we now call cover versions) to be made on payment of statutory royalty of 5 % of the price of the 'contrivance' with a minimum of ½d (Peacock and Weir 1975: 148). This more or less equated to the royalty paid per sale of sheet music until competition drove down the price of records in the 1920s; moreover, the development of two-sided records meant the statutory royalty had to be shared between the composers of all the works.[11] The 1911 Act was updated with the 1956 Copyright Act, which fixed the royalty at 6¼%. The compulsory licence was later deleted in the 1988 Copyright, Designs and Patents Act.

Another element of the mechanical right is the synchronization right (the 'dubbing' or 'synch' right) which was an extension for the use of music with a moving image, dating from the advent of the 'talkies' with the release in 1927 of the 'The Jazz Singer'. Music for film and other audio-visual products is now one of the main sources of income and growth in music publishing.

Mechanical rights provided an additional source of income to music publishers, nowadays distributed on a 50:50 split with the composer (or composer and

---

[11]Later 45s, LPs and CDs had multiple titles and and/or works by different authors. Streaming has reverted to a single track.

lyricist[12]), to whom they are paid directly. The decision (by both PRS and MCPS) to pay their share of the licence fee revenue directly to the composer and songwriter gave them a source of income independent of the publisher (Drysdale 2013). Music publishers along with composers and performers also benefitted from the formation in 1934 of PPL (Phonographic Performance Ltd), the collecting society for record companies, which licenses the public performance of sound recordings, for example, for broadcasts and discos. In principle, PPL licence fee revenues did not have to be distributed to music publishers but it was decided that an ex gratia payments of 10 % of net revenues from sound recordings would be made to them (Peacock and Weir 1975: 48–52). Publishers have traditionally exercised the mechanical right via MCPS and the 'majors' still do so but competition is appearing from smaller publishers and agencies that offer tailor-made data monitoring and cross-border licensing, developments which threaten collective rights management (Towse 2013).

3   The Value of Rights in Copyright

Following the 1911 Act, the composer had three sets of rights—the so-called 'copyright' for reproduction and distribution of printed music, mechanical rights and the performing right—and each had a different value in the marketplace. The values basically depended upon the use to which the work was put: for example, for a work in a sound recording there was a royalty for both the right to record a work (the mechanical right) and for its public performance (the performing right). The relative values of these rights have varied by genre over the years as markets changed. Evidence for 1971 is provided by the survey by Peacock and Weir into composers' incomes for categories of 'popular', 'serious' and 'light' composers. The contribution of the performing right to their incomes was 16, 24 and 26 % respectively, while sheet music earnings were 1.8, 3.6 and 1.1 % (Peacock and Weir 1975: 23).[13]

Those figures can be compared to the picture in 2012 (the latest figures available) for music publishing. The difference between the value of rights for popular and classical music is in evidence in Table 1.

In 2012, 37 % of revenues to UK music publishing came from foreign affiliates, demonstrating the significance international trade in music publishing (UK Music 2012). Smaller music publishers operate a system of contracts with sub-publishers for foreign sales and licensing, which remit revenues to UK. The major music publishers today are international conglomerates (see Sect. 5), which typically have offices in foreign capital cities. PRS revenues show a similar picture: in 2013, international revenues accounted for 30 % of the total and that was growing

---

[12]With songs mostly written by groups and teams of song-writers, as is present day practice, they have to share the writer's 50 %.

[13]See also the chapter by David Throsby in this book.

Table 1 Percentage of revenues in music publishing from various rights and sources by genre 2012

Popular music	
Mechanical royalties	40
Live performance and broadcasting	36
Synchronization fees	14
Other (ring tones, online, sheet music)	10
Classical music	
Sales of printed music	50
Hire fees	15
Mechanical royalties	12
Live performance and broadcasting	8
Synchronization fees	5

Source: MPA (unpublished)

significantly. In that year, revenues from collecting societies (PRS, MCPS, PPL) contributed 27 % and direct licensing (synchronisation rights, grand rights and permissions) contributed 26 %.

In Table 2 the relative importance of the different sources of PRS revenues over the period 1998–2013 are shown. 1998 predates the introduction of downloading technologies around 2000 and the table demonstrates the dramatic fall in the percentage of PRS/MCPS revenues from sound recording (Samuel 2014). By 2014, online revenues had increased to 18 % and recorded media had fallen by 22 % (PRS 2015). These figures demonstrate the shifting role of the values of the various right and the markets from which they come.

4 Contracts and Payments in Music Publishing

The switch of the business model from sales to rights management in music publishing was accompanied by an equivalent switch in the contract between composer and publisher from a single fee buyout of the copyright, which had been the norm from its very beginning, to the now prevalent royalty contract.[14] What is now considered to be a typical royalty contract between a music publisher and a composer or song writer, that is, one that pays a percentage of revenues from the sale or licence of a work, is a feature of the twentieth century. The contract the music publisher makes with the creator of a work is an essential part of the business model of all intermediaries and the complexity and variety of contracts in music publishing demonstrate their importance in that industry. The core competitive advantage in music publishing, as in the record industry, lies in signing up successful writers and performers early on in their careers and then hanging on to them by various contractual arrangements (Harrison 2011).

---

[14]The exception was the contracts of the 'grand' rights for staged performances of opera and musicals, which could include fees per performance as well as an upfront payment (see Rosselli 1984; Scherer 2004).

Table 2 PRS for music revenues by source: 1998–2013 (percentages)		1998	2013
	Sound recording etc.	37 %	12 % (online 9 %)
	Broadcast	27 %	24 %
	International	17 %	30 %
	Public performance	19 %	21 %

Source: extracted from Samuel (2014: 37)

The contract between and the music publisher is what determines the split of revenues that reaches each party and that is a means whereby a publisher can compete in the market for 'talent'. Drysdale (2013: 70) in his study of the composer Edward Elgar's earnings and contracts with his publisher Novello & Co. aptly writes: 'For Novello, the ideal situation was to pay a very small copyright sum to a struggling composer for a work which then became a huge success. For a composer the ideal situation was to be well established and able to command a very high royalty percentage on works which sold consistently well over a period of years'. This quote demonstrates the fundamental asymmetry between composer and publisher[15] and Drysdale provides several examples of the very different contracts Novello & Co had with their well-known composers in the late nineteenth century, ranging from complete buy-outs to profit-sharing deals, with various types of royalty agreements in between.

As publishers are keen to point out, though, hits are few and far between and they have to bear the cost of flops as well as successes—William Boosey, the head of Thomas Chappell & Co., suggested a figure of 40 for every 1 profitable title in the 1920s (Boosey 1931). Since fees, advances and royalty payments are an 'input' cost to the publisher, the incentive is to offer as low a rate as possible. In economic terms, the publisher's incentive is to pay the marginal amount that will keep the composer or songwriter with a track record 'in production' with the publisher. Signing talent is now the responsibility of the A&R (Artist and Repertoire) department of the publishing house and, though that term had not been coined in his day, William Boosey (1931) goes into considerable detail as to how he commissioned popular ballads by putting together lyricist and composer and matching them with singers in the days of popular concerts and music halls.

There were separate contracts for words and music of a song (and still are unless the song is written by the same author). At the end of the nineteenth century newly written, often commissioned, lyrics were being bought out 'all rights' for a flat fee (such as 2 guineas = £2.2/-; a guinea was 21 shillings).[16] There were several famous and prolific suppliers of lyrics for whom it was a pastime (notably Fred Weatherly,

---

[15]See Towse (1999) for a fuller analysis.

[16]Research on this and related topics was conducted in the Boosey &Hawkes archive kept at the Royal College of Music Library. I am grateful for the assistance of Peter Horton at the RCM library.

a barrister, who wrote the words for 3000 songs, including 'Danny Boy'[17]). There seem to have been few composers of songs in the UK who were fully employed in that activity, though there were some who produced a large number of hits, such as Liza Lehmann (a former singer), Amy Woodforde-Finden (a 'married woman') and Ivor Novello (actor and singer). Some classical composers produced highly popular works (such as Elgar's 'Land of Hope and Glory') and others produced popular works under a pseudonym (Michael Maybrick, who wrote the music of 'The Holy City', published as Stephen Adams).

It is possible that this state of affairs influenced contracts and payments. To some extent, 'amateur' composers and song-writers spoiled the market for those who intended to make it their sole profession (the case with Elgar, argues Drysdale 2013). As royalties were unlikely to offer sufficient income (then as now), composers usually had other professional activities, such as teaching or a job as a church organist, that offered regular and less risky incomes (Ehrlich 1985).

From the late nineteenth century a few 'classical' composers were paid a percentage of receipts from sales, however. Sir Arthur Sullivan (best known today for his operettas with Gilbert) composed 'The Lost Chord', one of the most famous pieces of its day, which sold 500,000 copies between 1875 and 1902. He was paid a royalty per copy by Boosey & Co., though no performing right royalty (Boosey and Hawkes' archive). In the few cases in which a royalty was paid, it was specified as 1d, 2d or 3d per copy sold, depending on the status of the composer. For popular songs, however, the standard deal was a buy-out of all rights with a single payment. In 1924, Roger Quilter, known today as a classical composer, was paid 2gns for all rights of one of his many songs (though a royalty for others) and Peter Warlock was paid 10 gns for all the rights of 'Two Short Songs' by Boosey & Co. Marjorie Kennedy-Fraser, however, had a 20 % royalty on sales of all her songs (many settings of folk songs).[18] Even here, though, there were hidden snags: it was trade practice to pay 13/12, meaning that one copy was not compensated for every 13 sold, and that was after typically 200 copies has been distributed 'free'.

Royalty rates are one thing but it is price and quantity sold that determines the revenue the parties to a contract receive. Prices for sheet music remained stable over a long period. They varied according to genre and the cost of production: printing a full score of an opera or oratorio was much costlier and the market relatively smaller than that for a single popular song (see Scherer 2004 for details on developments in printing technology). Novello & Co. specialised in producing cheap music of good quality for the Church and choral society market; in 1863 four books of Mendelssohn's 'Four-Part Songs' were sold for 1/- each; by 1866, the price had been reduced to 1/6d for all four books (Grove 1887: 85). By1887, Novello & Co. had a catalogue of over 21,000 works, half in octavo size with

---

[17]The tune of Danny Boy is traditional; nevertheless Boosey &Co. paid Weatherley royalties as both the author and composer (Boosey &Hawkes archive, *Publication Book of Copyright Works*). NB Boosey & Co. amalgamated with Hawkes &Co. in 1930 to form Boosey and Hawkes.

[18]All information from the Boosey & Hawkes archive (see above), researched by the author.

prices from 1d to 42/- (*ibid*: 141). At Boosey & Co. the typical price of a song was maintained at 2/- for a considerable period from the 1880s into the twentieth century. Accordingly, a per unit royalty payment of 3d was equivalent to 12.5 %. Kennedy-Fraser's 20 % royalty on her much loved song, the 'Eriskay Love Lilt' (still in print), was not worth much, however, at the rate of 2d a copy in 1922 (Boosey & Hawkes' archive).

Sporadic references to the number of copies sold relate only to the most popular songs. 'Soldiers of the Queen' (or 'King', depending on the incumbent) was one of the all-time popular hits (and is still performed today by military bands); at the height of the Boer War in 1898 it sold 238,000 copies. Anything over 200,000 was apparently considered by the director of Francis, Day and Hunter Ltd, the third major publisher of the late nineteenth century, to be a great success (Peacock and Weir 1975: 42). Stainer's 'Crucifixion' sold 1.25 million copies with a royalty of 2d to the composer[19] (Ehrlich 1985: 103).

Things began to change during the 1920s and by the 1930s, the royalty paid on newly contracted works was a percentage of sales revenue; a fee might still be paid for an arrangement, though.[20] There were 'mixed' cases, presumably reflecting the stage at which a work was first contracted: Eric Coates, whose published works of songs and 'light' music[21] date from 1908, was at first paid a fixed fee, then a 1d or 2d royalty, then eventually a percentage of sales revenue (Boosey and Hawkes' archive).

Today the percentage royalty contract by now seems to be standard, some with an advance. MPA members reported £133m. spent on 'investment in writers'[22] in 2012, which is largely for advances (MPA 2014). Advances are taken out of the composer or song-writer's royalties as they are earned but are a 'loss' to the publisher if the work is not successful. What is far from standard is the percentage share of the writer and the publisher: very successful writers (such as Paul McCartney) might even get a 100 % of all revenues while others receive a 75–25 % split or less, depending on the type of contract (Harrison 2011). A 50:50 share was normal in US music publishing for many years (Napier-Bell 2014). An exception is production music, which may be sold 'rights free' for a flat fee;

---

[19]'Since its publication in 1887' to quote Ehrlich (1985), p. 103—unfortunately the information is not precise enough to enable a modern calculation of what must have been a very high income. Stainer died in 1901 so the work would have entered the public domain in 1951. He retired as organist at St Paul's Cathedral in 1888, possibly with the prospect of these royalties.

[20]The story on arrangements is complex: in principle, the original author must give permission and the arrangement attracts its own copyright. In practice, if the publisher owned all rights he could commission an arrangement and acquire the copyright to it. It was common practice for publishers to commission piano or other arrangements to be made of an orchestral score, for which the original composer might receive a royalty on sales of the arrangements depending on the terms of her contract with the music publisher (Drysdale 2013).

[21]Known to many UK oldies as composer of 'Calling All Workers', the theme tune of 'Music While You Work' (the first music this author remembers from early childhood!) and of music for the film 'The Dam Busters'.

[22]Most on advances but also publishers run song writing camps, offering technical help to new writers.

alternatively the composer may assign the synchronisation right to the user and retain the performing right. Where a work is commissioned, the contract for the fee is normally between the composer and the commissioner but if a publisher has been involved, he will take a cut depending on the publishing contract (Harrison 2011).

5   Economic Organisation of Music Publishing

Music publishing occupies a midway position in the upstream/downstream configuration of the process of 'producing' music. Music printing began very soon after the adoption of the Gutenberg printing press in the late fifteenth century and indeed, methods remained remarkably similar with copper plates engraved with the musical notes and text being pressed first on to vellum, later on to paper. The input: output process in UK music publishing was more or less the same from the 1500s up the First World War. On the input side, a musical work was produced in manuscript by the composer/songwriter, usually freelance (and often an amateur); a contract was signed for a fixed payment between composer and publisher; a copyist edited the manuscript; the publisher contracted with an engraver to produce the plates for the press and then with a printer to print sheet music from the plates and bind the pages; finally, the publisher distributed the sheet music to a retailer and set about advertising the title. The output side of the business was (and is) promoting performances of the work with performers, theatrical promoters and concert organizers. Part of that business is the hire of orchestral/band parts.[23] The publisher also had arrangements made of a work, for example, in different keys, for different instruments or a piano reduction of an orchestral work or opera, thus exploiting the underlying musical work by differentiating the 'product' and enabling price discrimination. Until the twentieth century, as explained above, the publisher was the sole recipient of revenues from those sources but predominantly from the sale of sheet music.

It can be seen from this that some stages of the process of producing sheet music were bought in, in particular the highly specialized skill of printing music, which historically was protected by guild or trade union restrictions. Some printers in the UK were also publishers, however, and some publishers had their own printing shop (notably Novello & Co) but that seems to have been exceptional. In the eighteenth and nineteenth centuries there were a large number of both music printing and publishing companies (Humphries and Smith 1970). The business model changed over time: in the eighteenth century, published sheet music was often produced as a complement to other products, especially musical instruments; innovations in instruments enabled innovation in the music they could play. Innovations in printing technologies, especially the development of lithography, offered music publishers a

---

[23]Instrumental music for ensembles is usually printed for one specific instrument e.g. first violins, oboe, trumpet etc. The full score consisting of all the instrumental parts is used by the conductor. Vocal music is usually printed for all voices SATB (soprano, alto, tenor, bass). A piano arrangement of orchestral music is made for rehearsals e.g. for opera chorus and for ballet.

choice of different costs and quality of printing as did reductions in taxes on paper and its production costs (Scherer 2004). All these factors affected prices. By the nineteenth and early twentieth centuries, publishing houses in the UK had sorted themselves into higher priced (Boosey & Co., Chappell & Co.) and lower priced firms (Novello & Co, J. Curwen & sons). The chain of production outlined above still operates in classical music publishing for sales and hires (see Table 1), though they now represent only a small proportion of the overall music publishing business.

The twentieth century saw many mergers and acquisitions of publishing companies in this profitable industry and in the present day oligopoly, the 'majors' in music publishing—Imagem, Warner Chappell Music, BMG—are owned by international conglomerates, mega companies which own most of the older UK publishing houses, such as Boosey & Hawkes, Chappell & Co, Novello, and Francis, Day & Hunter; they in turn had previously absorbed older companies or acquired their catalogues. The brand names of the older publishing houses continue to be used in preference to that of the holding company. Some of the 'majors' have interests in sound recording, broadcasting and film (such as Warner/Chappell Music) while others are simply equity companies (for example, Imagem which acquired Boosey & Hawkes). Thus, there is both horizontal and vertical integration in music publishing downstream from the initial creation of the musical work. The long term trend to large-scale conglomerates suggests there are economics of scale and scope. As with most oligopolistic markets, especially those in the creative industries, though, there is a host of smaller independent music publishers that offer composers and song writers a nuanced service. The MPA had 260 members in 2015, representing 4000 catalogues.

A question for cultural economics today is whether digitization in the music business will support the survival of these smaller independent companies or even increase their number. New entrants in recent years specialise in 'bespoke' rights management with their own databases, potentially competing with the collecting societies by having superior IT and a system of licensing directly in all territories. The complexity of multi-territorial licensing by collecting societies and increased digital use makes these services increasingly attractive. Entry costs, in the form of new IT systems, however, are high and are also potentially disruptive of the established system collective rights management (Towse 2013).

The process of mergers and acquisitions in music publishing has been made simple by the combination of contract and copyright law. Historically, when all the rights in a musical work were bought from the composer by the publisher, he was free to exploit it (or not). A work could be sold on by the publisher with no obligations attached, and since he also owned the engraved plates of a title (a song or instrumental piece), both could be sold together to another publisher. 'Copyright auctions' were regularly held in London from the end of the eighteenth century and into the twentieth (Coover 1983; Towse 2016). These auctions greatly assisted entry of new firms into the industry as they cut through the need to contract with composers and song writers for new works and to have plates engraved, which could take some time. When royalty contracts became the norm, publishers typically required the assignment of all rights in a work in a contract. The contract was often for the life of copyright, that is, 50 (now 70) years after the death of the author. Those rights may then be reassigned to another owner who can exploit them (or not), often without further recourse to the composer. Thus copyrights are tradable assets, 'alienated' from the creator, and they are the basis of mergers and acquisitions in music publishing business. In economic terms music publishers could also be described market-makers or even as traders in copyright assets.

All copyrights do not have equal value, however, since every work is novel (new popular songs were called 'novelties') and music publishing is accordingly subject not just to normal risk in the economic sense but also to radical uncertainty, something it shares with the record industry and other creative industries (Caves 2000). Entrepreneurs in every industry have to deal with risk but the music industry is particularly subject to fickle tastes and difficulty in predicting what will please, especially in the popular music area which by far dominates music publishing. It seems that one explanation for the growth of large international corporations is that they are able to absorb uncertainty and by having a huge catalogue (often running into several million titles) to turn it into pooled risk. Extensions of the copyright term enable them to exploit successful works over a longer period. Moreover, with royalty contracts, risk is shared between the publisher and the composers/song-writer. Both invest in a musical work, the composer by her investment of time and human capital and the publisher by his outlays on production and promotion costs and any advance to the composer.

It has been argued that when revenues were paid directly to the composer for performing and mechanical rights, the composer was able to become more independent of the publisher (Montgomery and Threlfall 2007: Drysdale 2013). Both sources of revenue for both composer and publisher have grown considerably with the much greater scope of licensing to record labels, films, broadcasters, advertisers, games and internet uses. Moreover, technological progress has extended to the process of composition: software programmes, such as 'Sibelius Scorch' and 'Finale', enable composers and song-writers to produce their own printed music— even to hear the music as it is composed. Now composers are able to operate independently of a music publisher: some of the UK's most successful composers do not have a publisher.

Another feature of the economic organisation of music publishing has been the structure of international trade in musical works. Many musical compositions published in the UK were (and are) by foreign composers and, until the adoption of the Berne Convention in 1886, they were typically published without the authorization of the composer or foreign publisher. The practice was, however, mutual and 'piracy' of UK published music was normal elsewhere, especially N. America. Selling printed music by foreign composers was therefore even more profitable as no royalty payment was made for its use. This was standard practice and was not regarded as piracy as we now conceive of it and anyway, there was no international legal standard or effective means of enforcement. When it was ruled in the UK courts that the Berne Convention required permissions be obtained and foreign royalties paid, some UK publishers were severely pressed financially and a few went out of business (Boosey 1931). In order to better exploit their copyrights the major music publishers set up offices abroad, while others contracted with sub-publishers in other countries to collect revenues in foreign markets and protect their rights. These arrangements still prevail, largely due to the territoriality of copyright law. With improved enforcement of copyright and the growth of broadcasting channels worldwide royalties to UK publishers from 'foreign affiliates' has become a significant source of revenues ('international' in Table 2).

The economic organisation of music publishing is based on contracting. Of all the intermediaries in the creative industries, it probably has the greatest complexity and variety of contracts. And as a trader in rights, it is fundamentally reliant on copyright. These features are the basis of the industry and fertile ground for future research in cultural economics (see Barr and Towse 2015).

6 Conclusion

This chapter has traced the development of the main economic aspects of copyright in music as it relates to music publishing in the UK. It is evident from the treatment of the topic here how much the present author owes to the earlier research by Peacock and Weir (1975). Much of the material—institutional, empirical and economic—from that path-breaking book on musical composition has been reworked in relation to music publishing. The chapter presents evidence on the revenues associated with the various rights, in some cases updating the research by Peacock and Weir, and in other cases providing evidence on new sources of income and the associated rights. The relative value of the revenue streams have changed since they wrote because of developments in the technologies of delivering and accessing music and the resulting shifts in consumer demand. Music publishers have reacted to these changes by putting new arrangements in place for collecting those revenues. Responding to exogenous changes rather than initiating endogenous change has continued to determine music publishers' business models over the last two centuries.

The initial problem faced by music publishers was to effectively enforce copyright for sheet music and the performing right was dismissed as a nuisance and ignored until sales fell. As the market changed, music publishers combined to form effective organisations by the early twentieth century that both lobbied for new rights and enforced them. Internationalization of music markets led to setting up a network of licensing agreements to mutually protect musical rights in foreign markets. Copyright laws have been adapted to new technologies—the latest being the protection of digital rights in music—prompting changes in business models in music publishing. In the long run, the switch in music publishing to rights management as its central business model has enabled it to deal more effectively with digitisation, unlike other parts of the music industry.

A question that is often asked is: how important is copyright in the creation of music? It is widely held to be an economic incentive to the creation of artistic works of all kinds. Plant (1934), in perhaps the first article on the economics of copyright, was of the opinion that not only was it not needed as an incentive but that it created a moral hazard effect: copyright encouraged the production of 'extra-marginal' works by protecting ones that would not have been viable on the market by reducing risk. Scherer (2004), in his ambitious quantitative economic history of musical composition, concluded that copyright's role was unproven, that historically the choice of composition as a vocation had not been influenced by the existence of effective copyright laws. He even hinted that increased incomes due to the collection of performing right royalties had led to a 'backward-bending' supply curve on the part of some composers, for instance, Verdi (Scherer 2004: 194). The question we should ask here is: how important is copyright to music publishing? To that, the answer is: it is the bedrock of the industry. As intermediaries, the management and promotion of the use of rights is their sole objective.

A topic that has not been discussed here is what role was played by music publishers in lobbying for increased copyright protection over the years. We know that the Stationers Company lobbied for the 1710 Statute of Anne (Deazley et al. 2010); subsequent changes to copyright law were at the behest of publishers whose interests, as we have seen, were not always fully 'in harmony' with those of composers. Music publishers formed the MPA as a lobbying organisation for protection from piracy to defend their chosen business model of sales of sheet music. They responded quickly to the introduction of mechanical royalties but dragged their feet over performing right royalties as they stuck against the odds to the sales model—to the detriment of composers.

Another question we should consider is this: is copyright in music is the way it is because of music publishers' defence of their business models? Which is the chicken and which the egg: copyright law or the business model? Over the centuries, path dependency has set in, making them inseparably synergistic. When music publishers did move from sales to rights management, though, the costs did not seem to be very high. The same questions could be asked of the role of copyright in other creative industries.

Perhaps a newer question is: how important are music publishers in the market for digital music? Musical composition today does not require printing, copying, editing etc. as it can all be done using computer software. Song-writers and composers can easily and cheaply make a demo disc and release it via the internet. The difficulty is gaining access to markets and uncertainty of it all, as Caves (2000) perceived. Musical composition is an especially difficult case as performance is needed in order to reach consumers. Today, however, music publishers normally require a track record of performances of their works, or at least a contract with a performer or band, before they are willing to 'sign' a composer or song-writer—a tactic for reducing uncertainty to the publisher, while requiring a greater investment on the part of the composer.

A basic question that relates to all the creative industries is: what is the role of intermediaries today, why do they and will they persist? In the case of music publishing, the answer seems to be their ability to acquire and manage copyright assets and to spread and pool risks. Profitability in music publishing, which now attracts large international conglomerates, suggests that they have been successful for a very long time.

Acknowledgements The research for this article was financed by a grant from the UK's Arts and Humanities Research Board for the project 'Economic Survival in a Long Established Creative Industry: Strategies, Business Models and Copyright in Music Publishing' (AH/L004666/1) at Bournemouth University.

References

Barr K, Towse R (2015) Going for a song: theory and practice of music publishing contracts. Paper presented at SERCI annual conference, Glasgow

Baumol W, Baumol H (1994) On the economics of musical composition in Mozart's Vienna. J Cult Econ 18(3):171–198

Blaug M (2005) Why did Schumpeter neglect intellectual property rights? Rev Econ Res Copyright Issues 2(1):69–74

Boosey W (1931) Fifty years of music. Ernest Benn, London

Caves R (2000) Creative industries. Contracts between art and commerce. Harvard University Press, Harvard, MA

Coase R (1979) Payola in radio and television broadcasting. J Law Econ XXII(2):269–328

Coover J (1983) Music at auction: Puttick and Simpson (of London) 1794-1971. Harmonie, Detroit, MI

Deazley R, Kretschmer M, Bently L (eds) (2010) Privilege and property: essays on the history of copyright. Open, Cambridge

Drysdale, J. (2013). Elgar's earnings. Woodbridge: The Boydell Press

Ehrlich C (1985) The music profession in Britain since the eighteenth century. Clarendon, Oxford

Ehrlich C (1989) Harmonious alliance: a history of the performing rights society. Oxford University Press, Oxford

Grove G (1887/2009) A short history of cheap music. Cambridge University Press, Cambridge

Harrison A (2011) Music: the business, 5th edn. Virgin, Chatham

Humphries C, Smith W (1970) Music publishing in the British Isles, 2nd edn. Blackwell, Oxford

McFarlane G (1980) Copyright: performing right. City University, London

Montgomery R, Threlfall R (2007) Music and copyright: the case of Delius and his publishers. Ashgate, Aldershot

Music UK (2012) The economic contribution of the core UK music industry. UK Music, London

Music Publishers Association (MPA) (2014) Annual report 2013/14. MPA, London

Napier-Bell S (2014) Ta-Ra-Ra-Boom-De-Ay. Unbound, London

Peacock A (1993) Paying the piper: culture, music, money. Edinburgh University Press, Edinburgh

Peacock A, Weir R (1975) The composer in the market place. Faber, London

Plant A (1934) The economic aspects of copyright in books. Economica 1(2):167–195

PRS (2014, 2015) Annual reports. PRS, London. Online at www.prs.com. Accessed 04-02-2016

Rizzo I, Towse R (2015) In memoriam Alan Peacock: a pioneer in cultural economics. J Cult Econ 39(3):225–238

Rosselli J (1984) The opera industry in Italy from Cimarosa to Verdi. Cambridge University Press, Cambridge

Samuel M (2014) Winds of change. Journey of UK music from the old world to the new world. Rev Econ Res Copyright Issues 11(2):27–59

Scherer F (2004) Quarter notes and banknotes. Princeton University Press, Princeton, NJ

Towse R (1999) Copyright, incentives and performers' earnings. KYKLOS 52(3):369–390

Towse R (2013) The economic effects of digitization on the administration of musical copyrights. Rev Econ Res Copyright Issues 10(2):55–67

Towse R (2016) Economics of music publishing: copyright and the market. J Cult Econ. http://link.springer.com/journal/10824/onlineFirst/page/1

The Composer in the Market Place Revisited: The Economics of Music Composition Today

David Throsby

Abstract The book *The Composer in the Market Place* by Alan Peacock and Ronald Weir was published in 1975. In the first chapter of the book the authors give an account of the ways in which composers work in a difficult economic environment. The present chapter considers whether the economic circumstances of composers have changed over the 40 years since the book's publication. The chapter outlines changes in the music market on the demand side, the supply side, and in the operations of the market itself. Some hypotheses are put forward about the nature of composers' economic behaviour which are tested empirically using data from a survey of professional composers in Australia undertaken in 2009. The chapter shows that, despite the radical disruptions brought about by the spectacular advances in technology that have affected the processes of music production, demand, supply and distribution, the resulting incentive structure facing professional composers has changed little, such that economic outcomes in terms of composers' labour supply decisions and their relative levels of income remain much the same as they were in 1975.

1 Introduction

In 1975 Alan Peacock and Ronald Weir published a book entitled *The Composer in the Market Place*, a work praised by Asa Briggs for its analytical approach; "it pioneers the application of economic theory—concepts and methods—to musical composition", Briggs wrote in a Preface to the book. His positive assessment has been confirmed in the years since by the honoured place the book has come to hold in the literature of cultural economics. The book went about its investigations into the working life of the composer from a particularly well-informed perspective. Alan Peacock was himself a composer of no small talent and although he had not been obliged through his career to rely on his musical earnings—which he

D. Throsby (✉)
Macquarie University, Sydney, NSW, Australia
e-mail: david.throsby@mq.edu.au

© Springer International Publishing Switzerland 2016   153
I. Rizzo, R. Towse (eds.), *The Artful Economist*,
DOI 10.1007/978-3-319-40637-4_9

described as 'meagre'—he was well aware of the creative processes involved in composing serious music and of the problems and possibilities for the professional composer in turning these processes to pecuniary advantage.

The book is primarily an historical account of the development of the music market in the twentieth century, with its main focus, not surprisingly, on the definition, codification and enforcement of composers' intellectual property rights in their creative work. The importance of copyright in music is a matter beyond the scope of this chapter.[1] Here I want to concentrate solely on Chapter 1, to which Peacock and Weir (hereafter P&W) gave the title 'The Economic Characteristics of Music Composition'. In this chapter they gave a detailed account of the ways in which composers work in a difficult economic environment. The question I address here is: to what extent do their conclusions hold good today, and in what ways have the economic circumstances of composers changed over the 40 years since the book's publication?

The present chapter is structured as follows. Section 2 reviews the first chapter of P&W in detail, followed in Sect. 3 by an account of changes in the music market on the demand side, the supply side, and in the operations of the market itself. Section 4 puts forward some hypotheses about the nature of composers' economic behaviour; these are tested empirically in the following section using data from a survey of professional composers in Australia undertaken in 2009. Section 6 contains a brief discussion of the prospects for composition of 'serious' classical music today, the area of the field in which Peacock's own efforts as a composer were engaged. The final section of the chapter contains some conclusions.

2 The Economics of Music Composition

In outlining the economic characteristics of music composition, P&W applied the same approach to their analysis as that used by Baumol and Bowen (1966) almost a decade earlier, summarised as follows: if we interpret the production, exchange and consumption of the arts in economic terms, how can the theory and methods of economic analysis help us to understand the ways in which these processes are carried on, and what recommendations might we, as economists, suggest to improve their operation? In fact Baumol and Bowen paid only cursory attention to the situation of the composer (1966: 107–109), pointing mainly to the inadequacy of earnings and the difficulties composers face in having their work heard. The treatment in P&W (1975: 14–32) is much more detailed, covering the characteristics of the musical product, the market environment, and the reactions of composers to the conditions in which they work.

The first requirement in any economic analysis of an industry is to define the product. The authors identify three distinctive characteristics of musical output.

---

[1]See further in Ruth Towse's chapter in this book.

First, music has traditionally been a perishable service, with a live performance existing only in the moment; in earlier times the only source of revenue beyond the performance came from the sale of sheet music, printed scores, etc. However the performance of music can now, of course, be stored, such that composers' rights extend well beyond those that can be exercised over the immediate performance and the printed manifestations of their work, to encompass also the reproduction and resale of performances of their compositions.[2]

Second, music performance in certain formats can be interpreted as a public good. For example, free-to-air broadcast music is both non-excludable and non-rival. This leads to the third characteristic of music. The combination of both private-good and public-good properties inherent in the fruits of musical composition means that ownership rights are only partially enforceable by the person or group composing and/or performing the music. A complete capture by the composer of the monetary value of a work will require more complex mechanisms.

The second section of Chapter 1 of P&W looks at the market environment of the composer. The nature of the product as described above indicates that individual composers will not be able to negotiate with potential users of their work; even if rights are clearly defined, "their negotiation and enforcement could impose costs on the individual composer which in most cases would far outweigh the expected financial return" (p. 19). Thus some form of collective administration of composers' rights would be necessary. The authors point to the fact that in the UK a major user of music rights at the time was the BBC creating a near-monopsony on the demand side for the licence to broadcast music:

> The reaction to this situation by the producers of music and the consequential development of the system by which rights are negotiated with the media provides a fascinating case study in market economics in which ... the inevitable result has had to be state regulation of the terms on which bargains are arranged. (p. 20)

In the third section of Chapter 1 the authors consider the reactions of composers, both 'classical' and 'light', to the market environment. They see these reactions as falling into three groups: individual, cooperative and collective, although the latter two overlap to some extent. Individual action includes diversifying output so that revenues are not dependent on just a single market. One such avenue for diversification, as often practised in the nineteenth century, is for composers to double as performers. Other musical activities such as conducting, teaching, reviewing etc. have also been common means for spreading the sources of finance, as have the variety of jobs that composers may take in other spheres altogether—the authors mention Borodin, Rimsky-Korsakov and Ives in this respect. The chapter goes on to present some statistics on the amount of composers' earnings in the UK in the early 1970s; we return to these data in Sect. 5 below.

An additional form of individual action identified by P&W is product differentiation. Composers can take steps to promote their music individually, through

---

[2]An extensive account of the historical evolution of the music industry can be found in Tschmuck (2006).

self-advertisement that seeks to distinguish their work from that of competitors, for example through the marketing of demonstration tapes, etc. Composers of sufficient eminence or popular reputation may develop a 'circle' of supporters; P&W mention Benjamin Britten as a case in point, but nowadays this phenomenon is more evident in the fan clubs and followers' groups that proliferate in the social media.

The second and third types of composers' reactions to the market environment discussed by P&W, cooperation and collective action, can be conveniently considered together. A particular means of insuring against losses and fluctuations in incomes is via risk-sharing, an avenue traditionally found in the history of music in the financial relations between composer and publisher. In the twentieth century, with the emergence of mechanical and performance rights that had not existed hitherto, some conflicts of interest between composers and publishers emerged over ways in which copyrights in musical works should be exploited. Nevertheless, given the impracticality of forming supply-side cartels in music provision, market realities led inexorably to the formation of collection societies to enable rights-owners to negotiate collectively with users. Such societies could access the scale economies available to what are essentially natural monopolies, and provide an efficient service to both providers and users of musical product.

P&W point out that their review of methods of collective action by composers would be incomplete if they failed to mention public support measures that are provided, they presume, because the benefits of music composition to society are not fully recognised in the commercial operations of the music industry. The two principal providers of such support for composers in the UK in the mid-1970s were the Arts Council of Great Britain and the BBC, although the contribution of these two sources of funds to composers' earnings appeared in aggregate to be quite small.

In the final pages of P&W Chapter 1, the authors draw several conclusions from their analysis of the conditions of music composition in the UK at the time of their writing. They note that at the beginning of their careers, composers are typically totally unprepared for the problems they will encounter in making a living. The universities and other institutions that educate professional musicians would serve their students better if they provided some form of training in how to manage the business side of their careers.[3] According to P&W, the trauma induced by this lack of preparedness helps to explain the pervasive suspicion amongst composers at the workings of the market which they see as aligned against their interests. Despite this, the authors observe that composers have been remarkably successful in developing their countervailing power to protect themselves against exploitation by powerful purchasers and against the threats of technical innovation. They conclude that, notwithstanding their economic naiveté, composers have developed "an intelligent appreciation of their own economic interests" (p. 32).

---

[3]On the need for educating classical musicians in managing their own careers, see Bennett (2008).

3 Music Composition Today

How have the economic circumstances of music composition changed in the four decades since *The Composer in the Market Place* was written? In 1975 P&W observed that the major external influence on music composition and the music market up till that time was rapidly changing technology. In 2016 we can make the same observation. It is axiomatic that technological change has had a profound influence on all aspects of the music industry in the modern era. But there is one sense in which the recent historical record is different from that of the past: despite the significant effects of the introduction of radio, the tape recorder, etc. in the pre-1975 world, nothing occurring then can compare with the impacts of the new information and communications technologies that have been developed in the period since. The advent of personal computers followed by the introduction of the internet and then the continuing growth in the use of social media have transformed the music industry in ways that could scarcely have been imagined 40 years ago.

These developments have affected both the demand and supply sides of the market, as well as the operation of the market itself. Let us consider each of these aspects in turn. First, shifts in consumers' demand for music have been driven by both extrinsic and intrinsic factors. Not surprisingly the major external influence has been the growth of the world-wide web, which has enabled ready access to an enormous range of musical product, some of which can be purchased legitimately but much of which can be illegally downloaded without payment. As a result the volume of music piracy has increased enormously, greatly facilitated by file-sharing across peer-to-peer (P2P) networks.[4] In these circumstances, composers and performers as well as publishers, i.e. all legitimate rightsholders, are denied the payments to which they are entitled.

A further external influence of changing technology has been the invention of new means for listening to music electronically. The development of a variety of hand-held devices such as iPods and mobile phones allows music to be consumed on demand anywhere and everywhere.[5] The availability of associated software for transmitting, handling and storing music files has served to accelerate the growth of these new methods of music consumption.

It is not clear whether these externally-induced changes in the music landscape lead or follow shifts in consumer taste. No doubt both are true to some extent. Certainly the balance between consumption of live and recorded music is affected by technological change, although the net effects are difficult to predict. On the one hand recorded music can act as a substitute for live performance, indicating that demand for the latter is likely to decline over time in relative terms. On the other hand, there is evidence that listening to recorded music can stimulate demand for

---

[4]On piracy, see Waldfogel (2012), Liebowitz (2013), Koh et al. (2014); on digital consumption of music and P2P filesharing, see McKenzie (2013), Waelbroeck (2013).

[5]See, for example, Nguyen et al. (2014), Leung (2015).

the live product, since attendance in a concert hall, entertainment centre, pub, club or other music venue provides a different sort of experience for the consumer. In such a case recorded and live music become complements, not substitutes.[6]

There are likely also to be intrinsic shifts in preferences for music that are not so much technologically induced as part of a longer-term evolution of musical taste influenced by fashion, social pressures, changing demographics, etc. For example, it is often argued that demand for classical music is declining[7]; however, although this may be true in relative terms given the rise in popular music consumption that has been the primary beneficiary of the technological changes discussed above, it remains unclear whether demand for live or recorded classical genres is falling off in absolute terms, or simply remaining steady (see further in Sect. 6 below).

Finally on the demand side we can point to the emergence of new uses for music that provide a possible additional revenue source for composers. For example, there appears to be an increased intrusion of background music into public spaces such as malls, airports, etc. and in such uses as music-on-hold. These sorts of now well-established means for using music are subject to monitoring and enforcement of appropriate licensing requirements.

Turning to the supply side, we can note a number of ways in which new technologies have had a direct impact on the processes of music composition and on the actions that composers can take to promote and sell their work. When composers are working at the drawing board—or more precisely, the keyboard—they can avail themselves of a range of computer-related technologies. Electronic musical instruments can reproduce precisely the sound of a range of actual instruments, as well as a host of new sounds that extend a composer's palette beyond the usual repertoire. In addition, notation software can remove much of the sheer labour of writing down notes on manuscript paper. Indeed some composers produce music direct to recording or via live electronics, bypassing the need for a notated record altogether. When a printed score is in fact produced, photocopiers and scanners can turn out parts in an instant, rendering the age-old occupation of copyist obsolete.

Also on the supply side, the advent of the internet has opened up a range of new communication options for composers. They can interact directly with other artists and with consumers of their work via web-forums, blogs, etc. More importantly they can build up their own individual presence in the local, national or global music market place through a personal website, enabling the establishment of a direct promotional and marketing interface with music distributors and with individual consumers.[8]

A further supply-related issue concerns the ways in which composers can have their work performed. Here a difference is apparent between composers of classical and popular music. Unlike the situation that prevailed half a century ago, popular

---

[6] Aguiar and Martens (2013).

[7] Although classical composers increasingly write for film and television, as discussed further in Sect. 6 below.

[8] See Bockstedt et al. (2006).

composers nowadays are often the performers of their own compositions, so the route from composition to performance (and to the associated promotional opportunities) is likely to be a direct one. Classical composers, on the other hand, mostly have to rely on others to perform their works. Moreover there is usually little prospect in classical music for the many repeat performances that popular composer/performers can count on. The march of technology over recent years has opened up ever widening opportunities for popular composers to pursue such a composition/performance/promotion strategy, in contrast to the options available to classical composers. Thus technological change can be seen in this respect to have had a differential effect over time on composers across the musical genres.

It is in the music marketplace at large where some of the most obvious impacts of new technologies can be observed. Ongoing developments in recording and transmission technologies have been affecting publishers and record companies for many years, but it has been the growth of the internet that has brought about the most profound changes in the business models of these companies. Efforts by the multi-national majors to stem the tide of piracy that was undermining their very existence have included legal action against P2P networks and cooperation with internet service providers to block user access to copyright infringing websites. However, these strategies have proved inadequate, leading the majors to turn towards trying to capture a share of the online market for themselves.[9] At the same time a number of independents have managed to carve out a niche for themselves in a difficult international market.[10] All of these developments have been accompanied by significant shifts in prices and in revenues for all players in the industry, both large and small.

In conjunction with the changing structure, conduct and performance of the music industry at both international and national levels, there have been many developments in rights administration which are beyond the scope of this chapter.

4 Hypotheses

How have all these changes affected the economic circumstances in which composers work? Our basic hypothesis in considering this question as it relates to composers writing music at the present time is that technological change remains the most important factor in influencing their economic situation, since it has fundamentally altered the incentive structure that composers face in the production and marketing of their creative work. It can be seen that this is essentially the same hypothesis as that underlying the analysis by P&W of the economics of music

---

[9]For an account of the actions of major recording and music publishing companies in attempting to capture a share of the on-line music market, see IFPI (2015).

[10]These observations are relevant to the survival of music industries in developing countries; for some examples, see Throsby (2002).

composition in the mid-1970s. Furthermore we can hypothesise that the outcomes are likely to be similar to those observed by P&W. In particular we propose that

- There is continuing pressure on composers to diversify their income streams
- There is continuing pressure on composers to differentiate their product; however
- Despite composers' efforts to respond to these pressures, their earnings from musical composition are likely to remain low.

Moreover it can be argued that if technology is indeed the primary driver of change, economically successful composers will be those who embrace new technology, not those who ignore it.

The above hypotheses provide some propositions that can be tested empirically, a matter to which we turn in the next section.

5 Empirical Evidence

In this section we examine the above hypotheses with reference to data from a survey of practising professional artists carried out in Australia in 2009 (Throsby and Zednik 2010). Just over 1000 artists were sampled in the survey, classified by artform into eight occupational categories, one of which was composer. Artists assigned to the latter category were those who described their "principal artistic occupation" (PAO) as composer ($n = 93$). They can be divided into:

- Composers of classical/contemporary-classical/new-music (24 %);
- Composer/songwriters in jazz, rock, pop, hip-hop or other contemporary genres (23 %);
- Composer/songwriters for film, television or radio (not advertising commercials) (14 %);
- Composer/songwriters of folk music (8 %);
- Other composers (31 %).

It should be borne in mind that composing music is an activity also undertaken by members of other PAOs, notably those artists who give their PAO as musician. Indeed the crossovers between the PAOs of composer and musician are quite significant. Of those who were identified primarily as composers in the survey, 38 % had also engaged in serious concert performance as an instrumental musician, and 22 % had similar achievements as a singer, while 41 % of those classified as musicians had composed music of one sort or another during their careers.

In the following analyses we focus our attention solely on those whose principal occupational designation as an artist is as a composer. Given that our coverage of musical genres includes classical and a range of popular styles as indicated above, it is presumably similar in scope to that of the group with which P&W were themselves concerned. We look at data on incomes, labour supply and the use of new technologies, and go on to estimate an earnings function for Australian composers.

5.1   Composers' Incomes

In Chapter 1 of P&W the authors present data from a survey of British composers undertaken by the Performing Rights Society during 1972. The data indicate the relatively small proportion of composers who could rely on their earnings from musical composition as making up a significant component of their total income; at the other end of the distribution, more than half of the composers in the sample received only 20 % or less of their total earnings from this source. These results for the early 1970s in Britain can be compared with those for the Australian composers in 2009. The comparison is shown in Table 1. It is clear that little has changed, especially for the "classical" or "serious" composers in the two surveys; in both cases fewer than 20 % of these artists were able to earn most or all of their income from their compositions. When the sample is extended to cover all composers (including 'popular' and 'light' composers in P&W's terminology), the outcomes appear somewhat better for both the British and Australian groups, since the earnings of these other composers improve the overall mean. Indeed in the Australian case the earnings distribution across all composers shows a significantly smaller number in the lowest earnings quintile, compared with the corresponding quintile in the UK data; this result probably reflects the wider range of lucrative alternative outlets available to composers nowadays compared to 40 years ago (see further below).

To summarise, the conclusion we can draw from the evidence in Table 1 is: *plus ça change*. These results imply that the conditions under which composers work today will impose the same sorts of pressures on their work choices as in the past. So the question arises as to whether their responses will be similar to those observed by P&W, including taking action to diversify their income sources. Table 2 provides evidence of this for the Australian composers. The two main sources to which composers can turn are other music-related activities—teaching music, performing, reviewing, etc.—and work outside music and the arts altogether. In common with artists in other artforms whose creative incomes are insufficient, composers have a strong preference for the former alternative, i.e. for finding additional work within their artform rather than outside (Throsby and Zednik 2011). It is apparent as a result that, notwithstanding the relatively low returns to original creative work,

Table 1 Earnings from musical composition as a proportion of total earnings: distribution of numbers of composers (per cent)

	Peacock and Weir (1975)		Throsby and Zednik (2010)	
Earnings from composition as proportion of total earnings	Classical composers	All composers	Classical composers	All composers
Less than 20 %	61	53	50	33
20–80 %	25	22	33	36
More than 80 %	14	25	17	31
Total	100	100	100	100

Table 2 Distribution of sources of income of Australian composers: 2009 (per cent)

Income source	Classical composers (%)	Songwriters (%)	All composers (%)
Creative income	25.1	62.6	56.6
Arts-related income	58.1	13.5	22.4
Sub-total arts income	83.2	76.1	79.0
Non-arts income	16.8	23.9	21.0
Total	100.0	100.0	100.0
Total annual income ($A '000)	36.3	75.6	49.5

composers on average are able to earn the majority of their income (about four-fifths) from musical work of one sort or another. This result is broadly similar to that found in the British survey.[11]

5.2 Labour Supply

The actions taken by composers to diversify their income sources can be examined from the perspective of their labour supply decisions. As has become standard in the analysis of data on artists' working conditions, we separate out the three labour markets which generate the categories of earnings described above, i.e. the market for creative labour, that for arts-related labour, and the market for non-arts work. Table 3 shows the average distribution of weekly working hours across these three labour markets for the Australian composers. Again the diversified nature of composers' work portfolios is clear.

The disjunction between labour input and earnings produced is apparent in a comparison between Tables 2 and 3. We note, for example, that composers spend on average two-thirds of their working hours on creative work, yet earn little more than half their income from this source. By contrast, they earn one-fifth of their income from work outside the arts, with a time input of only one-tenth of their total working hours. These observations are consistent with the so-called work-preference model which proposes that creative artists will prefer to allocate more time to original creative work than to more lucrative but less artistically satisfying opportunities elsewhere.[12]

---

[11]See P&W, Table 1.1, p. 23.

[12]See Throsby (1994), Steiner and Schneider (2013).

Table 3 Composers' mean time allocation to different labour markets: 2009 (hours per week)		Hours/week	%
	Creative work	26	66.7
	Arts-related work	9	23.1
	Sub-total all arts work	35	89.8
	Non-arts work	4	10.2
	Total working time	39	100.0

5.3 Composers' Use of New Technologies

As noted earlier, the development of digital technologies over recent years has had a profound impact on artistic practice across all art forms, not least in the field of music composition. In the Australian survey, 85 % of composers report using the internet for any purpose "frequently" or "occasionally", and the great majority use other technologies regularly for a variety of purposes. When it comes to the use of new technologies in their creative practice, the numbers narrow somewhat. Nevertheless Table 4 shows that the proportions of composers who use various technologies frequently or occasionally in their creative work are still quite significant. Apart from the use in running their creative practice generally, some use digital technologies specifically to create art works. For example, 19 % of composers report using the internet to create collaborative or interactive compositions with other artists, and 15 % had created artistic work using social networking websites. Smaller numbers had generated artistic work in virtual environments or virtual worlds (5 %), or had created collaborative or interactive works with non-artists (4 %).

These data paint a striking picture of the fundamental changes that have overtaken the practice of musical composition since the P&W book was written. Nevertheless further evidence from the Australian survey shows a consistency with the same product differentiation hypothesis that P&W put forward, even though the contemporary means for pursuing this strategy are radically different. Respondents to the survey were asked about their usage of the internet to promote their work. The results indicate that a clear majority of composers use the internet frequently or occasionally to promote and advertise their work, either through their own personal website (61 %) and/or through another party's website (70 %). Amongst other outcomes, such strategies have the effect of 'branding' an individual's work and giving it a distinctive edge in a competitive marketplace. Furthermore, this market is a truly global one, such that interest in a composer's work might be sparked and demand created from anywhere in the world.

To investigate further the various propensities of composers to adopt new methods, i.e. to act as 'innovators', we can construct a score for each individual in the sample by counting the number of different types of usage of new technologies he or she is or has been engaged with.[13] We identify ten such items covering

---

[13]The impetus towards innovation amongst composers has a long history; see Leap and Williams (2015).

Table 4 Frequent use of new technologies in creative work by Australian composers (per cent)

	Proportion of composers (%)
Sound recording devices	75
Sound manipulation software	62
Sound player devices	61
Electronic musical instruments	67
Music composition and notation software	62
Multimedia software	32
Internet	40

the usages discussed in this section, and rank the sample according to this innovation index. The distribution of the index is shown in Table 5. It is apparent that the majority of composers could be described, according to this analysis, as only moderate innovators who prefer by and large to stick with the traditional ways of running their creative lives. On the other hand, at the other end of the spectrum there is a smaller but still significant proportion of composers who lead the way in adapting to the new technological environment. Whether a willingness to embrace the new technologies bestows an income advantage on individual practitioners will be examined in the next section.

5.4 Determinants of Composers' Earnings

The data from the Australian survey can be used to estimate a standard earnings function for composers. In line with the conventional approach in the specification of an appropriate model, we hypothesise that an individual worker's earnings are a function essentially of his or her human capital and labour supply, with relevant socio-demographic and other control variables included in the estimating equation. Thus we define the following explanatory variables:

- *Human capital*

  - Experience (dummy for "established")
  - Music training (dummy for trained at music school or conservatorium)

- *Labour supply*

  - Time spent at creative work (per cent of working time)
  - Time spent at non-arts work (per cent of working time)

- *Socio-demographics*

  - Age (years)
  - Gender (dummy indicating female)
  - General education (dummy for completed degree)

Table 5 Index of propensity to innovate among Australian composers (per cent)

Innovation index	Proportion of composers (%)
0–1	30
2–3	28
4–5	21
6–7	15
8–10	6
	100

- *Music genre*

    - Composer of classical music (dummy yes/no)
    - Songwriter (dummy yes/no)
    - Composer for film/television (dummy yes/no)

- *Innovation*

    - Innovation index (scale 0–10 as defined above)

The earnings function was estimated using ordinary least squares with robust standard errors, with composers' creative income (cf. Table 2) as the dependent variable. Results are shown in Table 6. Of the human capital variables, experience appears far more important than musical training in generating income. Indeed coefficients on both the music training and general education variables show negative signs although both are non-significant. The labour supply variables show the expected signs—positive for time spent at creative work and negative for time spent working outside—although the coefficient on the latter is non-significant.[14] It is not possible to draw any conclusions as to the effects of age and gender. However there are striking differences between the earning potential of work in classical music, and that for songwriting and composition for film and television, with the results for the latter two indicating the very lucrative opportunities in these areas. Finally, although the innovation index coefficient shows a positive sign, it is not significant. We are thus unable to say decisively that innovative composers make greater creative incomes than the rest, *ceteris paribus*.

---

[14]There may be differences between popular and classical composers in the effects of musical education and training on their prospects of success. Classical musicians are unlikely to be able to follow a successful professional career unless they have undertaken specialised post-school musical education or training of some sort, whereas some popular musicians achieve success without such preparation. Nevertheless such a differential, if it exists, may not necessarily be reflected in relative incomes. The sub-sample sizes are not large enough to enable this proposition to be tested using our survey data.

Table 6 Earnings function for Australian composers (dependent variable:creative income): 2008–09

Explanatory variables		Coefficient	Robust standard error
Socio-demographics	Age	−1.333	1.71
	Gender	−5.499	9.53
	Education	−12.420	13.41
Human capital	Experience	33.490***	12.30
	Music training	−1.640	13.05
Labour supply	Time at creative work	0.512**	0.21
	Time at non-arts work	−0.142	0.25
Genre	Classical	3.410	12.96
	Songwriter	26.340*	15.23
	Film/TV	32.840**	12.67
Innovation	Innovation index	6.766	4.50
Constant		−30.290	30.19
Adjusted R-squared		0.442	
F statistic		2.87***	
N		87	

Notes:
(a) For definitions of explanatory variables, see text
(b) Some non-significant explanatory variables omitted
(c) $*p < 0.1$, $**p < 0.05$, $***p < 0.01$

6   The Prospects for Classical Music

Evidence from the above analysis concerning the relatively poor income prospects facing composers of classical music raises questions about the future of this artform. If the financial rewards are so bleak, will composers continue to produce works in this genre? The first observation to make in addressing this question is that the revenues of classical composers have always been precarious, yet they have continued over centuries to pour forth a steady stream of fine music.[15] So the interesting issues relate to how the contemporary state of the world is affecting this genre of music production and consumption. Several factors can be seen to be at work.

   In the first place are trends within the artform itself which have an effect, one way or another, on demand. The history of music, as with the other arts, is replete with examples of practitioners eager to serve a market by producing works which were guaranteed to sell or to please a beneficent patron. But artists also follow their own visions, and this may result in their creating art without regard for how the

---

[15]There are innumerable accounts of the lives of great composers and of the financial insecurities that they faced. Of course not all composers spent lives of unremitting poverty, including Mozart; according to a modern economic assessment, he enjoyed periods when he was actually reasonably well off—see Baumol and Baumol (1994). For an account of the evolution of composers' income sources between the seventeenth and nineteenth centuries, see Scherer (2001).

output is to be received. In classical music, for example, it seems unlikely that the development of serialism and 12-tone composition by composers such as Schoenberg, Webern and Stockhausen was seen as a crowd-pleasing move. Indeed it can be argued that such music is now looked upon simply as a stage in the evolution of music theory and practice that has run its course, and although contemporary composers still call on atonality in various circumstances, the overall trend in classical music writing in recent times appears to be towards works that are more readily understood by conventional audiences.

The second issue relates to competition for consumers' attention. In the marketplace for musical experiences, either live or reproduced, the extent of competition for the listener's ear has grown considerably, such that classical music has to compete with a wider variety of other musical genres and other avenues for cultural consumption than ever before. To some extent the expansion in the range of cultural media available to consumers has had an upside for classical composers—it has opened up opportunities for them to write serious music for use other than in the traditional concert hall or recording studio. Writing music for film, for example, has long presented a creative challenge to classical composers, one taken up by such major figures in the history of twentieth century music as Walton and Shostakovitch.

In addition, opera companies and symphony orchestras have responded to trends in consumer demand by diversifying their offerings in an effort to attract new audiences and to shore up their precarious finances.[16] It is not unusual these days to find opera companies including one or two musicals amongst their traditional programming of Verdi, Puccini and Mozart, whilst some of the world's great orchestras perform with stars from popular music, or play crossover or fusion music in addition to their conventional repertoire. Moreover a range of possibilities exists for presenters of classical music concerts to make their offerings more attractive to new audiences, including enhancing feelings of inclusion and accessibility for first-time attenders.[17] However none of these presenter-driven innovations is likely to have had much effect on opportunities for the current generation of composers.

Notwithstanding the fact that the relative position of the classical genre in the musical landscape may have declined over the long term, it could well be that there will always be a baseload demand that will maintain a minimum level of activity, not only in the niche market of recorded classical music but also in the similarly small market for live classical performance. This proposition is supported in respect of the former possibility by observation of trends in record sales of classical and operatic music in Australia over the 10 year period since 2005. Data show that the proportion of classical and operatic sales have fluctuated between 3 and 5 % of total sales during this period, but have shown no clear trend upwards or downwards over

---

[16]Broadcasters of classical music face similar issues of declining audiences and shifting tastes, and may adopt similar strategies to attract new listeners; see further in Letts (2015).

[17]For some empirical evidence, see Dobson (2010).

this time (ARIA 2015). Such evidence for a baseload demand for classical music is clearly limited in time and place, but it is at least suggestive of the possibility that demand will not actually die out.

Ultimately, however, it can be argued that the survival of classical music is not dependent so much on the economics of musical supply and demand as it is on the fundamental significance of the intrinsic aesthetic qualities of this genre of music which extends, it must be remembered, well beyond the confines of the Western cultural tradition. Such an argument relates to the importance of music as a repository of meaning, a purveyor of civilising values, and a vehicle for cultural transmission through time. It resonates with the efforts made by cultural economists to differentiate between the cultural value of art and its economic value.[18] These considerations suggest that, despite the vagaries of the marketplace, the essential nature of art which classical music embodies will in the long term prevail.[19]

7 Conclusions

In this chapter we have reviewed the economics of musical composition as seen by P&W and updated their analysis to account for developments in the 40 years since their book was written. We have shown that, despite the radical disruptions brought about by the spectacular advances in technology that have affected the processes of music production, demand, supply and distribution, the resulting incentive structure facing professional composers influences them in ways that have changed little. We find that the economic outcomes in terms of composers' labour supply decisions and their levels of income remain much the same as always, such that the conclusions reached by P&W are, broadly speaking, as relevant today as they were in 1975.

The book that we have revisited in this chapter was a pioneer in applying the principles and methods of economic analysis to musical composition. In the detail that it provides of the circumstances in which music was being written and marketed in the mid-1970s, the book is a vivid reflection of its era. At another level, however, it can be seen as timeless in its relevance to long-standing issues facing composers as they struggle to make a living.

Acknowledgements I am grateful to Dr Tom Longden and Nick Vanderkooi for their research assistance and, with the usual *caveat*, to Dr John Carmody, Professor Victor Ginsburgh and Dr Richard Letts for insightful comments on an earlier version of this chapter.

---

[18]See, for example Throsby (2001) and contributions to Hutter and Throsby (2008).

[19]These arguments are discussed at length in a number of significant contributions to the literature, including Johnson (2002), Ford (2005), Fineberg (2006), Kramer (2007).

References

Aguiar L, Martens B (2013) Digital music consumption on the internet: evidence from clickstream data. Institute for Prospective Technological Studies. European Commission Joint Research Centre, Seville

Australian Recording Industry Association (2015) Australian wholesale sales for the years ended 31 December. ARIA, Sydney

Baumol WJ, Baumol H (1994) On the economics of musical composition in Mozart's Vienna. J Cult Econ 18(3):171–198

Baumol WJ, Bowen WG (1966) Performing arts: the economic dilemma. Twentieth Century Fund, New York

Bennett D (2008) Understanding the classical music profession: the past, the present and strategies for the future. Ashgate, Aldershot

Bockstedt JC, Kauffman RJ, Riggins FJ (2006) The move to artist-led online music distribution: a theory-based assessment and prospects for structural changes in the digital music market. Int J Electron Commerce 10(3):7–38

Dobson MC (2010) New audiences for classical music: the experiences of non-attenders at live orchestral concerts. J New Music Res 39(2):111–124

Fineberg J (2006) Classical music, why bother? Hearing the world of contemporary culture through a composer's ears. Routledge, New York

Ford A (2005) In defence of classical music. ABC, Sydney

Hutter M, Throsby D (eds) (2008) Beyond price: value in culture, economics, and the arts. Cambridge University Press, New York

International Federation of the Phonographic Industry (2015) Digital music report: charting the path to sustainable growth. IFPI, London

Johnson J (2002) Who needs classical music? Cultural choice and musical value. Oxford University Press, Oxford

Koh B, Murthi B, Raghunathan S (2014) Shifting demand: online music piracy, physical music sales, and digital music sales. J Organ Comput Electron Commerce 24(4):366–387

Kramer L (2007) Classical music still matters. University of California Press, Berkeley

Leap T, Williams DW (2015) Innovating during tough times: lessons from the great composers. Int Bus Res 8(1):191–196

Letts R (2015) ABC Classic FM as a dynamic force in art music. Music Trust, Sydney

Leung TC (2015) Music piracy: bad for record sales but good for the iPod? Inform Econ Pol 31:1–12

Liebowitz SJ (2013) Internet piracy: the estimated impact on sales. In: Towse R, Handke C (eds) Handbook of the digital creative economy. Edward Elgar, Cheltenham, pp 262–273

McKenzie J (2013) P2P file-sharing: how does music file-sharing affect recorded music sales in Australia? In: Tschmuck P, Pearce P, Campbell S (eds) Music business and the experience economy: the Australasian case. Springer, Berlin, pp 79–97

Nguyen GD, Dejean S, Moreau F (2014) Are streaming and other music consumption modes substitutes or complements? J Cult Econ 38(4):315–330

Peacock AT, Weir R (1975) The composer in the market place. Faber Music, London

Scherer FM (2001) The evolution of free-lance music composition, 1650–1900. J Cult Econ 25 (4):307–319

Steiner L, Schneider L (2013) The happy artist: an empirical application of the work-preference model. J Cult Econ 37(2):225–246

Throsby D (1994) A work preference model of artist behaviour. In: Peacock AT, Rizzo I (eds) Cultural economics and cultural policies. Kluwer, Dordrecht, pp 69–80

Throsby D (2001) Economics and culture. Cambridge University Press, Cambridge

Throsby D (2002) The music industry in the new millennium: global and local perspectives (Paper prepared for The Global Alliance for Cultural Diversity). UNESCO, Paris

Throsby D, Zednik A (2010) Do you really expect to get paid? An economic study of professional artists in Australia. Australia Council, Sydney

Throsby D, Zednik A (2011) Multiple job-holding and artistic careers: some empirical evidence. Cult Trends 20(1):9–24

Tschmuck P (2006) Creativity and innovation in the music industry. Springer, Dordrecht

Waelbroeck P (2013) Digital music. In: Towse R, Handke C (eds) Handbook of the digital creative economy. Edward Elgar, Cheltenham, pp 389–398

Waldfogel J (2012) Music piracy and its effects on demand, supply, and welfare. Innovat Pol Econ 12(1):91–109

Market Options and Public Action for Opera

Michele Trimarchi

Abstract Opera is a multi-dimensional cultural product. Its powerful theatrical and musical features attracted the leading social groups in the nineteenth century, while in the last decades its appeal proves limited to a small proportion of contemporary society. Its production is widely supported by public subsidies and private donations. Being endowed with a dramaturgic structure and an expressive language able to respond to society's emotional and cognitive expectations, opera could reinvent its traditional profile, without spoiling its creative identity but at the same time addressing the contemporary audience. This does not require special effects, but simply a more effective combination of its productive factors, exploiting its cross-media nature. Public action can prove crucial in a more advanced approach, shifting the focus of subsidies from the mechanical deficit coverage *à la* Baumol to the provision of in-kind support aimed at raising the entrepreneurial responsibility of opera managers. Market options could be increased along with the appraisal of opera by the complex contemporary society, continuity through infrastructure, technology and human capital training, in order for public action to reject paternalistic orientation and instead encourage opera producers to challenge the market.

1 Introduction

At my first meeting with Alan Peacock in his cigar-smelling office of the Vice-Chancellor at the University College at Buckingham, quoting Keynes, he warned me: "In economics it is preferable to be imprecisely right than exactly wrong". This has stayed with me ever since and informed my attitude to cultural economics (or economics of the arts, as it was known at the time—1983).

M. Trimarchi (✉)
University of Catanzaro Magna Graecia, Catanzaro, Italy

Fondazione Teatro Comunale di Bologna, Bologna, Italy
e-mail: michtrim@tin.it

© Springer International Publishing Switzerland 2016
I. Rizzo, R. Towse (eds.), *The Artful Economist*,
DOI 10.1007/978-3-319-40637-4_10

Cultural economics has crafted many views considering 'culture' as a set of objects (built heritage, the visual arts) and actions (the performing arts) finding common features amidst heterogeneity. Audiences are considered homogeneous in terms of their socio-demographic features, while the wide variety of subjective motivations among cultural consumers is often neglected.[1] Within this framework, price management, public subsidies, quality, even the impact of cultural production upon the local economy have often been faced with performance indicators demanding quantitative measurement. The emerging economic framework, variously defined (from 'knowledge' economy to 'sharing' economy), however, suggests the growing importance of complexity, based on a new value hierarchy in which relationships and experience prevail over competition and efficiency. From that perspective, the arts appear as a powerful laboratory in which desires are more important than needs, subjective taste prevails over acritical cloning and infrastructures can prove more effective than subsidies.

Opera, one of Alan Peacock's passions, can give us useful insights on how public, private and nonprofit actors can combine their strategies, actions and orientations within a synergic framework aimed at innovating views and tools in order for contemporary society's expectations to be effectively met. This chapter deals with opera as a specific 'product' endowed with multiple dimensions. The semantic, technical and social nature of musical theatre implies that its value is (or should be?) a balanced combination of musical performance, acting, singing, often dancing, along with and scenery and costumes, lighting effects and many other elements. Its technical complexity and artistic richness can strengthen its cultural value and meet the evolving expectations of contemporary society.

2 Tradition vs. Innovation

Opera, as with other cultural products, is often considered 'untouchable' due to the dogmatic conviction that the nineteenth century society in which it reached its zenith was highly cultivated and therefore able to digest its complex language and technicalities. It is often considered to be a form of art belonging to an extinguished past, valuable for the limited proportion of society already endowed with technical and aesthetic tools able to decipher its clubbish jargon.[2] Its language sounds odd and strange, its visual options are a potential source of conflict between two parties: on one hand those who expect opera to be faithfully reproduced as it was at the time

---

[1] A summary of the conventional views of audience motivations is offered by Swanson et al. (2008). For a discussion on the weakness of conventional audience studies see Trimarchi (2014b).

[2] Aria, cabaletta, soprano leggero, buffo, etc. are all labels that may sound strange to non-initiated consumers in a society where labels are progressively losing their meaning.

it was written, on the other hand those who prefer clear and often brave adaptations to the present human environment.

There is resistance on the part of some producers of opera and of audiences to any change. Critics, commentators and discussions in the press and online show that a proportion of the present day audience still appears reluctant to accept innovative opera staging and it does not want to acknowledge the need to address a society used to a higher threshold of acoustic and visual perceptions and to a greater variety of material and its presentation. Opera has and continues to evolve but merely preserving it ends up transforming it into a museum exhibit rather than a live performing art. Surveys of the repertoire most commonly performed in opera houses around the world are evidence of this static view (Heilbrun 2001).

That static view I believe to be unfounded. It anyway ignores some important features of opera. In those times when cinema, tv and the web had not even been imagined, opera was a major source of entertainment. It offered all round entertainment. In the eighteenth and nineteenth centuries opera houses' revenues were largely generated by the crowded foyer in which many people spent the evening gambling (chemin-de-fer was the preferred game), while the rest of the family was sitting in a box; intervals hosted acrobats and other circus attractions, just to keep the audience awake. Cinema put an end to its popularity and eventually, subsidy became the dominant source of revenues.

Can contemporary society be attracted by opera as musical theatre staging eternal human dilemmas and conflicts? From the economic perspective the question focuses upon the ability of opera to provide society and audience with a credible response to its needs and desires.[3] Although it may sound odd, opera actually offers a widely diffused and shared product if we consider its various basic plots, the dynamics occurring among characters, the combination of individual stories on a collective or historical background. It is still able to be attractive if its producers, rather than preserving opera as a static product, understand that demand for entertainment and knowledge (in every possible combination and reciprocal fertilization) has to be shifted from social rites in monumental theatres to emotional and cognitive exchange in a variety of places and tools.

The discussion about the nature of opera as a product becomes, then, crucial for the economic and policy implications concerning its provision. The factors that have to be taken into account are: the likely response of demand to various possible productions of the opera season; the design of prices (also for products such as programmes, digital reproductions, streaming, and so on), the selection and training of human resources combining artistic, technical and administrative personnel; the criteria and tools of public action and the evaluation system aimed at establishing the level of public support. These are all areas whose appropriate definition strongly depends upon the strategic choice focusing upon the multiple facets of opera as a specific product.

---

[3]For a critical discussion upon the growing relevance of desires and the fading centrality of needs in the economic approach see Holler (2015).

Opera production is dealt with by a variety of organizational models including public, non-profit and private legal status ownership and/or control. The adoption of either productive structure does not *per se* necessarily exert a crucial influence upon the cultural outcome (and, therefore, upon its ability to establish a dynamic and systematic dialogue with society). The overall effect depends on the existing incentives, which may alter the financial features of opera producers, affecting the dynamics of supply and demand. A dilemma between 'season' vs. 'repertoire' systems is often considered in the specialized discussions, but its subjective and controversial profile remains out of the scope of this chapter.[4]

The design of cultural policy aimed at supporting opera can be strongly influenced by the dilemma between tradition and innovation and its impact upon the audience-oriented strategy adopted by each opera producer. The nature itself of opera is complex: it is neither a sacred and sealed-off club good, whose special nature tends to exclude the non-initiated audience, nor an ordinary commodity whose dynamics are ruled by the textbook marketplace rules. Its specific features end up exerting a strong influence upon both its market options (the width and turnout of audience and its willingness-to-pay) and the strategies and mechanisms adopted by the cultural policy decision-makers. In this conflict, the product *per se* is not at all examined in its features (theatrical text and plot, musical language, eternal dynamics such as love, betrayal, passion, honesty, and so on)[5] though its appeal, if it is properly managed, could attract a wider and more varied audience.

We should observe that participation to opera does not depend upon its aesthetical choice; almost every opera house hosts various—and not necessarily consistent—stage approaches within the same season, therefore we cannot infer any probability of success from the traditional vs. innovative staging of operas. However opera is staged, figures reveal the existence of a systematic distance between opera production and society's expectations. The questions are, therefore, related to opera as a genre.

How can opera address contemporary society and attract consumers? The question is crucial to focus upon the likely market outcomes of a product still neglected by the majority of consumers (even on the part of those who show interest for other cultural activities). The attention to contemporary society and its emotional, cognitive and intellectual urges could elicit a wider and more systematic audience participation, justify stable public action, and attract corporate support and individual donations, making opera more sustainable than it is now. In most countries opera production normally adopts both views: in the same year

---

[4]The 'repertoire' system is adopted in Germany, where each opera house stages a high number of titles, with its stable singers covering various roles in a quite fast turnout; the 'season' system, adopted in the Mediterranean European countries, is based upon a sequence of titles; soloists are ad hoc hired for each single title as autonomous singers. There is a great deal of controversy about the pros and cons of either system, it remains beyond the scope and aims of this chapter. See Towse (2011).

[5]The issue of creative language remains quite controversial and delicate, as Trimarchi (2014a) argues.

conservative and innovative staging coexist, and they elicit various and often conflicting reactions on the part of the existing audience. New entries can be attracted not just with special effects: both old-fashioned and contemporary special effects aim at astonishment rather than at dialogue.[6]

3   The Economics of Opera

At the birth of cultural economics in the 1960s,[7] opera was the game of a minority. Even now, opera (together with dance performance and ballet) is among the least popular cultural activity in EU member countries.[8] Since the conventional acknowledgement of Baumol's Law[9] as the most powerful theoretical reason behind the case for public subsidies, opera has been considered, like many other areas of the arts and culture, endemically bound to failure when left to the rules of the marketplace. According to that view, public action is indispensable if society wants to rescue opera from progressive contraction and eventual extinction. In the light of the shared beliefs generated by Baumol's law[10] opera appears to be victim of an endemic financial weakness, as is every other area within the performing arts system. The problem is enhanced by the limited opportunities for reducing the artistic labour hired for each performance, given the impossibility (often, just the shared refusal) of eliminating characters, chorus and orchestra whose dimensions are normally quite large. Baumol's law has proved comfortable for those opera (and performing arts) producers who consider quantity as a credible proxy for quality.

At first sight opera appears to be condemned to failure unless external funds support its action; public subsidies are then aimed at granting survival to opera houses normally hosting a permanent orchestra and chorus, and also solo singers if the 'repertoire' system is the norm. The habit of pharaonic staging is seldom

---

[6]Does *Un ballo in maschera* need Riccardo's palace to become an electoral committee room? Does *Compare Turiddu* need to ride a Harley-Davidson? Symmetrically, does *Il barbiere di Siviglia* need shaving foam? Opera often indulges in superficial solutions and considers dialogue a sort of duty of the audience.

[7]The birth of cultural economics is not only conventionally identified with Baumol's and Bowen's seminal book Performing Arts: the Economic Dilemma (1996); we should consider that a few earlier works (such as Keynes's papers on public funding of the arts) were crafted upon a past social paradigm.

[8]On average, the participation is 18 %, with difference across countries, ranging from 34 % in Sweden to 8 % in Portugal and Greece (Eurobarometer 2013). A previous study on the former members and new entries in the EU shows that the audience of opera represents between 9 and 14 % of the adult population in the two areas (Eurobarometer 2003).

[9]For an extensive critical discussion on Baumol's disease see Towse (1997).

[10]Conventionally accepted as the main explanation of financial weakness of cultural organizations, and at the same time as the main justification for public subsidies to the arts, the law of unbalanced growth proves poorly supported by the empirical evidence (Peacock 1969), but also controversial and shortsighted, as Cowen (1996) argues.

discussed, for both the belief that opera cannot be frugal, and the reluctance to intrude in the creative freedom of stage directors. These end up as dogmatic and unjustified views, mainly due to the forced parallel between the quality of the performance (in any case subjective and controversial), on one hand, and the amount of expenditure devoted to superstars, luxury props and costumes, excess dimensions of orchestra and chorus on the other hand.

This apocalyptic view proved comfortable for the opera system, being supported by generous public budgets in Europe, and by substantial corporate sponsorship in the US. The possibility of relying upon external sources of funding ended up averting the need for entrepreneurial responsibility: audience feedback was not a priority and subscribers' fidelity was given much more importance than neophytes' participation; extension of audiences was simply ignored, clearly preferring Pavlovian consumers to reactive ones. It led the opera 'system' in those countries with high level of subvention to indulge in massive staging, superstar fees, wasteful competition aimed at capturing experts' attention rather than that of consumers. Generous public funds end up reducing the importance of attracting and consolidating a wide and possibly a dynamic audience. There are no incentives aimed at encouraging opera producers to exploit their market options. Moreover, the receipt of public funds is normally given as the acknowledgement of (presumed) high quality in programming rather than—as it should be—as an incentive to optimise the use and combination of productive resources.

The indirect effect of such an extensive external funding was, paradoxically, a very limited appeal of opera in society. Can opera abandon its museum-like features, and face the challenge of establishing a cultural exchange and interaction with contemporary society? Although the mission statement of many opera houses contains good intention of responding to evolving expectations, the present dimensions and composition of the audience in some countries shows that a gap still exists between formal commitments and actual action. The issue concerns the orientation of opera producers towards audience renewal aimed at growing sustainability. The challenge requires the rejection of some commonplace views according to which the low proportion of people actually participating in opera is considered cultivated while the others are not.

A static interpretation of cultural phenomena could lead to the belief that society is divided in cultivated vs. uncultivated individuals, and that between them there is a barrier, which obstructs any passage between the two. The simple knowledge of the theory of cultural addiction (Stigler and Becker 1977), however, should be sufficient for us to simply deny any foundation to this binary view. Cultivation is unavoidably a gradual and progressive accumulation of critical experience whose variety and versatility allow each individual to record a growing value in new cultural experiences, due to her/his growing ability to enjoy creative languages, styles, messages and meanings. This holds for every field included in the wide and diversified system that we label 'culture'. Opera fully belongs to it. Figures emphasizing the prevailing cultural participation of adult and 'senior' consumers[11] simply confirm that a long past experience is a powerful source of intensification for cultural experience.[12] This does not imply any preference for static opera staging, however: age is not necessarily the source of acritical and mummified views. The value of opera for contemporary society can be investigated, considering the perceptive, emotional and cognitive features of our time, as many opera houses are already experiencing in many countries. No product is being kept frozen for years, simply ignoring individuals' and society's changing needs and desires; if this is true even for merely functional products, it is much more important for products and actions whose core profile is creative and dialogic such as opera and the rest of cultural production.

As mentioned earlier, at the turn of the past century opera gradually lost its appeal, being replaced by more technologically advanced media such as radio, cinema and TV. Society simply started to craft new languages, and the period included within the two world wars radically and irreversibly affected cultural values, styles and expectations. Having enjoyed the position of the main entertainment for the bourgeois class, opera revealed itself as a magnificent and still seductive witness of the past and its staging ended up emphasizing preservation rather than creative innovation. Opera was not at all rejected by a barbaric new society, it simply was not inclined to adapt itself to the emerging expectations, whose complexity was satisfied by jazz and—eventually—rock music, cinema and television.[13]

This strongly changed the market options for opera, which no longer prevailed as the effective response to the demand for entertainment, becoming instead a major source for cultural and intellectual satisfaction for only a small proportion of the twentieth century's society. Public funding gradually dominated the sources of finance for opera. Box office revenues had never been sufficient, even in the glorious period when opera was the most prominent form of shared art; even then it relied on financial support from the rich and powerful, however. Eventually that source faded, giving a growing importance to either public funding (in the European experience) or a combination of corporate sponsorship and individual donations (in the US experience).

---

[11]However, the 'old' label can be given to various age brackets, also due to the increase of life expectation. Opera still records a prevailing proportion of over-50 consumers: recent evidence from the Metropolitan Opera audience reveals that subscribers' average age has slightly declined from 66.4 (2005) to 64.8 (2011). Including also occasional tickets, the overall audience age dropped from 60.4 (2005) to 57.7 (2011). Still much has to be done in order for younger (and therefore 'longer') consumers to raise (Glickel 2011).

[12]Income and education—whose high level usually corresponds to cultural participation—should be considered effective sources for the removal of constraints rather than actual motivations of cultural consumption.

[13]Paradoxically, the success of musical shows such as *Jesus Christ Superstar*, The *Phantom of the Opera* and the like (the list is quite long) should make it clear that the semantic and dramaturgic structure of musical theatre itself does not elicit hostility per se.

Opera is endowed with powerful dramaturgic dynamics, expressed in a cross-media technical and semantic framework; the plots have always been attractive for audiences of every time, they still provide writers and playwrights with solid inspiration; music is normally 'stolen' by movies, TV shows and advertisements, confirming opera's emotional strength. Properly addressed at contemporary society opera can enjoy a progressive increase in its audience. Some experiences (among which English National Opera, Teatro Real de Madrid, Fondazione Teatro Comunale di Bologna) are reshaping their seasons including many contemporary operas and hiring innovative stage directors. A few simple tools such as the students' last minute or the 'tweetseats'[14] are proving successful and their systematic adoption can attract new spectators who simply did never have any opera experience.

A wider and possibly heterogeneous audiences could represent a credible source for individual donations (in the US experience they represent the highest proportion of funds coming from the private sector), and would justify a new approach to public funding. Instead of mechanically rescuing opera from failure, it could offer a strategic incentive able to reward the flows of unfungible benefits generated by opera houses and opera production and encourage entrepreneurial responsibility on the part of opera decision-makers. The present features of public funding may act as an incentive to immobility or even to waste. According to Italian legislation, the amount of public subsidy depends upon the social security expenditure,[15] that is, upon the labour force, which represents a clear and powerful incentive to over-employment.[16]

In recent years opera performance has generated a diversified spillover of objects, services and actions to be sold in the market, not exclusively to the actual audience; the spread of digital channels and habits is multiplying the ways to expand opera in different markets, from cinema to web streaming; the opportunity to raise revenues is certainly much wider than the box office performance. New technologies offer a clear evidence of how unfounded Baumol's law conclusions are; in fact, opera houses are able to expand their market options diffusing their productions in movie theatres or through websites, showing that technology can be a helpful channel to address a wider audience.

---

[14] Adopted in 2015 by Arena di Verona, Opera di Firenze and Teatro Comunale di Bologna, the tweetseats allow spectators with a certain number of followers on Twitter to access opera for a very cheap ticket price, with the only condition that they will tweet their feelings and emotions, or simply tell the story, in real time, during the opera. This does not bother the rest of the audience (the tweetseats are in a specific area of the house), and conveys powerful emotional messages to non-attenders.

[15] In Italy, a mechanism aimed at establishing the amount of public subsidies to be given to each recipient active in the performing arts sector (whose final level partially depends upon some quality indicators) was introduced in Italy by the act n. 800, 14th August, 1967 still in effect.

[16] Also in Italy, the legislative decree n. 91, 8th August, 2013 prescribes the reduction of employees in the state financed opera foundations, due to their excess dimensions.

4   Public Action: Strategic Goals and Selective Tools

Public action should be crafted within a strategic framework in which institutional goals clearly determine the criteria and mechanisms for evaluation and sanctions. Potential and actual recipients should understand that their activity is contributing to the pursuit of public institutional goals. In the case of opera, this does not necessarily imply any influence upon the creative and expressive freedom of both the organisations and the individuals active in the system. Rather, it requires accountability, responsibility, possibly also an ambitious approach in seducing a complex society; at the same time it can avoid the usual self-referential view of many cultural professionals, who tend to justify their economic failures in the light of the imaginary ignorance of contemporary society.

Although public funding of the arts is often subject to critical views in response to a wider and more complex interpretation of the role and limits of public action in the economy, its basic features should be determined in the light of specific goals. As argued above, public subsidies merely aimed at opera survival actually lack any incentives; the identification of precise goals for public action can grant transparent and effective methods and tools. The present dynamics of opera exclude a wide proportion of society from its enjoyment (and therefore its appreciation and appraisal), require a traditional and static education and training for its professionals, and consider quality as the result of a conventional experts' evaluation. This may gradually widen the gap between opera and society, and drain its opportunity to address a growing audience.

Accordingly, public funds should aim at increasing access, innovation and excellence, as highlighted in Peacock (1994). These goals are formally stated in laws and regulations on public funding of the arts in most countries[17]; they are normally neglected due to the uncomfortable and delicate balance between productive choices and artistic freedom. The actual pursuit of these goals implies specific actions: access can be usefully pursued through a more even geographical distribution of opera, including devoting public buildings and areas to opera performances; at the same time it needs programmes addressed to new consumers, with a preference for young people whose time horizon is much longer, granting a more intensive 'addiction'. Innovation can be beneficial for both human resources, whose value will be raised by the adoption of new technologies, and the audience, whose appreciation will be enhanced by a more advanced expressive language from the musical and visual perspectives. Excellence depends upon professionality of artists and technicians, consistency with the cultural text, and the accessibility of opera's content. The belief that high quality culture can be digested only by the few is just a comfortable commonplace.

---

[17]With the notable exception of the UK, where they are formalised through funding agreements with each organisation in receipt of public subsidy in accordance with its agreed mission (see Towse 2001). Since 1989, the Arts Council has required its clients to include 'outreach' work in that mission.

The pursuit of increased access, innovation and excellence requires specific tools, possibly avoiding expert evaluation. The widespread convention of appointing commissions to provide public decision-makers with rankings among the potential recipients of public subsidies is simply the exercise of censorship: public funds depend upon such a subjective evaluation, and even their amount may be established according to the degree of experts' appreciation. In a democratic framework such a system should be banned. The challenge is to adopt effective tools in order for public action to provide opera with a sound basis without weakening its need to face the demand, to pursue qualitative goals, and to engage in audience promotion. That way the collective demand for culture can be consistently combined with its market orientation.

Among the major goals of subsidies is to help opera houses keep prices at a reasonable level, avoiding increases that could discourage demand and therefore lead to the contraction and the eventual extinction of opera, according to the apocalyptic view introduced by Baumol's disease. Prices are already varied in a wide range in every opera house; in any case their likely influence upon consumer choice is not mechanically linear, as Blaug (1978) clearly argues. Nevertheless, in order for the less wealthy audience to be attracted, the accessibility issue should be faced. According to an audience-oriented view this can be made possible shifting subsidies from the supply side to demand, through the introduction of vouchers aimed at making opera affordable for the low-income consumers. The value of vouchers would exactly compensate the gap between the market price and consumer's ability-to-pay with producers only being refunded for the missing proportion of price only for those who actually attended performances.[18]

The choice would therefore be left to demand: even the same level of public expenditure for vouchers would not imply any preferences among producers. In that way censorship would be avoided, the simple market appreciation would gain importance. From an abstract perspective the voucher scheme works, and in any case it appears preferable to the existing supply subsidies schemes. Distribution of public funds supporting existing demand has to be avoided, however. There are some weaknesses, as Peacock (1994) acknowledges: consumers may tend to self-select forming clusters of homogeneous demanders, producers' choice could strongly depend upon the existing pattern of tastes and taste formation could be limited and even eventually halted by the progressive draining of pluralism and diversification of the arts supply. This has been the main weakness of school vouchers where they have been actually introduced and made operational.[19] A further option could refer to a major feature of opera production: asymmetric information in both forms of adverse selection and moral hazard.[20] The process

---

[18]A topic discussed in detail in Forte's chapter in this book.

[19]The discussion on education vouchers has been intensive and sometimes driven by political convictions; for a sharp non-prejudicial analysis see Blaug (1984). Such problems could be faced with a selective design of the voucher mechanisms aimed at keeping pluralism in supply.

[20]For an extensive discussion on asymmetric information and its implications in the arts sector see Trimarchi (1993), where also the 'plasticity' issue is examined.

of opera production process is also endowed with a generous 'plasticity', in the light of which the same opera can be staged (produced) in a variety of ways without affecting its consistency. When the output cannot be effectively monitored it is preferable to anticipate public action upon inputs,[21] introducing in-kind subsidies, such as infrastructure (buildings, spaces, material inputs), audience dynamics (combining school programs with art projects and activities) aimed at increasing awareness; access to international markets (assessing quality and reliability of producers), technological endowment (wide band, connections, high-tech tools) aimed at innovation; human capital (on-the-job training, hybridization of skills and competences), access to credit (granting bank transactions) aimed at excellence.

The prevailing weight of in-kind support can relieve opera from many fixed costs, and provide it with skills, competences and tools able to improve its production and the relationship with the consumer. This does not imply the absence of financial subsidies; their coexistence with input support allows opera producers to allocate the tools of public action in order for input support to cover capital and current expenditure devoted to ordinary operations, and financial subsidies at feeding projects, and specific actions. In that way financial subsidies could depend upon the increase of audience through time, encouraging opera to stimulate a wider demand whose rise would be directly awarded by a corresponding rise in the amount of an ad hoc subsidy. The combination of input support and gradual monetary subsidies could provide opera with powerful incentives aimed at entrepreneurship and market effectiveness.

5   Concluding Remarks: A Future for Opera?

The system of funding presently adopted for the performing arts and opera sector in the Italian experience proves weak and often contradictory, acting as a powerful disincentive to innovation and strategy, since it supports the survival of the recipients rather than aiming at the needed equilibrated combination of public endorsement and entrepreneurial strategy. Cultural policy should refuse paternalistic action such as financial subsidies merely aimed at keeping the arts supply alive, independently of its impact upon demand. Refusal can be theoretically justified by both the philosophical framework based upon free choice, and therefore reluctance to believe in supply-induced reactions of demand, and the empirical awareness of the weak incentives associated with financial support of producers. If anything, subsidies should aim at facilitating choice and access: cultural addiction would do the rest. Whatever the area, the public sector should encourage any free and responsible choice aimed at facing society's reaction and market appreciation without relying upon ex ante monetary support.

---

[21] See Laffont and Martimort (2002).

The non-selective nature of the existing forms of support to opera and the performing arts may generate further problems, introducing waste and rents: in the arts system bad public action drives out good public action. Peacock (2000: 190) explicitly observes that

> the lack of correspondence between the prescriptions derived from welfare economics and the widespread intervention of governments in arts provision is the signal given to public choice economists (...) that attempts to rectify market failure may be frustrated by government failure.

Output subsidies imply quite a complex bureaucratic framework, with the likely effect of raising the opacity of public decision-making processes; input subsidies are transparent, since they do not depend upon any aesthetic and bureaucratic evaluation.

Moreover, the effective design of public action aimed at increasing access, innovation, and excellence can offset the contradictions between the map of social benefits on one hand, and income distribution on the other:

> The major question (...) is how the benefits of live performance can be diffused so that the poor of today and tomorrow are both able and willing to have access to them and are not to be asked to support the rich today and the sons of the rich tomorrow, and in the richest areas of the country (Peacock 1969: 331).

It may be important to grant the survival of cultural organisations, since it keeps employment and it can generate relevant exchanges; nevertheless, in a democratic system citizens/taxpayers must prevail.

The introduction of wider autonomy and responsibility in opera and performing arts production would give a growing importance to market dynamics and therefore could weaken the opera and performing arts organisations whose programs appear to be less seductive for wide audiences: experimental productions, neglected styles, innovative languages normally attract quite a limited number of spectators and therefore their box office revenues could prove insufficient in absence of financial subsidies granting deficit coverage. Such a danger is certainly possible in a steady society. In the recent years a growing interest for culture and the arts is being recorded; although an encouraging trend will be slow and gradual, the emerging economic and social paradigm offers new perspectives due to the rising value of knowledge, experience and relationship.

Opera is widening its productive and semantic scope and 'invading' urban spaces: recently the Teatro alla Scala performed *L'Elisir d'Amore* by Donizetti at Malpensa Milan Airport, and the Santa Cecilia Foundation started a long program of concerts at Fiumicino Rome Airport. The Palermo Teatro Massimo regularly offers outdoor live broadcasts of its productions, as many opera houses do in other countries. Language is being expanded, as the 'twitter opera' is being experienced in the 'Ignite' seasons at London Royal Opera House Covent Garden.[22] The

---

[22]See Carbone and Trimarchi (2012) for a discussion on crowdsourced opera as a form of 'commons', counterbalancing widespread creativity and intellectual property rights.

growing interest in culture showed by contemporary society, associated with the effort of opera houses aimed at expanding their relationships with a complex and dynamic audience, can represent an important signal of wider market options, and therefore for the need to re-design cultural policy aimed at supporting opera. In that way the present paternalistic and acritical mechanisms based upon mere deficit coverage could be substituted with input subsidies which would induce a higher attention to opera demand; monetary subsidies which would award measurable economic performances such as the increase in occasional spectators, the export of already staged productions, and so on; encouragement of individual donations and corporate sponsorship through accurate tax relief that could attract innovative forms of private funding. This would not imply any rise in the total amount of public expenditure devoted to opera; the eventual positive trend in the degree of sustainability of the opera system, associated to the growing role of input support, could require a decreasing amount of public funds. Opera would (partially) return to the market and it would depend upon society's choice, overcoming the typical paternalistic function of public funding, often "designed to give the public not what it wants but what it ought to have." (Peacock 1969: 323)

References

Baumol W, Bowen WG (1966) Performing arts: the economic dilemma. Twentieth Century Fund, New York

Blaug M (1978) Why are Covent Garden seat prices so high? J Cult Econ 2(1):1–20

Blaug M (1984) Educational vouchers—it all depends on what you mean. In: Le Grand J, Robinson R (eds) Privatisation and the welfare state. Allen and Unwin, London

Carbone A, Trimarchi M (2012) Opera 2.0: crowdsourcing the stage. In: Bertacchini E, Bravo G, Marrelli M, Santagata W (eds) Cultural commons. A new perspective on the production and evolution of cultures. Edward Elgar, Cheltenham, UK, pp 228–240

Cowen T (1996) Why I do not believe in the cost disease. J Cult Econ 20:207–214

Eurobarometer (2003) New Europeans and culture. Public opinion in the candidate countries. European Commission, Bruxelles

Eurobarometer (2013) Cultural access and participation. European Commission, Bruxelles

Glickel J (2011) Met opera inaccurately reports drop in audience age, reports says. DNA Info, 21 Feb 2011. www.dnainfo.com

Heilbrun J (2001) Empirical evidence of a decline in repertory diversity among American opera companies 1991/1992 to 1997/1998. J Cult Econ 25(1):63–72

Holler MJ (2015) Welfare, preferences and the reconstruction of desires. Int J Soc Econ 42(5):447–458

Laffont JJ, Martimort D (2002) The theory of incentives: the principal-agent model. Princeton University Press, Princeton

Peacock AT (1969) Welfare economics and public subsidies to the arts. Manchester Sch Econ Soc Stud 37:323–335

Peacock AT (1994) The design and operation of public funding of the arts: an economist's view. In: Peacock AT, Rizzo I (eds) Cultural economics and cultural policies. Kluwer, Dordrecht, pp 67–84

Peacock AT (2000) Public financing of the arts in England. Fiscal Stud 21(2):171–205

Stigler GJ, Becker GS (1977) De Gustibus Non Est Disputandum. Am Econ Rev 67(2):76–90

Swanson S, Davis J, Zhao Y (2008) Art for art's sake? An examination of motives for arts performance attendance. Nonprofit Voluntary Sector Q 37:300–323

Towse R (ed) (1997) Baumol's cost disease. The arts and other victims. Edward Elgar, Cheltenham, UK

Towse R (2001) Quis Custodiet? Managing the management: the case of the Royal Opera House Covent Garden. Int J Arts Manag 3(30):38–50

Towse R (2011) Opera and ballet. In: Towse R (ed) A handbook of cultural economics, 2nd edn. Edward Elgar, Cheltenham, UK, pp 313–319

Trimarchi M (1993) Economia e cultura. Organizzazione e finanziamento delle istituzioni culturali. Franco Angeli, Milano

Trimarchi M (2014a) Do the arts dream of society? The secret war of languages. Tafter J n. 76. www.tafterjournal.it. Accessed 9 Oct 2015

Trimarchi M (2014b) Urbs et Civitas: una mappa della cultura. In: De Biase F (ed) I pubblici della cultura. Audience development, audience engagement. Franco Angeli, Milano, pp 138–150

Part III
Economics and Cultural Heritage

Towards More Innovative Museums

Bruno S. Frey and Lasse Steiner

Abstract The situation in which museums find themselves is not unlike many other parts of society. Creative changes come to mind but are restricted by tradition, bureaucratic rules, as well as self-imposed constraints by positioning as icons and engaging in a particular architecture. This chapter discusses several suggestions for innovative moves such as flexibility in pricing, broader lending activities, or the possibility to sell objects.

1 Where Can Museums Be More Innovative?

According to the weekly Economist (2013), "museums are doing amazingly well… but can they keep the visitors coming?" Museums are in strong competition to other cultural institutions, the entertainment industry, and other attractions such as the large number of festivals of one form or other or sites listed in the United Nations World Heritage List (Frey and Steiner 2011).

There is also the question whether the young generation growing up with the internet, so called digital natives, is still so much interested in seeing original artworks, often at high cost and hassle. They may prefer to visit museum collections online. Such change in behaviour would fundamentally change the role of museums. The actual place is no longer relevant; it simply represents the origin where the online experience comes from. Superstar museums (Frey 1998) may lose importance compared to the virtual experience. As so often, it may be argued that exactly the opposite takes place. The online consumption of art may induce people to seek the 'real' experience of seeing the original art collected in museums. This

B.S. Frey (✉)
University of Basel, Basel, Switzerland

CREMA—Center for Research in Economics, Management and the Arts, Zürich, Switzerland
e-mail: bruno.frey@econ.uzh.ch

L. Steiner
CREMA—Center for Research in Economics, Management and the Arts, Zürich, Switzerland
e-mail: lasse.steiner@econ.uzh.ch

© Springer International Publishing Switzerland 2016   187
I. Rizzo, R. Towse (eds.), *The Artful Economist*,
DOI 10.1007/978-3-319-40637-4_11

seems to be rather unlikely because the online presentation of art is of high quality, and the art objects may be seen more clearly than the original in the museum. A pertinent example is the *Mona Lisa* (*Gioconda*) in the Louvre. The rather small painting is almost impossible to see due to the hundreds of admirers blocking the view.

Our chapter considers various possibilities to make museums more innovative and therefore more attractive to visitors, and discusses the implications. We distinguish three different areas: Sect. 2 flexibility in pricing; Sect. 3 broader lending activities; Sect. 4 selling objects.

The possibilities for innovations in these areas will now be discussed in turn based on the economic theory of museums as summarized in Frey and Meier (2006).

2 Flexibility in Pricing

2.1 Entry Prices

Most museums use differentiated prices to enter the museum. They focus on personal attributes, in particular offering lower entry prices for young and senior visitors, as well as for members of the respective museum society. In contrast, economists suggest that the additional cost produced by a visitor (the marginal cost) and the extent of reaction to price changes (price elasticity of demand) should be taken into account. When the marginal cost of admitting one more visitor is zero it is economically efficient to offer free entry (Peacock and Godfrey 1974). This holds especially for institutions operating below full capacity. The quality of a visit deteriorates when too many people want to see an exhibition. Overcrowding results in queuing, noise, and even an inability to see the objects on display. Empirical evidence suggests that congestion costs can be significant. Maddison and Foster (2003) estimated the congestion cost posed by the marginal visitors to the British Museum to be as high as £8.05. Thus, if a museum is rather empty in the morning hours, the marginal cost (direct cost and congestion cost) of a visitor is essentially zero; there are only fixed costs of opening the museum and guarding the objects exhibited. From that perspective, no entry price should be asked because the museum is not burdened while the visitors enjoy a welfare gain by being able to see the exhibits. Entry prices should also be discarded in those periods of the year in which there are few visitors.

Potential and actual visitors react quite differently to changes in entry price. In general, persons with higher income, education and age are less sensitive to a price increase. In contrast, families with children, low-income groups, persons with low education and the unemployed are likely to reduce their visits to a museum if the entry price is increased. Accordingly, these groups of persons could be attracted to visit a museum by asking a lower price.

Tourists have a low price elasticity, in particular for famous museums. To visit the Louvre when in Paris, the Prado when in Madrid, and the Vatican Museums when in Rome belongs to 'the programme' of most, if not all, organized tours as well as that of individual tourists. In many cases, tourists have spent large amounts of money to arrive at these and other cities, so that even a high entry price is small compared to these other costs. As a consequence, tourists could be asked a higher price than locals. This can also be justified by the fact that the locals pay income taxes with which museums to a large extent are financed. Today price discrimination based on residency is mainly applied by museums in developing countries, such as the National Museum of Costa Rica[1] or the temples of Angkor Wat in Cambodia.[2]

Few museums in developed countries sufficiently exploit the opportunity to ask tourists higher prices than locals. Annual cards may, to a limited extent, have such function. This is all the more surprising in the case of superstar museums such as the Louvre, Prado, the National Gallery in London, the *Kunsthistorische* Museum in Vienna, or the Vatican Museums. Most of the year, if not always, there are long queues of potential visitors. Instead of raising price and therewith securing higher revenue, admittance is rationed by having to book in advance on the internet. As there are nevertheless long waiting lines, scalpers get the opportunity to make money by selling overpriced tickets on the black market or even places at the beginning of the queue. Visitors' willingness to pay for a more quick entry (instead of having to wait often in the plain sun) does in this case not benefit the museum but rather only the scalpers. The scarcity of space in these superstar museums should be rationed off by setting higher prices for tourists. This need not be to the disadvantage to tourists as a whole because the museum could use the additional revenue to extend the opening hours, or to enlarge the facilities. At the same time the museums could set lower prices for locals but preferably only when the museums are less crowded. Locals have more opportunity than tourists to choose the time at which they wish to visit a museum.

Another way to skim the willingness-to-pay of visitors, and therewith increase welfare (through additional revenue for the museum) is to charge different prices for two different waiting lines: one with a higher price and a shorter waiting queue and another with a lower price and a longer queue. Having two separate entry points into the museum approximates the differentiation between people with a low price elasticity of demand, who should be charged higher prices than those with a high elasticity of demand.

---

[1]http://www.museocostarica.go.cr/en_en/visitas/horarios-y-tarifas-de-visitas.html?Itemid=110.

[2]http://www.telegraph.co.uk/travel/travelnews/11434648/Should-foreign-tourists-pay-more-than-locals.html.

2.2 Exit Prices

Exit prices are an innovative way to charge visitors of a museum (see also Frey and
Steiner 2012). Instead of charging visitors when they enter the museum, exit prices
are charged them when they leave it. The more time someone spends in the
museum, the higher the price she or he pays. Exit prices (the so-called car park
model) have rarely been considered in the debate about museum admission fees so
far. This is surprising, as they lower the entry barrier to visit and attracting more
visitors is one important goal of many museums.

To enable visitors to make a well-considered decision on the length of time to
stay, museums would have to make sure that visitors knew that there was an exit
price before they entered. The museum may indicate every 30 min costs 5 euros.
The price does not have to be calculated discretely; it also can be calculated
continuously, for example, per minute. The price a visitor has to pay for an
additional minute can be constant or decrease with time. Decreasing rates encourage a longer visit since the average-cost-per-minute is decreasing. The scheme is
not difficult from the administrative point of view as machines can easily do the
pricing. One change is that a booth would have to be moved to the exit.

One critical but usually disregarded characteristic of a museum is that the visit is
an experience good. Experience goods pose difficulties for consumers in accurately
making consumption choices, as it is difficult to observe product characteristics,
such as quality, in advance (Nelson 1970). This characteristic can justify charging
the visitors of a museum when they leave. Thus, exit prices have the major
advantage that they take into account how satisfied the visitors were with the visit
to the museum. As a side effect of being more satisfied, visitors may be willing to
spend more money at the museum shops and restaurant. Moreover, an exit price is
considered to be less unfair than an entry price. Those staying longer have profited
more and may find it fair to pay more than somebody staying only for a short period.

Exit prices also lower the external effects, namely congestion costs, imposed on
other visitors. The more time that a visitor spends in the museum, the more cost she
or he imposes on other visitors in terms of physical stress. A relevant additional cost
refers to the humidification of the air affecting the exhibits in a strongly negative
way. As mentioned above, congestion cost can be significant. In order to account
for the negative effects, it is justified to pay more the longer one stays. Furthermore,
the introduction of an exit price may be a good advertisement for the museum due to
the media coverage of the innovative pricing scheme.

The most common argument against exit prices is the incentive to minimize cost
by rushing through the museum. This conflicts with the idea of a cultural experience
being independent from economic necessities. However, by applying decreasing
marginal rates per minute, the total price a visitor would have to pay has a
maximum boundary (especially if the marginal rate is zero after a certain amount
of time). Even if the visitors lose track of time, they never pay a punitively high
price because there is a maximum price. By explicitly indicating this maximum
price at the entry, the perceived time pressure and incentive to rush can be mitigated

considerably. When discussing potential pressure induced by exit prices, one has to compare them with entry prices. It is possible that there is also emotional stress induced by high entry prices. If visitor have already paid the (high) entry price, they might feel obliged to stay longer than they wanted to.

It has to be mentioned that there are exit-pricing schemes for swimming halls or saunas, which provide joy and satisfaction to their visitors as museums do. Some overcrowded museums with entry prices already have a maximum visiting time, for example 15 min for Da Vinci's Last Supper. This can be seen as anecdotal evidence that paying for a cultural experience based on the amount of time it is enjoyed is acceptable to visitors.

2.3   Voluntary Contributions

In addition to varying the entry and/or exit prices following differences in marginal cost and price elasticities of demand museums may consider inducing visitors to make a voluntary donation. Such a procedure allows museums to raise revenue even when the law prohibits them to impose an entry price (as is the case for many important British museums such as the British Museum in London).

A voluntary contribution can be requested *before entering* a museum. This can, for instance, be done by requiring visitors to get an entry ticket and telling them that they are free to give as little or as much as they choose. Most visitors immediately ask what the "normal" sum is, in which case the museum should provide a price anchor. The cashier has to decide quickly whether to indicate a lower or higher amount depending on the considerations discussed above. It is also possible to ask for an additional (small) sum for a *specific* purpose. For example, the cashiers at the Royal Museum of British Columbia in Victoria asks entrants whether, in addition to the ordinary entry price, they are prepared to pay two Canadian Dollars to 'preserve exhibits'. Most persons (around 80 %) are willing to do so though it seems that 'preservation' belongs to the core activity of a museum and should not be financed by an additional collection (see Noble 1970).

A voluntary contribution can also be asked when persons are *leaving* the museum. It is important to "channel" the persons exiting in order to make them fully aware that they are invited to make a contribution. This could be combined by asking them before leaving to respond to the question "Did you like our museum?" Most visitors are prepared to contribute if they liked the museum as the situation of reciprocity is mildly imposed. Transparent boxes are possibly the best way to secure the greatest donation amounts since people are less likely to put money into 'a black hole' and are affected by the perceived donation behaviour of previous visitors. Unlike museums on the American continent, European and Asian museums rarely actively seek the support by the friends of the museum by providing social occasions, for instance by allowing them to visit a special exhibition first and being guided by an expert of the museum.

3 Broader Lending Activities

The lending activity between museums with the goal to undertake special exhibitions (which today is a major part of the activities of many museums) is *not organized in an explicit market*. It is impossible to find explicit prices for lending objects, for instance on the Internet. Rather, the exchange of objects takes place in an informal way, based on the personal relationships between the directors. Essentially, it is based on a *quid pro quo*: another museum receives an exhibit with the understanding that it is willing to reciprocate in the future. The implicit price is the expectation of reciprocation. Such an informal exchange strengthens the position of the directors, while it excludes outsiders. With few exceptions (for example for Russian museums which are in dire financial conditions) the exchanges are undertaken free of charge but sometimes the lender handles the cost of restoring the object.

The crucial question is whether an explicit market would result in an efficiency gain, and the extent to which it might produce significant external costs. This may well be the case but such costs should be explicitly discussed rather than rejecting the idea out of hand.

Museums exchange originals, that is, the lender wants to have a particular unique object attributed to a particular artist or historical period. This is surprising in view of the fact that today it is possible to produce *identical replicas*. Why should not such a replica be exchanged? Take Michelangelo's *Pietà* which was shipped from the Vatican to New York's World Exhibition. In view of the danger of being negatively affected by the transport or even get lost, an identical copy could have been sent. By definition, the beauty of the *Pietà* is in no way affected because no viewer is able to distinguish it from the original. The normal answer is that a copy does not have the 'aura' of the original. But the concept of 'aura' is highly questionable. For instance, a painting is often attributed an 'aura' even if it later turns out that it is a copy. The term 'aura' thus seems to just mean that it is an attribute of the original. Those arguing with the concept of the 'aura' should therefore carry all the mental cost when an original with its 'aura' gets damaged or is even lost while it is lent out. Would it not be preferable to exchange identical replicas?

The case of the Chauvet Caves shows that a broad range of visitors accepts exhibiting identical copies.[3] The Caves of Chauvet with its unique prehistoric art were discovered in 1994 but immediately concealed to public access. Instead a full-size facsimile of the Cave, the so-called 'Faux Lascaux', was built nearby and creates attracts huge numbers of visitors—who know that they don't get to see the original.

---

[3]See http://www.smithsonianmag.com/history/france-chauvet-cave-makes-grand-debut-180954582/?no-ist, Accessed 5.9.2015.

The exchange of copies would also overcome the legal restrictions faced by many museums prohibited to lend out anything (though such restrictions are not always fully observed).

4 Selling Objects

One of the major goals of museums is to present a well-arranged collection. At the same time, all museums have a stock of holdings with pieces that are not suitable for display. Major museums of art, such as the Prado, never exhibit over 90 % of their holdings. A large part of their collection remains in the vaults for good and is never shown to the public. As an exchange with other museums at present is quite restricted since it depends on the personal relationships of the directors, it would make sense to put the objects never exhibited on the market. This might not be possible with all artworks, as some donations were given with the restriction they should not be sold. The revenue gained would allow museums to acquire objects important for their own collection, or for any other purpose considered important to the museum directorate. At the same time, the objects sold may be a valuable addition to minor museums (see Montias 1973; Grampp 1989). Besides restrictions on donated artworks museums directors often use legal and institutional constraints as a shield to oppose a flexible approach for the sale and purchase of artefacts.[4] Being risk averse, they are not willing to undertake commercial transactions, which would put them under public scrutiny. This is particularly the case if they are allowed to devote the proceeds of sale to the purchase of other artefacts. Relying on public funding does not provide any incentive toward de-accessioning.

The next section deals with the issue whether the innovations suggested have a chance of being put into practice. As will be seen, this is unlikely to be the case.

5 Museums Are Conservative

5.1 Commitment to the Past

Museums are institutions *conserving and cherishing the past*. This is the very reason for their existence. They serve to collect what exists and is considered worth preserving (Peacock 1994). Museums are not future oriented, as they do not create but only preserve (but there are some art galleries that sometimes commission works of art). Despite this inherent feature they may be innovative with respect to the way they present their collections. This seems, however, to be a difficult task for them as shown, for example, by the long time it often took them to

---

[4]This line of thought goes back to Alan Peacock.

introduce cafeterias, restaurants, museum stores, and other amenities to make a museum visit more attractive.

5.2   Government Rules

Another reason why museums are conservative is their *dependence on government*. Institutions matter greatly in that they strongly determine how museum directors and other employees act. Most museums as part of the public sector are heavily subsidized by the government and are subject to many regulations. Large museums in most cases depend crucially on the financial support by government making them subject to a variety of political influences. Smaller museums in most cases have little revenue of their own and therefore are more or less a part of the local government administration. The public sector is known for its conservative tendencies and is rarely considered to be creative and progressive. Indeed, bureaucratic rules strongly restrict the activity space of museums. In the typical European model, if museums are able to raise their revenue by changing its entry or exit pricing, if they get additional voluntary contributions, or if they sell unused parts of their holdings, they run the great risk of losing these additional revenues. In a bureaucratic setting, the various subunits are generally not allowed to keep additional revenues but they are considered to be part of the public revenue solely administered by the central authority. This means that the directorate has little incentive to creatively search for additional revenues even if this was easily possible.

An alternative to reduce the influence of the government as originator of direct subsidies to museums would be to establish a system of vouchers (see Peacock 1993; Frey 2008). The recipients of these vouchers could be, for example, every resident of a country, city or all taxpayers. While the vouchers replace a part—or all—direct government subsidies to museums, their total value could be freely determined. The recipients use the vouchers to pay for access to selected museums the government deems worthy and puts on a corresponding list. The museums can then cash the vouchers they received at the Treasury. Vouchers incentivize museum directors to run exhibitions the population appreciates. These are most likely more innovative than the art preferred by more conservative bureaucrats. Vouchers do not necessarily induce suppliers of art to produce 'popular' art only. They can also display exhibitions only a minority is prepared to spend a large part of their vouchers on. As the directors can keep additional revenues, they are induced to advertise their services in an attractive way (and gain more visitors). Recipients of vouchers have a strong incentive to use them and visit a museum instead of wasting them. Thus, they are a suitable means to attract people who rarely or never visit a museum. Even if a voucher is not used by the recipients themselves, they could be given to a friend or sent to a museum.

Vouchers reflect the preferences of the population more strongly than direct subsidies. They also induce museum managers to cater to non-standard demand for the arts and to be more innovative.

5.3   *Constraints on Behaviour*

A third reason why museums tend to be conservative is partly *self-imposed*. Superstar museums have become icons whose features have been defined by tourist organizations in travel books and advertising. This position is undermined if an iconic museum is very creative as the visitors expect to see a particular kind of museum with a particular kind of exhibition and are disappointed if they are confronted with a 'new' museum.

Many museums pride themselves of their *architecture*. Famous architects are hired to establish uniqueness in order to attract the attention of the public. This mainly applies to superstar museums. A case in point is the spectacular Guggenheim Museum in Bilbao designed by Frank Gehry. The building clearly dominates the content of the exhibitions. There are also less well-known museums tending to rely on architecture as their defining feature. An example is the Beyeler Museum in Basel. It advertises itself as a *Sammlung der Klassischen Moderne im Museumsbau von Renzo Piano* (Museum of Classical Modern Art in a building designed by Renzo Piano). A new architecture such as Renzo Piano's supports creativity but once established the same strong reliance on the architecture reduces the scope for changes.

6   Conclusions

The situation in which museums find themselves is not unlike many other parts of society. Creative changes come to mind but are restricted by tradition, bureaucratic rules, as well as self-imposed constraints by positioning as icons and engaging in a particular architecture.

The suggestions made here for innovative moves as well as other new proposals for museums are therefore unlikely to materialize in the new future. However, newly founded museums have more freedom to pick up some of the ideas proposed here which then puts pressure on the established museums to follow suit. In this indirect way, museums may become more creative over time. A well-rounded discussion of the advantages and disadvantages of creative ideas is a prerequisite for their useful application in the future. It is important to learn from other institutions and countries.

Acknowledgments The authors are grateful for insightful discussions with the Director of the Swiss National Museum in Zurich, Dr. Andreas Spillmann, and a representative of the Royal Museum of British Columbia in Victoria, without implying them in any way with the arguments provided in this chapter. The discussion of exit prices builds on one of our previous papers (see Frey and Steiner 2012). The authors are grateful for helpful remarks especially to Francoise Benhamou, Isidoro Mazza, Anna Mignosa, Margit Osterloh, David Throsby, Ruth Towse, Michele Trimarchi and Ezra Zubrow.

References

Economist (2013) Museums. Temples of delight. December 21

Frey BS (1998) Superstar museums: an economic analysis. J Cult Econ 22:113–125, Reprinted in: Frey BS (2003) Arts and economics. Analysis and cultural policy, 2nd edn. Springer, Berlin, ch 5, pp 49–66

Frey BS (2008) Cities, culture and happiness. World Cities Summit Issue 1:9

Frey BS, Meier M (2006) The economics of museums. In: Ginsburgh V, Throsby D (eds) The handbook of the economics of art and culture, vol 1. Elsevier, Amsterdam, pp 1018–1047

Frey BS, Steiner L (2011) World heritage list: does it make sense? Int J Cult Pol 17:555–573

Frey BS, Steiner L (2012) Pay as you go: a new proposal for museum pricing. Mus Manag Curatorship 27(3):223–235

Grampp WD (1989) Pricing the priceless: art, artists and economics. Basic, New York

Maddison D, Foster T (2003) Valuing congestion costs in the British Museum. Oxf Econ Paper 55:173–190

Montias JM (1973) Are museums betraying the public's trust? Mus News 51:25–31

Nelson P (1970) Information and consumer behavior. J Polit Econ 78:311

Noble JV (1970) Museum manifesto. Mus News April:27–32

Peacock AT (1993) Paying the piper. Culture, music and money. Edinburgh University Press, Edinburgh

Peacock AT (1994) A future for the past: the political economy of heritage. Proc Br Acad 87:189–226

Peacock AT, Godfrey C (1974) The economics of museums and galleries. Lloyds Bank Rev 111 (January):17–28

Technological Perspectives for Cultural Heritage

Ilde Rizzo

Abstract The chapter investigates the effects of technology on the provision of cultural heritage services. A common tenet in the literature is that, because of technology, the scope and the mission of cultural organizations are changing and that overall education and cultural appreciation as well as cultural participation are enhanced. With respect to this conventional wisdom, the chapter offers a systematic analysis of the effects of technological advancements on the demand and supply of cultural heritage services, taking into account their different economic features and having also in mind the differences across cultural organizations (public, private) and their business models. Some empirical evidence drawn from European surveys offers an overview of the potentialities of new technologies for the future of cultural heritage.

1 Introduction

The chapter aims at investigating the effects of technology on the provision of Cultural Heritage (CH) services. A broad concept of CH is used, including built heritage, museums, libraries and archives and the different economic features of the related services—from private to public goods—are outlined. Technologies play many different roles for CH, ranging from diagnostics, conservation and restoration to Information and Communication Technology (ICT). Here, attention is mainly, though not exclusively, paid to digitization and ICT applications to CH. It is widely agreed that digital technologies play an important role for the innovation of the cultural sector (Borowiecki and Navarrete 2015) and that the effects of ICT on the cost structure, digital distribution and payment mechanisms have made it profitable to develop new business models in the cultural sector (Towse and Handke 2013).

When moving to the CH sector, the same conclusions cannot be taken for granted and the investigation of the effects of ICT requires the analysis of its

I. Rizzo (✉)
Department of Economics and Business, University of Catania, Catania, Italy
e-mail: rizzor@unict.it

© Springer International Publishing Switzerland 2016
I. Rizzo, R. Towse (eds.), *The Artful Economist*,
DOI 10.1007/978-3-319-40637-4_12

197

specific features. In fact, most CH organizations are somehow publicly funded and, therefore, have a mission to increase society's well-being, promoting, among the other things, education, engagement with society, innovation and knowledge, as well social inclusion and participation. Also in this field, it is widely agreed that ICT technologies bring about potentialities for new and more engaged audiences, new developments for art forms, new sources of economic and cultural value and new business models (Bakhshi and Throsby 2012). A common tenet in the literature seems to be that, because of technology, positive changes can be foreseen in terms of the scope and the mission of cultural organizations and that, overall, education and cultural appreciation as well as cultural participation are likely to increase.

With respect to this conventional wisdom, the chapter sketches the main effects of technological advancements on the demand and supply of CH services, taking into account the economic features of cultural services, the differences across cultural organizations (public, private) and their business models. At the same time, the inequality effects related to the occurrence of a cultural 'digital divide', across social groups and CH institutions, is outlined. From that perspective, some attention is also paid to the features of the decision-making process and to the role of ICT experts. Some empirical evidence drawn on European surveys, though drawn from a limited database, offers an overview of the potentialities for innovation and the future of CH, as well as some suggestions on the necessary research developments. The chapter is organised as follows: Sect. 2 investigates the impact of technological progress on the demand and supply of cultural goods and services and analyses how technological choices fit within the institutions' decision-making process; Sect. 3 offers some empirical evidence at European level of the technological behaviour of cultural institutions; Sect. 4 provides some policy implications and concluding remarks.

2   Economic Effects of Technology on Demand and Supply of CH

When dealing with technologies in the cultural sector one faces a very wide array of possible definitions. In very general terms, following Potts (2014: 218), technology can be defined "as a space that enables some transformation possibility", encompassing both the producer and consumer sides. Technologies play many different roles for CH and it is not easy to list all of them, ranging from diagnostics, conservation and restoration to ICT. Examples of ICT for cultural heritage are websites, mobile applications (based on the use of mobile devices, such as smart phones and tablet computers), and virtual reconstructions. In what follows we concentrate attention on digitization[1] and ICT applications, with the Internet revolution in the background.

---

[1]The concept of digitalization has evolved beyond the conversion of an analogue signal to a digital one and includes the whole system of digital platforms and standards (Henten and Tadayoni 2011).

2.1   Effects on Demand

Digital technologies and the Internet revolution have had a remarkable effect on the modes of approaching and consuming cultural heritage in recent years and significant changes have occurred not only in terms of access, sharing and re-use of all types of CH but also in terms of creation, participation, interaction and learning.

Cultural consumption patterns have changed, in quantitative and qualitative terms. In Western countries, electronic and digital media consumption of cultural goods has become very frequent and is increasing through time; according to NEA (2015), in the United States, 71 % of the adult population consumed art through electronic media in 2012 (much higher than the 54 % in 2002)[2] while the rate of attendance at live 'benchmark activities'[3] dropped from 39 % in 2002 to 33 % in 2012. Not surprisingly, young adults were more likely than adults in general to use electronic media to view, listen to, create, share, or edit art (80 %). Also in the European Union (EU) cultural consumption rates diminished significantly in recent years (with the only exception of cinema): for instance, 41 % visited a museum or a gallery in 2007 and that dropped to 37 % in 2013.[4] With respect to digital consumption, data are less detailed and the same survey shows that more than half of all Europeans use the Internet for cultural purposes, with a third doing so at least once a week (Da Milano and Righolt 2015).

According to Potts (2014: 216), "technological change does not just mean more, but also means different". Thus, variety and diversity in cultural consumption possibilities are increased; in fact, a new technology introduces new goods and/or enlarges the access to a wider range of cultural goods and services. Technology enlarges the possibility of distributing information about heritage and of improving knowledge about it. In fact, as result of the effort which many cultural institutions devote to the construction and update of their websites, a wide range of information becomes available for users, ranging from basic information about the services provided (opening hours, accessibility, prices, special events, and so on) to more elaborate ones about the heritage content. Thus, anyone can virtually visit a museum, an exhibition or an archaeological site while staying at home.

A side effect of technology might be the reduction of the asymmetric information, which characterizes the CH field (Rizzo 2011): the consumers' capability of comparing and valuating CH is likely to increase, limiting the overwhelming influence of

---

[2]The USA Survey of Public Participation in the Arts examines attendance at performing arts events (such as music, dance, or theater performances, or outdoor performing arts festivals) and at visual arts events or activities (such as art museums or galleries, craft fairs, and sites with historic or design value).

[3]'Benchmark' activities are: jazz events, classical music performances, opera, musical plays, non-musical plays, ballet, and art museums or galleries. These activities are identified as 'benchmark' because participation in them has been tracked since 1982.

[4]Analogously, 54% visited an historical monument or site in 2007 and 52% in 2013. This decrease is not only linked to the economic crisis since a major part of the EU population indicates lack of interest and time as major barriers to attendance.

experts.[5] Moreover, the possibility for public scrutiny, surveys and public enquiries increases, thereby introducing challenging incentives for suppliers so that they take into account the preferences of the public and become more accountable.

As Navarrete (2013) suggests, CH has become a marketable asset in the information market. Demand for digital cultural heritage increasingly relies on the search for the right information, in the right format, at the right place and time. The digital revolution has caused a shift from a distributor model, which is based on controlled access, to a network economy model, which relies on having large amounts of information available and a large number of users. Relationships between producers and consumers are more direct and new intermediaries manage information flows and control the interfaces through which users enter the network (Farchy 2011). A particular feature is that information is usually specialized since it is based not only on images but also on metadata, which describe the object and the context.

Peacock (1994: 7) emphasized the consumer's role as the 'producer' of her own utility in his definition of cultural heritage as "an intangible service increasing the utility of consumers, in which historic buildings and artefacts are inputs". Peacock's view somehow anticipates the wide range of possibilities of combining heritage inputs generated by technology. 'Virtual' individual cultural experiences can be replicated and may differ, depending on the consumer's ability to appreciate them, rather than on the changes in the features of the heritage itself (Peacock and Rizzo 2008). Digital technologies improve the understanding of heritage because they enlarge the possibilities for contextualising and stimulating active consumption: for instance, by organizing available metadata, users can create their own virtual collection and learn the stories related to each item.

Bakhshi and Throsby (2010) summarise the new dimensions of cultural experience linked to the technological change: interactivity (the possibility of two-way communication with users of cultural goods); convergence (for example, the possibility of accessing the good without time and space constraints) and connectivity (for example, direct communication between users and suppliers). New possibilities for participation and involvement of the audience—such as collaboration and co-curation—as well as for interaction with their community are also feasible. It is not possible to determine how active individuals actually are in their Internet access to cultural content and information; digital engagement is not necessarily less active than 'real time' attendance.

'Virtual' consumption is usually free except for the opportunity cost of time in terms of the reduction in other substitute activities. As cultural goods are experience goods, the strategy of free supply[6] can be an effective promotional tool. Virtual consumption makes the public more familiar with cultural content, generates a learning effect, thus encouraging future (paid for) consumption. In addition, other benefits may arise from knowledge transfers and from a technologically dynamic creative economy. For example, some museums, such as the Metropolitan Museum

---

[5]See below, para 2.3.
[6]The changing strategies of cultural producers are examined in Sect. 2.3.

of Art in New York and the Rijksmuseum in Amsterdam, provide open access to content (text, video, photo, music) generated by museum visitors on social networks, encouraging cultural exchange and communication among people. At the same time, the increase in heritage consumption and understanding is likely to positively affect the consumption of complementary goods.

Whether virtual visits are a substitute or a complement to real-time experience is an open question. As Guccio et al. (2016) argue, substitution or complementarity very much depends on the type of cultural consumption and on the underlying motivation. Substitution is more likely to occur for institutions such as archives or libraries where the motivation of study or research makes the access to a digitised document of good quality almost equivalent to the seeing the original. For museums or CH sites, where visits are mainly motivated by entertainment, the enjoyment deriving from the 'real' experience is unlikely to be substituted by a digital copy of a painting or by a virtual tour. In that context, Peacock (2006: 1138) has argued that technological changes are likely to create a "globalization of culture". Technological changes, rather than exerting a substitution effect on real visits to heritage sites or on performance attendance, seem to operate as a form of advertisement. As a side effect, they can generate international mobility of artistic productions and exhibitions, as well as of tourists, increasing the demand for heritage. However, there is no conclusive evidence across the different types of CH institutions, though there is some evidence that complementarity is likely to occur (Ateca-Amestoy and Castiglione 2014; Styliani et al. 2009). This is a topic for which more research is needed.

Saying that there are no space, time or physical constraints for cultural consumption and that cultural consumers are likely to be empowered does not necessarily imply that all potential users enjoy the same accessibility, however. In fact, an important question is whether electronic media lead to a real democratization of access or whether, contrary to conventional wisdom, they may increase inequalities and, therefore, worsen the position of the most disadvantaged.

There is evidence of a 'digital divide' in the access to cultural content depending on education, income, gender and age, with behavioural differences between digital 'natives' and the rest of the population (Ateca-Amestoy and Castiglione 2015). More generally, the 'digital divide' refers to individual disparities associated with socioeconomic resources, cognitive skills, demographic and motivational (trust in media) characteristics as well as with disparities related to ethnicity/race (Norris and Inglehart 2013).[7] Overall, the 'divide' implies the unequal representation of different social groups with negative effects in terms of social inclusion and participation. The 'divide' also depends on the different capabilities of individuals in evaluating the reliability and legitimacy of the sources of information that are related to their social status and level of education and have significant equity implications, which have not been adequately investigated and addressed so far (Krebs 2012).

---

[7]OECD (2001) outlines significant differences in the Internet access in the United States across groups from different racial, ethnic and cultural backgrounds which tend to persist through time.

2.2   Effects on Supply

Technology also affects cultural heritage supply in different dimensions. New approaches to detection and methods for recording the results strongly affect archaeological discoveries and, at the same time, heritage preservation benefits from improved techniques. In other words, because of technological changes, public goods, such as knowledge and preservation, become more widely available. ICT influences two crucial economic characteristics of CH services: 'rivalness' and 'excludability' (Giardina et al. 2016). In general terms, technology is likely to reduce 'rivalness' between conflicting objectives, such as preservation versus use. Actual use of specific heritage items, which are subject to deterioration (such as the visit to a heritage site, the consultation of a document or of a book) can make 'virtual' ones desirable. Taking an extreme view, one might say that technology reduces the economic constraints on the transmission of heritage to the future. If the material existence of an artefact and its physical transmission to future generations have no value *per se*, technology might offer an extreme solution to conservation problems: rather than investing resources in conserving an artefact, its image could be stored and preserved for the collective cultural memory (Peacock and Rizzo 2008). At a micro level, the extent of these effects varies depending on the type of institution, being more relevant to archives or libraries—where 'rivalness' is more pronounced than to museums, historical buildings or archaeological sites.

In a broad sense, the implications for 'excludability' may be also significant. In fact, the digitization of collections allows for the development of electronic applications and for the enlargement of the audience; for instance, an Internet portal, such as Europeana.eu, is an interface to almost 50 million artworks, artefacts, books, videos and sounds across Europe, with six million users per year and the target of increasing them by ten per cent annually.[8] As Guccio et al. (2016) point out, information and images are widespread in the web and, in most cases, though it is technically feasible, it would be pointless to impose restrictions on digital access; therefore, digital access to heritage is usually more 'public' than to the 'real' thing. Moreover, limiting access (for instance, through prices) might conflict with the institutional mission of heritage organizations, which aim at expanding the number of users and their knowledge and awareness about heritage.

Handke et al. (2013) suggest that copyright system and user ethics are the only barrier to 'free' use of proprietary items; the costs of obtaining permissions for works that are still in copyright and the problems of clearing of copyrights for 'orphan works'[9] still prevent the opening of some digital heritage archives in museums and libraries to the public. For the same reason, the digitization of the

---

[8]Data are provided by http://www.europeana.eu/portal/search.html.

[9]'Orphan works' are works like books, newspaper and magazine articles and films that are still protected by copyright but whose authors or other right-holders are not known or cannot be located or contacted to obtain copyright permissions. Directive 2012/28/EU sets out common rules on the digitisation and online display of these works.

content of large cultural institutions may be limited to content produced before the twentieth century.

New technologies increase the possibilities of preserving and exhibiting heritage and provide new services through the development of a wide range of applications on site and on the web,[10] which, however, are different for different types of institutions.[11] These applications allow for developing new strategies with respect to their audiences, in quantitative and qualitative terms, for example, enlarging the share of the population already attending, attracting new groups of population and improving the engagement of audiences.[12]

In principle, technology may have a significant impact on the business models of CH organizations, bearing in mind, however, that the extent of such effects in practice depends on their institutional features, which affect their missions and the incentives/constraints they face (see below). If CH organizations can rely on public funding and do not face sustainability problems, it is realistic for them not to put much effort in innovating the ways in which they identify their customers and their products, attract their consumers and generate value. On the contrary, when public funds decrease, CH institutions are forced to look for means of self-finance. The increasing competition with other cultural institutions, as well as with entertainment activities (for instance, home multimedia or theme parks) provide further incentives toward economy-oriented management schemes.

From that perspective, the need to increase and enlarge audiences and to attract sponsors, together with the opportunities offered by new technologies, may lead to changes in the scope and mission of CH organizations, with a major shift from an organisation-centred to a more customer-centred orientation. The development of Internet-based platforms may offer opportunities for activities of commercial nature as well as for non-profit-oriented activities (Minghetti et al. 2001).

---

[10]In the physical museum, examples are: simulation and virtual reality experiences; wireless connectivity enabling live feeds of information and tools; sound, laser and light shows; IMAX presentations, interactive kiosks and 'theme park-like' attractions. On the web, examples of applications range from the online access to collections and databases to online exhibitions; virtual exhibitions; downloadable and streamed multimedia content; interactive maps; dedicated sites, games and play spaces for children and young people; personalised spaces—creating own favourites and tagging objects; use of social media networks (Bakhshi and Throsby 2010).

[11]Sequeira and Morgado (2013) analyse the techniques and methods employed in virtual archaeology for imaging cultural artefacts and heritage sites; Styliani et al. (2009) survey the emerging technologies, which are widely used to create virtual museums, and explore the various kinds of virtual museums in existence.

[12]Bakhshi and Throsby (2012) report the experience of the use of the web by the British art gallery the Tate to provide access to a virtual presentation of an exhibition 'Colour Chart' in its Liverpool gallery. The website attracted 66,190 unique visits while only 19,000 visited the Tate Liverpool. The wider online audience includes mainly regular visitors to art galleries but also the existing clientele of the Tate's four galleries, but with a larger proportion of low income visitors than go to a gallery exhibition.

Apart from those in museums (Navarrete 2013), business models are still relatively unexplored in the other types of CH institutions—libraries,[13] archives, historical and archaeological sites. Building on the research on museums, several opportunities for business models can be suggested. The possibility of producing joint products with divisible private benefits, such as, for instance, DVDs and e-books, may enlarge the possibilities for private finance and reduce the dependence on public funds. Analogously, the sale of physical product online may be a significant source of revenue, especially for well-known museums, with an established brand that can attract online consumers. Digital distribution also enlarges the scope for specific web services with selective access, for targeted users, such as researchers, and for subscription models (traditionally used by art institutions and relying on 'friends of' associations) making price discrimination possible. Because of the Internet, geographical limitations are overcome and anybody can become 'friend of' without ever visiting the museum, library or archaeological site, enjoying the specific 'club goods', such as previews, dedicated lectures, special offers on merchandising and so on. Technical changes and social media may also enlarge the possibility and the scope for advertising: websites of major CH institutions can offer space for advertisers or sell banner-ads for sponsors. Following the logic of the two-sided market or of more complex multi-sided markets,[14] since the market value of advertising depends on the number of users of the 'free' service, such opportunities are especially valuable for major CH institutions, attracting large number of web accesses. Thus, as Handke et al. (2013) point out, business models based on multi-sided markets and network effects enhance the superstar features, which are already observed in the consumption of cultural products, with the implication that 'minor' CH organizations may not survive.[15]

The relationship with 'stakeholders', especially funders, is also enhanced: the above-mentioned 'globalization' of culture is likely to make sponsorships more attractive and, therefore, reduce the scope for public financing of heritage with a competitive advantage in favour of 'superstars'.

New technologies, therefore, are claimed to enable the development of new revenue streams, improving the organisation's financial sustainability. However, some empirical research would be helpful to assess the role of technologies in generating added value, since there is no evidence that ICT 'by itself' provides a direct stream of revenues, and the related distributional impact. In addition to economic value, technologies that provide new cultural experiences to consumers might also generate new forms of cultural value.

---

[13]Different types of libraries find different ways to adapt their model to new media (Salaün 2013).

[14]The two-sided market model is widely employed in creative industries, for instance in commercial broadcasting, which makes programmes available to viewers without direct payment and gets finance from selling airtime to advertisers and sponsors. The market value of advertising depends on the number of users of the 'free' service. Many applications on the Internet, such as search engines and social networks, are developing more complex, multi-sided markets.

[15]See below, Sect. 3.

Technological interactivity allows customers to coproduce cultural outputs and therefore to enlarge cultural supply: in other words, the boundaries between public and private production become blurred. Terms such as 'produsers', 'prosumption' and 'produsage' describe the sort of evolution that can take place independently of commercial entities ,which is beyond established industrial-age producer/consumer relationships (Bruns 2013).

To support new business models it is important to have information about consumers. CH organizations are increasingly interested in using web statistics, which are an inexpensive source of information. Web Analytics—compilation, measurement, study, and reporting of Internet data—offer new opportunities for strategic planning for CH institutions (Plaza 2011). They also seem to offer a new solution to the old problem of the revelation of preferences. Big data and user-generated data track and analyse visitors' current behaviours and thus are useful in anticipating future needs and predicting future behaviour of visitors.

2.3   New Technologies and the Decision-Making Process

In the analysis of the impact of technologies on supply, the beneficial effects on CH organizations in terms of innovation, new and more effective strategies toward audiences as well as new business models are almost taken for granted. In fact, the literature does not pay much attention to investigating how decisions about the use of technology fit within the various levels of decision-making process concerning CH.

Government has a prominent role in the heritage field, even in countries, such as USA or UK where public intervention is less prominent, and most of the major heritage organizations are somehow publicly funded; therefore, a political economic analysis can be useful for a better understanding of their behaviour. As Holler and Mazza (2013) point out, any cultural policy decision is the outcome of complex procedures involving several actors both on the supply and the demand side. On the supply side we find political representatives, heritage agencies (such as in UK) or state bureaucracies (such as in Italy), museums and galleries, which function at different levels of administration and are vertically and horizontally connected. On the demand side, we find the general public, organized—and often powerful—groups with a common specific interest, such as the museum associations, professional associations (of archaeologists, architects, urban planners, restorers and so on) and the personnel working on conservation. "Within this complex scenario, the rules of policy-making will be shaped by the legal framework, which defines competences of each institution, the link between central and peripheral bodies, and the balance between the political sector and bureaucratic and independent agencies, in a context of overlapping principal–agent relationships" (Holler and Mazza 2013: 20).

Decisions on whether to adopt technologies and to what extent to adopt them take place in the above framework and, among the several issues raised in the political economic analysis of cultural policies (Mazza 2011), it is useful here to recall the problem of asymmetric information and the role of experts in affecting the outcome of the decision-making process (Peacock 1994). The role of experts appears to be twofold when the decision-making process deals with new technologies, in the sense that not only 'traditional' heritage experts (architects, art historians, archaeologists and the like) but also ICT experts enter the picture.

On the one hand, the conventional wisdom about the behaviour of heritage experts—those whom Peacock (1997) labelled as 'cognoscenti'—highlights a bias in favour of an 'elitist' curatorial approach favouring preservation, at the expense of enhancing CH services and enlarging the number of visitors. From that perspective, 'virtuality', as a tool for the promotion of archaeological sites, historical artefacts or museum's collections, is likely not to be unanimously accepted, since mass communication methods are considered to downgrade the 'high' character of heritage and risk transforming sites into some vulgar form of 'theme' park (Peacock and Rizzo 2008). Therefore, even acknowledging the need for using digital technologies, especially if cultural policies are to pay attention to communication technologies, the 'elitist' approach might lead to highly specialized digital cultural content, with poor educational effects and scarce attention to the involvement of the public. Of course, to what extent CH organizations are able to exploit the enormous potentialities offered by digital technologies to be truly innovative as well as being responsive toward the public and accountable, varies across countries, depends on the incentives and constraints that society and funding bodies impose on them.[16] However, because of increasing public budget constraints, which strengthen the needs of legitimacy for public spending and enhance the search for additional funding, ICT can be helpful in promoting the aims of CH organizations, as a useful tool that improves public understanding and interest in supporting CH initiatives. Emphasizing the complementarity between visiting CH and museums and presenting their educational and cultural digital content can make the case for 'virtuality' to be taken into account in their public finance.

From that point of view, the great attention paid to ICT applications in the cultural field at the international level generates opportunities for funding and therefore may also influence CH institutions strategies towards the adoption of ICT. The EU has undertaken policy and funding actions[17] to promote the

---

[16]Methods of appointments, contractual arrangements, evaluation criteria and systems of finance are relevant in affecting CH institutions' behaviour.

[17]In this direction, for instance, the European Commission has issued the Recommendation on the digitisation and online accessibility of cultural material and digital preservation (2011/711/EU) and there are the related Council conclusions on the digitisation and online accessibility of cultural material and digital preservation adopted in 2012. There is also the Council Decision (2013/743/EU) establishing the specific programme implementing Horizon 2020—the Framework Programme for Research and Innovation (2014–2020), in particular Societal Challenge 6 (Innovative, inclusive and reflective societies). Moreover, the art. 5(2) c of Regulation 2013/1301/EU on the European Regional Development Fund considers "strengthening ICT applications for … e-culture" as an investment priority.

digitisation of cultural resources across Europe and to develop their economic potential, favouring the use of the Structural Funds for national activities in this area. In these EU funding programs, the traditional conservation or educational objectives of CH institutions are not necessarily priorities and this may impinge upon their mission: CH institutions might be induced to change their strategies in line with the EU requirements in order to enhance the probability of obtaining the funds.

On the other hand, it is also worth noting that new types of experts emerge, contending the space of the more traditional professionals in the field, with an impact on the outcome of the decision-making process. There is no reason to believe that the above-mentioned conclusions reached in the political economic literature do not apply to this too and therefore the same approach can be useful for a better understanding of the motivations of these experts and to investigate the set of incentives and constraints they face. Because of the different professional background and of their links with the industrial sector, other, and probably more influential pressure groups, enter the picture. Asymmetric information also occurs between CH organizations curators and ICT experts, especially for the most sophisticated (and costly) 'virtual' applications. Therefore, the use of technologies and its overall beneficial impact crucially depends on how influential is the role of ICT experts within the decision-making process; is technology a tool (for communication, research, education and so on) or is it considered as an aim, which is valuable *per se*, as most ICT experts would probably prefer? In the latter case the implementation of sophisticated technological content and applications would be considered valuable, independently of its marginal contribution to innovation and to the appreciation of CH, without taking into account its opportunity cost, in terms of other less 'fancy' alternative ways to use the same financial resources for the benefit of CH users. The outcome of such a process is likely to vary depending on the type of organization (private—not for profit—public), its mission, the incentives/constraints it faces and the related business model. Not to mention the role of industrial interest groups on the decision-making process. Collecting best practices and experiences across CH institutions and countries would be useful to fill the lack of knowledge about these aspects and to offer policy suggestions.

From that perspective, it might be also interesting to look at other sectors, which have experienced earlier the impact of technologies: for instance, it is worth noting that several studies show that the use of technology is one of the most important drivers of the increase of public expenditures on health (Smith et al. 2009). The economic dimension of the CH field is extremely small compared with the health sector but it is interesting to investigate this issue further. Labour represents more than half of the digitization related costs (69 % in archives and libraries and 98 % in museums) and some activities, such as the selection of objects to digitize, are labour-intensive since they have to be done manually (Navarrete 2013). Moreover, so far there is no evidence of any assessment of the cost-effectiveness of technological applications (3D, augmented reality and the like) in terms of their contribution to the appreciation of heritage. The scarcity of available resources would call for investigating closely the opportunity costs of technological choices for CH organizations but, almost paradoxically, as we have said above, funding opportunities strongly depend on technological implementation. To whom and to what this is beneficial is an open issue.

3 Some Empirical Evidence: *Much Ado About . . . What?*

A potentially important role of heritage content for creative uses is widely recognized by international organizations and at national level. Several reports as well as projects and programs promoted by EU, UNESCO and OECD deal with the issues of the digitization in the cultural sector (Frau-Meigs 2014).[18] Reading this wide array of documents it is difficult to say what their real impact is: in many cases, they seem to overlap on the same topics and the overall impression is that there is no coordination between them, since each organisation seems to pursue its own objectives with no great attention paid to those of the others.

At European level, notwithstanding the efforts carried out so far, CH institutions still have not moved very far in adopting digital technologies and becoming part of the information economy. Little research deals with the degree of innovation related to institutions that keep heritage collections and related large endowments of information. As Da Milano and Righolt (2015: 7) report, the digitisation of Europe's cultural collections "is still at an early stage, due to funding, organisational and/or legal problems. Poor metadata, lack of interoperability, persistent digital identifiers, agreed standards (for example, for 3D objects) or the absence of online rights' clearance platforms are other existing challenges." They also point out that in national reports,[19] heritage protection and the widening of access appear to be the main goals for the digitisation of cultural content, while awareness of the potential of digital media platforms for fostering participation and artistic creation is rather limited.

To date, information is rather scarce about the extent to which heritage organizations are able to innovate, or at least to adopt digital technology, in order to increase access to collections and to actively involve users. The lead indicator used at European level to measure the degree of digitization is the percentage of cultural collections digitised across Europe and made accessible online:[20]

---

[18]Frau-Meigs (2014) offers a mapping of reports as well as projects and programs of international organizations on the impact of digitization on the cultural sector.

[19]National reports are available in the Compendium of Cultural Policies and Trends in Europe (http://www.culturalpolicies.net/web/index.php).

[20]Other aspects under investigation refer to the implementation by Member States of the Recommendation on the digitisation and online accessibility of cultural material and digital preservation, using a number of good practices reported by Member States as indicators. Other indicators are the number of Member States making use of the EU's Structural Funds to co-fund digitisation and e-culture-related activities and the number of public-private partnerships creating new ways for funding digitisation of cultural material.

according to the figures provided by Enumerate Core Survey 3,[21] in 2015, only 17 % of heritage collections have been digitized (Nauta and van den Heuvel 2015). The data set includes information provided by each institution on: (1) the state of digitisation activity; (2) the collection; (3) access to digital collections; (4) its digital preservation strategy; (5) expenditure of digitisation by the institution.

Although great caution is in order in interpreting Enumerate figures, since the sample is not representative and suffers of self-selection bias, some snapshots of the main findings may be useful to get a clearer picture:

- 58 % of collections are catalogued in a collections database;
- 41 % of institutions declare they have an explicit digitization strategy;
- 23 % of heritage collections has been digitally reproduced;
- 32 % of digitally reproduced and 'born digital' heritage collections are online for general use;
- The most important reason to provide digital access to the collection is academic research; educational use is the second and sales and commercial licensing is the least important reason;
- 52 % of all institutions measure the use of digital collections, 91 % with web statistics and 38 % with social media statistics;
- 47 % do not have a solution yet for long term preservation based on international standards for digital preservation;
- There are large differences across institutional types: national libraries are 'front runners', followed by national archives; museums are far behind;
- About 52 % of the costs are incidental cost (referring to the initial creation or acquisition of a digital collection) and 47 % are structural costs (referring to the ongoing maintenance, enhancement and preservation of a digital collection);
- 74 % of the costs are in-house costs, 28 % are out-of-pocket costs for external service providers.

The Enumerate Core figures also show differences across European countries with regard to the degree of digitization and to online publication rates in Europe, represented by Table 1.

---

[21]Enumerate Core Survey 3 is the third edition of a European survey monitoring the status of cultural heritage in Europe. 1030 institutions belonging to 32 European countries participated to this third round (participants to Core Survey 2 were about 1400). The dataset includes information for each institution in 2015 with respect to: the state of digitisation activity, the dimension and characteristics of collections, digital access, preservation strategy and expenditure. Institutions are distinguished in 4 types (Museum, 34.47%; library, 33.59%; Archive/record office, 21.12%; other type, 10.78%). Almost all institutions have collections to be preserved and 84% have a digital collection (this percentage was 83% in Core Survey 1 and 87% in Core Survey 2). For more information, see http://www.den.nl/art/uploads/files/Publicaties/ENUMERATE_Report_Core_Survey_3_2015.pdf.

Table 1 Shares of digitized collections and of collections available online—per country

Country	% of collections already digitally reproduced	% of collections available online
Austria	24.46	25.92
Belgium	23.86	32.50
Bulgaria	35.00	0.00
Cyprus	25.00	25.00
Czech Republic	22.86	37.14
Denmark	18.86	41.43
Estonia	15.89	68.44
Finland	28.60	32.21
France	37.50	55.00
Germany	15.71	22.60
Hungary	13.87	40.50
Iceland	24.63	38.54
Ireland	24.70	45.70
Italy	31.50	44.51
Latvia	16.90	27.33
Liechtenstein	3.00	5.00
Lithuania	15.19	26.45
Luxembourg	86.00	66.50
Malta	10.00	0.00
Netherlands	29.74	27.80
Norway	2.00	20.00
Poland	22.50	53.29
Portugal	20.64	29.00
Romania	13.00	5.50
Slovak Republic		
Slovenia	19.98	27.35
Spain	27.06	35.53
Sweden	14.97	29.73
Switzerland	17.90	24.55
United Kingdom	15.93	36.13
Sample	22.86	32.19

Source: Enumerate Core Survey 3

These differences do not offer a precise quantitative representation of a 'digital divide' across European countries, because of the above-mentioned weaknesses of the available data, but they provide some evidence that the phenomenon requires a closer quantitative investigation. Further support in this direction is given by the fact that there exist important differences in ICT development and access in

European countries, which is a necessary condition for the application of digitization and of digital access to culture.[22]

From the qualitative point of view, there is a widespread concern (Paolini et al. 2013) that one major effect of the digital revolution is indeed the occurrence of a large cultural digital divide across countries and institutions, depending on visibility on the Internet: institutions which are culturally very important may be dominated by lesser ones. For instance, countries like Italy with outstanding heritage distributed over a huge number of sites/institutions (small villages, churches, historical sites, museums) are disadvantaged in providing an overall picture of their cultural endowment. So, the above-mentioned 'superstar' phenomenon is likely to exhibit particular features in such a context, not necessarily related to the quality of cultural endowment but just to the size of the digital resources and equipment.

Alongside the lack of resources, the business model may contribute to explain the 'divide': those institutions relying on a strong relationship with their audiences are likely to adopt ICT in a much more visible manner than those that do not since multimedia, the Internet and mobile devices are crucial to fostering communication. On the contrary, when the business model is based on public funding (subject to political preferences), the relationship with the audience is less important and therefore ICT adoption goes lower down the priority list (Paolini et al. 2013).

4 Conclusions

This chapter investigates the implications of technology on the provision of Cultural Heritage (CH) services, with the main attention paid to ICT technologies. Far from reaching clear-cut conclusions, it raises questions about the real relevance of ICT technologies for CH as well as about the related distributional effects and offers some suggestions to overcome limitations and shortcomings. First of all, despite the almost unanimous consensus on the relevance of technologies for the enhancement of the CH sector, it seems that some conclusions, developed for the wider cultural sector, are somehow taken for granted in the CH case and accordingly, further investigation is needed.

---

[22]In 2014 almost 20% of Europeans have never used Internet; with great differences between the North of Europe—where this percentage was below 5%—and the Mediterranean area—where it was about 30%. From a European perspective, the number of persons using the Internet has increased in the last decade: starting from 40% in 2003 it has reached an average of 75.2% in 2013. In terms of broadband connections, in 2014 the European average rate was 78% with differences between the North of Europe, (with an average close to 90%) and the South (with an average close to per cent) (Da Milano and Righolt 2015). Of course, disparities across continents are much wider as it is clearly showed, for example, by the fact that in 2011 in the world as a whole, more than 67% of individuals had no access to the internet, this percentage rising to more than 86% in Africa (Krebs 2012).

At the European level, notwithstanding the efforts carried out so far, CH institutions still have not moved very far in adopting digital technologies and becoming part of the information economy. Little research deals with the degree of innovation related to institutions keeping heritage collections and large information endowments related to them. Nor does it deal with the differences across these institutions. The availability of data on the subject is very poor. Any assessment of the relevance of technologies for the CH sector and of their economic, cultural and social implications would require more data and information on actual behaviour of individuals and institutions, a necessary condition for sound policy making. Thus, one wonders on what empirical evidence the 'mantra' on the relevance of technologies for CH is founded.

Second, the distributional implications of technologies deserve more attention. There is some evidence of the occurrence of a 'digital cultural divide' across social groups and CH institutions but its features need to be investigated to provide effective answers. On the one hand, cultural policy objectives such as social inclusion and participation are threatened and, on the other hand, the 'minor' (though not necessarily less culturally important) CH institutions might be at risk. The challenge goes beyond the future of the organization since it may have impact in terms of local and community social and economic development. Policy measures to promote innovative network projects to be undertaken by minor CH institutions could be useful to enhance these 'invisible' cultural resources.

Third, the enthusiastic acceptance and support for ICT in CH is probably intended to encourage change and innovation in a field, which would seem more inclined to look backward rather than forward. New types of experts emerge, yielding the space to the more traditional professionals in the field, with an impact on the outcome of the decision-making process. Therefore, there is a need for a better understanding, also from a political economic analysis perspective, of how these changes impact on the CH organizations' mission and what trade-off is established between new for-profit and old not-for-profit objectives. Assembling good practice and experience across different type of CH institutions in different countries might offer a starting point for a sound comparative analysis of effective incentives and constraints. Thus, comparative studies might be helpful to understand under what (institutional, social, financial, operational) conditions different examples of good practices take place and, therefore, to avoid duplicating them where the environmental conditions make them ineffective.

Summing up, new technologies bring about several positive challenging opportunities for CH institutions and to take full advantage of them, theoretical and empirical investigation is needed. The complexity of the situation is well put by the former secretary of the Smithsonian Institution saying that:

> Everybody can take part in the creative processes of institutions that once were not even in public view. However, this unprecedented and continuous shift has left many institutions struggling to adapt and is forcing them to rethink how to maintain their unique qualities while at the same time adding value. Today, no organization is immune to the disruptions caused by technological innovation. (Clough 2013: 2)

References

Ateca-Amestoy V, Castiglione C (2014) Live and Digital Engagement with the visual arts. https://editorialexpress.com/cgi-bin/conference/download.cgi?db_name=ACEI2014&paper_id=108. Accessed 30 Jan 2016

Ateca-Amestoy V, Castiglione C (2015) Digital cultural audiences. Should cultural managers worry about the digital divide? http://martin.falk.wifo.ac.at/fileadmin/homepage_falk/files/Ateca_Castiglione_EWACE_31_May.pdf. Accessed 30 Jan 2016

Bakhshi H, Throsby T (2010) Culture of innovation. An economic analysis of innovation in arts and cultural organization. NESTA, London

Bakhshi H, Throsby T (2012) New technologies in cultural institutions: theory, evidence and policy implications. Int J Cult Pol 18(2):205–222

Borowiecki KJ, Navarrete T (2015) Digitization of heritage collections as indicator of innovation. AWP-08-2015. http://www.culturaleconomics.org/awp/AWP-08-2015.pdf. Accessed 4 Feb 2016

Bruns A (2013) From prosumption to produsage. In: Towse R, Handke C (eds) Handbook on the digital creative economy. Edward Elgar, Cheltenham, pp 67–78

Clough GW (2013) Best of both worlds: museums, libraries, and archives in a digital age. Smithsonian Institution, Washington, DC

Da Milano C, Righolt N (2015) Mapping of practices in the EU Member States on promoting access to culture via digital means. EENC Report. http://acpculturesplus.eu/sites/default/files/2015/06/24/eenc_mappingofpracticesintheeumemberstates_on_promoting_access_to_culture_via_digital_means.pdf. Accessed 15 Jan 2016

Farchy J (2011) The internet: culture for free. In: Towse R (ed) A handbook of cultural economics. Edward Elgar, Cheltenam, pp 245–252

Frau-Meigs D (2014) European cultures in the cloud: mapping the impact of digitisation on the cultural sector. https://www.coe.int/t/dg4/cultureheritage/culture/digitisation/DFrau-Meigs1-Mapping_EN.pdf. Accessed 10 Oct 2015

Giardina E, Mazza I, Pignataro G, Rizzo I (2016) Voluntary provision of public goods and technology. International advances in economic research 22:321–332

Guccio C, Martorana MF, Mazza I, Rizzo I (2016) Technology and public access to cultural heritage: the Italian experience on IT for public historical archives. In: Borowiecki KJ, Forbe N, Fresa A (eds) Cultural heritage in a changing world. Springer, Heidelberg, pp 55–76

Handke C, Stepan P, Towse R (2013) Cultural economics and the Internet. http://ssrn.com/abstract=2310512. Accessed 10 July 2015

Henten A, Tadayoni R (2011) Digitalization. In: Towse R (ed) A handbook of cultural economics. Edward Elgar, Cheltenam, pp 190–200

Holler MJ, Mazza I (2013) Cultural heritage: public decision- making and implementation. In: Rizzo I, Mignosa A (eds) Handbook on the economics of cultural heritage. Edward Elgar, Cheltenham, pp 17–36

Krebs A (2012) Education and access to digital culture: the current situation and future directions for European culture. http://www.houseforculture.eu/upload/Docs%20ACP/educationdigitalencatcannekrebsENGL.pdf. Accessed 10 June 2015

Mazza I (2011) Public choice. In: Towse R (ed) A handbook of cultural economics. Edward Elgar, Cheltenam, pp 362–369

Minghetti V, Moretti A, Micelli S (2001) Re-engineering the museum's role in the tourism value chain: towards an IT business model. J Inf Technol Tourism 4(1):131–143

Nauta GJ, van den Heuvel W (2015) Survey report on digitisation in European cultural heritage institutions 2015. Europeana/ENUMERATE, DEN Foundation NL. http://pro.europeana.eu/files/Europeana_Professional/Projects/Project_list/ENUMERATE/deliverables/ev3-deliverable-d1.2-europeana-version1.1-public.pdf. Accessed 10 Jan 2016

Navarrete T (2013) Digital cultural heritage. In: Rizzo I, Mignosa A (eds) Handbook on the economics of cultural heritage. Edward Elgar, Cheltenham, pp 251–271

NEA (2015) A decade of arts engagement: findings from the survey of public participation in the arts 2002–2012. NEA Research Report n 58, Washington, DC

Norris P, Inglehart R (2013) Digital divide. In: Towse R, Handke C (eds) Handbook on the digital creative economy. Edward Elgar, Cheltenham, pp 90–101

OECD (2001) Understanding the digital divide. OECD, Paris

Paolini P, Mitroff Silvers D, Proctor N (2013) Technologies for cultural heritage. In: Rizzo I, Mignosa A (eds) Handbook on the economics of cultural heritage. Edward Elgar, Cheltenham, pp 272–289

Peacock AT (1994) A future for the past: the political economy of heritage. Proc Br Acad 87:189–226, Reprinted in Hume Occasional paper n.44, Edinburgh

Peacock AT (1997) Toward a workable heritage policy. In: Hutter M, Rizzo I (eds) Economic perspectives on cultural heritage. Kluwer, Dordrecht, pp 225–235

Peacock AT (2006) The arts and economic policy. In: Ginsburgh V, Throsby D (eds) Handbook of the economics of art and culture, vol 1. North-Holland, Amsterdam, pp 1124–1140

Peacock AT, Rizzo I (2008) The heritage game. Economics, policy and practices. Oxford University Press, Oxford

Plaza B (2011) Google analytics for measuring website performance. Tourism Manag 32 (3):477–481

Potts J (2014) New technologies and cultural consumption. In: Ginsburgh V, Throsby D (eds) Handbook of the economics of art and culture, vol 2. North-Holland, Amsterdam, pp 215–231

Rizzo I (2011) Regulation. In: Towse R (ed) A handbook of cultural economics. Edward Elgar, Cheltenam, pp 386–391

Salaün JM (2013) The immeasurable economics of libraries. In: Rizzo I, Mignosa A (eds) Handbook on the economics of cultural heritage. Edward Elgar, Cheltenham, pp 290–305

Sequeira LM, Morgado L (2013) Virtual archaeology in second life and open simulator. J Virt Worlds Res 6(1):1–16

Smith S, Newhouse JP, Freeland MS (2009) Income, insurance, and technology: why does health spending outspace economic growth. Health Aff 28:1276–1284

Styliani S, Fotis L, Kostas K, Petros P (2009) Virtual museums, a survey and some issues for consideration. J Cult Herit 10:520–528

Towse R, Handke C (eds) (2013) Handbook on the digital creative economy. Edward Elgar, Cheltenham

Archaeological Cultural Heritage: A Consideration of Loss by Smuggling, Conflict or War

Ezra B.W. Zubrow

Abstract Ever since ISIS, Daesh, Taliban and other terrorist organizations have been systematically destroying archaeological sites, questions of the size, scale and value of the loss has been discussed in the popular media and academic press. This chapter examines different ways to consider archaeological cultural heritage and in particular this loss. Archaeological cultural heritage is examined along a private to public continuum of property. Then, we argue that given contested definitions, a human rights conception is useful.

> There are risks and costs to action. But they are far less than the long-range risks of comfortable inaction. (John F. Kennedy)

1 Cultural Heritage

Heritage is the connection of identity to past place, community, religion, ethnicity or culture. Since it is past oriented, archaeology is frequently associated with one's heritage. Whether it is a real past or an imagined one makes little difference. What is important is that the connection is made, recognized, and operationalized in some way. Nostalgia, rituals, memories, stories, songs, and poems incorporate heritage. Archaeological and historical sites, memorials, museums, galleries, and monuments materialize them.

UNESCO divides heritage into both intangible and tangible forms of cultural heritage. It claims that "intangible cultural heritage includes the representations, expressions, knowledge, skills—as well practices as the instruments, objects, artifacts, and cultural spaces associated therewith-that communities, groups, and

E.B.W. Zubrow (✉)
University at Buffalo, Buffalo, NY, USA

University of Toronto (SO), Toronto, ON, Canada
e-mail: ezubrow@gmail.com

© Springer International Publishing Switzerland 2016
I. Rizzo, R. Towse (eds.), *The Artful Economist*,
DOI 10.1007/978-3-319-40637-4_13

individuals recognize as part of their cultural heritage"[1] (Stefano et al. 2012; Labadi 2013). An ethnographic viewpoint conceives intangible cultural heritage as a type of tangible heritage embodied in living peoples. However, most archaeological cultural heritage is tangible. Tangible heritage has been protected for a longer time[2] and includes immovables and movables. The former are "... archaeological and historic or scientific sites, structures or other features of historic, scientific, artistic or architectural value, whether religious or secular, including—groups of traditional structures, historic quarters in urban or rural built-up areas and the ethnological structures of previous cultures" and "ruins existing above the earth as well as to archaeological or historic remains found within the earth". Movables include "movable property of cultural importance including that existing in or recovered from immovable property and that concealed in the earth, which may be found in archaeological or historical sites or elsewhere".

Although somewhat elusive, cultural heritage and particularly archaeological cultural heritage is dynamic, invented and reinvented. It is seldom static or inert.

1.1 Value of Cultural Heritage

What is the value of cultural heritage? There are many ways to think about value of which only one is economic. Moreover, there is a long history of debate in economics over the question of value. The most widely accepted today is the neo-classical version, which bases measures of economic value on what people want—their preferences. Many economists assume that individuals are the best judges of what they want.[3] Thus, generally the theory of economic valuation is based on individual preferences and operationalized choices. Cultural economics accepts extensions of this theory to include external benefits and the recognition of the public good characteristics of heritage and then extends these notions even further. Cultural economists identify the 'existence' value, suggesting that people derive benefits from the very existence of heritage and the 'option' value to present generations who, for various reason, do not wish to express their preferences by paying directly for heritage but are anyway willing to support their existence and to contribute to their maintenance collectively. Similarly, present generations are willing to support heritage for the benefit of future generations. As previously noted, economic value is only one of multiple ways to define and measure value. It is useful for economic choices, for resource allocation, and for targeted decision making. In general, it is expressed as the exchangeability for other goods. For the purposes of estimation one should take into

---

[1] The UN does so in a series of conventions which are formal multilateral treaties signed by a large number of parties or signed by the international community as a whole such as the Convention on Intangible Property (UNESCO 2003).

[2] Recommendation concerning the Preservation of Cultural Property Endangered by Public or Private works, UNESCO, Paris, 19 November 1968.

[3] See the chapter by Forte in this book.

account all the relevant costs and social benefits. One might examine simply the real market,[4] the grey market,[5] or even the black market value.[6]

A third value, which is the topic of this chapter is the replacement value. It is that which is needed to replace an asset or a good (Malcomson 1975; Douglas 2001; Nwaeze 2005; Cabeza 2006; Schulz and Werwatz 2011; Notaro and Paletto 2012; Yatsenko and Hritonenko 2015). One needs to distinguish the replacement value from the replacement cost. The latter refers not only to the value of the replacement entity but includes the extra cost incurred by the replacement process. It is a type of loss in the solution value on top of the optimal cost solution. There is an assumption made when the 'replacement value' is discussed namely, for some archaeological materials there are no replacements.

1.2 Archaeological Cultural Heritage as an Asset

Cultural heritage corresponds well with the modern concepts of economic asset evaluation. The evaluation of assets is a central part of modern government, economic, and business analysis. The literature is full of economic methods and analyses for evaluating intangibles (Andersen 1992; Bianchi and Labory 2004; Lev 2005; Anson and Drews 2007; Zatzman and Islam 2007; Tomer 2008; Mackie et al. 2009; Kang and Gray 2011; Vallejo-Alonso et al. 2011; Moberly 2014) and tangible assets (United Nations Statistical Office 1979; Schmalensee 1981; Böhm and Vachadze 2008; Greco et al. 2013; Goto and Suzuki 2015). These methods have been applied to intangibles (Smith and Akagawa 2009; UNESCO 2009; Stefano et al. 2012; Kapchan 2014) and tangible cultural heritage.

However, cultural heritage is messy.

Alan Peacock believed that there is an unusual paradox about cultural heritage. He felt that the aim of public policy is consumer sovereignty and that it is used to justify the "provision of and also the demand for cultural services" such as museums, performing arts and the like. Some are paid for publicly others are not. He wondered "why such support, coupled with regulatory measures to control the provision and sale of historical artefacts, is found in the arts, whereas in other forms

---

[4]Bonham's auction house in the UK recently sold according to their website—an Egyptian wood canopic jar box for £139,250 in 2013, a Mesopotamian terracotta cuneiform cylinder for £264,00 in 2011, and a Roman marble relief panel for £490,400 in 2011. http://www.bonhams.com/departments/ANT/.

[5]Ebay sells antiquities such as "high quality ancient Roman gold intaglio ring of Mars 2nd century AD" $4750.00 or "Ancient Greek Hellenistic pottery Kylix 4th century" for $169.50 http://www.ebay.com/sch/Antiquities/37903/bn_1865503/i.html.

[6]In Hatay Province in Turkey, Mohamed is selling a looted ancient mosaic from Syria. "The mosaic was looted from Apamea, a city in northwest Syria with vast ruins that are under rebel control. Mohamed bought it for $21,000 from a dealer in Syria and hoped to sell it for $30,000." http://www.buzzfeed.com/mikegiglio/the-trade-in-stolen-syrian-artifacts#.ntXR6Pz2n.

of productive activity, such support is increasingly reduced, as instanced in privat-ization measures" (Peacock 2006: 1123). He assumed that this made it structurally similar to other 'subsidized' industries (Towse 2005). He believed the answer is that governments did not trust the consumers to choose for themselves (Ricketts and Peacock 1986; Peacock 2006).

Recently, there is evidence that even heritage and the arts are beginning to drift toward privatization (Dice 1999; Martin 1999; Masele 2012). Museums, archaeo-logical and other heritage sites have become more dependent upon their entrance fees and shops. Governments increasingly argue if the private sector cannot afford it then it is not worth having. If so, Peacock's paradox is becoming unraveled as support is reduced and perhaps regulation as well.

1.3 Cultural Heritage as a Human Right

Problems of contested views impact on the value of cultural heritage and thus some scholars have looked to human rights in international law for help.

We take it as given that most people believe in the importance of their own cultural heritage. They value it. How much varies. For some they will give up large amounts of time, labour, and wealth to ensure they participate or that the heritage continues from generation to generation. For others, it is far less important.

Whether they have or will extend that importance to others is far less certain. What the value is of the heritage of 'others' is in many ways essential to this chapter. Only a few people have systematically rejected all concepts and totally devalued their own heritage. Among this group the largest have been refugees or immigrants. Sometimes their antipathies to their homelands are so great that there is negative value. However, they usually accept the heritage of their new home or create a new, sometimes blended heritage (Deaux 2006; Akerlof and Kranton 2010; Mexar 2014). Thus, there is a true exchange—one for another.

1.4 Archaeological Cultural Heritage as a Human Right

Archaeology enhances cultural heritage in several ways. First, through material culture, it extends the time depth of one's heritage. Second, for societies with short or no historical records, it helps verify oral traditions. Third, for societies that are extinct and have left no historical or oral traditions, it brings their cultural heritage back to modern awareness and consciousness. Fourth, for the truly deep time origins of human evolution, it makes modern societies aware of the overriding uniformity of our heritage. All of us come out of Africa; all of us were once hunters and gatherers, all of us have generally common intellectual and physical capacities.

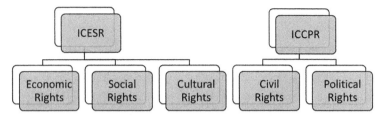

Fig. 1 The relationship of different human rights to the international conventions

Archaeological cultural heritage is a human right. There are fundamental characteristics to human rights. They apply to individuals, to all people globally, and involve the relationship between the individual and state.

Furthermore, certain principles apply to all human rights that we will see later in this chapter are critical to the archaeological record. They are universal adherence, inherent self-worth of each individual, autonomy and self-determination, equality for all, and preservation of freedom of individual through social support.

The key documents (United Nations. Office of the High Commissioner for Human Rights 2006) are the International Bill of Human Rights (United Nations 1978), Universal Declaration of Human Rights (1948) (UN Charter) (Asbeck 1949; United Nations 1949), the International Covenant on Civil and Political Rights (ICCPR)(Joseph and Castan 2013), the International Covenant on Economic, Social and Cultural Rights (ICESC) (United Nations 1967).

The relationships between the types of human rights and these documents are shown in Fig. 1. As you can see, there are cultural, economic, social, political and civil rights. For this chapter we will be concerned primarily with the first two.

Cultural rights provide the right for all individuals to take part in cultural life and to freely exercise cultural customs and beliefs. These would include such activities as participating in arts and recreation, expressing and practicing cultural identity and customs, self-determination, benefitting from scientific progress, and engaging in scientific and creative activities.

So, we can ask the question: why is archaeological cultural heritage a human right? It is embodied in the International Covenant on Economic, Social and Cultural Rights (ICESC). Like many important ideas, the argument is very straightforward, very simple and very parsimonious. It begins with all people have equal rights. Some populations have unfettered rights and access to their archaeological heritage. Accordingly, the same range of rights needs to be extended to all people. Therefore, the State Parties are required to enable all persons to overcome obstacles and disadvantages regarding these rights.

Not granting archaeological cultural heritage status as a human right is unacceptable. If one makes access to one's archaeological cultural heritage impossible—such as destroying sites as have ISIS, then one must do so for all populations. None may be privileged. That means all churches, mosques, synagogues, temples and all historic places that have ethnic meaning need to be equally destroyed. Not even the Soviet Union or Maoist China took this view.

1.5   Background for Cultural Heritage

We want to ask two related questions. If the past is an asset, who owns the past and what is the nature of the asset value of cultural heritage? There is a bit of a chicken and egg issue here. For how you see the nature of the value might be different depending on who owns the past. Also who may decide they wish to own the past may be dependent upon how the value is perceived.

However, sidestepping this issue of priority, we suggest that there is a continuum in 'owning' the past. This continuum applies to all cultural heritage including archaeological cultural heritage. The continuum ranges from being completely in the private domain to being in the public domain. Within this continuum you might think about four general positions. On one extreme end, there are those people who believe that archaeological cultural heritage belongs to the individual. This would be the most capitalist, private sector view and would imply that individuals have every right to own, administer, and sell archaeological cultural heritage in the same way as they may do with other commodities. In fact, archaeological cultural heritage is property and is no different than other forms-except possibly scarcer, less frequently available in the market and probably not renewable. One consequence of this viewpoint is that if the owner does not value the archaeological cultural heritage, he or she may modify it, sell it, or even destroy it. The issue of value is solely for the individual owner.

The next position, which is less individualistic, is to suggest that the community owns its cultural heritage. As a community, one would include such groups as towns, villages, religions, ethnic groups, sodalities, and other associations. Thus, various First Nations or Native Americans[7] will claim they own their heritage and thus all artefacts or archaeological sites that once belonged to them still do. Any archaeological cultural heritage should be returned to them and thus from this viewpoint one understands such legislation as the Native American Graves Protection and Repatriation Act (NAGPRA), Pub. L. 101-601, 25 U.S.C. 3001 et seq., 104 Stat. 3048, requires federal agencies and institutions that receive federal funding to return Native American 'cultural items' to lineal descendants and culturally affiliated Indian tribes.

The next position would be national ownership. It is the position that is most frequently on the international stage. The nation state or state party owns the entire cultural heritage including the archaeological cultural heritage. Each nation has the right to determine its own law about the administration and ownership of such cultural property. They may vary in terms of ownership or principles of administration dependent upon each countries values and history. Thus, in the case of the United States the viewpoint is very individualistic and the country sits close to the

---

[7]Some of these peoples will claim they are a nation state but the legal reality is that they are a "conquered nation state or culture living as a community within the conqueror's nation state."

private part of the continuum.[8] The UK (excluding Scotland) has a combined private and public position with the Crown maintaining more rights than in the United States in such acts as the 1996 Treasury Act. While some nation states such as Norway simply state anything that is greater than 100 years old belongs to the state (Zubrow 2002).

The infamous destruction of the Buddhas is justified in this nationalist perspective. As you remember the Buddhas of Bamiyan were monumental Persian statues in Afghanistan dating to about 535 AD. The national Taliban leader at the time Mullah Mohammad Omar ordered them to be dynamited and destroyed in March of 2001 because of nationally stated religious iconoclasm and as a national protest about international aid. Does a national government have a right to destroy 'its' archaeological cultural heritage or to sell it off? From this viewpoint the answer would need to be yes, if it is property owned by the state. The issues between the state position and the community position have been examined closely by such organizations as the United Nations and the European Court of Human Rights (2011).

The fourth position is the furthest towards the public domain on private to public spectrum. From this vantage point cultural heritage and archaeological cultural heritage belongs to everyone and thus it is a universal ownership. Whether I am Canadian, Italian, Rumanian or Chinese, I have a partial ownership in the bones of the earliest hominids, in the Classical buildings of Italy or the archaeological sites that span from the southern tip of Tierra del Fuego to the Northern parts of Baffin Islands. From this perspective ownership must rest in the international bodies such as the United Nations or in the International Treaties and Covenants. No individual, no community, no nation state may own, sell, or destroy archaeological cultural heritage without the agreement of international bodies representing humanity as a whole.[9]

The valuation of the archaeological artefacts and sites is a very complex process for the determining of the current worth is based on many variables—including age, rarity, access, provenience, and so on. Moreover, it is clear that the question of ownership heavily impacts on the valuation. The greater value of the antiquity to the greater number of people is intrinsic as one moves from individual's market value, to community importance, to national heritage antiquity or site, to world heritage antiquity or site.

---

[8]Even in the United States there is some variation. For example, east of the Mississippi the ownership of cultural heritage belongs to the individual owning the land on which it exists or was found. West of the Mississippi it is less clear because the Homestead Act gave each settler 40 acres but did not cede them sub surface rights unless they specifically asked for them. So more of the cultural heritage sites are on public land than in the East.

[9]One suggestion that is appropriate but which would need another article to expand upon is that 'archaeological cultural heritage' needs its own international legal representation. In the same way, as corporations are legally persons, archaeological sites could be considered people. As children in domestic law are provided with their own legal counsel, perhaps sites should be as well.

2   A Few Contextual Generalities

There are a few generalities that are central and need to be considered when thinking of archaeological cultural heritage.

First, as seen above, clearly cultural heritage's importance, value, and administration will vary from population to population, from society to society, and from where in the society one is situated.

Second, the value of archaeological cultural heritage is not a constant. It fluctuates. It fluctuates over space and over time. The same object will have different prices in different markets. The value of an object *in situ* is different than in a museum. It may have different values in India than in the auction houses of New York City.[10] Similarly, the age of the site or the object is relevant. The provenance frequently adds value and there is a tradition of creating 'fake' or 'intermediate pass through' proveniences to not only add value but to bypass national and international restrictions on allowing artefacts to even enter the market. Some would claim that it fluctuates with the market but to see its value limited to the changing market would be a mistake.

Third, regarding time: in almost all cases the value of archaeological culture heritage is incremental with time. As objects, sites, art, architecture, and all other forms of cultural heritage get older, they become more valuable. Part of the reason is that it is scarcer but part of the reason is that its relevance is greater to a larger population. The various historical and archaeological sites on the Temple Mount dating to before and at the time of Christ and Mohammed are more relevant to more people than the seventeenth century Golden Temple of Amritsar (approximately 2.2 billion Christians, 1.6 billion Islam, and 14 million Jews compared to 27 million Sikhs).

Fourth, the destruction of cultural value is categorical. While the value of archaeological cultural heritage over time is incremental, its destruction is neither decremental nor reversible. Once truly destroyed it has no value. Once valueless there is little probability that it will regain any value. So while the maintenance of cultural value is inherently value producing, its destruction is not.[11]

The destruction of archaeological cultural heritage needs to be differentiated from the lack of conservation, maintenance or support. For in these cases the value of archaeological cultural heritage may be decremental up to a point. Good con-

---

[10]See footnotes 3, 4, and 5.

[11]One should note that the end points of these processes are very different. Essentially there is no endpoint for incremental growth of archaeological cultural heritage. On the other hand, once the decremental lack of conservation, maintenance, and support goes beyond a particular threshold, the diminishing value continues inexorably until the inevitable categorical destruction is reached. Once crossing this threshold one only has deferred the inescapable.

servation, improved maintenance, and improved investment may return value to the archaeological cultural heritage.[12]

3 Stolen and Destroyed Cultural Heritage

There is a tradition that has long been practiced. It is sequential looting, smuggling, selling and buying of antiquities. To put it into context, of international crimes, art theft is the third highest grossing criminal trade surpassed only by drug smuggling and arms trading (Hollington 2014). And of this art theft, the illegal looting, smuggling, selling and buying of antiquities makes up 90 % of international art theft. The tradition goes back to antiquity. Within a few decades of King Tutankhamen's death in 1327 B.C., his tomb was plundered of its metals and jewels. The famous Triumphal Quadriga, the Horses on Saint Mark's of Venice, originally from Island of Chios, are well known looted spoils of war. They were in the Hippodrome of Constantinople until 1204 AD when pillaged by Venetian forces, and remained in Venice until Napoleon forcibly removed them five centuries later. They were in Paris from 1797 and were returned in 1815 (Szopa 2004).

Finally, it is difficult to determine the value of the cultural heritage asset that either has been destroyed or that has been looted through conflict and warfare.

We believe that essentially there are two ways of calculating the value destroyed or conflict ridden cultural heritage. They are:

First, calculate the value that is lost. When archaeological artefacts show up on the antiquities market, it is relatively easy to determine the 'market value'. One simply follows the antiquity from one market to the next. The rule of 10 usually applies. For example, statues worth $500 in Syria are worth $5000 along the route as in Sofia or Istanbul, worth $50,000 in Geneva or Brussels and finally top the market at $500,000 in London and New York;

Second, calculate what would have been made into the future if it had remained.[13]

For non-moveable sites that are being threatened or destroyed, the calculation is more difficult. One method is to examine proxies for the pre-destruction or pre-threat data and then extrapolate to what would have happened over time if the destruction, threat or conflict had not happened.

An archaeological site, a historic building may also be viewed as an asset. When an artefact is bought or sold, the income stream is measurable and comparable across cultures, across time, across space, and is somewhat independent of whether cultural heritage is seen as individually, community, nationally, or humanity owned.

---

[12]Given that once destroyed, the antiquity's value is equal to nothing means that investment into archaeological cultural heritage past the decremental threshold provides only ephemeral value.

[13]Our estimate for the Middle East is approximately one and half billion dollars a year lost.

Periods of positive and negative growth need to be taken into account. One projects the growth forward (and backward) through time giving one a predictions on what the maximum income per year should be if there had been continuous growth during the peaceful periods rather than the decline in income during periods of heightened tension. One would conservatively compare the projections to the actual data noting the size of the differences. Having done this for one or more sites then one would aggregate the results to get estimates for regional trends. Thus, one could extend one's research to a much larger area.

One could potentially add other 'causal variables'. There are more than 140,000 records in the Global Terrorism Database. It includes numerous variables including, incident information and location, attack information, weapon information, target and victim information, perpetrator information, causalities, and consequences. The time ranges from 1970 to the present and geographically includes all countries. Exemplary attack types include assassination, hijacking, kidnapping, barricade incidents, bombing, other explosions, armed and unarmed assault, facility or infrastructure attack. There are many other variables in its 62-page codebook.

With more economic determinant and consequence variables and an increased use of such databases, one could do standard factor and determinant analyses to tease out the causal variables. However, that is not for this chapter.

4   Conclusions

There are several.

First, there are many ways to conceive, operationalize, value and measure archaeological cultural heritage. Second, one way that is useful for contested definitions is to consider archaeological cultural heritage as human right based on UN and International Treaties regarding cultural and economic rights. Third, some suggestions for general ways to calculate loss are explained.

References

Akerlof GA, Kranton RE (2010) Identity economics. Princeton University Press, Princeton, NJ
Andersen A (1992) The valuation of intangible assets. Economist Intelligence Unit, London
Anson W, Drews DC (2007) The intangible assets handbook: maximizing value from intangible assets. American Bar Association, Section of Business Law, Chicago, IL
Asbeck FM (1949) The universal declaration of human rights and its predecessors (1679-1948). E. J. Brill, Leiden
Bianchi P, Labory S (2004) The economic importance of intangible assets. Ashgate, Aldershot
Böhm V, Vachadze G (2008) Capital accumulation with tangible assets. J Econ Behav Organ 68 (1):248–257
Cabeza MMA (2006) Replacement cost: a practical measure of site value for cost-effective reserve planning. Biol Conserv 132(3):336–342

Deaux K (2006) Negotiating identity beyond assimilation models. To be an immigrant. Russell Sage, New York

Dice G (1999) The privatization of culture. Soc Text 59:17–34

Douglas AVS (2001) Managerial replacement and corporate financial policy with endogenous manager-specific value. J Corp Finance 7(1):25–52

European Court of Human Rights (2011) Cultural rights in the case-law of the European Court of Human Rights. European Council, Strasbourg

Goto M, Suzuki T (2015) Optimal default and liquidation with tangible assets and debt renegotiation. Rev Financ Econ 27:16–27

Greco M, Cricelli L, Grimaldi M (2013) A strategic management framework of tangible and intangible assets. Eur Manag J 31(1):55–66

Hollington K (2014) After drugs and guns, art theft is the biggest criminal enterprise in the world. Newsweek, 18 July 2014. http://www.newsweek.com/2014/07/18/after-drugs-and-guns-art-theft-biggest-criminal-enterprise-world-260386.html

Joseph S, Castan M (2013) The International Covenant on Civil and Political Rights: cases, materials, and commentary. Oxford University Press, Oxford

Kang HH, Gray SJ (2011) Reporting intangible assets: voluntary disclosure practices of top emerging market companies. Int J Account 46(4):402–423

Kapchan DA (2014) Cultural heritage in transit: intangible rights as human rights. University of Pennsylvania Press, Philadelphia, PA

Labadi S (2013) UNESCO, cultural heritage, and outstanding universal value: value-based analyses of the world heritage and Intangible cultural heritage conventions. Alta Mira, Lanham, MD

Lev B (2005) Intangible assets: concepts and measurements. In: Kempf-Leonard K (ed) Encyclopedia of social measurement. Elsevier Academic, Amsterdam, pp 299–305

Mackie CD, National Research Council, Board on Science Technology and Economic Policy (2009) Intangible assets: measuring and enhancing their contribution to corporate value and economic growth. National Academies Press, Washington, DC

Malcomson JM (1975) Replacement and the rental value of capital equipment subject to obsolescence. J Econ Theor 10(1):24–41

Martin R (1999) Beyond privatization? The art and society of labor, citizenship, and consumerism. Soc Text 59:35–48

Masele F (2012) Private business investments in heritage sites in Tanzania: recent developments and challenges for heritage management. Afr Archaeol Rev 29(1):51–65

Mexar M (2014) Immigrant identity, social adaptation and post-secular society. In: Toğuşlu E, Leman J, Mesut Sezgin I (eds) New multicultural identities in Europe. Leuven University Press, Leuven, pp 73–94

Moberly MD (2014) Safeguarding intangible assets. Butterworth-Heinemann, Boston, MA

Notaro S, Paletto A (2012) The economic valuation of natural hazards in mountain forests: an approach based on the replacement cost method. J Forest Econ 18(4):318–328

Nwaeze ET (2005) Replacement versus adaptation investments and equity value. J Corp Finance 11(3):523–549

Peacock A (2006) The arts and economic policy. In: Ginsburgh V, Throsby D (eds) Handbook of the economics of art and culture, vol 1. Elsevier, North Holland, Amsterdam, pp 1123–1140

Ricketts M, Peacock A (1986) Bargaining and the regulatory system. Int Rev Law Econ 6(1):3–16

Schmalensee R (1981) Risk and return on long-lived tangible assets. J Financ Econ 9(2):185–205

Schulz R, Werwatz A (2011) Is there an equilibrating relationship between house prices and replacement cost? Empirical evidence from Berlin. J Urban Econ 69(3):288–302

Smith L, Akagawa N (2009) Intangible heritage. Routledge, London

Stefano ML, Davis P, Corsane G (2012) Safeguarding intangible cultural heritage. Boydell, Woodbridge, Suffolk

Szopa A (2004) Hoarding history: a survey of antiquity, looting, and black market trade. Univ Miami Bus Law Rev 13:55–89

Tomer JF (2008) Intangible capital: its contribution to economic growth, well-being and rational-
    ity. Edward Elgar, Cheltenham, UK
Towse R (2005) Alan Peacock and cultural economics. Econ J 115(504):262–276
UNESCO (2003) Convention for the safeguarding of the intangible cultural heritage. UNESCO,
    Paris, 17 Oct 2003, Article 2.1
UNESCO (2009) Representative list of the intangible cultural heritage of humanity. UNESCO,
    Paris
United Nations (1949) Universal declaration of human rights: final authorized text. United Nations
    Dept. of Public Information, New York
United Nations (1967) International Covenant on Economic, Social, and Cultural Rights and
    International Covenant on Civil and Political Rights, with Optional Protocol. HMSO, London
United Nations (1978) The International Bill of Human Rights. United Nations, New York
United Nations. Office of the High Commissioner for Human Rights (2006) The core international
    human rights treaties. United Nations, New York
United Nations Statistical Office (1979) Guidelines on statistics of tangible assets. United Nations,
    New York
Vallejo-Alonso B, Rodríguez-Castellanos A, Arregui-Ayastuy G (2011) Identifying, measuring,
    and valuing knowledge-based intangible assets: new perspectives. Information Science Refer-
    ence, Hershey, PA
Yatsenko Y, Hritonenko N (2015) Algorithms for asset replacement under limited technological
    forecast. Int J Prod Econ 160:26–33
Zatzman G, Islam R (2007) Economics of intangibles. Nova, New York
Zubrow E (2002) Conflict, heritage and place: problems of cultural ownership in the era of
    globalization. Man Dev XXIV 4:229–250

Theory and Practice of Cultural Heritage Policy

Anna Mignosa

Abstract The economic analysis of policies for cultural heritage has referred to the reasons for public intervention and the consequent institutional arrangements in place for the design and implementation of rules that would guarantee the conservation and enhancement of cultural heritage. The analysis of the changes in the last 20 years highlights a trend towards devolution of power to lower levels of government and an increasing role of the private (no profit) sector for the implementation of cultural policies. This trend has been somehow speeded up by the recent economic crisis. This chapter provides a brief overview of these changes. Using a cultural economics approach, it offers some reflections on the impact they have on the conservation and enhancement of cultural heritage.

> The true test of our love of the arts lies in what we individually and collectively are willing to give up to allow the arts to flourish and develop. Running our cultural affairs should engage the full support and interest of the public. This in turn requires radical reform. (Peacock 2001: 12)

1 Introduction

Policies for culture and cultural heritage have changed in the last 20 years showing a common trend characterised by devolution of power to lower levels of government and by an increasing role for the private (non profit) sector in the implementation of cultural policies (Klamer et al. 2006). The trend has been somehow speeded up by the recent economic crisis. This chapter provides a brief overview of these changes and a preliminary reflection on the impact they have had on heritage policies and their possible outcome. Specifically, the next section illustrates a brief overview of the cultural economics analysis of cultural heritage policy highlighting the main issues that have emerged. Section 3 looks at the models in

A. Mignosa (✉)
Department of Economics and Business, University of Catania, Catania, Italy

Erasmus School of History, Culture and Communication, Erasmus University, Rotterdam, The Netherlands
e-mail: a.mignosa@unict.it

© Springer International Publishing Switzerland 2016
I. Rizzo, R. Towse (eds.), *The Artful Economist*,
DOI 10.1007/978-3-319-40637-4_14

place for the implementation of heritage policies, paying special attention to the changes that have characterised the sector. The role of the private sector is covered in Sect. 4, where the importance of bottom-up processes and the role of the Public-Private-Partnership (PPP) is illustrated. Section 5 provides some concluding remarks.

2 The Theoretical Analysis of Cultural Heritage Policy

In cultural economics, the analysis of cultural heritage policies has traditionally been characterised by a general agreement on the case for public intervention of some kind and thus several authors reflected on the reasons for public intervention, considering its pros and cons (Peacock 1994; Towse 1994, 2010; Throsby 1997, 2010; Benhamou 2011, 2013; Rizzo and Throsby 2006). The institutional arrangements in place for defining and implementing cultural heritage policy are discussed in Mignosa (2005), van der Ploeg (2006) and Klamer et al. (2013). Looking at the reasons for public intervention beyond the usual market failure cases of public goods, externalities and information problems (Mueller 2003), cultural economics puts forward other arguments for intervention in the cultural heritage sector connected to its role in promoting national prestige, and in the option, bequest and existence benefits (Throsby 2001; Towse 1994). The presence of these external benefits explains why consumers have no incentive (or no capacity) to reveal their preferences regarding cultural heritage or to pay for maintaining it. Thus, governments need to step in if cultural heritage is to be preserved. The market would fail in providing the socially optimal amount of culture that would satisfy consumers' demand, given these externalities. The approach to cultural heritage policies adopted here first points out in detail the main reasons for market failure and then concentrates on the tools of intervention (direct and indirect expenditure, regulation) and the institutional settings in place for the implementation of the policies.

Identifying Cultural Heritage In the case of cultural heritage the starting point for the analysis concerns its nature. It is still debated whether it should be considered as a good or a service. What is the 'product' supplied and consumed when visiting a museum, a heritage site, a monument, a historical centre? The visit itself? The pleasure of the visit? The additional services offered? The difficulty increases because heritage is not a fixed concept. The same notion of what is considered as heritage has been changing through time and is still changing (Rizzo and Mignosa 2013; Vecco 2010). There are two aspects to the change: one in the perception of what is heritage and the other related to its role for policies.

Starting with the latter point, the European Commission (2014) considers the role of cultural heritage beyond cultural policies, highlighting its economic impact, its importance for creativity and the creation and enhancement of social capital, and to achieve the Europe 2020 strategy goals. This approach seems to consider the needs of European societies which are becoming increasingly heterogeneous and where attention is paid to the inclusion and representation of minority cultures. The EU documents point to the role of public cultural institutions in promoting cultural diversity, intercultural dialogue and cultural participation (see for example European Commission 2014: 4).

The identification of cultural heritage is the result of a process of interpretation and selection (Gamboni 2001; Peacock 1994) whose outcome is not unequivocal and predictable. Normally, this process results in the compilation of national or international lists for policy purposes. At the national level, responsibility for listing varies: for example, lists may be the responsibility of central government (France), local government or agencies (such as English Heritage, now Historic England in England).[1] At the international level, the most famous is the World Heritage List (WHL) of UNESCO, which has become a reference point also for national policies.[2]

The focus of UNESCO has changed through time. The Convention for the Protection of the World Cultural and Natural Heritage (UNESCO 1972) initially focused on a 'traditional' or 'Eurocentric' concept of heritage looking at tangible heritage and more specifically at archaeological areas, castles, palaces, ancient constructions, and so on. With the passing of time it first opened up to natural heritage and later to 'less traditional' examples of heritage. Looking at the sites included in the WHL in chronological order, it is evident that there has been a change in the type of heritage included. Initially, the list consisted of 'traditional' heritage but, with the passing of time, natural and mixed sites, old factories, harbours and industrial sites started to be included: there has been an extension in the typology of cultural heritage. UNESCO emphasises the importance of including recent sites and structures not only for their artistic or historical importance but also for their technological and social importance (Operational Guidelines, par. 24). The Convention for the Safeguarding of the Intangible Cultural Heritage (UNESCO 2003) brought to international attention the notion of intangible heritage or *living heritage* intended as 'the practices, representations, expressions, knowledge and skills transmitted by communities from generation to generation' (UNESCO 2016a). Following the 2003 convention intangible heritage came on the agenda of national and local government.[3]

---

[1]For a survey of the different models of decision-making for the identification of cultural heritage see Klamer et al. (2013).

[2]Since 2013, the European Commission has introduced the European Heritage Label which includes (as for March 2016) 29 sites 'selected for their symbolic value, the role they have played in the European history and activities they offer that bring the European Union and its citizens closer together' (European Commission 2016).

[3]See for instance Nederlands Centrum voor Volkscultuur en Immaterieel Erfgoed (VIE) (2012) for the Netherlands and Regione Siciliana (2016) for Sicily (Italy). The notion was already known in far Eastern countries, for example, Japan where it has been the focus of specific policy measures since 1950 (Goto 2013).

Looking at national and international lists, the variety and variability of the criteria used for listing are evident. Illustrations of this come from the WHL: it is not always clear what is of 'outstanding universal value' or a 'masterpiece of human creative genius'. Researchers (Frey and Steiner 2013) as well as UNESCO (2016b) acknowledge the limitations of these criteria and recognise that the List fails to represent all countries and all types of heritage; other rules may influence decisions. The inclusion in a list (national or international) guarantees, or should guarantee, the preservation of a heritage site or item (in the case of movable cultural heritage) by the state. Listing is the result of an often long procedure whose result is not certain and which sees a high degree of 'competition' among different heritage sites. The process of selection itself might be the main cause hindering inclusion in the list. The reason, then, is political and not related to the qualities of the artefacts. As a consequence, 'valuable' heritage items might not be listed if located in politically weak countries. The inclusion in a list may entail a displacement effect. Attention concentrates on the superstar heritage with the risk of neglecting minor sites and thus the risk they will disappear if not protected. At the international level, richer countries may (and actually do) succeed in getting more heritage protected.

Role of Experts The ambiguities of the various definitions of cultural heritage, in fact, give discretion to those who actually make the selection, i.e., the experts. As Peacock (1994: 8) puts it "... [artefacts] become identified as heritage goods usually by archaeologists and historians who have obtained some form of official recognition or public acceptance of their status as experts in determining their artistic or historical significance (...)". The role of these experts is crucial but is also the object of some criticism within cultural economics (Peacock 1994; Throsby 1997, 2001; Rizzo 1998; Benhamou 1996). As a matter of fact, the lack of clear criteria to define cultural heritage transforms the selection process into a "professional or expert discourse whose practitioners will become the arbiters of what comprises heritage and what does not" (Throsby 2001: 75). The experts' background and personal preferences will influence their choices and the implementation of policies. Other stakeholders, like the public, are left out of the process. Still, experts' decisions affect the public and implicate the use of funds, public funds when government intervention is dominant. Experts therefore have the power to distribute resources between different cultural heritage items, determining the qualitative and quantitative composition of the stock of cultural heritage (Throsby 1997; Rizzo 1998).

The nature of heritage explains and somehow justifies the dominance of experts: it is an experience good. Consumers need to have some information before consuming it to appreciate it, but they lack the necessary information. Experts, on the other hand, possess information and can transfer it to consumers, saving them the time and cost necessary to acquire it. This asymmetry explains experts' power to decide which heritage should be supplied. They act as gatekeepers. Blaug (2001) considers this a case of 'supply-induced-demand': the expert (the supplier) decides what to offer and consumers demand it on their recommendation. Economists consider experts' hegemony over choices of heritage in contrast to the principle of consumer sovereignty; taxpayers finance heritage, yet their preferences are not taken into consideration. Hence, some economists (Peacock 1994; van der Ploeg 2006) propose the use of vouchers to let consumers choose directly which museum, heritage site to visit (or cultural 'product') to consume.[4]

Who Decides-Who Pays-Who Benefits? This leads to one of the core issues in the economic analysis of cultural heritage: those who take decisions about cultural heritage are not necessarily those who pay or who benefit from cultural heritage. In fact, several stakeholders participate in the heritage conservation and enhancement process (Throsby 1997) bearing different and, often, conflicting values.[5] The identification of these stakeholders is not easy.

It is possible to make some distinctions between each group of stakeholders. Those who pay can be divided between those who directly bear the costs of preservation, for instance in the case of private ownership or donations, and those who contribute indirectly through tax expenditures. When there is an entrance fee or when heritage is privately owned, those who pay for it are also those who benefit. However, in case of entrance fee, it covers only a small percentage of the costs, thus it is taxpayers who bear most of the costs. In the case of private owners, they may receive subsidies or tax benefits (Benhamou 1996); again, taxpayers are the ones covering at least some of those costs. The same holds true in the case of donations: when donors get a tax waiver discount, the donation is partially covered by taxpayers (Feld et al. 1983).

Depending on the institutional context, decision-makers in the case of heritage might be central or local governments, public institutions, arm's length bodies, private (profit or non-profit) organisations, international institutions, private owners of heritage, etc. Experts still have a key role: they decide what should be considered as heritage and can limit the power of private owners of heritage by imposing rules, regulations and constraints. This can (and often does) lead to conflicts among the various stakeholders. Decision makers therefore should take into consideration all the values that may be attached to heritage to be sure that their choices match the preferences and needs of the different groups who may benefit from and pay for cultural heritage. However, those who decide are not necessarily representative of the wider public interest. Often, decisions are taken through 'top-down processes', and the values considered 'tend to be those of elite or dominant groups such as heritage professionals, bureaucrats and politicians' (Throsby 2001: 85). The risk is then that cultural heritage not representing the value important for the local communities relates only to an elite instead of being a tool for cultural participation and social inclusion.

---

[4]The issue of vouchers is discussed in the chapter by Forte.

[5]The list of activities related to cultural heritage is wider and diversified including research, excavation, preservation, conservation, enhancement, digitalization, and so on. However, following Avrami et al. (2000) who use a wide definition of conservation, here the term is used together with 'enhancement' to indicate the full spectrum of activities related to cultural heritage.

Owners of cultural heritage and local communities might 'simply' want to use a cultural heritage site because they live there, like the people living in the houses on the Amsterdam canals or the Australian aboriginals who have traditionally used Kakadu, which is a sacred mountain, for religious rites or for economic reasons (including mining). Local communities may focus on the prestige or identity value, whereas other groups may consider the spiritual value. These people's interests are not always taken into consideration and can conflict with the conservation stance of national or international institutions. Then there are individuals who actually visit cultural heritage, or who want the option of being able to visit sometime in the future. The latter benefit from the existence of heritage, though they are not able to express the value to them via the market. Another group may desire to allow future generations to enjoy heritage and thus focuses on its bequest value. The educational value may be important for a heterogeneous group including, among others, experts, government officials, and the general public. Archaeologists, art-historians, architects and experts in general would focus on the scientific (artistic, architectural, historical, anthropological) value. The importance of economic value seems to have been increasing, given the attention given to it by governments, local populations, real estate companies, the tourism industry and so on. It is evident, therefore, that not only visitors and owners benefit from cultural heritage.

These different sources of value often clash, causing conflict among different groups of stakeholders. The cultural value of heritage and the conservation stance often conflict with the economic, prestige or spiritual values attached to it, as becomes clear with some World Heritage sites. For instance, the delisting of Dresden from the WHL represents the consequence of the contrast between the values of the local inhabitants and those of UNESCO. The same clash led to the threat of delisting Edinburgh's historical centre from the WHL following its Haymarket and Carlton area development plan. Peacock (2008) was rather critical of the UNESCO's threat as it did not consider the general public but was influenced by pressure groups. He suggested that Scottish local authorities would know better than UNESCO which heritage policy would suit Scotland confirming his positive stance towards decentralisation as the arrangement favoured by government, the private sector and the public (Peacock 2008; Rizzo 2015).

What Are the Policy Objectives? Looking at the objectives of cultural heritage policies (and wider cultural policy) it is possible to identify the underlying values in a specific context (Klamer et al. 2006). The analysis of policies, and especially of their evolution through time, shows a shift of focus or rather the widening of their objectives. In fact, whereas preservation and conservation are still high on the agenda, recently other objectives, such as reorganisation of heritage institutions, the definition of clearer criteria for listing, heritage tourism, education, accessibility, social and economic impact and sustainability have come into consideration. In addition, the need to involve the private sector and, thus, the introduction of tax incentives to stimulate its involvement, have captured the attention of policy makers (Klamer et al. 2013). It is suggested that these objectives reflect the underlying values prevailing within a community, a region, a country, an organisation or a group of decision makers. UNESCO conservationist stance seems to consider option, existence and bequest value. When cultural heritage policy focuses on tourism, one can suggest that economic as well as prestige value play an important role.

Heritage has come to be seen as a 'process and experience' (Ashworth 2013: 367). As mentioned, recent changes have led it to be considered as a "resource for sustainable development and quality of life in a constantly evolving society" (Council of Europe 2005a: 2) underscoring the importance of cultural heritage for the 'contribution it can make to other policies' (Council of Europe, ibid). This rhetoric was put forward already at the end of the 1990s by UNESCO (1996) and the Council of Europe (1997), leading to the emergence of a notion of culture and cultural heritage as instruments for cultural, social and economic development (European Commission 2014). This shift has brought issues as social cohesion, community capacity building, civil society, etc. to the core of policies reflecting also the changes characterising societies.

Thus, cultural heritage is often chosen as an instrument to reach other objectives: boosting tourism, stimulating the construction industry, creating jobs in a moment of economic recession and fostering social inclusion. Rypkema (2007) highlights the economic impact of cultural heritage that can be seen in the rehabilitation of historic buildings as well as increased property value of historic buildings and revenues from heritage tourism. The choice of the prevailing objectives is the responsibility of experts; their power and role vary depending on the institutional model in place; however. They might be working for a central ministry or the cultural office of a local government, for an arm's length body or a private trust, for a public or a private cultural organisation. Understanding these models is important to understand how policies are designed and implemented.

3   Trends in Cultural Policy

3.1   *Institutional Arrangements for Cultural Heritage Policies*

There is a great variety in the institutional arrangements for cultural and cultural heritage policies (Cummings and Katz 1987). Countries may be grouped in three models, according to the degree of centralisation of control by the state. The first comprises countries of continental Europe, where direct government provision and finance of cultural heritage has traditionally played the lion's share. In contrast to this is a model where direct intervention is reduced to the minimum and indirect support plays an important role for the financing of cultural heritage. The third model has an intermediate position; here direct public intervention in the form of financing and direct provision is combined with indirect support and a wide participation of the private sector. In this case, the government plays a guiding role, steering the activity of the other stakeholders involved in cultural heritage conservation and enhancement; Great Britain belongs to this type, for instance.

Public intervention takes place in different ways depending on the type of organisational setting, the tools used and the 'space' left to the private sector. The institutional arrangements put in place indicate which type of organisation is responsible for cultural policies—public authorities, the market, non-profit organisations. Also which level of government—centralized or decentralized—and which type of institutions (for instance, arm's length bodies). A study on cultural heritage policies of EU and non-EU countries (Klamer et al. 2013: 54) shows that those with a centralized organization, where the central ministry has most of the responsibility are still the majority.[6] Lower levels of government (regions, counties, municipalities, and so on) share (some) responsibilities for defining and implementing cultural heritage policies with different degrees of authority, depending on the institutional settings in place. In some countries, a decentralized/federal structure prevails and the lower levels of governments have more power than the central level and are responsible for policies.

The combination of tools of public intervention used varies also. As mentioned, direct public expenditure often corresponds to the direct provision of cultural heritage services through public institutions or the distribution of funds (in the form of subsidies, awards and grants) to public and private cultural institutions, private owners, or arm's length bodies. Another widely used tool, though one not favoured by economists (Throsby 2001), is regulation, that is norms and rules that influence and/or limit activities related to cultural heritage. Governments may also decide to use incentives as tax incentives to involve other actors in the finance of cultural heritage. In that case, to stimulate private individuals or companies to finance cultural heritage or to support no profit organisation the government foregoes taxes. Depending on how the rules are designed, government can steer the private sector intervention towards supporting a specific heritage site or a specific initiative. The different combination of direct expenditure, regulation and indirect expenditure can lead to totally different outcomes of heritage policies.

3.2   Recent Trends in Cultural Heritage Policies

International comparisons of the organisation of cultural policies (Klamer et al. 2006, 2013; www.culturalpolicies.net) show that a process of decentralisation and *désétatisation* is taking place. The trend towards decentralisation has

---

[6]Other ministries are often involved in the definition, implementation and, especially, finance of cultural policies. For instance: the Ministry of Economic Affairs set specific funds for heritage projects in Italy; in Germany, the Federal Ministry of Transport, Building and Urban Development responsible for urban design issues and energy efficiency of buildings also deals with cultural heritage; the Japanese Ministry of Economy, Trade and Industry has responsibilities over intangible heritage together with the Ministry of Culture.

corresponded to a reduction of central governments' expenditures in recent years and to changes in the laws delegating authority for the financing of and decision making about cultural heritage to the lower levels of government, even in traditionally centralized countries (for example, Italy and France). Thus though centralised organisation still prevails, as mentioned before, some form of decentralisation that corresponds to different levels of engagement of the lower levels of government is being introduced. The implementation of this reform is leading to different outcomes even within the same country. A case in point is Italy, where some authority on cultural matters has been delegated to the regional government. Some regional authorities have been introducing standards in the museums belonging to local levels of government (Garlandini 2006).[7] Though some experiences have attracted a lot of attention and been the cause of reflection, there is the risk of having different standards and, thus, different quality in museums. The example shows that besides a policy of delegation, there has to be coordination of policy measures to avoid duplication of activities and expenditure, otherwise, public resources are scattered and their potential effectiveness is reduced.

Furthermore, there is a trend towards a stronger involvement of the private sector. This policy is not new in Anglo-Saxon countries where non-profit institutions, such as foundations and trusts, have traditionally played a fundamental role in the conservation, management and enhancement of cultural heritage, bringing into practice the idea of the 'private provision of public goods' (Bergstrom et al. 1986).[8] However, the idea is still quite new in other countries where the responsibility and authority for cultural matters rests with the public authorities (central or local levels of government depending on the institutional tradition of each country). In these countries (for example, Italy) rules have been introduced that involve the private sector—both profit and non-profit—in the management of cultural heritage sites and museums including those that are publicly owned.[9] The third sector, 'described as 'nongovernment, social, and community-based institutions, and (...) people living near a heritage site' (Macdonald and Cheong 2014: 2) including what Carmel and Harlock (2008) define the 'quasi-private realm of voluntary and community organisations and their activities', has an important role.[10]

While the involvement of the private sector often raises fears of 'commercialisation' of cultural heritage, the involvement of the third sector offers the possibility of boosting finance for heritage preservation and enhancement in a period of increasing constraints for the public sector. Participation by third sphere organisations can overcome market failure, as people would have a chance to

---

[7]In Italy, Lombardy, Tuscany, Emilia Romagna have introduced interesting schemes adjusting them constantly.

[8]As testified, for example, by the importance of the National Trust in England and the role of volunteers in UK.

[9]Private individuals and organizations often own cultural heritage and are thus responsible for it (Fidone 2012; Seaman 2013; Rizzo and Towse 2002).

[10]Klamer uses the term 'third sphere' to refer to this wider notion of third sector (See Klamer and Zuidhof 1998).

support the heritage they value, especially at the local level. This could ensure the preservation of minor items cherished by local communities. However, it could also risk that attention would focus mainly on the more popular items neglecting others. Eventually, a combination of public, market and third sphere action seems the best option. The government would still have to play a fundamental role to steer and coordinate the other actors involved (Boorsma et al. 1998).

In addition assigning a more active role in heritage conservation and enhancement to private actors, countries have also introduced various forms of tax incentives in order to stimulate private intervention in the financing of cultural heritage. This is not something new: indirect support has played an important role for the financing of culture in various countries for some time (notably, the USA). Still, it is interesting that countries where that has not previously been the policy are now considering the possibility to use tax waivers as an element in cultural policy. A case in point is Italy, tax incentives have been present since 1980s and now the last government has increased efforts to spread information about them.[11]

4 The Role of the Private Sector

The question then is to find the right combination between public and private provision of culture and cultural heritage. The need for this has become even more evident following the financial crisis of 2008 and the reduction of public budgets as well as of private resources devoted to the sector. However, this is not something new, Matarasso and Landry (1999) were already reflecting on this issue at the end of the 1990s. By then, however, the debate about private intervention typically focused on two main options: sponsorship and philanthropy. The spectrum is much more complex now as it involves a wider array of possibilities as mentioned above.

These changes are still taking place and at a different pace in different countries. They testify a rising interest towards projects that involve firstly local communities instead of international crowds of tourists attracted by the new superstar museum, blockbuster exhibition, or event. Bilbao is the case that is referred to more often, where the construction of the new museum was the occasion to regenerate the city (Plaza 1999), thanks to the cooperation between the municipality of Bilbao and the regional government with the Guggenheim Foundation. The less famous case of Guimaraes in Portugal is another example of regeneration of the historical centre, which has first of all looked at improving the living conditions of the local community in the centre. The success of the project, promoted by the Guimarães Municipality involved the private sector (real estate companies and community

---

[11]There are even advertisements on the magazine distributed on one of the Italian airlines, see https://www.alitalia.com/content/dam/alitalia/files/IT/volare/news_rubriche/ulisse_megazine/Ulisse_dicembre_2015.pdf#

organisations) and was recognised by a series of prizes—the Europe Nostra Award (1985), the first prize of the Association of Portuguese Architects, in 1993, for the best work of conservation, the Real Fundación de Toledo Prize in 1996—and led to the inclusion of the town in the WHL in 2001 (Castanheira and Bragança 2012).

4.1 Public Private Partnership

This shift corresponds to the spread of 'bottom up' projects that have blossomed especially in urban regeneration but also in theatre management and cultural heritage conservation and enhancement (Barbieri et al. 2012; Dubini et al. 2012; Macdonald and Cheong 2014). It is not a totally new phenomenon; as mentioned earlier trusts and foundations have traditionally had an important role for cultural heritage conservation, management and enhancement, as shown by those in the UK. In some cases, the preservation of some heritage sites has been made possible thanks to the initiative of a group of individuals. In the case of Dutch windmills, for instance, the introduction of steam engines made windmills unnecessary; they occupied spaces that could have been exploited for agriculture thus people started demolishing them. A group of individuals started a campaign to stop the demolition, claiming that windmills should not disappear: they were part of the Dutch landscape and history. These people formed a *Stichting* (foundation) that bought the windmills from the owners, thereby preventing the destruction of an important part of Dutch heritage. Interestingly, the Dutch government then stepped in by appraising the value of windmills and becoming directly involved in their preservation. The importance of windmills was acknowledged at the international level in 1997 when UNESCO put the windmills of Kinderdijk-Elshout on the World Heritage List (Stokhuyzen 1962). Something similar happened in the UK where Railway Preservation Societies '… bought stretches of redundant railway lines from the nationalised railway system in order to cater for a pronounced sentimental interest in old steam trains' (Peacock 1998: 18). In both cases little groups with a specific interest in a historical period or item took action to preserve it for the public at large.

What is different now is that there seems to be a different attitude among decision-makers, who tend to involve local people more. They also are favouring projects that raise awareness among communities, even ones directly initiated by communities who try to '(re)-appropriate' their heritage (Barbieri et al. 2012; Macdonald and Cheong 2014). The involvement of the private sector, as mentioned, has been accompanied by the introduction of different laws and legal arrangements. It has also been made possible thanks to the creation of various forms of public-private-partnerships (PPP) involving both the profit and non-profit sector (Grossman 2008; Macdonald and Cheong 2014; Newman and Smith 2000), which see the collaboration of the public and private partners for the conservation, management and enhancement of cultural heritage (Macdonald and Cheong 2014; Ferri and Zan 2015; Newman and Smith 2000).

According to the National Council for Public-Private Partnerships (2016), a PPP is a contractual agreement between a public agency (federal, state or local) and a private sector entity. The skills and assets of each sector (public and private) are shared in delivering a service or facility for the use of the general public. Moreover, each party shares in the risks and the potential rewards. PPP is not a new construction and has been frequently used for infrastructure or industrial projects in developed countries and to privatize large service companies (UNESCO 2013; Dubini et al. 2012), it has also been widely adopted in urban regeneration projects to face the reduction of public resources on the one side and to involve local communities on the other (van Boxmeer and van Beckhoven 2005).

More recently, at the international level PPP has been increasingly considered an innovative tool for cultural heritage policy (Ferri and Zan 2015; Macdonald and Cheong 2014). The Council of Europe (2005b) suggested the need for guidelines about best practice of public–private partnerships in heritage conservation. According to UNESCO (2013: 1)

> [t]he cultural sector offers a great and unexplored potential for partnerships. Partnerships in the area of culture can bridge the funding gap of public entities, provide interesting investment opportunities for the private sector, but require environmentally and socially sound approaches that respect and benefit local communities.

In theory PPP is able to bring together the best of both worlds: each partner would contribute its competencies and expertise. The public sector would have a fundamental regulatory role while providing administrative support and facilitating investment. The private sector could bring in financial and human resources as well as the expertise and competencies that the public sector may lack. The coordination of public and private actors, the acknowledgment of mutual competences and the sharing of responsibilities are considered as the justification of the projects not only for heritage preservation but also, and especially, to promote the involvement of communities. In the literature there is consensus about the need for a division of 'tasks' between the private and the public sector (Dubini et al. 2012; Sciullo 2009). The former should have authority on all the activities necessary to guarantee the preservation and protection of heritage, whereas the private sector should get responsibility on enhancement activities.

A study by the Italian Ministry of Culture and Tourism (Ministero dei Beni e delle Attività Culturali e Turismo 2015) illustrates several cases of PPP relating to Sicily, a region where there is a special decentralisation of power from the national ministry to the regional government. Some studies (Dubini et al. 2012; Ferri and Zan 2015) concentrate on the Herculaneum Conservation Project (HCP), a partnership agreement between one public partner, the Special Superintendence for Pompeii, Herculaneum and Stabia and two non-profit partners, the Packard Humanities Institute and the British School at Rome for the conservation of the archaeological site of the ancient Roman city.

Another PPP worth mentioning is that between the University of Catania (I) and a private association—*Officine Culturali*, aimed at guaranteeing the enhancement of a World Heritage Site at which one of the departments of the university is based.

The Association aims to open the monastery to the widest public possible making its story and structure comprehensible to everyone. To do this it organises various initiatives and events as well and runs a daily service of guided tours based on international museum standards. All these activities promote social inclusion and development not only for the visitors but also for the members of the organisations who got the contracts to run them. The university, in accordance with the law, gets a percentage of the income from the sale of tickets and other activities of the association. The board of managers is chosen by the same members of the association and plans all the activities with an eye to the economic sustainability and public involvement.[12] The partnership has been indicated as one of best practice as for the management of a heritage site belonging to a university (Pirrelli 2015). Still, it confirms the analysis of the Ministry of Culture and Tourism (2016) about the need for clear rules and arrangements to maximise the advantages connected to this new form of arrangements available in the cultural sector.

4.2   Critiques of PPP

Some scholars (Hodge and Greve 2007), however, suggest that PPP is simply a 'word' designed to cover up other strategies, such as contracting out and privatization. Indeed, the variety of arrangements includes cases that may have side effects. A common critique to PPP relates to the fear that private involvement would lead to the commercialisation of cultural heritage, that is, an exploitation that would neglect cultural value in favour of the economic value. This would be in contrast with the positive view of PPP as a tool to stimulate communities' involvement and to offer the chance of considering the value they assign to 'their' cultural heritage. A second consideration relates to the risk of 'crowding-out' the public sector. It would pass the buck to the private (non profit) sector, giving up its responsibilities and authority on matters of public concern. It seems to be a problem that could affect 'young democracies' where the distribution of power is not balanced (van Boxmeer and van Beckhoven 2005). This issue is particularly sensitive in Italy as well, where the non profit sector is very active in taking care of cultural heritage projects but is still trying to find a balance in its relationship with public institutions.[13]

These tensions point to the need for a different approach: governments should have a leading role in influencing and steering the process, working with a range of different partners—public,   private   for   profit,   non-profit   organisations,

---

[12]For a thorough description of the activities of the association see Mannino and Mignosa (2016).

[13]The Italian Ministry for Culture and Tourism (Ministero dei Beni e delle Attività Culturali e Turismo 2016) analysing the role of PPP for culture, underlines the need for clear rules and the problems that still accompany this arrangements.

communities, and suchlike—in order to guarantee a wider range of activities to conserve and enhance cultural heritage, while taking into consideration the benefits for all the stakeholders (Matarasso and Landry 1999).

5 Concluding Remarks

If we think about the experience of the National Trust in England, it is evident that PPP is not a new phenomenon. What is new is the attention paid to this collaboration and the increased number of PPP projects (Macdonald and Cheong 2014). A possible explanation is the reduction of public resources that has followed the financial crisis of 2008 and the consequent need to find new arrangements to overcome it. This has led to a multiplication of the initiatives started by the private sector and, often, to the introduction of different set of rules in those countries (for example, in Italy) where the private sector was active in cultural heritage conservation only when it owned it.

Peacock favoured tax incentives and this tool has become widespread. He was a strong supporter of people's involvement and, as mentioned, the spread of PPP is (or could be) a way to stimulate people's participation in projects related to cultural heritage. In relation to that, the third sector occupies a special position, possibly in combination with regulation and subsidies. The gatekeeping role of experts is somewhat limited because of the decision-making processes that include non-government organisations that characterise PPP. Though, of course, conflicts can and do still happen, as shown by the case of Panmure House, Adam Smith's last residence which was bought by Edinburgh Business School in order to restore it. It turned into a long endeavor, as illustrated in Peacock (2013). The School bought the house in 2008 but restoration work started only in July 2015,[14] because of a series of rounds of consultation and objections (later dismissed) from Historic Scotland, the agency responsible for decisions on cultural heritage conservation in Scotland.[15]

Can we say that the radical reforms that Peacock (1994, 2001) called for have taken place and culture and cultural heritage are now run with the 'full support and interest of the public'? He was in favour of devolution of decision-making and finance of cultural heritage that he believed offer taxpayers the chance to be more involved in the process. Devolution also allows healthy competition to take place between fiscal authorities. Peacock was in favour of a specific model of ownership and management for heritage, as well as of cultural policy. He suggested that what can be called the National Trust model—membership organisations indirectly supported by the state through tax waivers—would maximise consumer sovereignty and ensure that the public's preferences are taken into account in choices

---

[14]See http://www.panmurehouse.org.

[15]In 2015, Historic Environment Scotland was created. The new agency includes the responsibilities of Historic Scotland and the Royal Commission on the Ancient and Historical Monuments.

about heritage. That is not the typical model in most countries, especially those in which heritage is owned and managed directly by the state. In these countries, experts take decisions about preservation, often without consideration of the number or choices of visitors, who have no mechanism for expressing their preferences. Even this model has been changing in recent times, however, and the entry of PPPs is loosening bureaucratic control, though not necessarily the ownership, of cultural heritage.

This chapter has looked at these questions through the lens of cultural economics. The question whether it is possible to provide evidence on which to base policy advice remains. A considerable body of qualitative information based on case studies provides information on successful measures, always considering that policy has an objective and that may be different in different cases. Another possible approach would be to use quantitative data to compare the outcomes of different models, for example, data on visitor numbers to comparable heritage sites, studies of willingness to pay (which are already conducted for cost benefit analysis evaluation of the value of heritage), a comparison of public expenditure per visitor. Such information could be used to make judgements on the social efficiency of the different measures and models adopted to preserve our cultural heritage.

References

Ashworth GJ (2013) Heritage and local development: a reluctant relationship. In: Rizzo I, Mignosa A (eds) A handbook on the economics of cultural heritage. Edward Elgar, Cheltenham, UK, pp 367–385

Avrami E, Mason R, de la Torre M (2000) Values and heritage conservation. Research Report. The Getty Conservation Institute, Los Angeles

Barbieri N, Fina X, Subirats J (2012) Culture and urban policies: dynamics and effects of cultural third sector intervention in Barcelona. Mètropoles 11. http://metropoles.revue.org/4605. Accessed 17 Feb 2016

Benhamou F (1996) L'economie de la culture. Editions La Découverte, Paris

Benhamou F (2011) Heritage. In: Towse R (ed) A handbook of cultural economics. Edward Elgar, Cheltenham, UK, pp 229–235

Benhamou F (2013) Public intervention for cultural heritage: normative issues and tools. In: Rizzo I, Mignosa A (eds) A handbook on the economics of cultural heritage. Edward Elgar, Cheltenham, UK, pp 3–16

Bergstrom TC, Blume LE, Varian HR (1986) On the private provision of public goods. J Publ Econ 29:25–49

Blaug M (2001) Where are we now on cultural economics? J Econ Surv 15(2):123–143

Boorsma PB, Van Hemel A, Van Der Wielen N (1998) Privatization and culture: experiences in the arts, heritage and cultural industries in Europe. Kluwer Academic, Dordrecht

Carmel E, Harlock J (2008) Instituting the 'third sector' as a governable terrain: partnership, procurement and performance in the UK. Pol Polit 36(2):155–171

Castanheira G, Bragança L (2012) Urban renovation of Portuguese historical centres. In: Bragança L, Fangueiro R, Ramos LF (eds) Construção e reabilitação sustentáveis—Soluções eficientes para um mercado em crise. Livro de Atas, Workshop Guimarães, 21 Sept 2012, Universidade do Minho. http://hdl.handle.net/1822/22417. Accessed 22 Mar 2016

Council of Europe (1997) In from the margins—a contribution to the debate on culture and development in Europe. www.coe.int/t/dg4/cultureheritage/culture/resources/Publications/InFromTheMargins_EN.pdf. Accessed 1 Feb 2016

Council of Europe (2005a) Framework convention on the value of cultural heritage for society, Faro 27 Oct 2005. Council of Europe Treaty Series—No. 199. http://conventions.coe.int/Treaty/Commun/QueVoulezVous.asp?NT=199&CM=8&CL=ENG. Accessed 20 Apr 2014

Council of Europe (2005b) The private management of cultural property. http://assembly.coe.int/Mainasp?link=/Documents/AdoptedText/ta05/EREC1730.htm. Accessed 10 Sept 2014

Cummings MC, Katz RS (eds) (1987) The patron state—governments and the arts in Europe. Oxford University Press, Oxford

Dubini P, Leone L, Forti L (2012) Role distribution in public–private partnerships. The case of heritage management in Italy. Int Stud Manag Organ 42(2):57–75

European Commission (2014) Mapping of cultural heritage actions in European Union policies, programmes and activities. http://ec.europa.eu/culture/library/reports/2014-heritage-mapping_en.pdf. Accessed 22 Mar 2016

European Commission (2016) European heritage label. Europe starts here! http://ec.europa.eu/programmes/creative-europe/actions/heritage-label/index_en.htm. Accessed 22 Mar 2016

Feld AL, O'Hare M, Schuster JMD (1983) Patrons despite themselves: taxpayers and arts policy. New York University Press, New York

Ferri P, Zan L (2015) Partnerships for heritage conservation: evidence from the archeological site of Herculaneum. J Manag Govern 19:167–195

Fidone G (2012) Il ruolo dei privati nella valorizzazione dei beni culturali: dalle sponsorizzazioni alle forme di gestione. AEDON. Accessed 29 Jun 2016

Frey B, Steiner L (2013) World heritage list. In: Rizzo I, Mignosa A (eds) A handbook on the economics of cultural heritage. Edward Elgar, Cheltenham, UK, pp 171–186

Gamboni D (2001) World heritage: shield or target? Conservat Getty Conservat Inst Newslett 16 (2):5–11

Garlandini A (2006) L'intervento delle regioni a favore dei musei: uno scenario in profondo cambiamento. Aedon 2. http://www.aedon.mulino.it/archivio/2006/2/garlandini.htm. Accessed 24 Mar 2016

Goto K (2013) Policy for intangible heritage in Japan: how it relates to creativity. In: Rizzo I, Mignosa A (eds) A handbook on the economics of cultural heritage. Edward Elgar, Cheltenham, UK, pp 567–585

Grossman SA (2008) The case of business improvement districts: special district public–private cooperation in community revitalization. Publ Perform Manag Rev 32(2):290–308

Hodge GA, Greve C (2007) Public–private partnerships: an international performance review. Public Adm Rev 67(3):545–558

Klamer A, Zuidhof PW (1998) The values of cultural heritage: merging economic and cultural appraisals. In: de La Torre M, Mason R (eds) Economics and heritage conservation. Getty Conservation Institute. Getty Center, Los Angeles, pp 23–61

Klamer A, Petrova L, Mignosa A (2006) Financing the arts and culture in the European Union. European Parliament, Brussels, www.culturalpolicies.net/web/files/134/en/Financing_the_Arts_and_Culture_in_the_EU.pdf. Accessed 20 Jan 2016

Klamer A, Mignosa A, Petrova L (2013) Cultural heritage policies: a comparative perspective. In: Rizzo I, Mignosa A (eds) A handbook on the economics of cultural heritage. Edward Elgar, Cheltenham, UK, pp 37–86

Macdonald S, Cheong C (2014) The role of public-private partnerships and the third sector in conserving heritage buildings, sites, and historic urban areas. The Getty Conservation Institute, Los Angeles

Mannino F, Mignosa A (2016) Public private partnership for the enhancement of cultural heritage: the case of the Benedictine monastery of Catania. In: Ateca Amestoy VM, Ginsburgh V, Mazza I, O'Hagan J, Prieto-Rodriguez J (eds) Enhancing cultural participation in the arts in the EU – Challenges and methods. Springer, Heidelberg (in press)

Matarasso F, Landry C (1999) Balancing act: twenty-one strategic dilemmas in cultural policy. Cultural Policies Research and Development Unit. Policy Note No. 4 Council of Europe Publishing

Mignosa A (2005) To preserve or not to preserve? Economic dilemmas in the cases of Sicilian and Scottish cultural heritage. PhD thesis, Erasmus University Rotterdam

Ministero dei Beni e delle Attività Culturali e Turismo (2015) Soggetti privati e cultura. Indagine sul contesto siciliano. http://www.retepoat.beniculturali.it/wp-content/uploads/2015/05/POAT_MiBACT_Soggetti-privati-e-cultura.-Indagine-sul-contesto-siciliano-08052015.pdf. Accessed 20 Mar 2016

Ministero dei Beni e delle Attività Culturali e Turismo (2016) Il partenariato pubblico privato nel settore culturale. http://www.retepoat.beniculturali.it/download/il-partenariato-pubblico-privato-nel-settore-culturale/. Accessed 18 Mar 2016

Mueller D (2003) Public choice III. Cambridge University Press, Cambridge

National Council for Public-Private Partnerships (2016) 7 keys to success. www.ncppp.org/ppp-basics/7-keys. Accessed 23 Mar 2016

Nederlands Centrum voor Volkscultuur en Immaterieel Erfgoed (VIE) (2012) Intangible cultural heritage—Chances and opportunities for policy. http://immaterieelerfgoed.nl/Lectures_64.html. Accessed 20 Jan 2016

Newman P, Smith I (2000) Cultural production, place and politics on the South Bank of the Thames. Int J Urban Reg Res 24(1):9–24

Peacock AT (1994) A future for the past: the political economy of heritage. Proc Br Acad 87:189–226, reprinted in Hume Occasional paper n. 44, Edinburgh

Peacock AT (1998) The economist and heritage policy: a review of issues. In: Peacock AT (ed) Does the past have a future? The Institute of Economic Affairs, London, pp 1–26

Peacock AT (2001) Calling the tune: a critique of arts funding in Scotland. Policy Institute, Edinburgh

Peacock AT (2008) UNESCO's role is rather like that of the Good Food Guide. The Scotsman, 28 August

Peacock AT (2013) 'Adam Smith has returned to live in Edinburgh': a case study. In: Rizzo I, Mignosa A (eds) A handbook on the economics of cultural heritage. Edward Elgar, Cheltenham, pp 491–498

Pirrelli (2015) Atenei, Scrigni ricchi d'arte da scoprire, Il Sole 24ore, Sabato 19 December:27

Plaza B (1999) The Guggenheim-Bilbao Museum effect: a reply. Int J Urban Reg Res 23(3):589–592

Regione Siciliana (2016) Registro eredità immateriale. www.regione.sicilia.it/bbccaa/dirbenicult/info/news/REI/index.html. Accessed 20 Jan 2016

Rizzo I (1998) Heritage regulation: a political economy approach. In: Peacock AT (ed) Does the past have a future? The political economy of heritage. The Institute of Economic Affairs, London, pp 55–74

Rizzo I (2015) A 'naughty' cultural economist. In: Alan Peacock dissenting. Essays in memory of the founder of The David Hume Institute. The David Hume Institute, Edinburgh, pp 34–39

Rizzo I, Mignosa A (eds) (2013) A handbook on the economics of cultural heritage. Edward Elgar, Edward

Rizzo I, Throsby D (2006) Cultural heritage: economic analysis and public policy. In: Ginsburg VA, Throsby D (eds) Handbook of the economics of art and culture. Elsevier, Amsterdam, pp 983–1016

Rizzo I, Towse R (eds) (2002) The economics of heritage. A study in the political economy of culture in Sicily. Edward Elgar, Cheltenham, UK

Rypkema (2007) Public-private partnerships for heritage buildings. UNECE United National Economic Commission for Europe on Promoting Successful Public-Private Partnerships in the UNECE region. www.unece.org/fileadmin/DAM/ceci/ppt_presentations/2007/ppp/rypk.pdf. Accessed 15 Mar 2014

Sciullo G (2009) Novità sul partenariato pubblico-privato nella valorizzazione dei beni culturali. AEDON. http://www.aedon.mulino.it/archivio/2009/2/sciullo.htm. Accessed 30 Jun 2016

Seaman B (2013) The role of the private sector in cultural heritage. In: Rizzo I, Mignosa A (eds) A handbook on the economics of cultural heritage. Edward Elgar, Cheltenham, UK, pp 111–128

Stokhuyzen F (1962) The Dutch windmill. Merlin P in association with CAJ van Dishoeck

Throsby D (1997) Seven questions in the economics of cultural heritage. In: Hutter M, Rizzo I (eds) Economic perspectives in cultural heritage. Macmillan, London, pp 13–30

Throsby D (2001) Economics and culture. Cambridge University Press, Cambridge, UK

Throsby D (2010) The economics of cultural policy. Cambridge University Press, Cambridge, UK

Towse R (1994) Achieving public policy objectives in the arts and heritage. In: Peacock A, Rizzo I (eds) Cultural economics and cultural policies. Kluwer, Dordrecht, pp 143–165

Towse R (2010) A textbook of cultural economics. Cambridge University Press, Cambridge, UK

UNESCO (1972) The convention for the protection of the world cultural and natural heritage

UNESCO (1996) Our creative diversity. Report of the World Commission on Culture and Development. http://unesdoc.unesco.org/images/0010/001055/105586e.pdf. Accessed 20 Feb 2016

UNESCO (2003) Convention for the safeguarding of the intangible cultural heritage

UNESCO (2013) Background note (PDF) on public private partnerships in the culture sector. www.unesco.org/new/fileadmin/MULTIMEDIA/HQ/CLT/images/PublicPrivatePartnershipENG.pdf. Accessed 22 Mar 2016

UNESCO (2016a) Intangible cultural heritage. http://en.unesco.org/themes/intangible-cultural-heritage. Accessed 19 Mar 2016

UNESCO (2016b) Global strategy. http://whc.unesco.org/en/globalstrategy/. Accessed 19 Mar 2016

Van Boxmeer B, Van Beckhoven E (2005) Public–private partnership in urban regeneration: a comparison of Dutch and Spanish PPPs. Int J Hous Pol 5(1):1–16

van der Ploeg F (2006) The making of cultural policy: a European perspective. In: Ginsburgh VA, Throsby D (eds) Handbook of the economics of art and culture. North-Holland, Amsterdam, pp 1183–1221

Vecco M (2010) A definition of cultural heritage: from the tangible to the intangible. J Cult Herit 11:321–324

On Judging Art and Wine

Victor Ginsburgh

Abstract In this chapter, I show that evaluating wine is very close to evaluating art, but that the gradings or rankings that follow often result in bullshit, within the meaning given to it by philosopher Harry Frankfurt (On bullshit. Princeton University Press, Princeton, NJ, 2005).

> A book of verses underneath the bough
>> A flask of wine, a loaf of bread and thou
>> Beside me singing in the wilderness
>> And wilderness is paradise now.
>> (Omar Khayyam, *The Rubaiyat*)

1 Introduction

I always find it hard to say what a great painting, or a great piece of music is. The more I see and hear, the more I change my mind, and start hesitating whether what I liked yesterday is still what I like today. I prefer Mozart's *Don Giovanni* that I heard yesterday to his *Magic Flute* that I listened to a couple of weeks ago, though I know that I will change my mind when I go back to the aria of the Queen of the Night. And it also happens that I will prefer Alban Berg's five *Altenberg Lieder* to both operas.

The same, if not worse, happens with wines. I like, or I dislike a wine, but never can distinguish what makes it likeable and what makes it bad, except when it is corked. It looks as if the only (negative) property that I can distinguish in a wine is the taste of cork. Not really, since I can also recognize sweet wines,[1] clarets and Burgundies, which I like in certain contexts, and dislike in others. I cannot even understand what an expert taster (Robert Parker) means, and adds to a wine

---

[1] Try *Assyrtiko* from the Greek island of Santorini. It is good, and helps Greek exports. See http://www.nytimes.com/2015/08/05/dining/wine-school-assyrtiko.html?emc=eta1&_r=1.

V. Ginsburgh (✉)
European Center for Advanced Research in Economics and Statistics (ECARES), Brussels, Belgium
e-mail: vginsbur@ulb.ac.be

© Springer International Publishing Switzerland 2016
I. Rizzo, R. Towse (eds.), *The Artful Economist*,
DOI 10.1007/978-3-319-40637-4_15

245

(a Châteauneuf du Pape) that he describes as follows[2]: "Deep ruby color includes purpose nuances. Closed aromatically, hints of crème de cassis and black cherries. Cuts broad swath across the palate with considerable depth and concentration. Tannic as well as broodingly backward." I am unable to say whether I will like such a wine or not, since I cannot reconstruct mentally the taste of 'cassis and black cherries', not to speak about the taste of 'closed aromatically' or 'broodingly backward'. Probably I would not even notice the nuances if I were drinking the wine. Journalist Bianca Bosker (2015) published a long paper in the *New Yorker* concerning wine tasting and concludes "as extravagant tasting notes have become de rigueur in the marketing world, they've also arguably lost their practical function as consumer guides."

As David Hume (1965 [1757]: 5) reminds us in his essay on the standard of taste, wine tasting was different in the times of Cervantes and Don Quixotte:

> It is with good reason, says Sancho to the squire with the great nose, that I pretend to have a judgment in wine: This is a quality hereditary in our family. Two of my kinsmen were once called to give their opinion of a hogshead, which was supposed to be excellent, being old and of a good vintage. One of them tastes it; considers it; and, after mature reflection, pronounces the wine to be good, were it not for a small taste of leather, which he perceived in it. The other, after using the same precautions, gives also his verdict in favour of the wine; but with the reserve of a taste of iron, which he could easily distinguish. You cannot imagine how much they were both ridiculed for their judgment. But who laughed in the end? On emptying the hogshead, there was found at the bottom an old key with a leathern thong tied to it.

Though the two experts did not agree, each of them discovered what he considered as being a property of the wine, while, with the exception of Parker himself, nobody knows whether the properties that he describes have much meaning.

As we shall see, evaluating art and wines are quite similar, though the few art philosophers who also write on wine[3] draw interesting distinctions. Immanuel Kant who enjoyed wine, separates it from art: There is a difference, he writes, between the 'agreeable' or the 'nice' such as the taste on the tongue, the palate, where everyone has his own taste, and the 'beautiful', which can be made 'universal' using cognitive arguments and the reason to convince others to agree.[4] But,

> the niceness of Canary wine lacks 'universal voice': as far as judgments of niceness and nastiness are concerned, anything goes. If you do not like smoked salmon, you are not lacking in judgment in the way you are if you do not appreciate the beauty of the Alhambra... People may sometimes say that others are wrong to like certain food or drink, but, in contrast with the aesthetic case, this is not something that they insist on for

---

[2]Quoted by Weil (2007: 137).

[3]To my knowledge, wine experts do not often discuss art.

[4]See Kant (1790).

long when faced with those with radically different likes or dislikes. The normative claim of aesthetic judgments has a certain *robustness* in the face of radically different judgments.[5]

Art philosopher Scruton (2009: 61) invokes 'intention' which is present in artworks, but not in wine. He takes music as example, but the argument can easily be extended to all performing and visual arts as well as to literature:

> The comparison between wine and music helps us also to understand why wine is not an art form. The notes in music are also gestures, marked by intention. In listening to them we encounter an act of communication, an intentional *putting across* of an imagined state of mind . . . Other things that we produce intentionally are not *marked* by intention as works of art are marked. The lettuces that grow in my garden were grown intentionally, and I worked to ensure that they had the shape and flavour that they have. In that sense their shape and flavour are intentionally produced. But the taste of the lettuce is not the taste of my horticultural intention, in the way that the sound of the kettledrum at the start of Beethoven's violin concerto is the sound of musical intention. We don't taste intention in lettuce as we hear intention in music. And that goes also for wine. However much the tastes in a great wine are the result of an intention to produce them, we don't taste the intention in tasting the wine, as we hear the intention in music. Wine results from the mind, but never expresses it.

The chapter proceeds as follows. Section 2 discusses evaluation in general, and tries to compare how one proceeds in the arts and for wines. Section 3 concentrates on wine tasting competitions, and analyses the famous 1976 Judgment of Paris, where Californian wines dethroned French wines. Section 4 briefly concludes.

2 Evaluation: The Views of Philosophers, Economists and Sociologists

It is convenient to distinguish between those who believe that properties lie in the object itself (realism) and those who, like Hume (1965 [1757]: 6), believe that properties are "no quality in things themselves: [they exist] merely in the mind which contemplates them; and each mind perceives a different beauty" (anti-realism).

2.1 Realism: Properties Lie in the Object

If properties lie in the work (or commodity) itself, it can be decomposed into parts (characteristics in the language of economists, properties in the one of philosophers) and each part can be valued; their individual valuations could be used to compare and perhaps rank the works.

---

[5]Zangwill (2003: 71). The consideration on Canary wine is by Kant, and so is the expression 'universal voice'. In Kant's time, Canary wine was considered a delicate wine. See also Zangwill (2014).

This is what, in the second half of the twentieth century, analytical philosophers suggested—though, as we shall see later, art critic Piles (1708) had also played with such an idea in the beginning of the eighteenth century, and so did Richardson (1719). Beardsley (1958), for instance, claims that there exist standards that make a work good. He considers three properties, unity, intensity and complexity such that if one of them is present in a work, the work is better. There also exist 'secondary' properties that will make a work better in a certain context, and worse in others. Beauty or quality may thus be contextual ("a beautiful ox would be an ugly horse", Sartwell 2014). Levinson (2003: 6) quotes some properties that belong to an open-ended list: Beauty, ugliness, sublimity, grace, harmony, balance, unity, etc., but he also adds that the "demarcation of the class is subject to dispute." Vermazen (1975), and Dickie (1988, chapter 9) take the idea a step further by suggesting that properties can be graded. However, they also point out that properties are incommensurable, and even if they are graded, can, therefore, not be aggregated to compute a total value, unless one gives arbitrary weights (for example equal weights) to the properties and computes a weighted average. But different weights will lead to different total values, and possibly change the ranking.

Economist Lancaster (1966) took a similar approach, by considering a commodity to be a bundle of characteristics. Since there are no markets for individual characteristics, these cannot be bought but consumers can choose among varieties (of computers for instance) to construct their preferred choice(s). Producers—including artists or winemakers—provide bundles of choices by producing different varieties, and consumers pick the one that provides the characteristics they find closest to their preferred combination.

This view led to a refinement of the economic theory of product differentiation (introduced by Chamberlin in 1933), which distinguishes vertical and horizontal characteristics in goods. Vertical characteristics are those on which every consumer can agree that more is better (or worse) than less (or more), other things, including price, being equal: Characteristics are monotonic in quantity. The size of the memory of a computer is a vertical characteristic. But some consumers prefer black computers, others prefer them silver: The colour of a computer is a horizontal quality. Adam Smith had already suggested distinguishing "differences of things which in no way affect their real substance," but yield pleasure, guide choices and drive "the whole industry of human life."[6]

The total value of the commodity (its price for economists) can in principle be reconstructed by computing a weighted sum of the prices of the characteristics. This is the way a price is set by the producer who also adds his profit margin. Economists go the other way and retrieve the value of individual characteristics by running a hedonic regression of total prices on the quantity of each characteristic (size of the memory, speed, dimensions, weight, perhaps colour, etc). The estimated parameters are the weights with which each characteristic contributes to the total price. The results of what can be called 'reverse engineering' (a dual approach to the one

---

[6]See De Marchi (2009: 97).

considered by philosophers) can inform consumers whether the price of a certain good is over- or underrated by comparing it to the weighted sum of the prices of the characteristics. If the price is larger (smaller) than this weighted sum, the consumer price is too high (low).

Peacock (1993: 80–85) plays with the close idea that funding bodies could use to make decisions in their funding of concerts, instead of considering the total number of concerts only. He divides concerts into seven categories (properties): total number, number of educational concerts, number of concerts with one, two or three new works (three categories), number of concerts with 'local' music and number of 'out of town' concerts. He then imagines different sets of weights given to the categories that are supposed to represent possible choices of implicit weights that could be used by the funding body to value each concert.

2.2 Anti-realism: Properties Lie in the Eye of the Beholder (or of the Taster)

Other philosophers "locate the ground of judgments of taste, not in some object which is the target of the judgment, but in the maker of the judgment" (Shiner 1996: 237) and seem to reach a minimal agreement on the following arguments already developed in Hume's classic essay on taste:

(i) Quality assessments should be left to experts who are familiar with the experience of the class of objects they have to value. Following Hume (1965 [1757]: 17–18)

> though the principles of taste be universal, and nearly, if not entirely, the same in all men, yet few are qualified to give judgment on any work of art, or establish their own sentiment as the standard of beauty ... Some men in general, however difficult to be particularly pitched upon, will be acknowledged by universal sentiment to have a preference above others.

(ii) Hume (1965 [1757]: 17) also lists the qualities that such experts should be endowed with: "strong sense, united to delicate sentiment, improved by practice, perfected by comparison, and cleared of all prejudice[7]; and the joint verdict of such ... is the true standard of taste and beauty."[8]

---

[7]Kant also strongly emphasized "disinterestedness" of judges.

[8]This is obviously not what Peacock (2006: 1139) thought of his fellow economists who do not pursue the public interest. He "regards it as essential that economists will retain a watching brief on those who claim that their expertise entitles them to pride of place in policy decisions. If we do not continue to demonstrate that their judgments of value are arbitrary, then we must not be surprised if they continue to invent the economics for themselves", instead "of being concerned with the immediate realities of improving the human condition."

Some philosophers and art critics thus put on experts the burden of proving quality, while economists often argue that the choice should be left to consumers. Bentham (1818 [1789]: 254) for example, was very critical of experts. According to him, they reduce the choice of consumers and "are really only the interrupters of their pleasure."[9]

Bourdieu (1983, 1996) argues that evaluation, and thus value, is arbitrary, because it is based on motivations imposed by the social and political structures of the cultural hierarchy.[10] It is objective but *only* as a social fact: the (artistic) field is contained within the field of power, which is itself situated within the field of class relations (Bourdieu 1983: 319). Accordingly, there exist no criteria that allow determining the intrinsic quality of a work, but only professional judges or experts who "possess the socially accepted authority to ascribe specific properties to a work … and how it should be ranked" (Van Rees 1983: 398). This is exactly what happens with the usual way of grading and ranking artworks and wines, to which we turn in Sects. 2.4.2 and 2.4.3.

2.3   The Test of Time

A test that is often used in the arts, but for obvious reasons much less so in wines,[11] is the test of time, introduced as follows by Hume (1965 [1757]: 9):

> A real genius, the longer his works endure, and the more wide they are spread, the more sincere is the admiration which he meets with… [E]nvy and jealousy have too much place in a narrow circle; and even familiar acquaintance may diminish the applause due to [the artist's] performances: but when these obstructions are removed, the beauties immediately display their energy; and while the work endures they maintain their authority over the minds of men.

This is how Peacock (1994: 8) interprets the test of time, though he is closer to Bourdieu's scepticism concerning the choice of experts:

> a large proportion of artefacts are not produced with the idea of reminding us of our past […] They become identified as heritage goods usually by archaeologists and historians who have obtained some form of official recognition or public acceptance of their status as experts in determining their artistic or historical significance.

What art historians have written on artists and their works at different points in time eventually lead to 'canons', that broadly speaking consist in lists of names and titles of works that belong to history. Given the short life of wines (with a few exceptions, and unless one can retrieve a couple of amphorae of Opimian wine

---

[9]Quoted by Goodwin (2006: 44).

[10]See also Hutter and Shusterman (2006: 193).

[11]Though the famous 1855 classification for Bordeaux wines is still in use today, but here causality may go in the other direction. Works of art that pass the test of time are celebrated works. For wines, it may well be that the heirs of winemakers whose wines had been ranked in 1855 still make efforts not to lose their "accreditation." See Ginsburgh (2014).

produced by the Romans in 121 BC, a very famous vintage), the test of time is hardly applicable. For further philosophical insights, see Savile (1982). Applications of the test and the way canons emerge can be found in Ginsburgh and Weyers (2010, 2014).

2.4   Evaluation in Practice

We distinguish two situations. If properties exist, they can be used to rank artworks or wines, though the ranking may not be complete (not all objects under consideration can be ranked). In most cases, the task of grading or ranking is left to art or wine experts who sometimes do implicitly use properties and explain their choices, but this is not always (and not necessarily) the case. If there is only one judge, the distinction between grading and ranking does of course not matter, since it leads to the same result. Once there is more than one judge, ranking and rating may lead to different results, and aggregating ranks or rates becomes problematic, unless a dictatorial judge imposes his or her choices.

2.4.1   Properties Exist and Are Used to Grade or Rank

We use a very simple example to show that it is not always possible to rank artworks or wines, even if their properties can be defined and graded, and even if there is a unique judge. Assume that we want to rank two works (or wines) a and b endowed with the same three properties A, B and C. Numbers between 0 and 20 represent the marks given to each property. Hence (17, 19, 18) means that work a gets 17 on property A, 19 on B and 18 on C. If the properties are incommensurable, one cannot compare work a with work b which has been given (17, 18, 19), since it gets a lower mark on property B and a higher one on C than work a.

Dickie (1988: 167–182) suggests constructing tables that allow comparisons with respect to a given work, say c, as long as the works to which c is compared have more of one property, and not less of any other, or less of one property and not more of any other. Work c endowed with properties marked (16, 15, 17) is 'better' than the four works that are located below c, and worse than those located above c in the following table:

	(17, 19, 18)
	(17, 18, 18)—(16, 19, 18)
	(17, 15, 18)—(16, 16, 17)
work c	(16, 15, 17)
	(15, 15, 15)—(16, 14, 17)
	(15, 13, 17)—(16, 15, 16)

In fact, Dickie constructs orderings, but in general these will be partial, and not complete: it is not possible to rank all the works. For example, we cannot decide whether work d with marks (16, 17, 14) is better or worse than c.

Table 1 Piles grading of properties for ten of his 56 painters

Painter	Composition	Drawing	Colour	Expression
Raphael	17	18	12	18
Rubens	18	13	17	17
Primaticcio	15	14	17	13
Domenichino	15	17	9	17
The Carraci	15	17	13	13
Le Brun	16	16	8	16
Van Dyck	15	10	17	13
Corregio	13	13	15	12
Poussin	15	17	6	15
Vanius	13	15	12	13

Source: Piles (1708)

Table 2 Piles grading. Some partial orders

Painter	Composition	Drawing	Colour	Expression
Raphael	17	18	12	18
Le Brun	16	16	8	16
Rubens	18	13	17	17
Van Dyck	15	10	17	13
Primaticcio	15	14	17	13
Van Dyck	15	10	17	13
Rubens	18	13	17	17
Corregio	13	13	15	12
Raphael	17	18	12	18
Domenichino	15	17	9	17
Poussin	15	17	6	15

Source: Own calculations

Interestingly enough, 300 years ago, the French art critic Piles (1989 [1708])
tried to describe the quality of painters on the basis of four properties: composition,
drawing, colour and expression. He graded on a scale between 0 and 20 each
property for 56 painters and constructed a table that he called 'the balance of
painters', but he avoided ranking the painters themselves (he did not aggregate
the grades). Table 1 illustrates his grades for ten painters from his and previous
times.

A couple of partial orderings are shown in Table 2 where, for instance, Raphael
obtains grades that are all larger than those of Lebrun. But these orders are partial,
and the reader can check that it is impossible to order all ten painters using this
method. This may even get more difficult as the number of objects (here painters)
increases, and if several experts are asked to grade the objects, since one would also
have to 'aggregate' the opinions of experts, and encounter Arrow's impossibility
result (see Sect. 2.4.4).

2.4.2 Voting on Quality

Voting by a jury is of course the most common method used to grade or rank both works of art and wines. This is so in most competitions such as the many musical competitions, the Oscar awards for movies, the Man-Booker Prize for novels, as well as for wines. Most competitions proceed in several stages in which the jury (which consists of several judges, sometimes up to 5000 for the Oscars) selects a subset of the competing subjects or objects and carries them to the next stage. In the one before the final stage, judges are faced with a small number of subjects (twelve finalists in the Queen Elisabeth competition for piano or violin, only six in the Tchaikovsky competition) or objects (five nominated movies, five or six titles for the Man-Booker Prize, ten to 20 wines). For musical competitions and wines, judges must sit together and listen or taste (though they are not necessarily the same during the whole competition, because they may not have the time to be present during all the stages, or because they get drunk). This is not necessarily so for movies and books that they can watch or read wherever they are, though they may have to gather for the last stage in which winners are selected. The names of the wines are of course hidden (the tasting is said to be blind). This may also be so for competitions in which orchestras have to choose musicians (who play behind a curtain), but is not so for musical competitions in general.[12]

The last stage consists in choosing the unique winner (Oscars, Man-Booker Prize)—the other finalists are 'nominated'—or in grading or ranking the candidates (musical competitions, wines). In some musical competitions, such as the Queen Elisabeth, 12 candidates are selected to participate in the finals. Until 1993, all 12 were ranked. Later on, only the first six are ranked while the other six are finalists but not ranked. In the Chopin and Tchaikovsky musical competitions, it happened that some prizes (for instance, the 'first' or the 'fourth') were not attributed. And W. H. Auden once closed the Yale Young Poets competition (of which he was the sole judge) without handing out any prize. But Auden was well known for having been a dictator!

Detailed opinions of judges are usually not revealed, and only the winner (Oscars, Man-Booker Prize) or the final rankings (in most musical competitions) are made public. The only way to compare winners and nominees is what happens to both once time has erased the immediate urgencies and possible favours.[13] This is not so in the case of wines (and some sports, such as artistic skating or diving, in which ratings are made public while the competition is under way), where many details of the proceedings are available, as we shall see in Sect. 3.

---

[12]Which may be unfortunate, since in one competition at least the final ranking was shown to depend on the order in which candidates performed. See Ginsburgh and van Ours (2003). Though one can also think that judges find important to observe body movements (musical gesture) of the musicians.

[13]See for example Ginsburgh (2003) and Ginsburgh and Weyers (2014).

2.4.3 Aggregating Judgments Resulting from Competitions

The common method used to rank n objects (wines, books, musicians, movies) evaluated by m judges works as follows. Each judge grades each of the n objects. Grades are added and the sum of the grades over judges leads to a unique ordering (though there may be ties). Since individual ratings are usually not disclosed, I illustrate the discussion using a wine tasting that changed the world of wines (more on this in Sect. 3).

The results of the competition of $n = 10$ red wines (columns A to J) by $m = 11$ judges (whose names appear in the rows) are given in Table 3. Each judge had to grade each wine on a 0–20 scale.

As already mentioned, there are problems in ranking on the basis of grades. First, some judges are generous, and give high grades; some are less so and give low ones. As one can check in Table 3, the most generous judge had an average grade of 13.8,

Table 3 The Paris 1976 wine tasting: red wines, judges and ratings

Judges	Wines									
	A	B	C	D	E	F	G	H	I	J
Pierre Brejoux	14	16	12	17	13	10	12	14	5	7
Aubert de Villaine	15	14	16	15	9	10	7	5	12	7
Michel Dovaz	10	15	11	12	12	10	11	11	8	14
Patricia Gallagher	14	15	14	12	16	14	17	13	9	14
Odette Kahn	15	12	12	12	7	12	2	2	13	5
Claude Dubois-Millot	16	16	17	13.5	7	11	8	9	9.5	9
Raymond Olivier	14	12	14	10	12	12	10	10	14	8
Steven Spurrier	14	14	14	8	14	12	13	11	9	13
Pierre Tari	13	11	14	14	17	12	15	13	12	14
Christian Vanneque	16.5	16	11	17	15.5	8	10	16.5	3	6
Jean-Claude Vrinat	14	14	15	15	11	12	9	7	13	7
Average grades	14.14	14.09	13.64	13.23	12.14	11.18	10.36	10.14	9.77	9.45
Implied ranking	1	2	3	4	5	6	7	8	9	10
Average ranks	1.5	3	1.5	4	5	7	6	10	8	9

Source: Taber (2005) and own calculations

Wines: (A) Stag's Leap Wine Cellars, 1973; (B) Château Mouton-Rotschild, 1970; (C) Château Montrose, 1970; (D) Château Haut-Brion, 1970; (E) Ridge Vineyards Monte Bello, 1971; (F) Château Léoville Las Cases, 1971; (G) Heitz Wine Cellars, 1970; (H) Clos du Val Winery, 1972; (I) Mayacamas Vineyards, 1971; (J) Freemark Abbey Winery, 1969 while the strictest averaged only 9.2. Secondly, the range of grades used by judges can vary dramatically. Indeed, one judge graded between 2 and 17, while another chose the range 8–14. As noted by Ashenfelter and Quandt (1999: 17), this "may give greater weight to judges who put a great deal of scatter in their numerical scores and thus express strong preferences by numerical differences."[14] To avoid these problems, they suggest transforming the grades given by each judge into ranks which avoid the problem of scatter, and adding ranks instead of grades to compute the aggregate ranking.

And indeed, the aggregate ranking based on the judges' ranks is different from the one based on their grades. This is shown in Table 3 which gives the grade of each judge for each wine. Adding the grades over judges and dividing by 11 (the number of judges) leads to the average grades and the implied ranking reported in the one before the last row of the table. Replacing grades by ranks and proceeding as before by adding ranks and dividing the result by 11 produces the ranking reported in the last line of Table 3. The two methods lead to different final rankings. In particular, wine C is ranked before B (and ties with A), G is ranked before F, and H before I and J, which becomes last. But this may have changed many issues, since the use of ranks would have produced a tie between Californian wine A and French wine C, and France's honour would have been saved!

All these methods, including the simple grading or ranking, are very demanding, since if an expert has to grade or rank all the wines that appear in a flight, she also has, in principle, to compare them two by two. And indeed, in wine tasting parties, one can see experts going back and forth between glasses.

In what follows, we suggest a method that is less demanding, and which is an extension of what Borda (1781) called *approval voting*,[15] in which each judge casts a vote for a set of size k, $0 \leq k \leq n$ of candidate objects (wines, musicians, ...), without necessity to rank or grade them. The votes are then added. This results in each object getting a certain number of votes (including as many as there are judges, and possibly no vote) and a final ranking can be computed.

The problem with approval voting is that a judge who chooses to vote for a large group of objects is exercising more political or strategic influence—since she expresses as many votes as there are objects to grade—than the one who chooses to vote for a unique object. The solution proposed by Ginsburgh and Zang (2012) is to let each judge have one vote, which she can use to vote for one object only or a set of k objects. If she votes for a group of objects, each object receives a fraction $1/k$ of her single unit of voting, and these fractions add up to 1.

These fractions are added object by object, as in approval voting, and an aggregate unique ranking (possibly with ties) is computed. The argument for equal sharing of votes is that the judge votes for a group of object without expressing preferences over the members of the group. It turns out that the total "amount of votes" (AV) associated to each object, is its Shapley Value (Shapley

---

[14] See also Quandt (2006).

[15] See also Balinski and Laraki (2010).

1953) in a related cooperative game.[16] AVs of objects reflect their relative contribution to overall quality, or their attractiveness. The Shapley Value is known for satisfying the following set of weak and natural properties:

Property 1. Full Distribution. The total AV, cast by the judges, is fully distributed among the participating objects.

Property 2. Symmetry. If an object contributes the same additional value (measured by its AV) to each group of objects,[17] then this will be the AV assigned to this object.

Property 3. Anonymity. The AVs, allocated to the various objects, do not change if one changes the order in which the objects are processed within the competition.

Property 4. Additivity. If the judges are split into two classes (say California and French wine experts), and the AVs, assigned to the various objects by each class of judges are computed, then the sum of those two AVs would yield the AV obtained by applying the process to the whole un-split population of judges.[18]

Using these four properties as *requirements* leads to the unique value system where the AV of each object is its Shapley Value. The Shapley Value allocation is, in general, quite difficult to compute once the number of candidates or objects becomes large. It turns out, however, that for this particular structured application, the computation is straightforward,[19] and obtains as described above.

2.4.4 Arrow's Impossibility Result

The persistent problem encountered when one has to aggregate choices made by *several* individuals or judges is neither due to the quality of beholders, listeners or tasters, nor to the method used—though simpler is usually better—but to Arrow's (1953) Impossibility Theorem. Arrow shows that if there are at least three choices (whether artworks, wines, or policy options), there exists no aggregate ranking (or grading) method that can simultaneously satisfy the following four (reasonably mild) axioms:

Axiom 1. Unrestricted domain. All individual preferences are allowed.

---

[16]See Ginsburgh and Zang (2003) for a proof of the result.

[17]Consider for example a particular wine, say A, and consider the total AV obtained from the judges who choose a certain group, say $W = \{B,C,D\}$. Suppose that this number is 10. Consider now the total AVs that were used by those judges who voted for the expanded group $\{A,B,C,D\}$ (that is, the group W plus wine A). Suppose that this number is 11.50. The difference between the two is 1.50. We then say that wine A contributes an AV of 1.50 to the subgroup $W = \{B,C,D\}$ of wines. If 1.50 is the AV contribution of wine A to each subgroup of wines (that excludes wine A), then the symmetry property says that its overall AV has to be 1.50.

[18]This implies that the sharing is immune to any "class manipulations."

[19]See Ginsburgh and Zang (2003).

Axiom 2. Pareto efficiency. If every judge ranks *A* before *B*, then the aggregate order must rank *A* before *B*.

Axiom 3. Independence of irrelevant alternatives. If *A* is ranked before *B*, then introducing a new choice *C* (or discarding a choice *C* from the list of choices) must not lead *B* to be ranked before *A*: *C* is irrelevant in the choice between *A* and *B*.

Axiom 4. Non-dictatorship. No judge can impose his or her own ranking.[20]

Arrow's axioms and Impossibility Theorem prevent us from constructing a method for aggregating choices. "Lasciate ogni speranza, voi ch'entrate."[21]

3 Evaluating Wines

Wines are evidently endowed with properties. Some are physical (real) and can be measured with great accuracy (degree of alcohol, content of sugar, acidity, tannin, etc.),[22] but many are more subjective, such as the colour of the wine, its 'balance' or its 'body' (the 'look' of the wine). These properties could also be evaluated individually, and aggregated to obtain a grading or a ranking, though this is rarely the case.[23] Evaluating wines is essentially left to experts, some of whom are close to what Hume had in mind (they have the qualities required to set the standard of taste), others are closer to Bourdieu's description. They may of course implicitly grade their idiosyncratically chosen properties and aggregate them using idiosyncratic weights, but they are not asked to disclose how they managed to get their numbers, though some write 'tasting notes' that are often found useless.[24] According to Weil (2007: 137) "(non expert) wine drinkers cannot match better than chance wines with their descriptions. Wine words used by critics to convey analogy to fruits, vegetables, minerals, and odors have no value".

---

[20]Not even W. H. Auden.

[21]"Abandon all hope, you who enter here." Dante, *Inferno*, Canto I.

[22]These look like the vertical characteristics suggested by the theory of product differentiation, though wine characteristics are not necessarily monotonic in quantity. For each of them, there is an optimum that may be different for each taster (some like more acidity, other like less) and may be contextual (more acidity may be better in some wines than in others).

[23]Note that art (and wine) philosopher Scruton (2009: 125) does not believe that decomposing a wine into its various savours, makes it any better.

[24]Kant suggests that the appreciation of an artwork can be made universal by convincing others, while this is not so for wines (and food in general).

3.1   Wine Tasting

Wines are tasted in two ways. There exist professional wine critics (Robert Parker, Jancis Robinson, among the most famous) who taste wines one by one, and publish their assessments (under the form of grades and tasting notes) in magazines or books used by wine merchants and consumers to make their buying decisions. They can choose to base their grades on all the information that is available on the wine (name, vintage, etc.). This is very different from wine competitions in which tastings are usually blind and tasters have no information on the wines they are supposed to grade—a so-called *flight* that consists of several (almost empty) glasses. The process of tasting is nevertheless close in both cases: Most experts use their eyes to judge the appearance of a wine (its colour, the way it sticks to the glass when it is tilted),[25] their nose to capture aromas, their mouth (though not their throat since they are not supposed to swallow the liquid), and the finishing stage in which they judge the aftertaste.

Blind tasting does not fully take into account what judges actually know about the wine. Ashenfelter and Jones (2013: 293) show that grades based on (blind) tasting only "are not efficient predictors of the prices of mature Bordeaux wines because they do not incorporate all the publicly available information", in particular the vintage and weather conditions and of course the name of the wine.[26]

It should therefore not be surprising that the blind assessments made during competitions are often inconsistent. Hodgson's (2009a) conclusions, for instance, are based on the analysis of 13 wine competitions including 4167 wines, of which 375 were tasted in at least five competitions. Judgments were so inconsistent that a statistical test carried out using the 375 often-tasted wines shows that those which received Gold Medals could as well have been chosen randomly.

But even tasting by renowned experts, which is usually not blind, is random to some extent. Ashton (2013) studies the correlations between the grades given to a common set of wines by the 15 pairs of six famous experts (Robert Parker, Jancis Robinson, Michel Bettane and Thierry Desseauve, James Suckling, as well as *Decanter* and *Revue des Vins de France*) for all vintages between 2004 and 2010. He finds that there is more concordance among them when judging classified growth wines (with an average correlation coefficient of $r = 0.63$) than non-classified ones ($r = 0.51$). Still, the coefficient may be very small in some cases. For instance in 2005, the correlation between Parker and Robinson is 0.34, and even drops to 0.22 between Robinson and *Revue des Vins de France* for the same 2005 vintage. Cardebat and Paroissien (2015) extend the analysis to 12 judges[27] (the

---

[25]In some competitions in which red and white wines are judged together, glasses may be non transparent (usually black). I have often been told that under such circumstances, it happens that experts cannot even recognize the colour of the wine they taste.

[26]See also Cardebat et al. (2014).

[27]Actually 13 judges, since they take into account two classifications by *Decanter*, one which gives grades between 0 and 20, another between 0 and 100.

same as above, plus Jacques Dupont, Neal Martin, Jeannie Cho Lee, Antonio Galloni, Jeff Leve and *Wine Spectator*) and 15 years (2000–2014). The average coefficient of correlation between pairs of judges over the whole period is 0.60, but it may get quite small between some pairs ($r = 0.14$ between Robinson and Galloni).

Ashton (2012) reaches a similar conclusion in a meta-analysis of expert judgments. He shows that reliability and consensus are lower for wine expertise than for other fields, such as meteorology, medicine, clinical psychology, auditing and business based on data that are more objective than those resulting from subjective wine tasting.[28]

To top things off, Hodgson (2008, 2009b: 241) shows that judges do not only disagree, but are also *inconsistent*; a judge can often not repeat his scores on identical wines:

> What do we expect from expert wine judges? Above all, we expect consistency, for if a judge cannot closely replicate a decision for an identical wine served under identical circumstances, of what value is his/her recommendation? In addition, we expect an expert wine judge to have the ability to discriminate across a broad range of quality... This study as well as that of Gawel and Godden (2008), suggest that less than 30% of *expert* wine judges studied are, in fact, 'expert'.

This is also the Klimmek's (2013: 320) conclusion that "two tasting notes for the same wine may differ to such an extent [that] it is not clear they are both about the same wine;" he suggests some algorithms that can be used to produce more meaningful notes. Hodgson and Cao (2014) even develop a test that allows evaluating the performance of wine judges, and consequently to accredit good experts only.

Still, wine experts seem to enjoy a good life and may even get rich.[29] This is probably less so for philosophers, though they were the first to argue about whether properties (such as beauty, elegance, agreeableness, delicacy) do or do not exist in an object, starting with Plato's *Symposium*, which in Ancient Greece, was in fact a wine drinking party.

3.2   The Paris Wine Tasting

Let us now turn to the so called Paris wine tasting that changed the world of wines since it put a Californian and not a French wine at the top of the ranking. A few words about what became an international 'event' are useful.

---

[28] See Storchmann (2012) for more on such failures.

[29] In 2012, Robert Parker sold the major stake in *The Wine Advocate* to Singapore-based investors for US$15 million. See http://www.thedrinksbusiness.com/2012/12/parker-sells-wine-advocate-stake-for-15m/

In 1976, Steven Spurrier, a well-known English wine trader and owner of the Caves de la Madeleine in Paris, and American born Patricia Gallagher from the French Académie du Vin, organized in Paris a blind tasting of white Burgundies and red Bordeaux (four in each case),[30] and Californian wines (6 whites and 6 reds). The eleven judges were all extremely competent wine connoisseurs (sommeliers, producers of famous wines, wine journalists, and owners of Michelin starred restaurants). The tasting ended up electing a Californian wine as winner, both for white wines (Chateau Montelena) and red wines (Stag's Leap Wine Cellars). Table 3 reproduces the results of the tasting for red wines. The outcome boosted the reputation of Californian wines and this second *Judgment of Paris*—recall that the first one initiated the Trojan War—changed the traditional view, shared by experts that only French wines can be of high quality. It led to an increase of competition between French and Californian wines, and quickly extended to the discovery of quality wines in many other countries and continents, including Australia, South America and South Africa. *Times Magazine*'s journalist George Taber who was present at the tasting, described the Paris tasting in a book that is highly worth reading (Taber 2005).

We already discussed in Sect. 2.4.3 how a change in the aggregation method (aggregating ranks instead of rates) would have changed the final ranking. Ashton (2011), Borges et al. (2012), Cardebat et al. (2014), Cicchetti (2004a, b, 2009) suggested other methods. Cardebat and Paroissien (2015) try to reconcile experts who grade on a scale of 0–100 (actually 50–100) and those who grade between 0 and 20.

Using approval voting corrected to embody Shapley's axioms is likely to make evaluations in competitions less burdensome, since, though all the wines in a flight must be tasted (which is the pleasurable stage), not all have to be graded or ranked. This may result in more consistent agreements between experts in a competition, and also across competitions, and avoid the pitiful conclusions reached by Hodgson (2009a) that the wines that were awarded Gold Medals in 13 competitions featuring the same wines could as well have been chosen randomly.

Since the voting procedure of the original competition was not organized on the basis of approval ranking but of grading, one cannot observe for which wines judges would have voted had they *not* been forced to rank all ten wines. Ginsburgh and Zang (2012) simulated the number of wines chosen, but take into account the information contained in the grades that each judge had actually given.

In all experiments and for each judge, they first generated the size of the group (number of wines) she would have recommended, and then assigned to this group the top wines from her list. In the first experiment, they ran three simulations assuming that each judge would have chosen a unique wine, or two wines, or three wines.

---

[30]Meursault Charmes Roulot, 1973, Beaune Clos des Mouches Drouhin, 1973, Puligny Montrachet Leflaive, 1972 and Batard-Montrachet Ramonet-Prudhon, 1973 for white wines, and Châteaux Haut-Brion, 1970, Mouton-Rothschild, 1970, Leoville Las Cases, 1971, and Montrose, 1970 for red wines.

In the second experiment, they picked the number of wines chosen by each judge at random. The numbers were generated from a Gaussian distribution with mean three and standard deviation one. Non-integer numbers were rounded to the closest integer. Five such simulations were computed, each time with a newly generated set of random numbers.[31]

In the third experiment, they started, for each judge, with the highest grade and then went down, until they reached a gap of two points. Those wines that were graded before the gap occurs were selected. Consider Judge Brejoux in the Paris tasting. He gave 17 to wine D, 16 to wine B, and then there is a gap of two points, since the wine that comes next is A with a grade of 14. So Ginsburgh and Zang assumed Brejoux would have chosen only wines B and D. They run this procedure for each judge, and add for each wine the shared votes.

The results expressed in terms of aggregate rankings obtained using the various methods appear in Table 4, which also contains the results of grading and ranking based on the grading shown in the last rows of Table 3. Each method leads to a somewhat different ranking. One should notice, however, that wines A, B, C, D, and E belong to the group of better wines (with the exception of random simulation 4) whatever the ranking method used. The ranking of wines F, G, H, I, and J is unstable. In some sense, this means that good wines are easier to rank than medium ones, and organisers of competitions should take this into account and stop announcing the ranks of the wines that appear at the end of the list, since their ranks are not stable. This is what the organisers of the Queen Elisabeth musical competition started doing a couple of years ago: There are 12 finalists, but only the first six are ranked, the others are cited as finalists, without being distinguished one from the other.

Shapley's axioms and Value do not save us from Arrow's curse. It does unfortunately not suggest a method that satisfies Arrow's axioms (Sect. 2.4.4), but some other reasonable conditions, which grading and ranking do not share once there is more than one judge. After all, we can perhaps soften Dante's "Abandon all hope, you who enter here," the first verse of Canto I of his *Inferno* and go to the first strophe of Canto I of his *Purgatorio*, which prepares our way to *Paradiso*:

> O'er better waves to speed her rapid course
>> The light bark of my genius lifts the sail,
>> Well pleas'd to leave so cruel sea behind;
>> And of that second region will I sing,
>> In which the human spirit from sinful blot
>> Is purg'd, and for ascent to Heaven prepares.

---

[31]In both cases, there is a problem with ties that appear quite frequently, as can be seen from Table 3. Judge Brejoux gives the same marks to wines A and H (14), and to wines C and G (12). Judge Kahn gives identical marks to wines B, C, D and F (12). When there are ties and the tied wines have to be chosen among the one, two or three wines, we introduced all the wines that were tied. This usually results in forcing us to choose more than one, two or three wines. Take for example the case of Judge De Villaine, in the case in which we decide to simulate approval voting with two wines. He gives a mark of 16 to wine C, and 15 to wines A and D. This leads us to accept all three wines as being "approved", while there should only be two.

Table 4 The Paris 1976 wine tasting: Ranking wines using different methods

	Wines									
	A	B	C	D	E	F	G	H	I	J
Average grades (Table 3)	14.14	14.09	13.64	13.23	12.14	11.18	10.36	10.14	9.77	9.45
Average ranks (Table 3)	1.5	3	1.5	4	5	7	6	10	8	9
Shapley rankings										
Forced no. of choices										
One choice only	3	4.5	1	2	4.5	9	6	9	7	9
Two choices only	1	4	2	3	5	10	6	9	7	8
Three choices only	1	3	2	4	5	10	7	6	8	9
Random no. of choices										
Simulation 1	2	4	1	3	5	10	7	8	6	9
Simulation 2	1	3	4	2	5	10	6	9	7	8
Simulation 3	2	1	3	4	5.5	9.5	7	8	9.5	5.5
Simulation 4	4	3	1	2	6	10	8	9	7	5
Simulation 5	2	4	3	1	5	9	6	10	8	7
Gap of two points	1	2	3	5	4	9	10	8	7	6

Source: Own calculations
Wines: (A) Stag's Leap Wine Cellars, 1973; (B) Château Mouton-Rothschild, 1970; (C) Château Montrose, 1970; (D) Château Haut-Brion, 1970; (E) Ridge Vineyards Monte Bello, 1971; (F) Château Léoville Las Cases, 1971; (G) Heitz Wine Cellars, 1970; (H) Clos du Val Winery, 1972; (I) Mayacamas Vineyards, 1971; (J) Freemark Abbey Winery, 1969

4   Conclusions

This chapter is based on previous work to understand how art and wines are evaluated. I eventually realized that both types of evaluation are very close, and that wine is close, but not identical, to art, and in particular to music, which Peacock knew as well, given his knowledge and experience of music (Peacock 1993).

Sir Alan's sense of humour lead me to surmise that he was sceptical about evaluation and quality rankings or ratings, and would probably have accepted Robert Pirsig's (1974: 184) questioning[32]:

---

[32]Pirsig is the author of *Zen and the Art of Motorcycle*, a work that was rejected by 121 publishers before being accepted, and of which five million copies sold. Does quality matter? And who is able to judge it?

Quality ... you know what it is, yet you don't know what it is. But that's self-contradictory. But some things *are* better than others, that is, they have more quality. But when you try to say what the quality is, apart from the things that have it, it all goes *poof*! There's nothing to talk about. But if you can't say what Quality is, how do you know what it is, or how do you know that it even exists? If no one knows what it is, then for all practical purposes it doesn't exist at all. But for all practical purposes it really does exist. What else are the grades based on? [...] What the hell is Quality?

Another of my surmises is that after reading about the wanderings of evaluation, Peacock had read philosopher Harry Frankfurt (2005) who on the first page of his pamphlet notes: "One of the most salient features of our culture is that there is so much bullshit. Everyone of us contributes his share." And it may well be that Sir Alan did not want to add more.

Fare well, dear Alan. I am sure that where you are now, you can choose among many good wines, and perhaps even order some *ambrosia*—the drink of the immortals in Greek mythology.

Acknowledgments I am grateful to the editors for their careful comments and references on what A. Peacock had written on judges and experts. They both forced me to think deeper about what was common between evaluating art and evaluating wine. And finally, they briefed me on writing in English. I. Mazza briefed me on Sir Alan's tastes in wine and S. Weyers briefed me on aesthetics. I did not do much else than thinking about Alan's wit and smile while I was writing the chapter.

References

Arrow KJ (1953) Social choice and individual values. Cowles Foundation Monographs, New Haven, CT

Ashenfelter O, Jones J (2013) The demand for expert opinion: Bordeaux wine. J Wine Econ 8:285–293

Ashenfelter O, Quandt R (1999) Analyzing a wine tasting statistically. Chance 12:6–20

Ashton R (2011) Improving experts wine quality judgments: two heads are better than one. J Wine Econ 6:160–178

Ashton R (2012) Reliability and consensus of experienced wine judges: expertise within and between. J Wine Econ 7:70–87

Ashton R (2013) Is there consensus among wine quality ratings of prominent critics? An empirical analysis of Red Bordeaux, 2004-2010. J Wine Econ 8:225–234

Balinski M, Laraki R (2010) Majority judgment. Measuring ranking and electing. MIT Press, Cambridge, MA

Beardsley M (1958) Aesthetics: problems in the philosophy of criticism. Harcourt, Brace, New York

Bentham J (1818) [1789] The rationale of reward. In: The works of Jeremy Bentham, vol 2. William Tait, Edinburgh

Borda JC de (1781) Mémoire sur les élections au scrutiny. Mémoires de l'Académie des Sciences, Paris, pp 657–664

Borges J, Real A, Cabral S, Jones G (2012) A new method to obtain a consensus ranking of a region's vintages' quality. J Wine Econ 7:88–107

Bosker B (2015) Is there a better way to talk about wine? The New Yorker, 29 July 2015. http://www.newyorker.com/culture/culture-desk/is-there-a-better-way-to-talk-about-wine. Accessed 9 Sept 2015

Bourdieu P (1983) The field of cultural production, or the economic world reversed. Poetics 12:311–356

Bourdieu P (1996) The rules of art. Polity, Cambridge

Cardebat JM, Figuet JM, Paroissien E (2014) Expert opinion and Bordeaux wine prices: an attempt to correct biases in subjective judgments. J Wine Econ 9:282–303

Cardebat JM, Paroissien E (2015) Reducing quality uncertainty for Bordeaux 'en primeur' wines. AAWE working paper 180

Cicchetti D (2004a) Who won the 1976 blind tasting of French Bordeaux and U.S. cabernets. Parametrics to the rescue. J Wine Res 15:211–220

Cicchetti D (2004b) On designing experiments analyzing data to assess the reliability and accuracy of blind wine tastings. J Wine Res 14:221–226

Cicchetti D (2009) A proposed system for awarding medal at a major wine competition. J Wine Econ 4:242–247

De Marchi N (2009) Reluctant partners: aesthetic and market value, 1708-1871. In: Amariglio J, Schilders J, Cullenberg S (eds) Sublime economy. On the intersection of art and economics. Routledge, London, pp 95–111

Dickie G (1988) Evaluating art. Temple University Press, Philadelphia, PA

Frankfurt H (2005) On bullshit. Princeton University Press, Princeton, NJ

Gawel R, Godden P (2008) Evaluation of the consistency of wine quality assessments from expert wine tasters. Aust J Grape Wine Res 14:1–8

Ginsburgh V (2003) Awards, success and aesthetic quality in the arts. J Econ Perspect 17:99–111

Ginsburgh V (2014) Is Bordeaux à la 1855 defensible? Aust New Zeal Grapegrower Winemaker 605:73–80

Ginsburgh V, van Ours J (2003) Expert opinion and compensation: evidence from a musical competition. Am Econ Rev 93:289–298

Ginsburgh V, Weyers S (2010) On the formation of canons: the dynamics of narratives in art history. Empir Stud Arts 28:37–72

Ginsburgh V, Weyers S (2014) Nominees, winners and losers. J Cult Econ 38:291–313

Ginsburgh V, Zang I (2003) The museum pass game and its value. Games Econ Behav 43:322–325

Ginsburgh V, Zang I (2012) Shapley ranking of wines. J Wine Econ 7:304–319

Goodwin C (2006) Art and culture in the history of economic thought. In: Ginsburgh V, Throsby D (eds) The handbook of the economics of art and culture, vol 1. Elsevier, Amsterdam, pp 25–68

Hodgson R (2008) An examination of judge reliability at a major U. S. wine competition. J Wine Econ 3:105–113

Hodgson R (2009a) An analysis of the concordance among 13 U. S. wine competitions. J Wine Econ 4:1–9

Hodgson R (2009b) How expert are "expert" wine judges? J Wine Econ 4:233–241

Hodgson R, Cao J (2014) Criteria for accrediting expert wine judges. J Wine Econ 9:62–74

Hume D (1965) [1757] Of the standard of taste. In: On the standard of taste and other essays, by David Hume. Bobbs-Merrill, Indianapolis

Hutter M, Shusterman R (2006) Value and the valuation of art in economic and aesthetic theory. In: Ginsburgh V, Throsby D (eds) The handbook of the economics of art and culture, vol 1. Elsevier, Amsterdam, pp 169–208

Kant I (1790) The critique of judgment. Translated by Denis Dutton. http://denisdutton.com/kant_third_critique.htm. Accessed 10 Oct 2015

Klimmek M (2013) On the information content of wine notes: some new algorithms. J Wine Econ 8:318–334

Lancaster K (1966) A new approach to consumer theory. J Polit Econ 74:132–157

Levinson J (2003) Philosophical aesthetics. In: Levinson J (ed) The Oxford handbook of aesthetics. Oxford University Press, Oxford, pp 3–24

Peacock AT (1993) Paying the piper. Culture, music and money. Edinburgh University Press, Edinburgh

Peacock AT (1994) A future for the past: the political economy of heritage. Proc Br Acad
    87:189–226, reprinted in Towse R (ed) (1997) Cultural economics: the arts, the heritage and
    the media industries, vol 1. Edward Elgar, Cheltenham, pp 189–226
Peacock AT (2006) The arts and economic policy. In: Ginsburgh V, Throsby D (eds) The
    handbook of the economics of art and culture, vol 1. Elsevier, Amsterdam, pp 1123–1140
Piles R de (1989) [1708] Cours de peinture par principes. Gallimard, Paris
Pirsig R (1974) Zen and the art of motorcycle maintenance. William Morrow, New York
Quandt R (2006) Measurement and inference in wine tasting. J Wine Econ 1:7–30
Richardson J (1719) An argument in behalf of the science of a connoisseur. W. Churchill, London
Sartwell C (2014) Beauty. In: Zalta E (ed) The Stanford encyclopedia of philosophy. http://plato.
    stanford.edu/archives/spr2014/entries/beauty/. Accessed 10 Sept 2015
Savile A (1982) The test of time: an essay in philosophy and aesthetics. Oxford University Press,
    Oxford
Scruton R (2009) I drink therefore I am. A philosophers' guide to wine. Continuum, London
Shapley L (1953) A value for n-person games. In: Kuhn H, Tucker W (eds) Contribution to the
    theory of games, vol II. Princeton University Press, Princeton, NJ, pp 307–317
Shiner R (1996) Hume and the causal theory of taste. J Aesthet Art Critic 53:237–249
Storchmann K (2012) Wine economics. J Wine Econ 2:1–33
Taber G (2005) The judgment of Paris: California vs. France and the historic 1976 Paris tasting
    that revolutionized wine. Scribner, New York
Van Rees CJ (1983) How a literary work becomes a masterpiece: on the threefold selection
    practiced by literary criticism. Poetics 12:397–417
Vermazen B (1975) Comparing evaluations of works of art. J Aesthet Art Critic 34:7–14
Weil R (2007) Debunking critics' wine words: can amateurs distinguish the smell of asphalt from
    the taste of cherries? J Wine Econ 2:136–144
Zangwill N (2003) Aesthetic realism 1. In: Levinson J (ed) The Oxford handbook of aesthetics.
    Oxford University Press, Oxford, pp 63–79
Zangwill N (2014) Aesthetic judgment. In: Zalta E (ed) The Stanford encyclopedia of philosophy.
    http://plato.stanford.edu/archives/fall2014/entries/aesthetic-judgment/. Accessed 2 Sept 2015

Afterword

On Giving Economic Advice

Giacomo Pignataro

Abstract The paper explores the most intriguing points raised in Peacock's work on advicing giving, considering in particular the relevant trade-offs economic advisers have to face in developing their consultancy work.

Alan Peacock spent part of his professional life in an advisory capacity. He played the role of adviser when he served as the Chief Economic Adviser to the Department of Trade and Industry of the United Kingdom in the mid-1970s. At that time he wrote several papers on the topic, based on his own experience but also looking at several theoretical issues that involved in the discussion of that topic. In this paper I will try to recall some of what I believe are the most intriguing points raised in Peacock's work on advice giving, considering in particular the significant issue of the nature of the appointment of advisers. These are surely eternal truths that are with recording for the future.

For long time the view of the role of advisers has been based on the 'progressive' idea of the public decision making process. This idea was founded on the need to separate politics from the process of administration. Politics is the realm of value judgments and objectives, which, for instance, are there to drive the discretionary choices on how to allocate resources. Administration, instead, is to be dominated by efficiency considerations (and other technical evaluations): for instance, once the amount of resources to be devoted to pursue given objectives it is chosen on the basis of political value judgments, their actual destination is to be decided on the basis of their most efficient use. Whenever an economist is called in for advising the decision-maker, he acts (should act) as a neutral technician to contribute to the efficiency of public choices as oriented by policy objectives.

The above view is clearly represented in the Seventies' debate about the nature of economic evaluation and, more specifically, cost-benefit analysis. At the time, there were several economists, particularly those contributing to the manuals used by the international organizations for the application of cost-benefit analysis to the

G. Pignataro (✉)
University of Catania, Catania, Italy
e-mail: giacomo.pignataro@unict.it

© Springer International Publishing Switzerland 2016
I. Rizzo, R. Towse (eds.), *The Artful Economist*,
DOI 10.1007/978-3-319-40637-4_16

267

evaluation of projects in developing countries,[1] arguing that a set of distributional weights should be used in the computation of costs and benefits of projects, depending on their distribution across different social groups. Ezra Mishan (1982) strongly opposed the use of distributional weights in cost-benefit studies, which would undermine the 'integrity' of the evaluation criterion as based on Paretian principles. Mishan regards the efficiency criterion as backed by a sort of ethical consensus and, consequently, he believes that it is representative of what society prefers. Therefore, the economic analyst must not distort the efficiency analysis with any value judgment, otherwise society's preferences risk being bent to any political position.

The idea of a clear-cut dividing line between the realm of politics and the one of technical evaluation, and the consequent 'independence' and separation of the latter with respect to the former, is not well founded and can obscure the real problems in the relationship between the different areas of decision making and, specifically, for what is of interest in this paper, between politics and advising—the problems at the centre of Alan Peacock's interest in the topic. First of all, this idea draws the implication that the efficiency analysis can be regarded as a sort of technical 'objective' analysis, a value-judgment-free evaluation: the analyst is then the 'minister' of economic truth. Unfortunately, there is no such thing as an 'objective' technical analysis of policy choices and, more generally, of the phenomena at the heart of most economic advising jobs. Methodologies and models of economic (efficiency) analysis are not unique, even when they are based on the same assumptions: there can be severe divergence across the conclusions reached by different analysts (which motivates the traditional jibe of "five economists with six opinions, two of them Keynes's"). Even an 'objective' technical instrument, with a strong theoretical basis, like cost-benefit analysis, is based on value judgments. Ralph Turvey (1963), discussing the issue of the choice between the internal rate of return and the present value as the right investment criterion, clearly stresses that this choice should help government in selecting projects that maximize whatever the government wishes to maximize within the relevant constraints. Turvey is aware that "the choice of maximand and constraints involves value judgments" and he believes that "the value-judgments made by economists are, by and large, better than those made by non-economists!" Alan Peacock (1992: 1217), reporting Turvey's view, remembered that "he was severally critical of his view at the time", but he conceded that "economists who adopt a position of 'highbrow agnosticism' in formulating policies are not likely to be listened to". I believe that Alan's brief comment on Turvey opens the right perspective on discussing the role of economic advisers in policy making. There cannot be autonomy (a separate realm of admin-istration, as governed by efficiency principles) and supremacy (economists' value judgments are better than the ones of anyone else) of economic evaluation. How-ever, there are important trade-offs economic advisers have to face, which are

---

[1] Among the others, the United Nations Industrial Development Organization (UNIDO) manual by Dasgupta et al. (1972) and the World Bank one by Squire and Van der Tak (1975).

condensed in Peacock's comment (highbrow agnosticism vs. effectiveness in being listened to), that deserve to be developed.

The trade-offs an economic adviser faces in his job depend on his objective function and the different constraints he has to deal with. I will not go into the details of this analysis, which strongly relies on the identification of the nature of advisers' appointment, whether they are part of a government's office or act as external consultants. This issue is developed in Pignataro (1993). Let us instead focus on the situation of external consultants because of the relevance of their professional environment in what they do as advisers. Profession is important for advisers for several reasons, the main one being the impact of advising output on professional reputation.

Peacock (1992: 1213) recognizes that "professional output and advice output display elements of complementarity ... much advice-giving requires not only a broad knowledge of economic analysis but often specialised knowledge in areas in which one may have made a contribution. Indeed the very experience of advice-giving may improve economic analysis in ways which satisfy academic criteria". At the same time, he acknowledges the different objectives of advisers:

> economists are no exception in wishing to satisfy not only their 'customers' in either the private or public sector but also their peer group ... advice-giving economists may attach importance to long-term income prospects and to public prestige, but self-respect and what Alfred Marshall called 'the desire for excellence' can be sufficiently important for them to wish to maintain their professional reputation (Peacock 1992: 1213)

Given this starting point of our analysis, the main trade-off to be considered is the one between professional reputation and effectiveness/credibility of advice: it may take several routes.

First of all, advice giving may require an effort, which is not sufficiently appreciated by the profession. Peacock (2004: 166), discussing the credibility of cultural economists' advice, states: "the researcher has to consider the pay-off of working in an area which is outside the normal ambit of interest and expertise of academic colleagues who have a say in the researcher's long-term career prospects. This applies as much in research consultancies as in academic institutions". Moreover,

> to invent a structure of social accounting for cultural activities ... seems to me a necessary logical pre-requisite particularly if governments regard themselves as responsible for supplying cultural services and financing those services provided by private bodies. I find considerable agreement amongst colleagues on this issue, but a marked lack of enthusiasm about undertaking this task. The reason does not lie in scepticism at the usefulness of such exercise but because it is hard and unsatisfying work which one prefers someone else to carry out (pp. 169–170)

I think this is one of the reasons that may discourage academics from carrying out advising, above all in fields like the cultural sector, where the exploitation of the sort of complementarities between professional and advising output, recalled by Peacock (1992), is harder than in other ambits, because of the still limited academic relevance of cultural economics research. This difficulty is exacerbated by the general standard of professional evaluation adopted for the acceptance of professional work in academic and scientific publishing and the correlated impact on academic carrier prospects.

A second way an adviser has to face the trade-off between his professional reputation and the effectiveness of his advice is concerned with the techniques and the language used. If one tries to carry out the advising job without 'diverting' from the methodology and the language used for his professional output in order to avoid any cost in terms of professional reputation and payoff, the likely implication is that technical knowledge, for appropriate or even excellent professional work, is not suitable to convey information understood by decision makers. Again Peacock (2004: 173):

> the main difficulty facing the economic investigator is achieving acceptance of familiar methodology, widely practised in studies of the economic impact of government funding. The use of historical time series which quantify the relevant variables may be understood by sponsors, but the construction of alternative scenarios to examine the relative impact of arts funding is an open invitation for those disliking the conclusions to attack any hypothesis about 'what would happen if...'.

Thirdly and more important, the employer of advisers may have a strong interest in a specific outcome of the economic evaluation: in other words, he knows the answers before he asks for the questions. There can be, therefore, an 'interest' of the sponsor for the outcome of the consultancy and the adviser runs a risk of being a 'hired gun'. Peacock (2004: 171) was quite conscious of this risk:

> Even with official blessing and, of course, funding, you are likely to find that your sponsors will wish to bargain with you over the terms of reference of your enquiry, sometimes going so far as to suggest (in the nicest possible way) what your conclusions might be. One has to be careful in such a situation not to be too insistent on your professional rights to use your own methodology and come to your own conclusions, though this is not to suggest that you should make compromises.

Peacock himself experienced such situations when he acted as Chief Economic Adviser at the Department of Trade and Industry. The arguments he had with Mr Benn are very well known, since the latter recalls several episodes in his diaries (1990). His experience as Chair of the Committee on Financing the BBC is also well documented by Peacock himself (Peacock 1993).

Finally, the economic adviser has to consider that, in carrying out his work, he may have to do not only with government officials and ministers, but also with other experts. This is the case, for instance, when the economic adviser is called in the field of arts. Peacock (2004) stresses the role of arts interest groups (for example, public sector managers of museums, galleries, theatres, and so on) and their "patrician view of their role as guardians of the public interest". The economist's view is different, since his analysis is usually based on the assumption of consumer sovereignty, which is of course in conflict with experts' assumption that they know what is best for the public.[2]

---

[2]On this issue, see also Peacock (2006).

Summing up, the credibility and effectiveness of advisers depends on the equilibrium between the different interests at stake in their relationships with decision-makers and other players.

> The economist who wishes to be heard has to work his passage with (often) highly experienced and intelligent people who will not be impressed solely by the quality of economic analysis. The customers are much more likely to be receptive to advice if its instigator understands, even articulates for them, their objectives and is prepared to enter into what may be a long and difficult dialogue on how objectives might be achieved, often requiring several different scenarios. There is nothing inherent in such collaboration which requires the economist to trim his analysis to suit the client; and a sensible and perceptive client will not be looking for a hired gun (Peacock 1992: 1221).

Is the economist really interested? "The government of the world is a great thing, but it is a very coarse one, too, compared with the fineness of speculative knowledge" (Marquess of Halifax 1969).

References

Benn T (1990) Against the tide: diaries 1973-79. Arrow, London

Dasgupta P, Marglin SA, Sen AK (1972) Guidelines for project evaluation. UNIDO, Vienna

Marquess of Halifax (1969) Moral thoughts and reflections. In: Kenyon JP (ed) Halifax: complete works. Penguin, London

Mishan EJ (1982) The new controversy about the rationale of economic evaluation. J Econ Issues 16:29–48

Peacock AT (1992) The credibility of economic advice to government. Econ J 102:1213–1222

Peacock AT (1993) Paying the piper: culture, music and money. Edinburgh University Press, Edinburgh

Peacock AT (2004) The credibility of cultural economists' advice to governments. In: Ginsburgh V (ed) Economics of art and culture. Elsevier, Amsterdam, pp 167–178

Peacock AT (2006) The arts and economic policy. In: Ginsburgh V, Throsby D (eds) Handbook of the economics of art and culture, vol 1. North-Holland, Amsterdam, pp 1124–1140

Pignataro G (1993) The role of analysts in the public investment decision-making process. In: Williams A, Giardina E (eds) Efficiency in the public sector. The theory and practice of cost-benefit analysis. Edward Elgar, Aldershot

Squire L, Van der Tak HG (1975) Economic analysis of projects. Johns Hopkins University Press, Baltimore, The World Bank

Turvey R (1963) Present value versus internal rate of return—an essay in the theory of the third best. Econ J 73:93–98

Printed by Printforce, the Netherlands